PARTNER VIOLENCE

A Comprehensive Review of 20 Years of Research

Edited by

Jana L. Jasinski
Linda M. Williams

with

David Finkelhor
Jean Giles-Sims
Sherry L. Hamby
Glenda Kaufman Kantor
Patricia Mahoney
Carolyn M. West
Janis Wolak

Foreword by
Murray A. Straus

SAGE Publications
International Educational and Professional Publisher
Thousand Oaks   London   New Delhi

For information:

 SAGE Publications, Inc.
2455 Teller Road
Thousand Oaks, California 91320
E-mail: order@sagepub.com

SAGE Publications Ltd.
6 Bonhill Street
London EC2A 4PU
United Kingdom

SAGE Publications India Pvt. Ltd.
M-32 Market
Greater Kailash I
New Delhi 110 048 India

Printed in the United States of America

Library of Congress Cataloging-in-Publication Data

Partner violence: a comprehensive review of 20 years of research/
    editors, Jana L. Jasinski, Linda M. Williams with David Finkelhor
    . . . [et al.].
        p.   cm.
    Includes bibliographical references and index.
    ISBN 0-7619-1317-3 (cloth: acid-free paper). — ISBN
0-7619-1318-1 (pbk.: acid-free paper)
        1. Conjugal violence—United States.   I. Jasinski, Jana L.
    II. Williams, Linda Meyer.
    HV6626 .2.P37   1998
    364.15′553—dc21   97-33919

        00   01   02   03   04   10   9   8   7   6   5   4   3

Acquiring Editor:	C. Terry Hendrix
Editorial Assistant:	Dale Mary Grenfell
Production Editor:	Michèle Lingre
Production Assistant:	Karen Wiley
Typesetter/Designer:	Rebecca Evans
Indexer:	Julie Grayson
Cover Designer:	Candice Harman

Contents

Foreword

MURRAY A. STRAUS

This book reflects not only the insights and analytical skills of its authors, but also a truly remarkable development in social science. There has been an explosion of research and knowledge about partner violence on a scale and place that may be unprecedented. In the period from 1974 to 1996, the output of just one research group—the Family Research Laboratory at the University of New Hampshire—included 35 books and almost 300 articles on family violence. One can get a broader idea of the enormous growth of research on family violence from the fact that ten new journals on this topic began publication since 1985. As a result of this outpouring of research, the authors of this book were able to compile a bibliography of 1,557 references on just the partner violence part of family violence.

What can explain the explosive growth in research on partner violence and the impressive body of knowledge documented in this book. It cannot be explained on the basis of increases in partner assault because the available evidence suggests that partner violence has been decreasing (Straus & Gelles, 1986; Straus & Kaufman Kantor, 1994). Rather, the growth in research has been in response to the "social construction" (i.e., public recognition) of partner violence as a major problem. This recognition occurred as a result of major changes in society and in the social sciences (Finkelhor, 1984; Straus, 1992). I will list some of them in approximate chronological order:

- The social activism of the 1960s, which championed oppressed groups, was extended to the oppression of children and women.
- The rising homicide, rape, and assault rate, violent political and social protest and assassinations, terrorist activity, and the Vietnam war, sensitized people to violence.
- Disenchantment with the family in the 1960s and early 1982s facilitated perceiving negative features of family life, including violence.
- The growth in paid employment by married women provided the economic means to no longer tolerate the abuse that had long been the lot of women.
- Studies by Levinger (1966) and O'Brien (1971) demonstrated that violence was a factor in 40% of divorces. The increased legal, economic, and social acceptability of divorce also helped make it possible to no longer tolerate abusive behavior.
- Professions with a stake in intervening in the family grew extremely rapidly. For example, the American Association of Marriage and Family Therapists went from 3,375 members in 1975 to 25,000 in 1995. These professions created an audience receptive to findings on family violence (Finkelhor, 1982).
- Social activist baby-boomers were entering graduate school and they were interested in using social science as a means of social activism.
- The women's movement created two new social institutions: rape crisis centers and shelters for battered women. Both did more than provide medical and psychological assistance and safety. They were also ideologically important because they crystallized and publicized phenomena that had previously been ignored (Straus, 1974).
- There was a convergence of certain aspects of the conservative agenda of the 1980's with the agendas of the feminist movement and of sociologists engaged in research on family violence. The conservative demand for "law and order" and use of punishment to correct social problems coincided with the demands of women to end the virtual immunity of wife beaters from legal sanctions. The sexual repression that is a traditional aspect of conservatism coincided with feminist campaigns against pornography.
- Changes in theoretical perspectives in sociology put the consensus model of society under attack by conflict theory and feminist theory. The inevitability of conflict in all human groups, including the family, was recognized, along with the violence as a conflict tactic.
- Certain enduring characteristics of one of the disciplines (sociology) meshed with these historical circumstances. Sociology has a tradition, dating at least to the time of August Comte, of seeing sociology as as a vehicle of social improvement. Also part of the sociological tradition is a concern for the underdog and liberal political leanings. Finally, sociology has a strong debunking tradition (Berger, 1973). Research on family violence was consistent with these three elements of the culture of this discipline. It held out the hope of improving families and society,

it came to the rescue of oppressed women and children. It debunked the view of the family as a "haven."

- A growing number of women entered academic life during this period. One of the benefits was attention to gender roles and research on male oppression, including violence in maintaining male dominance (Dobash and Dobash, 1979; Straus, 1973, 1976; Yllö and Straus, 1990; Yllö and Bograd, 1988).

These changes in society created a demand for scientific findings on family violence, and the research community responded. Their book makes the findings from this remarkable growth in research available, and it does so in a way that is scientifically accurate, understandable, and hopefully useful in ending an ancient scourge.

References

Berger, P. L. (1973). *Invitation to sociology: A humanistic perspective.* Woodstock, NY: Overlook Press.

Dobash, R. E., & Dobash, R. (1979). *Violence Against wives.* New York: Free Press.

Finkelhor, D. (1984). *Child sexual abuse: New theory and research.* New York: The Free Press.

Finkelhor, D. (1982). Sexual abuse: A sociological perspective. *Child Abuse & Neglect, 6,* 95-102.

Levinger, G. (1966). Sources of marital dissatisfaction among applicants for divorce. *American Journal of Orthopsychiatry, 26*(October), 803-807.

O'Brien, J. E. (1971). Violence in divorce-prone families. *Journal of Marriage and the Family, 33,* 692-698.

Straus, M. A. (1973). A general systems theory approach to a theory of violence between family members. *Social Science Information, 12,* 105.

Straus, M. A. (1974). "Foreword". In R. J. Gelles (Ed.). *The violent home.* Newbury Park, CA: Sage.

Straus, M. A. (1976). Sexual inequality, cultural norms, and wife-beating. In E. C. Viano (Ed.). *Victims and society* (pp. 543-559). Washington, DC: Visage Press.

Straus, M. A. (1992). Sociological research and social policy: The case of family violence. *Sociological Forum, 7*(2), 211-237.

Straus, M. A., & Gelles, R. J. (1986). Societal change and change in family violence from 1975 to 1985 as revealed by two national surveys. *Journal of Marriage and the Family, 48,* 465-479.

Straus, J. A., & Kaufman Kantor, G. (1994). *Change in spouse assault rates from 1975 to 1992: A comparison of three national surveys in the United States.* Paper presented at the 13th World Congress of Sociology, Bielefeld, Germany.

Yllö, K., & Bograd, M. (Eds.). (1988). *Feminist perspectives on wife abuse.* Newbury Park, CA: Sage.

Yllö, K., & Straus, M. A. (1990). Patriarcy and violence against wives: The impact of structural and normative factors. In M. A. Straus & R. J. Gelles (Eds.). *Physical violence in American families: Risk factors and adaptations to violence in 8,145 families* (pp. 383-399). New Brunswick, NJ: Transaction.

Acknowledgments

We have many people to thank for their contributions to this book. First we wish to thank C. Terry Hendrix, senior editor at Sage Publications, whose commitment to the field of child abuse and family violence is reflected in his tremendous support of professionals and authors.

We would also like to thank members of the 1996 Family Violence Research Seminar, Family Research Laboratory, University of New Hampshire for their helpful comments on earlier drafts of the chapters. These members include Victoria L. Banyard, Tracy L. Dietz, E. Milling Kinnard, Steve Kelly and Liza Little. We also thank Murray Straus for his comments, feedback and foreword to the book. Other Family Research Laboratory staff and associates supported this project including Doreen Cole, Kelly Foster, Kaushalia Tailor, Sigliende Field, Sarah Hamilton, Alex Boros, David Malone and Susanne Hebert. David Sugarman, who permitted us to use a bibliography he compiled for an earlier project, also deserves our hearty thanks.

This project was partially supported by National Institute of Mental Health Training Grant 5-T32-MH15161. Parts of this book were also derived from an earlier project "US Air Force Domestic Violence Literature Review," supported by the US Department of Agriculture Cooperative Research Education and Extension Service Cooperative Agreement No. 95.EXCA-3-0414, University of Missouri and the United States Air Force. Although the points of view and opinions expressed in this book are the authors' own, we wish to acknowledge the important comments and feedback provided for some of the chapters by a team of scholars and clinicians assembled by the Air Force. This team was ably lead by Albert Brewster and Geoffrey Leigh and included: Joel Milner, Craig Allen, James Daley, Louise Parker, Sandra M. Stith, Tina Balderrama, Terri Weaver, Denise Marantes, Jean Metzker, Barbara Froke, Sharon Wright and Judy Branch.

Finally we wish to thank our families, colleagues and friends for their encouragement and support while undertaking this project.

Introduction

JANA L. JASINSKI
LINDA M. WILLIAMS

The history of research on family violence is relatively short. Early empirical research on family violence was based primarily on a few cases or special populations, such as students or shelter residents. Although this research gave insight into the complexity of family violence and its meaning for victims, no data were available for estimating the magnitude of the problem. In 1975, the first National Family Violence Survey was conducted to measure the extent of violence in the family, to try to understand what the violence meant to the participants, and to determine what caused the violence to take place (Straus, Gelles, & Steinmetz, 1980). This was the first attempt by researchers to measure intrafamily violence in a large, nationally representative sample. This survey found that individuals faced the greatest risk of assault and physical injury in their own homes by members of their own families.

More than 20 years after the first national survey on family violence, considerable difficulties remain in arriving at consensus about how to define and measure family violence, whether and how psychological abuse is incorporated into the definition of violence, how

Parts of this book were derived from an earlier project—United States Air Force Domestic Violence Literature Review, Synthesis, and Implications for Practice—supported by the United States Department of Agriculture Cooperative Research Education and Extension Service Cooperative Agreement No. 95-EXCA-3-0414, the University of Missouri, and the United States Air Force. Points of view or opinions expressed within this book are those of the authors and do not necessarily represent the official position or policies of the United States Department of Agriculture or the United States Air Force.

it is measured, and the validity of distinguishing between types and degrees of severity of partner violence, as well as violence perpetrated by males and females. Much debate also continues about the application and influence of differing theoretical perspectives to research and practice in the field of family violence. Finally, because the field has been unable to state definitively the causes of violence, a great deal of debate remains about the significance of intergenerational transmission of violence. Each of these areas affects the social response to violence and, as a result, has created another controversy: What works to stop violence?

The 20-year history of research on violence in the family has contributed to an increasing awareness of the scope and significance of this problem. Since 1974, hundreds of articles and many books have been published. A comprehensive, interdisciplinary review of this research was needed, however. That is the aim of this book. This book synthesizes the accumulated knowledge of more than 20 years of research in the area of partner violence, summarizes the major findings of the research, and delineates its strengths and limitations. In addition, recommendations based on the research are made for the field, especially in the area of prevention and treatment.

Part of the literature review process involved in preparing these chapters included reaching agreement on terminology to be used. We chose to use the term *partner violence* when referring to violence between two married or cohabiting adults. Although the term *domestic violence* is often used to refer to this phenomenon, we agreed that *partner violence* more accurately captured the literature we wanted to review. *Domestic violence* may generally refer to other types of violence in the family, including child abuse. Another commonly used term, *marital* or *spousal violence,* implies consideration of only the violence that occurs between married individuals. *Partner violence,* though, takes into account violence in nonmarital relationships, such as cohabiting relationships. Although this book focuses on partner violence and we had much literature to review on this topic, we come from a long-standing tradition of examining violence in the context of the entire family and anticipate that future efforts in this area will integrate discussions of partner violence, child abuse, and sibling violence.

This review is organized into seven chapters. Chapter 1, "Dynamics and Risk Factors in Partner Violence," introduces the literature review by focusing on prevalence rates of partner violence, dynamics of abusive relationships including typologies of batterers, documented risk markers, and the importance of assessing violence in different life stages. A comprehensive understanding of these risk factors and their different impact at various life stages is essential because they are at the heart of successful prevention and intervention models.

Partner violence has dramatic consequences for the perpetrator and victim, the family, and the entire community. Chapter 2, "The Aftermath of Partner Violence," reviews the literature on the consequences of partner violence, with particular emphasis on the emotional consequences for victims and other family members, the economic costs of treatment, the costs from loss of work or school, the consequences for family norms and community standards, and the transmission of violent behaviors from one generation to the next.

Chapter 3, "Children Exposed to Partner Violence," looks at how partner violence affects the children who witness it or who live in the families where it occurs. The effects of partner violence on children deserve special attention because of the vulnerability of children and the importance of interrupting possible intergenerational transmission effects.

Chapter 4, "Sexual Assault in Marriage: Prevalence, Consequences, and Treatment of Wife Rape," examines another form of partner violence in addition to physical assault: marital rape. Sexual violence deserves special attention because of the special shame and secrecy that surround it and the crossover in the sexual assault and partner violence literatures.

Partner violence affects certain populations in unique ways that need to be understood for effective policy and intervention. Two chapters are devoted to the examination of partner violence in specific populations. Chapter 5, "Leaving a Second Closet: Outing Partner Violence in Same-Sex Couples," considers the stressors associated with being gay or lesbian. In addition, it looks at the incidence and characteristics of same-sex partner violence.

Chapter 6, "Lifting the 'Political Gag Order': Breaking the Silence Around Partner Violence in Ethnic Minority Families," focuses on the incidence and prevalence of intimate violence in the four largest ethnic groups in the United States: African Americans, Latinos, Asian Americans, and American Indians. This chapter also discusses historical circumstances and social and cultural factors that put these populations at an increased risk for partner violence.

Although each chapter addresses prevention and treatment issues that are suggested by the literature, Chapter 7 is focused specifically on the literature that addresses these issues. This chapter examines the literature on primary, secondary, and tertiary prevention and treatment and how successfully we as professionals can deal with and respond to the relevant dynamics, risk factors, and outcomes of partner violence. This chapter focuses specifically on several important prevention and intervention issues, as well as current controversies regarding the use of some types of intervention and treatment. Primary prevention, community and legal interventions, and mental health treatments are all discussed.

Implications for the Future

After more than 20 years of empirical research on partner violence, many questions remain unanswered. On the basis of what is known from the existing research, however, we are able to discuss the implications of this knowledge. Our recommendations fall into the three broad domains of prevention, treatment, and research.

Prevention

Although this review found evidence of an extensive and varied history of local, state, and federal prevention programs for partner violence, the effectiveness of these programs remains essentially unknown. These programs need to be evaluated so that those that do work can be maintained and new programs can be developed to replace those that do not work. The research does suggest that prevention programs for partner violence may need to begin earlier than high school. One of the most consistent risk factors for partner violence is experiencing or witnessing violence in the family of origin. Identifying such children and adults and providing support for them may be one way to prevent violence from continuing into the next generation.

This review demonstrated that the impact of partner violence reaches beyond the individual and into the community. Efforts to stop family violence should, therefore, be undertaken at the community level, as well as at the individual level. These efforts could take the form of public education and promotion of awareness that violence is not an acceptable form of conflict resolution. Nonviolent skills for conflict resolution should be taught. The establishment of an integrated task force composed of community members, practitioners, and researchers would make a coordinated effort to stop partner violence a realistic goal.

Treatment

Additional resources also need to be invested in the evaluation of treatment programs. To conduct these evaluations successfully, however, practitioners and researchers must agree on the definition of treatment success. Treatments should be designed that recognize that the range of violent behaviors may require a range of treatment options. Treatments may need to be tailored to the individual, the family, and the community. There is no such thing as the "one size fits all" treatment. Culturally appropriate assessments and treatment programs are needed. Programs that were developed for upper-class white individuals may not work for other individuals. In addition, although one individual may present with the offending behavior, in any treatment program it is important to consider all members of the family because of the important consequences for witnesses of violence, as well as for the direct victims and perpetrators. Treatment should also take into account stages in the life cycle and impact and risks for re-offense.

It is also important at this juncture to recommend that more attention be paid to the negative impacts of partner violence on women and children and that treatment programs focused on reducing these negative consequences and on promoting strengths and resiliency be designed and evaluated.

Research

Future research efforts should be aimed at answering today's questions. In particular, very limited longitudinal research has been conducted even though violence differs in its dynamics and impact for individuals and families in different stages of the life cycle. Longitudinal studies would also offer insight into patterns of escalation or cessation of partner violence. Research on partner violence among ethnic minorities is also in its infancy. Research is needed that focuses on minority families. Program evaluations are needed to aid

practitioners and policy makers by learning which programs or policies work to stop violence and to keep the violence from reoccurring.
We also need research that follows up victims and perpetrators of
partner violence to document the impact of treatment on the pattern
and course of the violent behavior over time. Existing research focuses on characteristics of the perpetrator that increase the risk for
violent behavior. Future research should also consider characteristics
of the victim and victim strengths that may point the way to important interventions for victims and children who witness violence.
Finally, more research efforts are needed to identify and understand
the social and community impact of partner violence.

Although the research conducted during the past 20 years has
added much to the understanding of partner violence and especially
documented its incidence and prevalence, as this review indicates,
many unanswered questions will require the attention of researchers
and practitioners from a diverse array of disciplines and backgrounds.

CHAPTER ONE

Dynamics and Risk Factors
in Partner Violence

GLENDA KAUFMAN KANTOR
JANA L. JASINSKI

Questions about how much violence occurs in families, the severity of the violence, and the nature of victim-offender relationships in families are primary concerns of those engaged in efforts to
reduce and control intimate violence. Studies have documented the
severity and pervasiveness of violence against intimate partners in
the United States and in other countries, but at times the incidence
rates range widely and investigators differ in their opinions on appropriate theoretical explanations, relevant risk factors, and the gender equivalence of violence in intimate partner relationships. When
variations in rates or severity occur across studies, the inconsistencies often reflect differences in study design and methodology, such
as the population studied, the time dimension during which abuse is
assessed, or the method of interviewing or measuring abuse. Populations may differ in the extent to which they possess particular risk
factors for violence, such as youth, poverty, or family history of abuse.
Johnson (1995), for example, made a distinction between common
couple violence that is found in general population samples and the
more extreme "terroristic" violence that is typically experienced by
shelter populations of battered women. The ability to identify the
terrorist and intimate offenders who pose an ongoing risk of future

1

severe assaults is critical to establishing effective interventions (Straus, 1993). This chapter examines current research on the dynamics and patterns of family violence, the types of abuse, and the major known risk factors for partner violence because this knowledge is fundamental to prevention and intervention.

We have come to fear the headlines heralding the worst possible scenario related to intimate violence—the death of a woman murdered by her spouse or a husband killed by his long-battered wife. The two primary sources of figures on wife battering—the National Family Violence Survey and the National Crime Victimization Survey—illustrate both the extensiveness of intimate violence and the gender inequalities of intimate violence, as well as its lethal potential. At least 2 million women are beaten by their partners each year (Bachman & Saltzman, 1994; Straus & Gelles, 1990b), and evidence from the National Crime Victimization Survey (Bachman & Saltzman, 1994) indicates that one in five attacks on women by either a stranger or an acquaintance involved the use of a weapon. Although strangers who assaulted female victims were more likely than intimates to carry or use a weapon, injuries were twice as likely to occur if the assault was perpetrated by an intimate, rather than by a stranger (Bachman & Saltzman, 1994). In addition, as many as half of all female homicide victims are killed by their husbands or boyfriends (Kellerman & Mercy, 1992). It is rare for male homicide victims to be killed by intimate partners. Only about 3% of such homicides are perpetrated by wives, ex-wives, or girlfriends (Bachman & Saltzman, 1995).

Although the incidence of lethal perpetration is greater for men than for women, data from the 1975 and the 1985 National Family Violence Surveys indicate that women assault their partners at least as often as men do (Stets & Straus, 1990; Straus et al., 1980). Parity between intimate partners may end, however, with the similarity in occurrence of aggressive acts. Studies by Straus and associates (1980) found that assaulted women were several times more likely than men to require medical care after severe assaults and were significantly more likely than assaulted husbands to experience psychological injuries related to their abuse (Stets & Straus, 1990).

In this chapter, we first examine current knowledge in the field on the types and dynamics of abusive relationships, including characteristics of batterers and victims. We then examine theoretical frameworks for marital assault and their relevant risk markers. We also consider particular aspects of the life course as risk markers for marital assault or the cessation of assault. Last, we consider implications for policy and practice.

Patterns and Dynamics of
Abusive Relationships

The Patterns

A cycle of violence is often discussed as an integral component of the battered woman syndrome and the dynamics of partner assault. The cycle, first described by Walker (1979), is said to include a period of tension building followed by battering. The batterer may express remorse, and a period of relative calm ensues. The cycle is reactivated after a period when tensions increase or stresses resurface. The assumption underlying the cycle theory is that all partner violence increases in frequency and severity over time. Most of the evidence describing the cycle is clinical and anecdotal, however, or based on shelter populations. In fact, intimate violence that is relentless, is cyclical, results in measurable physical injury, or becomes progressively more severe over time may not be characteristic of the majority of intimate violence reported in general population surveys of families. Rather, these severe patterns may reflect the more extreme end of the intimate violence continuum. In his exploration of these issues, Johnson (1995) concluded that a pattern of battering that escalates in frequency and intensity may better characterize the patriarchal, terroristic form of wife abuse. Dutton and Starzomski (1993) suggested that borderline personality disorder may account for the intermittent abusive rage of batterers described by the cycle theory of abuse.

On the basis of clinical observations, Douglas (1991), for one, found that, in the early stages of the violence cycle, interim periods still include some good times and caring feelings between partners. Over time, the pattern of conflict becomes set, recurring issues between partners are unresolved and frequently replayed, and then the intensity of conflict increases. The ongoing violence erodes the relationship, and any positive aspects of the relationship diminish. Next, according to Douglas, is the severe stage in which violence is "deliberate, dangerous, premeditated," and there is no relief from punishing, dominating behaviors, extreme jealousy, and criticisms. The husband may become increasingly possessive and controlling and may isolate the woman from her family and friends (Douglas, 1991; Frieze & Browne, 1989; Walker, 1979). As we discuss below, however, the forms and patterns of physical violence may not be the same in all families. A pattern of violence in which the severity escalates progressively over the course of the relationship may, in fact, represent one of the more severe and less common forms that intimate violence takes.

The Psychodynamics

A common dynamic of conflicted intimate relationships is an inability of the couple to communicate or negotiate in rational, nonjudgmental ways. Verbal arguments occur in which the partners attack each other "in ways that diminish self-esteem, create feelings of vulnerability, and activate fears of rejection and abandonment" (Douglas, 1991, p. 528). Either or both partners may use responses that escalate the conflict in ways that differ from those in couples in which violence does not occur. Gelles and Straus (1988) also assert that attacks on a partner's vulnerabilities often precipitate violence. This is illustrated by the following comment by a husband:

> If I want to make her feel real bad, I tell her how stupid she is. She can't deal with this and she hits me. (Gelles & Straus, 1988, p. 79)

Men, particularly those with low self-esteem, may defend themselves against feelings of frustration, vulnerability, and personal attack by using violence against a partner. Male physical violence can serve to intimidate, control, and silence the partner to gain the upper hand in a relationship. Physical violence may also be a strategy of first resort or last resort among men lacking verbal communication and problem-solving skills. Holtzworth-Munroe (1992) found that men engaging in marital violence were more likely than nonviolent men to lack adequate responses to situations posing perceived challenges or rejection on the part of the wife. Additionally, even so-designated behaviors, such as "poor housekeeping" on the part of wives, may inflame husbands who view meals not cooked to their tastes or rooms not cleaned to their satisfaction as a "sign of the wife's disregard" (Barnett, Miller-Perrin, & Perrin, 1997, p. 241).

Violence may serve to relieve tensions, create emotional distance because of fear of intimacy, impending loss of control, or anxiety (Browning & Dutton, 1986); or as Douglas (1991) suggests, may be used to facilitate intimacy, as in the case of "making up" by engaging in sex or even forcing sex as a continuation of the violence. To some, this may make the sex appear to be more intense and exciting (Douglas, 1991). In another severe manifestation of violence, extreme episodes of rage can emerge with absolutely no apparent stimulus:

> When I got violent, it was not because I really wanted to get violent.
>
> It was just because it was like an outburst of rage. I was a real jerk for almost a year. And anything would set me off.
>
> I was like uncontrollably violent. I would slap her, knock her down, choke her, and call her a slut and a whore. (Ptacek, 1988, p. 143)

Male Dominance, Control, Family Power, and Societal Norms

Some evidence suggests that the way the family unit is organized (e.g., male dominated vs. equality between partners) plays an important role in family functioning (Coleman & Straus, 1986; Straus et al., 1980). For example, the results from previous research suggest that wife beating is more common in households where power is concentrated in the hands of the husband or male partner (Coleman & Straus, 1990; Levinson, 1989; Straus et al., 1980; Yllö & Straus, 1990). In these households, physical violence may be used to legitimate the dominant position of the male (Babcock, Waltz, Jacobson, & Gottman, 1993). At the societal level, cultural norms supporting unequal family power structures or traditional gender roles may help explain some variations in rates of spousal violence. In other words, males are socialized to use violence to maintain control. Aggression can also emerge from frustration over an inability to control the female partner (Fagan & Browne, 1994). One might also consider normative approval of violence as a risk factor for spousal violence. Previous research has demonstrated a significant relationship between self-reported approval of the use of violence toward a spouse and actually using violence (Jasinski, 1996; Kaufman Kantor, Jasinski, & Aldarondo, 1994; Straus & Gelles, 1990b).

Other research on the more individual-level concepts of dominance and power found that higher levels of dominance were associated with higher levels of violence (DePuy, 1995; Hamby & Sugarman, 1996). Studies comparing wife assaulters with nonassaultive men, matched on demographic characteristics, found that assaultive men demonstrated higher needs for power (Dutton & Strachan, 1987). One explanation for this phenomenon is that men who feel powerless because of low self-esteem or who feel little control over others or the events in their lives have high needs for power. Another mechanism is suggested by Dutton and Strachan (1987). They hypothesize that men who view intimacy with women as dangerous, threatening, and uncontrollable can become highly anxious and angry. These feelings of psychological discomfort may then lead to behaviors such as violence to control their partners and to reduce the men's anxiety and anger.

A further elaboration of the dynamics of power and control are provided by Prince and Arias (1994). They assessed the relationship between control and self-esteem among abusive and nonabusive men and found two relationship patterns. In the first pattern, men had high self-esteem but a poor sense of control over their lives and used violence with the intention of gaining control. In the second pattern, men had low self-esteem and felt powerless but became violent in response to frustration. The study authors concluded that when different dimensions of control are examined—interpersonal control, on the one hand, and control over life events, on the other hand—the latter is a more significant predictor of wife assault. This finding is also important because it helps explain the importance of socioeconomic factors such as unemployment to intimate violence.

Female Perpetrators and Mutual Violence Between Intimate Partners

It has been suggested that offender-victim roles in intimate relationships are not sex-specific. However, the participants in intimate violence may be equally assaultive, the men may be the sole perpetrators of violence against their partners, or the women may be the lone aggressors in the relationships. Given widely held beliefs that aggression is primarily a masculine behavior, it is not surprising that research on aggression by women is relatively recent. Aggression by wives has been studied less than aggression by husbands, and findings of equal rates of violence by wives (Stets & Straus, 1990; Straus, 1993; Straus et al., 1980) have been regarded as controversial and challenged by some feminist scholars (Dobash, Dobash, Wilson, & Daly, 1992; Pleck, Pleck, Grossman, & Bart, 1978). Underlying the concerns of the feminist protest is the belief that such a focus detracts attention and resources from the more serious problems of battered women. Feminists maintain that historically and culturally rooted inequalities of power are the underlying cause of male violence against women and that women are the real victims of intimate violence. It has been argued that physical violence by husbands and wives cannot be equated because of the greater potential for physical injury by husbands, given their usually greater size and strength. For example, women are six times more likely than men to require medical care for injuries sustained in family violence (Kaufman Kantor & Straus, 1987; Stets & Straus, 1990). Furthermore, women are less able than men to leave violent relationships because of numerous social constraints, including greater economic dependency and responsibility for children, and because women are socialized into believing that they are responsible for the well-being of a relationship. Culturally scripted messages persist that wives should stay in unhappy marriages "for the sake of the children." Culture and religion may also influence the organization of traditional gender roles in families, and family integrity may be valued more than the cost of enduring abuse. Cultural differences may also exist in the extent to which women engage in acts of aggression.

Research on Gender and Aggression

Maccoby and Jacklin's (1974) comprehensive review of gender differences in children found few gender differences other than more aggression by boys. More recent reviews investigating gender differences in aggressive behavior by adults suggest either inconsistencies or fewer gender differences in aggression and identify factors that mediate gender aggression relationships (Eagly & Steffen, 1986; Frodi, Macaulay, & Thome, 1977). Eagly and Steffen (1986), in their meta-analysis, concluded that women's and men's beliefs about the consequences of their aggression are the major factor accounting for variability in gender-differentiated aggressive behavior. Greenblat (1983) found greater tolerance for wives slapping husbands than the reverse because it is believed that women are less likely than men to do physical harm. This is illustrated by the following comment regarding hitting by a wife from a husband interviewed in the Greenblat study:

> I'd say that it doesn't matter that much. . . . because it's rare that a wife can hurt her husband, just hurt his emotions. I wouldn't feel that bad as a husband, because I would say she's angry and it doesn't hurt me at all, so let her get her anger out. (Greenblat, 1983, p. 254)

Many criticisms of the Conflict Tactics Scale (CTS; Straus, 1979, 1990), the most widely used instrument for measuring spousal violence, were elicited in response to the findings on violence perpetrated by women. More than 30 studies examined gender differences in rates of violence in nonclinical populations. All, including follow-up data from the National Youth Survey (Morse, 1995), found approximately equal rates of violence (in both frequency and severity of acts) by the women (Gelles & Straus, 1988; Straus, 1993). These findings seem implausible to many because of the cultural image of women as less violent than men, which in turn is bolstered by women's much lower rate of violent crime outside the family. It is also based on the fact that at least 90% of police reports of domestic violence involve male offenders.

Straus (1993) believes that the controversy over assaults by women stems largely from the implicit assumption by those doing community epidemiological survey research that their findings on comparable rates of spousal assault by men and women also apply to cases known to the police and to cases that come to the attention of shelters. Clinical researchers have made similar unwarranted assumptions. Straus argues that the discrepancy between the findings from surveys of family problems (both those using the CTS and other measures) and findings based on criminal justice system data or the experiences of women in shelters for battered women does not indicate that one set of statistics is correct and the other not. Both are correct. They apply to different groups of people, however, and reflect different aspects of domestic assault. Community and epidemiological data, as well as clinical sample data, are valid.

Is Mutual Combat a Valid Description of Intimate Violence?

Descriptions of marital assaults as mutual combat and of women as equal to men in their violent acts have resulted in extremely contentious debate. Fagan and Browne (1994), for example, argue that because of methodological problems in marital violence research, "it is misleading to characterize marital violence as mutual violence" (p. 169). Although recent studies of clinical samples suggest that acts of marital violence by both partners are typical (e.g., Langhinrichsen-Rohling, Neidig, & Thorn, 1995), recent empirical examination of the notion of reciprocation in marital violence needs to be considered further. Generally, marriages described as mutually violent in the National Family Violence Surveys are those in which either the male or female respondent for a household reported that both he or she and the partner engaged in any minor or seriously assaultive act toward the other. Additionally, the 1985 National Family Violence Survey included one context (incident) specific question to measure who initiated the physical conflict. Three national surveys of family violence have reported that between one half and three quarters of all intimate violence is mutual, although as mentioned, these numbers are based on data from one partner per family household (Kaufman Kantor & Asdigian, 1996; Straus & Gelles, 1990b; Straus et al., 1980). Moreover, an analysis of the specific incident data (Stets & Straus, 1990) found that gender made no difference in offender-victim roles as measured by initiation of minor physical conflicts (mainly slapping or throwing things). An often neglected point of this research is that the study also found men's acts of serious physical violence (punching, choking, use of weapons) to be much higher when reported by women. This suggests that men underreport their severe assaults and that interviews based solely on male reports must be treated cautiously.

Vivian and Langhinrichsen-Rohling's (1994) study elaborates on the mutuality issue by considering whether bidirectionally violent couples are mutually victimized. Their research sample consisted of 57 clinical couples (with communication problems as their presenting complaint) in which both partners reported partner aggression. The findings of this study support prior research regarding the more severe effects of male aggression on women victims. The study authors found that wives had more injuries and more negative psychological effects from the husbands' aggression. Additionally, their statistical analysis categorized couples into types based on evidence of different *dimensions* of aggression. Over one half of the couples were categorized as belonging to a subgroup in which both partners engaged in low levels of mutual violence. Among a second subgroup (26%), the wives reported higher levels of victimization than the husbands; and in a third subgroup (18%), the husbands reported higher levels of victimization than the wives. Additionally, the authors concluded that the greatest distress was found in the asymmetrical relationships among highly victimized men and women regardless of gender.

Johnson (1995) helps reconcile some of the debate over women's physical violence and the mutuality of violence. As noted in the discussion above, he argues that two distinct forms of violence occur in U.S. families. Data from large-scale national surveys show a predominance of one form of violence, "common couple violence," largely reflecting more "minor" violence and a reciprocity of assaults between partners. In the second form of violence, data from shelter, clinical, and criminal justice samples reflect an interpersonal dynamic in which women are systematically terrorized and subjected to serious and frequent beatings and women's violence is self-defensive in nature. Johnson views these two forms of assaults as virtually non-overlapping in nature.

Overall, although less evidence documents the patterns of women's violence in intimate relationships, it appears that women's violence toward intimate partners does exist but is different in nature from that of men. Indeed, available evidence suggests that women's physical violence is less injurious and less likely to be characterized as motivated by attempts to dominate or terrorize the partner. For example, domination and control of women in intimate relationships may take multiple forms that can coexist. These multiple forms encompass abuse in physical, sexual, emotional, or economic spheres of a woman's life. So, for example, battered women may be abused in other ways, such as being kept under surveillance or not permitted to work but provided with only limited access to money (Hanmer, 1996). No evidence in the literature (that we are aware of) describes a comparable *system of victimization* for men in intimate heterosexual relationships. The notion of different types or dimensions of intimate violence has important implications for policy and practice and needs to be examined in greater depth.

Assessing Types of Abusive Relationships

Male Perpetrators

A hit is a hit is a hit, or is it? Although the general consensus is that no aggression by intimate partners should be tolerated, more recently disagreement has arisen about whether the "one size fits all" approach to defining battering and batterers is appropriate. Often, early research based on varying samples or solely on the reports of battered women depicted batterers as regular guys with poor impulse

BOX 1.1 Different Types of Batterers

Assaultive Type	Characteristics
Family Only	High dependency on partner
	Low levels of impulsivity
	Poor communication skills
	Family-of-origin violence
Dysphoric/Borderline	Parental rejection
	Child abuse (family-of-origin violence)
	High dependency on partner
	Poor communication
	Poor social skills
	Hostile to women
	Low remorse
Generally Violent/Antisocial	Family-of-origin violence
	Delinquency
	Deficits in communication, social skills
	Violence viewed as appropriate response to provocation

control and drug/alcohol problems or as sadistic psychopaths (Gondolf, 1988b). The theoretical and clinical importance of distinguishing between different types of violent men has also been well documented in Holtzworth-Munroe and Stuart's (1994) review of the evidence on different typologies of male batterers. Their own typology distinguishes three types of maritally violent men: (a) family only, (b) dysphoric/borderline, and (c) generally violent/antisocial. The types differ in background and other characteristics (see Box 1.1) and in the nature of mental health and other services. The family-only abuser (perhaps similar to the common couple phenomenon described above) is described as less deviant or deficient on some indicators, including impulsivity, substance abuse, criminal behavior, and social skill deficits. Relative to nonviolent men, these abusers do have a history of exposure to aggression in the family of origin and are hypothesized to have poor communication and social skills, high levels of dependence on their partners, and low levels of impulsivity. The dysphoric/borderline batterer is hypothesized as having a history of parental rejection and child abuse, some history of delinquency, a high level of dependency on his partner, poor communication and social skills, a hostile attitude toward women, positive attitude toward violence, and low level of remorse for his violence. The generally violent/antisocial batterer represents the most aggressive, impulsive, and antisocial behavior. Risk factors include family-of-origin history of abuse and involvement with delinquency. For these men, deficits in all areas mentioned above are more profound than those found in the other types of batterers. These men likely view violence as an appropriate response to any provocation.

The authors of 14 of the typologies reviewed by Holtzworth-Munroe and Stuart (1994) all concluded that the different types require different services. For example, it has been suggested that treatment for personality disorder is central to work with the generally violent/antisocial type but is rarely needed by the family-only type of batterer. As is the case in child sex offender research, however, controlled studies examining different treatment strategies for the various offender typologies have rarely been conducted. Although the typologies provided by Holtzworth-Munroe and Stuart need to be tested empirically, they appear to be consistent with other emerging research about different typologies of batterers. For example, Johnson's (1995) discussion of family violence types was addressed above, and recent research on physiological differences among batterers (Gottman et al., 1995; to be discussed below) adds to our understanding of the ways batterers vary.

Theoretical Explanations for Partner Violence

Theories on the causes of partner violence provide a framework for understanding and responding to this phenomenon. Additionally, different theories point to particular variables or risk markers that might alert clinicians to the potential for partner violence in an intimate partnership. Thus, the more integrated and encompassing the theoretical model, the more valid the model for the purpose of predicting intimate violence. The latter approach is not without its critics, however, and currently dispute rages over the relative importance of one framework over another (e.g., a social-structural framework over an emphasis on psychopathology; Dutton, 1994; Miller, 1994; Renzetti, 1994). Early theoretical development on the causes of partner abuse (Gelles & Straus, 1978) identified 15 theories, organized into three broad categories—intraindividual theory, sociocultural theory, and social-psychological theory (Bersani & Chen, 1988)—that provide guidelines for the risk factors that need to be considered.

Intraindividual theory has emphasized the role of alcohol and other drugs and psychological traits such as self-esteem (Hamberger & Hastings, 1986; Hudson & McIntosh, 1981; Roy, 1977) and antisocial personality disorder (Holtzworth-Munroe & Stuart, 1994) in partner violence. The contribution to later intrafamily aggression of individual biological and neurological factors such as childhood attention deficit disorders or head injuries (Elliott, 1988; Warnken, Rosenbaum, Fletcher, Hoge, & Adelman, 1994) as risk markers for relationship aggression are not often incorporated into sociological, feminist, or even psychological theories and research on intrafamily aggression. A growing body of research, however, suggests the importance of including personality, neurological, and even physiological factors into models of relationship aggression (Miller, 1994). Increasingly, attention is being drawn to variations in psychological pathology among batterers (Dutton, 1994; Gondolf, 1988b; Holtzworth-Munroe & Stuart, 1994).

Sociocultural theories focus on the influence of social location (social class, education, income) on partner violence and have attempted to integrate social-structural and family processes (Kaufman Kantor et al., 1994; Straus, 1973). Feminist explanations of women's victimization are related to, and also underscore, sociocultural factors. In the feminist view, the central factors that foster partner assaults include the historically male-dominated social structure and socialization practices teaching men and women gender-specific roles (Pagelow, 1984; Smith, 1990; Ylló, 1984). The major constructs in a feminist analysis of wife abuse are the structure of relationships in a male-dominated (patriarchal) culture, power, and gender (Bograd, 1988). Consequently, the units of analysis in feminist research may also be at the societal level, rather than at the intrapersonal level.

Social-psychological approaches have stressed social learning through experience and exposure to violence in the family (Kalmuss,

BOX 1.2 Three Broad Categories of Intimate Violence Theory and Their
Risk Factors

Theoretical Explanations	Risk Factors
Intraindividual	Factors within the individual: e.g., excessive drinking; personality disorders, biological or neurophysiological disorders
Sociocultural	Importance of social location: social class; education; income, employment status
	Social-structural and family processes: traditional gender roles in families
Social-psychological	Social learning: exposure to violence in the family one grows up in

1984; O'Leary, 1988; Straus et al., 1980). For an example of the latter,
O'Leary's (1988) social learning model of partner violence suggests
five major variables, or risk factors, for physical partner violence:
(a) violence in the family of origin, (b) aggressive personality style,
(c) stress, (d) alcohol use and abuse, and (e) marital dissatisfaction.
A major focus of our discussion in this chapter is on risk factors at
the individual level; we also take into account risk markers reflecting
the three broad categories of intimate violence theory (see Box 1.2).

It is important to note that, for the most part, the theories pertain
to explanations of the *perpetrator's* violence. Thus, the discussion
that follows is focused mainly on the major risk markers associated
with male-perpetrated violence. Where the literature allows, risk
markers related to characteristics of female victims are also addressed.

Risk Markers for Partner Violence

Risk factors or *risk markers* refers to characteristics associated
with an increased likelihood that a problem behavior will occur. An
important caution, however, is that the presence of one or more risk
markers is not equivalent to a causal relationship. It simply means
that the odds of an associated event (in this case, intimate assaults)
are greater when one or more risk markers are present. Hotaling and

Sugarman's (1986) analysis of risk markers for partner violence found that eight characteristics were consistent risk markers of the husband's violence toward the wife:

1. Sexual aggression toward the wife/partner
2. Violence toward the children
3. Witnessing parental violence as a child or teen
4. (Working class) Occupational status
5. Excessive alcohol usage
6. (Low) Income
7. (Low) Assertiveness
8. (Low) Educational level

Analyses from three national U.S. surveys (Gelles & Cornell, 1990; Kaufman Kantor et al., 1994; Straus et al., 1980) also show that particular risk markers are enduring and generally consistent predictors of intimate violence across several years of survey research conducted among several thousand families in the general population. These risk markers include cross-generational violence (childhood abuse, witnessing parental violence), occupational status, excessive alcohol use, and socioeconomic status (Aldarondo & Sugarman, 1996; Kaufman Kantor & Asdigian, 1996; Kaufman Kantor & Straus, 1989; Straus & Gelles, 1990b; Sugarman, Aldarondo, & Boney-McCoy, 1996). Whereas research based on clinical populations, such as male batterers in treatment for relationship violence, has supported the significance of the latter "sociological" risk markers from survey populations, the body of clinical, mainly psychological research has also emphasized the importance of personality variables as major risk markers (Dutton, 1994; Gondolf, 1988b; Holtzworth-Munroe & Stuart, 1994). In this chapter, in our discussion of risk markers, we emphasize violence across generations (parental violence), socioeconomic risk factors (income, education, occupational status), and alcohol and personality factors (sexual aggression is discussed in Chapter 4). We also consider additional risk markers (gender, biology, the life course) that have emerged from current research as notable areas of inquiry.

Gender as a Risk Marker

Are women placed at risk for victimizations by the same complex of factors that place their partners at risk for perpetrating the violence?

Our ability to answer this question is limited because most research on risk markers for intimate violence has focused on the male perpetrator. Some have argued that research on victim characteristics is an inappropriate focus and constitutes a form of blaming the victim. For the most part, theories of partner violence pertain to explanations of the perpetrator's aggression. This theoretical emphasis on the perpetrator is supported by analyses of risk markers that revealed that eight characteristics were consistently associated with being *an abuser*, whereas only one factor (witnessing violence as a child or adolescent) was consistently associated with being *a victim* of wife abuse (Hotaling & Sugarman, 1986). Yet, stereotypes persist that partner abuse occurs because of the victims' masochism or because women do things to provoke assaults. The question commonly asked by the general public, "Why do they stay?" implicitly suggests that victimization occurs because something is wrong with battered women. In fact, women remain in abusive relationships for many complex reasons, including economic dependency, ambivalent feelings toward their violent partners, and their traditional socialization. Moreover, Dobash and Dobash (1979) pointed out that blaming the victim of wife beating provides a justification for batterers' violence. As a result, when women nag or try to have an equal say in family decisions or refuse sex, husbands may believe that they are justified in using force (LaRossa, 1980) to keep the wives in line. In such a case, the woman is blamed by her husband for her own victimization (e.g., "She had it coming").

For these reasons, scant research examines victim characteristics that may be risk markers for abuse. The research that does exist is subject to erroneous attribution that is really the effects of abuse on women's personalities and mental health (see Chapter 2). In other words, it has not been clear whether the personality characteristics of battered women are the "effects, correlates or causes of abuse" (O'Leary & Murphy, 1992, p. 37). O'Leary and Murphy (1992) have also argued, however, that personality similarities are often the rule among married partners.

Violence Across Generations as a Risk Marker

A history of violence in the family of origin is probably the most widely accepted risk marker for the occurrence of partner violence (Arias, 1984; Kalmuss, 1984; Straus et al., 1980). On the basis of their initial study of 2,000 U.S. families, Straus and associates (1980) presented strong empirical evidence for the social learning of violence within families. A basic thesis underlying this work is that the family is the training ground for violence and that even the use of ordinary physical punishment such as spanking is associated with child abuse and wife beating. The two National Family Violence Surveys found increased rates of physical punishment, child abuse, and wife abuse by male and female partners subjected to high rates of physical punishment as children. Thus, multiple forms of family violence relate both across generations and within generations. Additionally, witnessing interparental violence is significantly associated with adult marital assaults. Studies based on clinical populations—usually battered women in shelters—support the national survey data and report high proportions of cross-generational violence in 42% to 81% of families of male batterers (Bowker, 1983a; Fagan, Stewart, & Hansen, 1983; Walker, 1984).

The primary mechanism believed to be involved in intergenerational transmission of violence is that of modeling the parental behaviors observed (Arias, 1984; O'Leary, 1988). Stith and Farley's (1993) analysis expanded on the dynamics of this process. Their analysis of male spousal violence in a treatment sample of male batterers and male alcoholics indicated that observation of parental violence in childhood diminishes men's self-esteem. In turn, the authors suggest, lowered self-esteem increases marital stress, alcoholism, and approval of marital violence. Normative approval of marital violence was also directly influenced by the process of social learning in the study findings. Alexander, Moore, and Alexander (1991) suggest that the development of attitudes toward women is also affected by having witnessed parental marital violence.

Abuse in childhood or exposure to marital violence in the family of origin may similarly increase women's risks of victimization. For example, women who have been assaulted by their partners are at least twice as likely to have grown up in a violent home, when compared with nonassaulted women (Kaufman Kantor & Straus, 1989). O'Leary (1988) suggests, however, that this relationship is a less consistent predictor of women's victimization than it is a predictor of men's violence. Where intergenerational effects exist, the mechanism may be that repeated attacks by parents can lead to damaged self-esteem and suppression of rage. These effects may be different for men and women and may be compounded by the current life situation. Women who were harshly punished in childhood or who

witnessed parental violence are more likely to be victimized as adults
because they have low self-esteem and have learned that assaults
from a loved one are legitimate or because they are more likely to
engage in mutual assaults with their spouses (Straus & Kaufman Kantor, 1994). According to some researchers, wives were more likely
than husbands to blame themselves for the first incident of violence
and were also more likely than husbands to report being beaten as
children. For both men and women, recollections of maternal beatings
predicted their perpetration of marital assaults, but recollections of
paternal beatings predicted marital victimization. The authors speculate about the possibility that maternal violence carries with it a violent message about appropriate styles of conflict resolution but that
paternal violence leads to a sense of helplessness (Langhinrichsen-
Rohling et al., 1995).

An important conclusion of research on the intergenerational
transmission of partner violence is that many risk markers for current
partner violence are interwoven in family-of-origin experience. For
example, because alcoholism and family violence are so intertwined,
both women and men exposed to violence at home may also have
suffered the effects of parental alcoholism (Widom, 1993). Intergenerational transmission of parental rejection and depressed mode
can also occur (Whitbeck, Hoyt, Simons, Conger, & Elder, 1992). Abuse
and the proclivity for violence may be transmitted along with problems such as having had a cold and unresponsive father (Shupe,
Stacey, & Hazlewood, 1987). One study concluded that women subjected to abusive parenting may develop a "hostile, rebellious orientation" and, consequently, be more likely to affiliate with and marry
similar men (Simons, Johnson, Beaman, & Conger, 1993). This mechanism could also be mediated, however, by the partners' shared history
of similar delinquent behavior (e.g., alcohol other drug use) or current
shared lifestyle factors.

Can the Cycle of Abuse Be Broken? Discussions of intergenerational violence are often frustrating because they imply an unbreak-
able chain of events. Of course, few absolutes are found in social
behavior; what is transmitted is a vulnerability to victimization or
perpetration of aggression. The vulnerability is heightened by the
double whammy effect of exposure to both parental child abuse and
witnessing parental spousal assaults. Widom (1989) suggests that
protective factors include the following:

- Age of exposure: The older the better
- Gender: Boys may be more vulnerable for criminal behavior
- Temperament
- Intelligence
- Cognitive appraisal

In regard to cognitive issues, perceptions of the abuse as caused by external reasons, rather than by internal reasons such as rejection, are associated with more positive outcomes. Similarly, Caesar's research (1988) comparing maritally violent and nonmaritally violent men (both family-history positive for violence) found that nonviolent men were less likely than batterers to view their mothers as victims in marital fights between parents that they had witnessed. Nonviolent men seemed to have been more aware of parental shortcomings; that is, they did not idealize and were not protective of violent parents, as were the batterers. They also did not choose sides between parents. Additionally, Caesar described those men who broke the cycle of abuse as having better coping mechanisms; for example, they had constructive outlets for their emotions, such as sports or running.

Personality as a Risk Marker

Our discussion of violence across generations provides some understanding of how personality is shaped by the family-of-origin experience and contributes to future attributes and behaviors conducive to both victimization and violence. For example, the excessive controlling behaviors of maritally violent men may be caused by their feelings of helplessness and dependency stemming from abusive childhoods (Shupe et al., 1987).

The literature on personality factors associated with male battering is large. Men who batter are often emotionally dependent, insecure, low in self-esteem and empathy, and exhibit low impulse control and poor communication and social skills (Gondolf, 1988b; Holtzworth-Munroe, 1992; Holtzworth-Munroe & Stuart, 1994; Murphy, Meyer, & O'Leary, 1994; Rounsaville, 1978; Shields, McCall, & Hanneke, 1988) and are often irritable and belligerent (Dutton, 1988; Gottman et al., 1995; Margolin, John, & Gleberman, 1988; Shupe et al., 1987). Aggressive and hostile personality styles are also reliably found in many studies of maritally violent men (Heyman, O'Leary, & Jouriles, 1995).

Neidig, Friedman, and Collins (1988) used assessments of self-esteem, attitudes toward women and others, and empathy and authoritarianism in their study of male military personnel. The findings revealed that abusive men differed from nonabusive men only in regard to the lower self-esteem of abusive men and their low trust in others.

Use of the Minnesota Multiphasic Personality Inventory (MMPI; Hathaway & McKinley, 1967) and Millon Clinical Multiaxial Inventory (MCMI; Millon, 1987) evaluations or other psychological inventories that are used with batterers reveals elevations on measures of borderline symptomatology, passive aggressive and aggressive tendencies, narcissistic and antisocial characteristics, anxiety, depression, and somatic complaints (Dutton & Starzomski, 1993; Else, Wonderlitch, Beatty, Christie, & Staton, 1993; Flournoy & Wilson, 1991; Hastings & Hamberger, 1988; Maiuro, Cahn, Vitaliano, Wagner, & Zegree, 1988; Murphy, Meyer, & O'Leary, 1993). An important caution in summarizing or generalizing from the results of standardized assessment tools is that scale elevations vary across studies. Consistent with our discussion of typologies, no singular profile defines all abusive men (Hamberger & Hastings, 1986). Furthermore, men without any abnormal findings in clinical assessment tools may engage in violence toward their partners.

Personality Risk Markers in Male Batterers

- Emotional dependence
- Insecurity
- Low self-esteem
- Low empathy
- Low impulse control
- Poor communication and social skills
- Aggressive and hostile personality styles
- Antisocial personality
- Narcissism
- Anxiety
- Depression

Substance Abuse as a Risk Marker

What Role Do Alcohol and Other Drugs Play in Intimate Violence? Alcohol is the drug most commonly associated with violence (Fagan,

1990, 1993), and substance abuse is a consistent finding in many of the profiles of abusive men. Other psychoactive drugs, such as barbiturates, amphetamines, opiates (withdrawal), phencyclidine, cocaine, and alcohol-cocaine combinations, have been associated with aggression (Fagan, 1990; Goldstein, Belluci, Spunt, & Miller, 1989). All together, the aggressive effects of psychoactive drugs other than alcohol have been investigated less, and the results have been inconsistent. Taylor and Chermack's review (1993) found that drugs with depressive effects are most likely to facilitate aggression, and Fagan (1990) found solid evidence of a psychopharmacological basis only for the combined effects of an alcohol-cocaine combination. Aldarondo (in press) found that a lifetime history of any "hard drug" use (e.g., cocaine, amphetamines, heroin) by the husband was associated with a more persistent pattern of abuse in intimate relationships. Physical violence, however, is not an inevitable consequence of any intoxicant usage. Because of the consistency with which alcohol has emerged as a risk marker in general research on aggression and specific research on wife assault, our primary focus in this section is alcohol-related wife assault.

Conventional wisdom about the alcohol-violence linkage has emphasized alcohol's powers as a disinhibitor or drunkenness as an excuse for violence (see Kaufman Kantor & Straus, 1989). Attributing alcohol's effects on marital aggression to disinhibition, however, understates the complexity of the relationship. Experimental laboratory studies examining alcohol effects on aggression have generally demonstrated both direct effects of alcohol on aggression and indirect effects mediated by beliefs about alcohol's ability to change behavior (Bushman & Cooper, 1990; Gustafson, 1986; Lang, Goeckner, Adesso, & Marlatt, 1975; Pihl, Zeichner, Niaura, Nagy, & Zacchia, 1981; Taylor & Leonard, 1983; Zeichner & Pihl, 1979). Reviews of research on alcohol and wife assaults, however, yield wide-ranging estimates suggesting that from 6% to 85% of wife assaults are alcohol involved. One or both of the parties is more likely to be intoxicated at the time of an assault when the husband is a heavy daily drinker or binge drinker (Kaufman Kantor, 1993; Kaufman Kantor & Straus, 1987; Leonard, 1993). This was found to be the case for about one half of the violent families interviewed in the 1985 National Family Violence Survey (Kaufman Kantor & Straus, 1987).

Alcohol-related family assaults have been explained in many ways pointing to the importance of social context (e.g., fights over a

spouse's drunkenness that lead to partner violence). Kaufman Kantor's
(1990, 1993) examination of the relationship between alcohol consumption patterns and intrafamily violence revealed significant effects of a family history of violence and current family alcohol use
on the incidence of child abuse and wife abuse. The author concluded
that aggressive beliefs about the effects of alcohol and the appropriateness of inflicting violence while under the influence may both be
learned from the family. For example, an adult may recall being beaten
by an intoxicated parent or recall violent encounters between parents
when one or both were drinking. One result of such exposure is an
increased likelihood that these experiences will be reenacted in the
second generation because of modeling influences.

Kaufman Kantor and Asdigian's research (1996) found that although some evidence supports contentions that men drink to be
violent (Gelles, 1974), this represents only one possible scenario. Furthermore, it assumes harmful intention and ignores the many factors
potentially present in a drinking situation, such as drinking or aggression by the other partner. In addition, it is possible simultaneously
to hold competing expectancies about alcohol's effects (Rohsenow &
Bacharowski, 1984). For example, people may choose to drink or get
drunk to forget their troubles. But because each drinking situation is
composed of many situational variables, such as the amount drunk,
the partner's drunkenness, and issues raised by either partner when
drinking, aggression does not necessarily follow from drunkenness.

The pharmacological effects of alcohol often tend to be minimized
in much of the research and theorizing about alcohol's importance to
wife assaults. Despite ongoing debate about the precise pharmacological
effects, the consensus is that alcohol disrupts cognitive functioning
by diminished ability to reason, reduced ability to perceive or calcu-
late consequences of aggressive behaviors, and enhanced perception
of threat (Pihl, Smith, & Farrell, 1983; Taylor & Chermack, 1993). All
the latter mechanisms bear upon the process of social interaction and
are likely mechanisms that could increase the risk of partner violence. It is clear that aggression may be a consequence of alcohol's
impairment of perception, judgment, and memory. Distorted perceptions increase the likelihood of miscommunications, developing resent-
ment, and ability to take into account the consequences of aggressive
actions (Kaufman Kantor & Asdigian, 1996).

Heavy drinking by women is found infrequently in surveys based
on general population samples (Kaufman Kantor & Straus, 1987). Re-

search examining clinical samples of alcoholic women, however, does suggest that such women have high rates of victimization over multiple relationships. In a review of the research on intoxication and women's victimization, Kaufman Kantor and Asdigian (1996) concluded that such victimizations appear to be more of a function of the male partner's drinking and propensity to violent behavior.

Biology and Physiology of Intimate Violence as Risk Markers

Does Intimate Violence Have a Biochemical Basis? Aside from alcohol's acknowledged importance to aggression and family assaults, the contributions of biology or physiology to violence in the family have received little attention. Few studies attempt to integrate biological, social, and psychological perspectives (McKenry, Julian, & Gavazzi, 1995). At least one treatment program for violent men, however, incorporates a diet for hypoglycemia (low blood sugar). Deschner (cited in Shupe et al., 1987) suggests a link between blood sugar level and neurochemical imbalance leading to depression, rage, and other emotional disturbances. Shupe and associates (1987) caution that male batterers provided with such treatment tend to use the hypoglycemia notion to rationalize their violence. Research on the biochemical links to aggression has considered other physiological pathways. For example, Lindman, von der Pahlen, Ost, and Eriksson (1992) conducted serum analysis of ethanol (an alcohol by-product), testosterone (a hormone), cortisol (a hormone elevated in stress), and glucose (blood sugar) in 16 men arrested by police after spousal assault incidents. They found elevated levels of ethanol and glucose, low serum testosterone, and high cortisol levels in the arrested men, compared with their sober state later. The authors also caution readers, however, that cortisol may have been temporarily elevated by hangover or withdrawal stress or that economic hardship and frequent marital conflicts can pose chronic stressors that increase cortisol levels. The authors concluded that there is little effect of intoxication because no differences were found in ethanol levels in a nonaggressive control group of men drinking in a bar. They also did not find effects of testosterone but believe that their findings do not preclude the possibility that high testosterone levels contributed to aggressive coping styles before the onset of alcohol abuse patterns. Moreover, they concluded that aspects of the conflict, drinking, and arrest situation were most likely responsible for changes in blood chemistry.

Elliot (1988) acknowledged that neuropsychological causes of wife assault are often overlooked. We know that organic deficits can affect cognition, perceptions, emotions, and behaviors but rarely relate these factors to the occurrence of intimate violence. Elliot's review of this literature identified a wide range of causes of neuropsychological disorders associated with persistent criminal aggressive behavior, including borderline syndromes, schizophrenia, antisocial personality disorders, and brain defects. He also identified other important potential organic causes of violence, including temporal lobe epilepsy and head injuries. He hypothesized that organically based minimal brain dysfunction might be related to violent behavior because the associated cognitive problems can interfere with communication patterns. Two other potentially disruptive types of behavior patterns fall into the latter group: episodic dyscontrol (unpredictable attacks of rage) and antisocial personality disorder. These have been discussed above as factors affecting the dynamics and patterns of abuse. Attention deficit disorder is also linked with an early onset type of aggressive behavior that can continue into adulthood. This syndrome includes attention deficits, hyperactivity, impulsivity, learning defects, and some associated neurological symptoms.

Systematic research on the prevalence of organic and neurological problems among batterers is scant. Elliot's data on the prevalence of minimal brain dysfunction among batterers suggest that it was present in 40% of cases of episodic dyscontrol in the family. His was a sample of patients seen in specialized clinics for reasons other than family violence, however, which raises questions about generalizability. Therefore, no conclusions about prevalence can be accurately drawn from these data. A recent study by Rosenbaum and associates (1994) compared groups of men (53 partner-abusive men and 32 maritally discordant men) and found that head injury significantly increased the odds of marital assaults by male batterers. Slightly more than one half of abusive husbands had experienced a head injury, compared with one quarter of the other men studied. Although these authors concluded that head injury may play a role in marital aggression, they also cautioned that a third variable cause, antisocial behavior disorder, may actually be increasing the rate of both head injuries and marital aggression because antisocial men may be more likely to get into fights with others, leading to head injuries, as well as engage in assaults on their wife.

One recent experimental laboratory study examined the relationship among physiological indicators, emotionally aggressive behavior, and general violence in batterers. Gottman and associates (1995) used changes in the male batterer's heart rate reactivity to differentiate types of violent men. Men designated as Type I batterers *decreased* their heart rates during marital conflicts, whereas Type II men increased their heart rates during laboratory conflict situations. Type I men were described as more verbally aggressive toward their wives, more belligerent and violent toward others, rated high in antisocial behavior and sadistic aggression, and were more often drug dependent and lower in dependency than Type II men. Type I men were also more likely to have witnessed violence between their parents. On 2-year follow-up, none of the Type I marriages had ended. Type II men were not less violent in their marriages, compared with Type I men, but they were not likely to be violent toward others. Interestingly, the separation-divorce rate for Type II men at 2 years was 27%, whereas none of the Type I men had gotten separated or divorced. Gottman and associates (1995) suggest that the reason for the greater stability of the Type I marriages, a seemingly paradoxical finding in the light of the sadistic aggression and drug dependence, is that (a) women are more fearful of leaving such men and are less likely to express anger toward them and (b) women married to Type I men are themselves more often antisocial and may be more conditioned to a violent relationship than other women.

The results of the body of research on the biology and physiology of aggression show some promising areas for future consideration. There is also a need to consider the total picture, however, including the fact that social factors can shape biology and physiology related to antisocial behavior and family assaults.

Socioeconomic Risk Markers

What Is the Relationship Between Educational Attainment and Violence? The relationship between educational attainment and partner violence is complex and inconsistent. Hotaling and Sugarman's (1986) review of more than 400 empirical reports on husband-to-wife violence found that higher educational level was associated with less violence in more than one half of the studies examined in their analyses. Other research has found a mixed relationship between educational attainment and partner violence. Straus and associates (1980), for example, found that partner violence was most common among individuals with high school diplomas or at least some high school education. More recent research suggests that the absence of a college education is associated with a high frequency of both moderate and severe violence (Downs, Miller, & Panek, 1993). Rollins and Oheneba-Sakyi's (1990) research on Utah households, however, found no differences between violent and nonviolent families on the basis of education. Education may be most important as it relates to the likelihood of finding employment in a stable and well-paying job.

Are Employment and Occupational Status Risk Markers for Violence? Previous research has suggested that households in which the husband is unemployed or employed only part-time have increased rates of violence, particularly severe violence (Gelles, 1978; Gelles & Straus, 1978; Hornung, McCullough, & Sugimoto, 1981; Jasinski, 1996; Kaufman Kantor et al., 1994; McLaughlin, Leonard, & Senchak, 1992; Steinmetz & Straus, 1974). Unemployment or part-time work with few, if any, benefits is very stressful economically for families and may increase the likelihood of partner violence. Other research, however, has found no relationship between employment status and violence among intimates (Hotaling & Sugarman, 1990; Rollins & Oheneba-Sakyi, 1990). Evidence also suggests that, in addition to unemployment, occupational class or status is related to partner violence. For example, rates of violence between husbands and wives have been found to be twice as high in families of blue-collar workers than in families of white-collar workers (Kaufman Kantor & Straus, 1987; Stets & Straus, 1989; Straus et al., 1980). McLaughlin et al. (1992) also found that rates of moderate aggression were twice as high among working- and middle-class husbands, compared with upper-class husbands.

Are Occupational and Social Status Discrepancies Risk Markers for Violence? Occupational and social status discrepancies have been established as risk markers for partner violence. Some evidence suggests that households with status incompatibilities are at a greater risk for partner violence than those without incompatibilities. Smith (1988), for example, found that households in which the wife works, or works more than her male partner, may be at a greater risk for spousal violence. One explanation for this finding suggests that men may use physical violence to compensate for their inability to be the primary breadwinner in the family (Straus et al., 1980). Some evidence also suggests, however, that violence is more likely to occur in couples in which the husband has a much higher status than his wife (Hornung et al., 1981). Yllö and Straus (1990) have suggested that, on the one hand, in a couple in which the wife has the higher status, the husband may feel threatened by this and use violence to restore his authority. In a couple in which the wife has a much lower status than that of her husband, on the other hand, he may use violence as a mechanism of control and dominance. The results of these studies provide strong evidence that inequalities of status and power are undesirable in marriages at minimum and, at maximum, increase the probability of partner assaults.

Is Income a Risk Marker? Research evidence suggests that income, particularly poverty, is an important risk marker for partner violence (Dibble & Straus, 1980; Hotaling & Sugarman, 1986; Kaufman Kantor, 1990; Straus & Smith, 1990b). Straus and associates (1980) found that families living at or below a family income of $20,000 had a rate of violence 500% greater than families with incomes greater than $20,000. Families living in poverty may suffer from stress because of an inability to meet their needs with the resources available to them. This stress may then lead to frustration and possibly aggression (Conger et al., 1990). Stress-producing events such as unemployment and other economic problems associated with it, such as the stresses of daily survival, are also more likely to occur in low-income families (Gelles & Straus, 1978), who may be ill-equipped to deal with them.

As with many of the other risk markers considered thus far, economic, educational, and occupational deprivation are strong predictors, but they are not sufficient causes for intimate violence. Our discussion above on the dynamics of power and control suggested that multiple dimensions often come into play, such as the combination of low self-esteem, feelings of lost interpersonal control from unemployment, and not enough money to support the family's needs. When these factors coexist with a history of violence in the family of origin, the risks of intimate violence are increased.

Life Course Risk Markers

An analysis of life course dynamics provides a useful framework for examining changes in marital conflict resolution patterns over the life span of a relationship. For example, courtship, early marriage, pregnancy, and middle and late marriage may each carry differential risks for the likelihood of marital assaults. Unfortunately, scant prospective research explicitly examines the effects of life course transitions on marital violence trajectories. Analyses, primarily of cross-sectional studies based on large national surveys, however, support the existence of greater violence in the earlier phases of marriage and a decline in marital violence across the life course (Suitor, Pillemer, & Straus, 1990).

The stability of violence patterns over the course of a relationship is an important area that requires further investigation. A study of stability in marital patterns by O'Leary and associates (1989), for example, found a moderate association between aggressive behavior in courtship and similar behavior 30 months after marriage. Aldarondo (1996), however, found that, in many relationships, physical assaults against women may stop completely or may occur inconsistently over the course of the relationship. Other researchers have found relatively high rates of desistance (cessation of the assaults) among perpetrators of partner violence (Feld & Straus, 1990; Woffordt, Mihalic, & Menard, 1994).

Patterns of desistance may differ vastly for criminal justice samples of batterers or the terroristic batterer, as described above. Studies assessing the recurrence of violence among men who have undergone either voluntary or court-mandated treatment for wife battering find that treatment effects, at best, range from small to moderate and are dependent on a host of individual and program-related factors. Reviewers of this research (Burns, Meredith, & Paquette, 1991; Shepard, 1992) report re-arrest rates for spousal assaults ranging from 4% to 20% for posttreatment periods between 6 months and 5 years. These rates are conservative and most likely underestimate the true incidence of recidivism because all spousal assaults are not reported to, or acted on by the police. Indeed, studies examining partner reports of violence have found that up to 54% of men continue to be physically abusive within a 6-month to 1-year period following treatment.

It is difficult to make any definitive conclusions about the stability of partner violence over the life course because of the lack of longitudinal research, the methodological problems associated with locating severely violent individuals, and differences that exist across samples. It is possible, however, to make some generalizations based on research that specifically focuses on one stage of the life course. This body of literature is examined below.

Courtship Violence Risk Markers

What Is the Prevalence of Courtship Violence? Most studies addressing partner violence have focused primarily on married couples. The study of marital violence, however, has expanded to include intimate, nonfamilial relationships such as cohabiting and dating or courtship relationships. We prefer the term *courtship violence* for the phenomenon to be discussed in this section because it seems more applicable to the initial relationship phase of adult intimate partners. Although dating/"courting" relationships may involve a high degree of intimacy, they are often not considered official relationships either socially or legally (Deal & Wampler, 1986). A review of 17 separate studies (Sugarman & Hotaling, 1989) on lifetime prevalence estimates of dating violence among college students reported that an average of about one third of students surveyed reported dating violence involvement. Although these estimates are informative, much of the research examining courtship violence uses nonrandom samples of college or high school students, making it impossible to generalize about the actual extent of courtship violence. Additionally, respondents are often asked to recall instances of physical aggression that may have occurred in their most recent dating relationship even if it was several years prior.

Researchers hold discrepant views about whether the theoretical model used to describe marital violence is applicable to the courtship period. Notably, dating couples are not economically or contractually bound or bound by children (Carlson, 1987). Also, despite substantial evidence for the existence of sexual inequality and cultural norms favoring violence against women (Straus, 1976), some authors argue against the applicability of this theoretical model to courtship violence (Arias, Samios, & O'Leary, 1987; Lloyd, Koval, & Cate, 1989). The reason for this differing view is related to the findings of some studies that many women admit to aggression against dating partners. There is also evidence, however, that females suffer more injuries than males (Makepeace, 1984), that females are more likely than males to describe their aggressive behavior as self-defensive, and that males are more likely than females to describe their aggressive behavior as

motivated by needs to intimidate, control, or coerce the other
(DeMaris, 1987; Makepeace, 1984; Olday & Wesley, 1983). The discrepant views of appropriate theoretical explanations of dating violence and the finding of reciprocal aggression in dating violence suggest to us that a more integrated theoretical model is needed that
includes gender inequalities and cultural norms, as well as the social
learning of violence.

What Are the Risk Markers for Courtship Violence? Studies examining the etiology of courtship violence have established risk markers
for abusive behaviors similar to those discussed for marital violence
(e.g., societal norms, along with exposure to violence in the home,
parental divorce, and contextual factors such as stress, jealousy, alcohol and other drug use, and the seriousness of the relationship;
DeMaris, 1987; Foo & Margolin, 1995; Makepeace, 1983; Riggs &
O'Leary, 1989; Sugarman & Hotaling, 1989; Tondonato & Crew, 1992).
Research examining dating violence, however, has lacked consensus
on the importance of a history of abuse to adolescent relationship
violence (Foo & Margolin, 1995; Smith & Williams, 1992), although
several studies do show that having experienced child abuse increases the likelihood of being violent toward dating companions
(Laner, 1983; Marshall & Rose, 1988; Sigelman, Berry, & Wiles, 1984).
In addition, characteristics of a "battering personality" commonly
discussed in the literature on married couple violence have also been
found to be associated with courtship violence (Ryan, 1995).

Both the number of dating partners and the frequency of dating
have been found to increase the risk for violence (Bergman, 1992).
This is most likely a function of greater time at risk, as well as greater
odds of increasing intimacy developing with frequent contacts. The
more time spent together, the greater the possibility of conflict occurring. However, intimacy may also carry with it a greater presumed right
to influence the partner (Laner & Thompson, 1982). Generally, more
serious and emotionally intense relationships have greater chances
of conflicts developing, but even relationships of short duration carry
with them the chance of serious violence (Makepeace, 1989).

Does Courtship Violence Carry Over Into Marriage? An important
area of investigation that we need to be concerned with here is the
continuity of violence into the marital or cohabiting relationship. Evidence from shelter samples of women abused in their marriages in-

dicates that one half or more had been physically assaulted in a court-ship relationship as well (Roscoe & Benaske, 1985; Star, Clark, Goetz, & O'Malia, 1979). A study of couples in their first marriage found that 31% of men and 44% of women reported engaging in aggression against a courtship partner prior to their marriage (O'Leary, Arias, Rosenbaum, & Barling, 1985); 30% of respondents said they eventu-ally married someone who had abused them in courtship.

Early Stage of Marriage as a Risk Marker

Youth is probably one of the strongest risk markers for aggression, and therefore we might expect that the prevalence of marital assaults is highest among youthful partners in the early stage of marriage. In a longitudinal study of couples surveyed 1 month prior to their mar-riage and at 18 and 30 months thereafter, O'Leary and associates (1989) found that 27% of men and 36% of women indicated they had engaged in aggression 1 ½ years after their marriage. After another year, prevalence rates decreased slightly to 25% and 32%, respec-tively. Other research has found similar rates of partner violence among young adults (Elliot, Huizinga, & Morse, 1986). These rates are three to four times higher than those found by Straus and associates (1980) and Kaufman Kantor and associates (1994), neither of whom focused exclusively on the early marriage period. Others (McLaughlin et al., 1992; Straus et al., 1980), however, did find that the highest rates of partner violence were among those 30 years old and younger, and in particular the group 18 to 24 years old (Fagan & Browne, 1994).

In addition to youth, other factors may be associated with higher rates of violence in early marriage. Leonard and Senchak (1993) ex-amined alcohol, marital aggression, and relationship satisfaction among young couples (ages 18 to 29) applying for marriage licenses. This study, conducted in an urban setting, found that higher levels of relationship aggression in early marriage were associated with the husband's heavy alcohol use, marital dissatisfaction, the husband's hostility, and beliefs that alcohol excuses aggression. This study il-lustrates that other risk factors may interact with life course status to affect the probability of intimate violence.

Pregnancy and Marriage as Risk Markers

An important stage in the course of a relationship occurs if the woman becomes pregnant. Some evidence suggests that the changes taking place with pregnancy have implications for marital violence. Prevalence estimates of violence during pregnancy range from 7% (Amaro, Fried, Cabral, & Zuckerman, 1990; Campbell, Poland, Walder, & Ager, 1992) to 20% (Bullock & McFarlane, 1989). Much of the information regarding the relationship between pregnancy and wife assault comes from research using hospital samples without a comparison group of women who are not pregnant (Bullock & McFarlane, 1989; Campbell et al., 1992; Stark & Flitcraft, 1995; Stewart, 1994). Results from this research, together with anecdotal reports from victims, have suggested that pregnancy may be a time of increased risk for wife assault. Research using national probability samples, however, indicates that, once the analyses control for the effects of age (Gelles, 1990; Jasinski & Kaufman Kantor, 1997), pregnant women may be at no greater risk of experiencing wife assault than women who are not pregnant.

What Are the Dynamics of Violent Relationships During Pregnancy? Although evidence does indicate that pregnant women are at risk for marital violence, there is little agreement as to the dynamics of these violent relationships. Some evidence, for example, suggests that pregnancy is a time of respite for previously abused women and that violent attacks by their partners stop while they are pregnant (Campbell, Harris, & Lee, 1995; Campbell, Oliver, & Bullock, 1993). Other evidence suggests that violence may actually escalate with pregnancy (Campbell et al., 1992; Campbell, Harris, & Lee, 1995; Helton, 1986) or postpartum (Stewart, 1994). Campbell and Alford (1989) confirmed that many victims of marital rape report sexual assaults during pregnancy or soon after delivery (see Chapter 4 for more information on marital rape).

Research has indicated motives for men who abuse their pregnant partners. Campbell and associates (1993; Campbell, Harris, & Lee, 1995) found that jealousy of the unborn child and anger toward the unborn child were two motives. These were occasionally manifested in the type or location of the abuse (e.g., beatings aimed at the woman's abdomen). The results of their research also indicated that men may see pregnancy as interfering with the women's roles and duties as wives, such as their caretaking of the men. In this line of thought, the violence, though pregnancy specific, is not directly aimed at the child. Men may also see pregnancy as a threat to their definition of manhood that does not include taking care of babies (Campbell, Harris, & Lee,

1995). For some men, pregnancy may not change the amount or type of violence they inflict on their partners (Campbell et al., 1993).

Regardless of the dynamics of abuse against pregnant women, one consequence is that women involved in violent relationships enter prenatal care later in their pregnancy than do women in nonviolent relationships (Parker, 1993). They are also twice as likely to begin prenatal care in their third trimester (McFarlane, Parker, Soeken, & Bullock, 1992). Battered women are more likely than nonbattered women to give birth to preterm and low-birthweight infants (Bullock & McFarlane, 1989), to have miscarriages (Berrios & Grady, 1991; Stark & Flitcraft, 1995; Webster, Chandler, & Battistutta, 1996), and to incur preterm labor, fetal injury, and fetal death (Bohn, 1990).

Separation and Divorce as Risk Markers

Divorce and remarriage represent important stages in some relationships and could have important implications for partner violence. Some evidence suggests that divorced individuals are more likely to report violence (Levinger, 1966) or that separation may be a result of partner violence (Fagan et al., 1983; Kurz, 1996). In a random sample of 129 divorced women, for example, Kurz (1996) found that 19% of women left their marriages because of the violence. The termination of an intimate relationship may also pose an increased risk for violent behavior or more serious violence by partners who may not want the relationships to end (Ellis, 1987; Feld & Straus, 1990). Risks for sexual violence (Finkelhor & Yllö, 1985) and serious or lethal violence may also be greater when individuals try to leave relationships (Browne, 1987; Wallace, 1986; Wilbanks, 1983; Wilson & Daly, 1993). Evidence indicates that this risk is disproportionately incurred by women (Wilson & Daly, 1993). Moreover, death threats may extend to other people outside the couple as an attempt to prevent one member from leaving (Browne, 1987). Victims of partner violence may even stay in abusive relationships out of fear of retaliation or death (Browne, 1987).

After a separation or divorce, individuals may enter new relationships, creating new family units. This also represents an important stage in the life course that may be associated with partner violence. Individuals who were violent in previous relationships may also be violent in subsequent relationships because of the patterned nature of behavior. Another interpretation is that the stress of a new family may increase the risk for partner violence. Kalmuss and Seltzer (1986), using a national survey, found that violence was twice as likely to occur in remarried, compared with intact, families.

Late Stage of Marriage as a Risk Marker

What Is the Prevalence of Elder Partner Abuse? Limited empirical research documents the extent to which elderly persons are abused by their spouses or partners. Much of the research on elder abuse focuses on abuse by caretakers, such as adult children (Goldstein, 1995; Wolfe, Zak, Wilson, & Jaffe, 1986), or in institutional settings (Shiferaw et al., 1994). Moreover, such research often includes financial abuse and neglect, as well as physical violence. Two surveys that have examined partner abuse, one conducted in the United States (Pillemer & Finkelhor, 1988) and one in Canada (Podnieks, 1992), have found rates of physical violence ranging from 5 per 1,000 (Podnieks, 1992) to 20 per 1,000 (Pillemer & Finkelhor, 1988). Other research has found that from 23% to 33% of abusers of elderly persons were spouses (Hageboeck & Brandt, 1981; Wolf & Pillemer, 1989; Wolf, Strugnell, & Godkin, 1982). The limited research on partner violence among elderly persons may be partly a result of the lack of consensus and clarity of the definition of abuse (Lachs & Pillemer, 1995; McCreadie & Tinker, 1993; Wolf, 1988). It has also been suggested that older abused women are essentially an invisible population (American Association of Retired Persons [AARP], n.d.). Although the actual extent of elder partner abuse is unknown, some researchers estimate it is lower than other forms of violence in the family (Pillemer & Finkelhor, 1988).

What Are the Risk Markers for Elder Partner Abuse? There is some debate about whether elder abuse is a unique phenomenon (Wolf & Pillemer, 1989) or simply a continuation of physical abuse that began at an earlier point in the relationship (Matlaw & Spence, 1994). Assaults against older women may also begin as a result of age-related stresses such as retirement, failing health, caregiver burdens, or increased dependency (AARP, 1992). Wolf and Pillemer (1989) argue that the vulnerability of the elderly to abuse, the nature of the abuse suffered, and the relationship of the elderly to society make elder abuse a separate category from partner abuse. Others have compared abuse of the elderly to child abuse (AARP, 1992; Johnson, 1979). Some risk markers for abuse of the elderly have also been established as risk markers for partner violence of non-elderly persons (Harris, 1996). These include substance abuse (Pillemer & Finkelhor, 1989; Wolf, Godkin, & Pillemer, 1986), intergenerational transmission of violence (Steinmetz, 1977), external stress (Pillemer & Finkelhor, 1989; Podnieks, 1992), social isolation (Pillemer, 1985), and dependency (Paveza et al., 1992; Pillemer, 1985; Wolf et al., 1986). Other risk factors, such as disabilities, may be more particular to older individuals (Lachs, Berkman, Fulmer, & Horwitz, 1994). Wolf and Pillemer (1989), for example, found that almost one half of the 328 elderly victims of abuse they studied used walkers, canes, or wheelchairs.

Older victims of partner assaults may not self-identify as victims, thus creating a barrier to achieving safety. Other barriers include fear of retaliation, of having to appear in court, of being placed in a nursing home, of having decision-making rights taken away, and of having to leave home. Health concerns and problems associated with aging may also make victims dependent on their assaultive partners for such things as transportation, mobility, and socialization (AARP, n.d.).

What Is the Prevalence of Spousal Homicide? The most serious outcome of partner violence is spousal homicide. In 1988, 540 spousal murder cases were reported in the 75 largest counties in the United States (U.S. Bureau of Investigation & U.S. Department of Justice, 1995). In 1993, 5% of murders and nonnegligent manslaughters known to the police were of spouses and 4% were of dating partners (U.S. Department of Justice, 1995). Most of what we know about spousal homicide comes from studies of police records or from databases such as the Uniform Crime Reports. This information, though valuable, is somewhat limited in its ability to provide the context in which a murder took place. The Uniform Crime Reports also rely on the ability of police departments to consistently categorize victim-offender relationships and to provide this information to the national collection center. The information that does exist, however, has demonstrated that important gender differences exist in the risk of lethal assault by a spouse (Browne, 1987; U.S. Department of Justice, 1995; Wilson & Daly, 1993). In particular, wives are 1.3 times more at risk than husbands (Mercy & Saltzman, 1989). Several studies have also examined gender differences in perpetration of homicide and found that men were more likely to kill acquaintances and strangers and that women were more likely to kill intimate partners (Browne &

Williams, 1989; Jurik & Winn, 1990; Kellerman & Mercy, 1992; Wilbanks, 1983)

What Are the Risk Markers for Spousal Homicide? The information obtained from official records and other sources has indicated some risk markers for murder of a spouse. Mercy and Saltzman (1989), for example, found that homicides increased with a gap in age between the husband and the wife (Mercy & Saltzman, 1989). Alcohol has also been established as a risk marker for partner homicide (Wilbanks, 1983). Other research has suggested that homicides are often preceded by domestic quarrels (Jurik & Winn, 1990). Aldarondo and Straus (1994) reviewed clinical studies of extreme marital violence and summarized factors associated with life-threatening violence:

- High frequency of violence
- Dependency
- Physical injuries
- Violent behavior outside the home
- Rape of partner
- Physical violence in family of origin
- Possession or use of weapons
- Threats to hit and/or kill partner
- Having killed or abused pets
- Controlling and psychological maltreatment

Browne (1987) found a similar pattern of variables, as did Aldarondo and Straus (1994). Her research identified seven variables that distinguished between battered women who killed or seriously injured their abusive partners from battered women in the nonhomicide group:

- Frequent intoxication by the man
- Drug use by the man
- Frequent abuse
- Severe injuries to the woman
- Rape or threatened sexual assault by the man
- Threats to kill by the male partner
- Threats of suicide by the woman

The complex dynamics and characteristics of intimate partner violence that have a lethal ending are similar regardless of gender of the perpetrator. It should also be noted that the risk markers for lethal violence by men are consistent with the characteristics of Type I batterers identified by Gottman and associates (1995) as discussed above.

Implications for Practice and Policy

What Professionals Can Do

Screening for Victimization and Assessment of Risk

Some risk markers for partner violence can be identified by professionals who might come into contact with individuals or couples involved in violent relationships. Physical signs of abuse, such as bruises or other questionable injuries, should be noted and inquired about. In addition, general questions about marital satisfaction and quality can also be asked in a nonjudgmental and non-victim-blaming manner. Questions about violence, both current and in the family of origin, should become part of the documented family history because they indicate elevated risk. The mental health practitioner should also routinely ask questions such as the following:

- Is anyone in your family hitting you?
- Does your partner threaten you? your life?
- Does your partner prevent you from leaving the home, from getting a job, or from returning to school?
- What happens when your partner does not get his or her way?
- Does your partner threaten to hurt you when you disagree with him or her?
- Does your partner destroy things that you care about (e.g., your family photographs, your clothes, your pets)?
- Are you forced to engage in sex that makes you feel uncomfortable?
- Do you have to have intercourse after a fight to "make up"?
- Does your partner watch your every move? call home 10 times a day? accuse you of having affairs with everyone? (Schecter, 1987)

Other risk markers that should be assessed include excessive alcohol/illicit drug use by one or both partners and the presence of life stressors, such as a change in employment status (e.g., more responsibility at work, reduction in work load, reassignment to another job), pregnancy, and problems with children. Affirmative responses to threats of violence and of death, and destruction of property and pets are signs of potentially lethal violence. Immediate intervention may be necessary in such cases. In a group therapy session, professionals should watch for the relationship dynamics of the couple and guard against one partner controlling the other. Signs to watch for include one partner constantly speaking for the other and the demand by one partner to always be present when discussing the relationship. If possible, partners should be interviewed separately to allow each to feel free to speak openly about their relationship.

Professionals who deal with pregnant women are in a unique position to screen for marital violence and to initiate intervention if needed because pregnant women must come in periodically for checkups (Sampselle, Petersen, Murtland, & Oakley, 1992). During these visits, professionals can note any physical signs of abuse, such as bruises, as well as ask questions regarding abuse as part of both an oral and a written history (Campbell et al., 1993). Research evidence suggests that this process should involve more than one question regarding abuse. For example, Helton (1986) found that, of 68 self-identified battered women, 78% checked no to the first abuse-focused question in a written history. Because many batterers may attend doctor visits with their partners, written questions or a private interview may be a more appropriate mechanism for assessing risk for abuse (Campbell, Pugh, Campbell, & Visscher, 1995).

A particularly risky period for women in violent relationships occurs when they try to leave (Ellis, 1987; Feld & Straus, 1990). In particular, risks for lethal violence may be greatest when individuals try to leave relationships (Browne, 1987; Wilbanks, 1983; Wilson & Daly, 1993). Professionals who counsel victims of partner violence should watch for signs of escalating abuse, including more frequent and severe episodes of violence, and should be aware of any threats of violence or use of weapons. Such behavior may indicate an increased risk for lethal violence.

The ability of therapists to recognize the risk markers for lethal violence is extremely important. Some evidence, however, suggests that more training is needed in this area. Hansen, Harway, and Cervantes (1991), for example, found that, in a sample primarily composed of family therapists who were presented with case studies containing evidence of violence, almost one half did not address this violence as a problem.

Assessment of Male Partners. Counselors of abusive men suggest that specific questions are needed to assess the extent of violent behavior (Emerge, n.d.). Guidelines developed by counselors from Emerge, the first program in the United States for treating male batterers, suggest the need for concrete questions such as, What happens when you lose your temper? Did you become violent? What about grabbing or shaking? Have you hit her? When you hit her, was it a slap or a punch? They also suggest that violence needs to be defined to the men as any actions that force a partner to do things that she does not wish to do or that make her afraid. Therefore, questions should be posed about whether he ever threatened her, took away her car keys, threw things in her presence, damaged her property, or punched walls or doors. He should also be asked about when the violence occurred and against whom it was directed. Aldarondo (in press) cautions about the need to use language carefully. Because men often do not consider pushing and shoving to be violent behavior, the therapist should avoid using the term *violent.* Many of the behavioral items mentioned above are already included in the Conflict Tactics Scale (CTS; Straus, 1990); clinicians may wish to use or adapt this most frequently used assessment tool for couple violence or the recently revised version of the CTS (Straus & Hamby, 1996). Counselors should ask direct questions about the man's violence to help him take responsibility for his actions, as well as to understand the nature and extent of the abuse.

Assessment Tools for Abusive Behavior

Aldarondo (in press) suggests several tools for assessing abusive behavior in addition to the Conflict Tactics Scale, noted above. They are as shown in Box 1.3.

Assessment Tools for Alcohol and Other Drug Use

One limitation of the assessment tools is that none of the tools mentioned include measures of other risk markers, such as alcohol or other drug use. Because of the importance of substance abuse as a risk marker in serious intimate assaults, we recommend that clinicians routinely identify alcohol and other drug use patterns and continue to monitor them during treatment as well.

BOX 1.3 Tools for Assessing Abusive Behavior

Selected Measures of Intimate Violence	Source
The Abusive Behavior Inventory: 30-item self-report measure of physical, psychological abuse and control.	Sheppard and Campbell, 1992
The Aggression Scale: 19-item self-report measure of physical and psychological aggression.	Snyder and Snow, 1995
The Danger Assessment Instrument: 20-item, interviewer-administered measure. Asks women to use calendar for obtaining history of abuse. Limits to use for legal purposes.	Campbell, 1995
Spouse Specific Aggression Scale: 29-item self-rated scale measuring aggressive, assertive, and passive aggressive behaviors.	O'Leary and Curley, 1986

Problem Drinking Measures. Problem drinking may be assessed in several ways. One approach is to use the Michigan Alcoholism Screening Test (MAST; Selzer, 1971). Shortened versions of the MAST (10 items) have been found to be as effective as the complete instrument in discriminating between alcoholics and nonalcoholics (Pokorny, Miller, & Kaplan, 1972). This inventory of alcohol-related drinking problems includes items such as "Have you ever attended a meeting of Alcoholics Anonymous, or A.A., for your own drinking problem?" "Have you ever gotten into fights when drinking?" and "Have you ever neglected your family or your work for 2 or more days in a row because of your drinking?"

Another approach is to use standard beverage-specific questions about the quantity, frequency, and variability of alcohol consumption. By "beverage-specific questions," we mean that persons should be asked the same series of drinking questions for wine, beer, and then again for distilled alcohol beverages.

Illicit Drug Use Measures. In our own research, we have used standard items measuring the type and frequency of illicit drug use in the past year or ever. The items are based on those used in the National Household Drug Survey (Miller et al., 1982) and by drug researchers (Elinson & Nurco, 1975). The Diagnostic Interview Schedule (Gleason,

1993) also is a potential source of items that measure drug dependency. Questions may be repeated to assess the partner's usage.

Summary

This chapter examined current research on the dynamics and patterns of family violence, the types of abuse, and the major risk markers for intimate assaults and emphasized implications of these findings for assessment. Major findings included the following:

1. The forms and patterns of family violence are not the same for all families experiencing violent conflict. Patterns of common couple violence are more prevalent among general population samples, and patterns of severe, "terroristic" violence are more typical of clinical samples.

2. The cycle of violence associated with the battered woman syndrome may be typical only of the more severe form of intimate violence.

3. Common interaction dynamics include violence as a response to loss of control, unmet dependency needs, fears, anxiety, frustrations, and threats to self-esteem. Extreme, severe, and intermittent episodes of rage (with no apparent stimulus) may be associated with particular disorders of personality.

4. Aggression by women, though studied less than aggression by men, differs in regard to the greater incidence of physical and psychological injuries experienced by female victims compared with male victims. Women also appear at greater risk for a system of victimization that includes physical, sexual, emotional, and economic forms of abuse.

5. Recent typologies of male batterers distinguish three types of maritally violent men: family only, dysphoric/borderline, and generally violent/antisocial.

6. Major risk markers for intimate violence include violence in the family of origin; socioeconomic factors; personality variables such as low self-esteem; substance abuse; biology; and situational factors related to the life course.

7. Many risk markers in the family of origin are interwoven and can be passed on to future generations. These include exposure to abuse, alcoholism, and hostile/depressed personality-style parents.

8. Aggression does not inevitably follow from alcohol intoxication, but alcohol is the drug most consistently related to intimate assaults. Alcohol facilitates aggression in many ways, including pharmacologic effects that interfere with reasoning, perceptions, calculations of the consequences of behavior, and perceptions of threat.

9. A potential biological component to intimate violence is suggested by findings of organically based correlates, including head injury, attention deficit disorder, and differences in heart rate reactivity among different types of violent men.

10. An analysis of life course risk markers found that rates of intimate violence are increased during courtship and early marriage, pregnancy, separation, and divorce. Elders are also at risk for abuse by caretakers, although these rates are lower than for other forms of family violence.

11. The risks for spousal homicide are greatest when the spouse is also violent outside the family, rapes the partner, kills or abuses pets, severely injures the partner, and/or threatens to kill the partner.

Implications for Intervention, Policy, and Research

The information presented on the different types of abuse points to the need for varying interventions. The most important distinction is whether the abuse patterns fit the common couple dynamic or the terroristic dynamic. The limitations of traditional family systems therapy, couples therapy, or even psycho-educational approaches are all too evident when the abuser fits the terrorist profile (Walker, 1995). The research on psychological characteristics, alcohol abuse patterns, and biological risk markers points to the need for both a variety of assessments, as well as a variety of approaches to intervention. Because more severe and injurious abuse is likely to be associated with numerous psychological problems and with alcohol or other drug abuse problems, specialized clinical skills are required. It should not be assumed that a program focused mainly on "anger management" is sufficient to end the more serious types of intimate violence or, for that matter, that substance-abuse-focused treatment alone is sufficient. Sobriety may not be enough to end the assaults by all batterers. At the same time, there is a need for more and better research on effective treatment and other deterrence strategies.

The Vivian and Langhinrichsen-Rohling (1994) study, in particular, points to the need to characterize offender-victim relationships. The findings of this research, while documenting the rarity of women as the sole "batterers," also showed that victimization of either spouse, even by low levels of aggression, significantly increased psychological distress. The study authors went on to suggest that instances in which victimizations are truly mutual and mild may be amenable to couples therapy. Research that addresses the specific issue of marital aggression is still needed. In cases of asymmetrical aggression (one perpetrator or one primary aggressor), gender-specific treatment of individual partners is advisable.

Our review of the research found scant systematic examination of victim characteristics, risk markers, or research on victim-specific interventions. This gap in the research suggests that more information on victims is needed. Women who have experienced abuse, particularly severe or long-term abuse, may need assistance in understanding and processing their experience so that they can move ahead with their lives (Walker, 1995). There is also a need to assess whether the welfare of victims has improved or declined longitudinally (McCord, 1992). Research to date has rarely considered the well-being of women in the follow-up. Clinical evidence based on reports of battered women service providers, however, suggests that the safety mechanisms and psychological counseling provided in battered women's shelters are central to women's recovery (Walker, 1995).

We identified particular gaps in the literature in regard to batterer-specific and victim-specific interventions and victim risk markers. At the same time, the discussion of this chapter drew on almost three decades of research that clinicians can use to enhance their practice with clients at risk for intimate violence. The strengths of our knowledge base as detailed above include improved ability to identify offenders that pose an ongoing risk; improved understanding of the psychodynamics of violent relationships; better understanding of gender similarities and differences in the forms that partner violence takes; and gains in knowledge about how to break the cycle of abuse.

The Aftermath
of Partner Violence

JEAN GILES-SIMS

A Social Problem

In the last two decades, researchers and practitioners together have changed the meaning of an assault by a spouse from a private family matter to a social problem. In part, this shift occurred because of the weight of the evidence of negative psychological and social consequences that partner violence has for victims and families. On an individual level, there is pain, trauma, fear, helplessness, depression, anxiety, loss of self-esteem, suicide, and alcohol problems ranging from mild and temporary to lifetime (Dutton, 1993; Gelles & Harrop, 1989; Gleason, 1993; Kaufman Kantor & Asdigian, in press; Orava, McLeod, & Sharpe, 1996; Pagelow, 1984; Stets & Straus, 1990; Straus & Gelles, 1990b; Walker, 1979). Families suffer marital disruption and less satisfying and responsive marital and parental relationships (Giles-Sims, 1983; Mahoney, 1991). The social community suffers from high costs for the criminal justice and mental health systems, lost work and lower worker productivity, and lower educational and economic achievement for victims and family members (Browne, 1987; Miller, Cohen, & Wiersema, 1996; Straus & Gelles, 1986). Much of this suffering, family disruption, and cost to the social community could be reduced or eliminated through prevention programs and effective intervention (Straus & Gelles, 1990b).

First, this chapter examines how researchers have defined and measured consequences of partner violence and how different definitions of scope and methodology have produced different perspectives on the problem. Second, the chapter documents the extent and severity of psychological outcomes of partner violence presented in different studies and explores factors that mediate between partner violence and outcomes. These factors are particularly important for prevention and intervention. Next, this chapter reviews the social impact of partner violence on marital relations, the medical and criminal justice systems, and intergenerational family patterns of violence. Finally, the chapter concludes with some implications of the research for constructive intervention in the problem of partner violence (also see Chapter 7).

How Are Consequences of Partner Violence Defined?

The individual impact of partner violence includes a long list of possible psychological problems, and research has assessed this impact in different ways relying on different samples and methodologies. Each assessment method has its own strengths and drawbacks, and each has been associated with different research populations and approaches. Early studies on the impact of violence (Dobash & Dobash, 1979; Giles-Sims, 1983; Martin, 1976; Pizzey, 1974; Walker, 1979) were primarily based on shelter populations by using battered women's descriptions of their feelings and experiences of the psychological impact of the violence. This type of qualitative description relied on focused interviews with individual victims and gave respondents considerable latitude in directing the range of topics to be covered and the depth of attention to each. Qualitative research was designed for understanding violent behavior, for learning about the experience of violence from the victims' perspective, and for describing the consequences for victims, including the complex interrelationships of individual, family, and social factors.

Early surveys of clinical or volunteer populations tended to use some form of self-report measure of self-esteem and depression problems to indicate the psychological impact of partner violence (Gayford, 1976; Gelles, 1974; Pagelow, 1984; Roy, 1977; Stark & Flitcraft, 1988).

Other surveys used somewhat structured assessment techniques, including nominal checklists of physical and psychological symptoms (Straus & Gelles, 1990b; Walker, 1984). These typically included sleep problems, anxiety, eating problems, depression, crying, and feelings of helplessness, worthlessness, and despair. Analyses of nominal checklist data provide information on the type and level of symptomatology and problems experienced. Responses are compared for groups with different rates of violence to examine the psychological consequences associated with partner violence. Comparing outcomes under different individual and social conditions (e.g., frequency and severity of violence, level of social support) further specifies the consequences of violence. Even more precise models control for other social and demographic factors that may contribute to negative psychological consequences. Survey analyses are designed to answer questions such as, "Do all victims of violence experience psychological problems, the same pattern of problems, or the same levels of problem, or do outcomes vary by other social factors?"

More recently, studies have used standardized measures that also have established (a) norms for the general population and (b) both reliability and validity. These include the Center for Epidemiological Studies of Depression Scale (CES-D; Radloff, 1977; Rounsaville & Weissman, 1978), the Minnesota Multiphasic Personality Inventory (MMPI; Rosewater, 1988), the Self-Rating Depression Scale (SDS; Sato & Heiby, 1992), the Diagnostic Interview Schedule (DIS; Gleason, 1993), and measures of post-traumatic stress disorder (PTSD; Houskamp & Foy, 1991; Saunders, 1994b) to identify precisely how many victims suffer clinically relevant problems and under what conditions. Standardized measures allow a more specific description of symptoms, more definitive diagnosis for clinicians, comparability across research studies, and standardized norms to identify clinically significant symptomatology.

Although it is likely that violence affects almost every aspect of family and social life and community well-being, it is more complicated and difficult to assess these social impacts of partner violence than it is to assess individual well-being. Researchers have primarily measured the social impact of partner violence indirectly, counting the costs of programs that aid or provide services to victims and their families. These indicators present a picture of social losses to the community in work, education, marital stability, and medical and criminal justice resources (Browne, 1987; Mahoney, 1991; Miller et al., 1996; Shepard & Pence, 1988; Straus & Gelles, 1986).

Consequences of violence as measured in each of these ways using case studies, surveys of individual experiences, clinical assessments, and calculation of community service costs tend to present a consistent picture of negative psychological and social consequences of partner violence. However, different methodologies produce different perspectives on outcomes of partner violence.

How Do Different Methods Produce Different Perspectives on Outcomes?

Researchers using data from victimization surveys and victim services interviews have highlighted large gender differences in negative consequences of partner violence, whereas researchers who have focused their analyses on rates of family violence in the total population have reported that men and women are equally violent (Kurz, 1989; Straus & Gelles, 1990b). These differences illustrate a distinction between types of violence (patriarchal terrorism vs. common couple violence) that helps put these differences in perspective (Johnson, 1995). Understanding that these are at least partially distinct types of violence illustrates the need for different types of research studies that complement each other to provide a more complete understanding of the impact of different types of partner violence.

Different perspectives on the impact of partner violence developed as changes occurred over time in methodology, including types of samples and measurement techniques used in the study of partner violence. Initial attempts to describe the problems of partner violence relied on case studies and anecdotal accounts of individual abuse histories. These brought attention to the most serious cases of male abuse of females and, naturally, increased the focus on men as perpetrators. Studies of clinical samples from shelters and emergency social and medical services also contributed to a conviction that the victims of partner violence were most significantly women. Women report victimization and seek help for psychological distress, depression, and other psycho-physiological symptoms at much higher rates than men. Men, however, may be less likely to report victimization because of stigma or may seek private sources of support that do not get reported.

Researchers who have analyzed national surveys to identify more general patterns of partner violence have used different methodologies

that have led to very different perspectives on the nature of the problem, the extent of the problem, and particularly the extent to which
severe battering is limited to men and negative consequences to women
(Kurz, 1989; Straus, 1976; Yllö, 1984, 1988; Yllö & Straus, 1990).

Different methodologies also have produced different types of information about the processes and outcomes of partner violence.
Generally, case studies and surveys of clinical populations have provided more in-depth descriptions of processes that culminate in severe psychological and social impacts for battered women. Studies
using national sample surveys have identified the particular proportion of the total population that experiences specific outcomes and
have allowed comparisons of battered and nonbattered subgroups
from the same database. Within the family violence research community, controversy exists about whether the primary focus should be
on the severely victimized population of women and the male/female
context of the partner violence or on the larger problem of family
violence in a context of social norms and family conflict (Kurz, 1989;
Straus & Gelles, 1990b). The perspective of this chapter is that all
types of methodologies and their resulting perspectives are valuable
to an understanding of the impact of partner violence. This chapter,
therefore, is organized to evaluate information on outcomes available
from a wide variety of studies with different methodologies.

The research on partner violence includes both women and men
as victims, but in general the emphasis is on giving first attention to
wives as victims (Straus & Gelles, 1990b; Straus et al., 1980) because
men's use of force, threat of force, and overall control of women's
activities results in more clearly defined consequences for women.
The impact of violent acts on men or associated costs of such violence
have not received as much study. However, women's problems influence men's psychological condition, as well as their work and other
activities. Partner violence and its consequences affect the entire family system.

What Are the Psychological
Consequences of Partner Violence?

As indicated above, research on the frequency and nature of the psychological consequences of partner violence evolved historically,

starting with case studies and then moving to clinical surveys and then surveys of nationally representative samples. The trend reflects a move to greater standardization of measures and an increased focus on representative samples and generalizability to the U.S. population (or the population of other countries). Each type of research, however, offers its own contributions to understanding violence processes and outcomes.

What Do Victims Say About the Impact?

Battered women in shelters often tell incredible stories of beatings, rapes, torture, and constant terror. Hearing or reading their life stories in their own words effectively conveys the negative impact of violence, raises consciousness, and convinces others of the need for help. Thus, case studies often accompany news reports, funding proposals for programs, and research grant proposals. Case studies allow victims to identify their own experiences and the full context of the violence. Under what conditions does violence happen? How does violence escalate? Do similar patterns of violence occur across time? How do victims react to violence across time? What processes lead to either leaving or changing a relationship?

Qualitative analyses of case studies can lead to an understanding of the complexity and meaning of violence. Presentation and analyses of case studies stimulated much of the early program development for battered women (Dobash & Dobash, 1979; Giles-Sims, 1983; Martin, 1976; Pizzey, 1974; Walker, 1979).

Each woman victim has her own individual description of what beatings have done to her psychologically. For example, Paula reported:

> I wouldn't feel anything. I'd keep low. I didn't want to do anything and I didn't want to go anywhere. I didn't want to visit anybody. Especially when he was around I was more depressed than ever. I didn't want to do anything that would make him angry. I was like a robot. I didn't feel anything. I didn't want to feel anything. (Giles-Sims, 1983, p. 107)

Elizabeth also felt the helplessness and confusion when she came to a shelter, seeking help for herself and her children:

> I felt helpless. I don't know what was happening to me. At the time, I just couldn't stand my kids with me. I loved them, but I just couldn't

cope with them around me at the time. I felt like putting my fist
through something or jumping out a window or . . . quitting. (Giles-
Sims, 1983, p. 99)

Case studies have offered women the opportunity to express their
own feelings and to explain the meaning and context of the violence
and their reactions. Many advocates for women emphasize that a
complete understanding of women's victimization must include
qualitative analyses of accounts in their own words (Kurz, 1989). But
case studies are costly and can provide information only on relatively
small samples. There is also a restriction on the range of analytic
processes that can be used in these studies. Thus, many researchers
have conducted surveys to identify more general patterns of violence,
social and psychological causes of violence, and subsequent impact
on individuals and the social community.

What Are the "Cycle of Violence" and the "Battered Woman Syndrome"?

Analyses of the similarities and patterns of violence revealed by
case studies and, later, by more structured interview studies led
Lenore Walker (1979) to characterize the process of repeated tension
buildup, battering, and contrition as the *cycle of violence.* Her research found that this repeated cycle led to severe psychological
symptoms for the victims of this violence, such as sleep disturbances,
eating problems, fatigue, and psycho-physiological indicators of
stress such as headaches, back pain, skin reactions, high blood pressure, and heart problems. These symptoms may result from the inconsistency of men's behavior during the cycle of violence and
women's inability to control their own fates. According to this tension-
violence-contrition cycle, an abusive partner gains power through
violence, making the victim the accused. Reconciliation relieves the
victim of the role of guilty person (Serra, 1993).

Walker (1984) also found a pattern of psychological consequences
developing in women as chronic battering relationships became increasingly serious, uncontrollable, and unpredictable over time. *Battered woman syndrome* describes the effects of violence as learned
helplessness, reexperiencing the trauma, intrusive recollections, generalized anxiety, low self-esteem, and social withdrawal.

Recently, both legal experts and researchers have explored and tried to refine further the concepts of "cycle of violence" and "battered woman syndrome." Dutton and Painter (1993) presented research on battered and emotionally abused women, suggesting that the intermittency of the abusive behavior may be a more reliable predictor of psychological symptoms than the predictability of violence suggested by the cycle of violence theory. Dutton (1993) also pointed out some lack of clarity in this concept and sought to redefine battered woman syndrome for lawyers. The syndrome needed redefinition and expansion for two reasons. First, the courts often examine the totality of battered women's experiences, including more than their psychological reactions to violence. For example, attorneys seek testimony about a victim's prior responses to violence, the outcomes of her attempts to get help, and the context within which responses were made, in addition to her psychological reactions. Second, battered women's psychological reactions do not always fit the one particular profile identified by battered woman syndrome (Dutton, 1993). In addition, "feeling helpless" may not be a psychological characteristic or attribute of the person, but rather a realistic response to the situation (Webersinn, Hollinger, & DeLamatre, 1991), and not all women's experiences of violence follow an intermittent cycle of violence. Many report a constant state of siege, with little relief from the fear and terror (Dutton, 1993). When these women have sought help, research indicates, this often does not stop the violence and may make the women less likely to seek police intervention in subsequent episodes (Bachman & Coker, 1995). The history of help seeking and responses to those attempts reflect on both the women's psychological state and the societal responses to the problem.

Survey Research: Reactions to Battering

Survey research with clinical samples has consistently identified numerous psychological problems among battered women. Among the problems are anxiety, depression, anger and rage, nightmares, dissociation, shame, lowered self-esteem, somatic problems, sexual problems, addictive behaviors, and other impaired functioning (Campbell, 1989a; Dutton, 1993; Hilberman & Munson, 1977-1978; Koss, 1990; Mitchell & Hodson, 1983; Orava et al., 1996; Prescott & Letko, 1977; Rounsaville, 1978; Rounsaville & Weissman, 1978; Stark, Flitcraft, & Frazier, 1981; Trimpey, 1989; Walker, 1979, 1984). For example, when Follingstad and associates (Follingstad, Brennan, Hause, Polek, & Rutledge, 1991) presented 234 physically abused women with a checklist of 12 physical and psychological symptoms, most of the sample (65%) reported 3 to 7 symptoms. Only 3% reported no symptoms, and one woman reported all 12. Most frequently cited were depression (77%), anxiety (75%), persistent headaches (56%), back and limb problems (54%), and stomach problems (54%). Other studies of victims confirm the rates of about 75% to 80% for depression and other problems (Dutton, 1993; Gelles & Harrop, 1989; Goodman, Koss, & Russo, 1993).

Analyses comparing battered women's responses on the DIS with group norms for the general population do confirm that the major components of battered woman syndrome are much more common among the battered sample (Gleason, 1993). A very large majority of the battered women in both a shelter sample and a community volunteer sample reported major depression (63%–81%), psychosexual dysfunction (87%–88%), and phobias (63%–83%). In comparison, depression rates in the normative population were 7%, and for simple phobias, 15% (Gleason, 1993). Obsessive-compulsion, anxiety, PTSD, dysthymia, alcohol and other drug abuse, panic disorders, and antisocial personality among battered women were also significantly higher than in the normative population.

Shelter samples of battered women may differ in important ways from survivors of wife battering in the general population. Shelter samples include women who have sought help and do not include women who could not or would not seek help. Findings, however, indicate few differences among battered women living in shelters and those in the community (Gleason, 1993). Another concern is that women in clinical samples may suffer from other conditions that could account for some of their problems or even antedate the victimization. Surveys of clinical samples provide scant data to address the issue of causal ordering of abuse and symptomatology. Most survey research relies on correlational rather than longitudinal data. But at least some data indicate that abuse of longer duration led to more symptoms than did short-term abuse and that when women left a relationship, declines in medical and psychological health ceased but did not return to preabusive relationship levels (Follingstad, Brennan, et al., 1991).

Data on consequences of partner violence from clinical or volunteer samples present significant limitations when researchers seek the answers to questions related to the consequences of all levels of violence (violence ranging in severity) in the general population. To address these broader questions, large-scale national surveys like the 1975 and 1985 National Family Violence Surveys (Straus & Gelles, 1990b; Straus et al., 1980) are needed.

Rates of Psychological Distress
Measured in National Surveys

The 1975 National Family Violence Survey (Straus et al., 1980) focused on violent behaviors toward spouses and children by using the Conflict Tactics Scales and stressed causal factors associated with violent behavior. Limitations of this survey were noted in regard to assessment of the impact of violent acts. As a result, the 1985 resurvey included several questions focused on the psychological outcomes of partner violence (Straus & Gelles, 1990b). The resurvey assessed psychological distress by measuring days in bed because of illness, psychosomatic symptoms, depressive symptoms, and stress.

Do Psychological Distress Levels From Violence Differ for Men and Women? Few studies of outcomes of partner violence allow direct comparison of male and female victims. Both male and female victims of severe violence experience considerable psychological distress, as indicated in the 1985 National Family Violence Resurvey (Straus & Gelles, 1990b). Even minor violence was associated with elevated stress levels, and the level of symptoms escalated sharply with increases in violence rates. But the women victims suffered about twice the number of consequences as men. Specifically, under conditions of severe violence, (a) 23% of women and 15% of men reported any days in bed because of illness, (b) 44% of women and 26% of men reported high levels of psychosomatic symptoms, (c) 61% of women and 34% of men reported high levels of stress, and (d) 58% of women and 30% of men reported high levels of depressive symptoms (Stets & Straus, 1990). For both men and women, each of these four measures reveals rates of symptomatology that are at least twice as high under conditions of severe violence as they are under conditions of no violence. The proportion of women experiencing these problems, however, was significantly higher than was the proportion of men reporting such symptoms, and the increases in levels of symptoms were much greater for women (Stets & Straus, 1990). In short, both women and men suffered psychological problems, but rates were much higher for women than for men when subjected to comparable levels of partner violence. Women also reported rates of symptoms that escalated more sharply with increasing violence than did men. Seriously assaulted women reported double the number of headaches, four times the rate of depression, and five and one half times more suicide attempts than women experiencing no violence (Straus & Gelles, 1990b).

Even when couples reciprocate aggression, females suffer more negative consequences. One study of clinical victims indicated that 71% of couples reported some violence in the past year and that 86% of that violence was reported as reciprocal (Cascardi, Langhinrichsen, & Vivian, 1992). But wives were more likely than husbands to sustain severe injuries and to be negatively affected. Many wives reported clinical levels of depressive symptoms.

Cross-sectional survey data, even of a nationally representative population, cannot satisfactorily address issues of causal ordering. But these data are consistent with many other studies that have found a strong association between assaults and psychological injury, particularly for women victims. As indicated above, several early interview studies of battered women found psychological problems associated with violence (Hilberman & Munson, 1977-1978; Roark & Vlahos, 1983; Rounsaville & Weissman, 1978; Star et al., 1979; Walker, 1979).

Cross-sectional survey data can provide the benefits of control groups and representative populations. Gelles and Harrop's (1989) review article, for example, found research that improved on the methods of earlier studies by including control groups. This research also found associations between partner assaults and psychological distress on more specific measures (Back, Post, & D'Arcy, 1982; Christopoulos et al., 1987; Dalton & Kantner, 1983; Derogatis, 1977). More definitive research, however, requires comparison groups and controls for social and demographic factors associated with higher levels of psychological distress that may account for some of the psychological symptoms found among battered women.

Do Social and Demographic Factors Influence Consequences? Data from the 1985 National Family Violence Survey included measures of marital conflict, income, education, number of children, and health that were used in analyzing and further clarifying the relationship between violence and symptoms in a complex model that took into account these social and demographic factors (Gelles & Harrop,

1989). The summary measure of psychological distress combined depression, stress, and somatic symptoms. This outcome measure, divided into moderate and severe distress subscales, was compared across three groups reporting either no violence, minor violence, or severe violence. When those subjected to severe violence were compared with those subjected to no violence, a very strong relationship between experiencing violence and negative psychological impact was found. Distress scores of those in the severe violence group averaged so high that they equaled those in the 80th to 90th percentile of respondents subjected to no violence (Gelles & Harrop, 1989). When the contribution of all the social and demographic variables (marital conflict, total family income, highest level of husband-to-wife violence, health of wife, and age of wife) was taken into account statistically along with the effects of violence, the researchers established that partner violence contributed to negative psychological impact in addition to the contributions of other social and demographic factors.

On this basis, one can conclude that although violence may be found more commonly in groups with multiple social problems, violence is associated with psychological problems over and above the negative effects of these other factors. These data cannot establish causation because of the cross-sectional design, which does not allow for examination of the causal ordering of the violence and symptomatology, but as associational evidence mounts, confidence in the causal relationship continues to grow. Controlled longitudinal studies are still needed to advance knowledge in this area.

Does More Frequent and Severe Abuse Lead to More Problems?

Comparing psychological reactions in groups of women with varied histories in terms of length and severity of battering is one way to examine causal relationships. Theoretically, more frequent or more severe abuse or both would be related to more frequent and more severe distress symptoms if violence causes the distress. This theory suggests the need for research relating outcomes to the severity and frequency of abuse. One particularly well designed study tackled this issue by first dividing a sample of 234 physically abused women into two groups: (a) those with three or fewer incidents of violence and no further incidents for at least 2 years (26% of the sample) and

(b) those in long-term, ongoing abusive relationships (74%). The researchers compared rates of physical and psychological symptoms across the two groups (Follingstad, Wright, Lloyd, & Sebastian, 1991). Women who experienced more severe and frequent abuse experienced more symptoms. Abuse of longer duration predicted more symptoms than did short-term abuse, and those with long-term abuse sustained more injuries requiring medical treatment. An important finding is that when women left a relationship and the abuse ended, the decline in physical and psychological health associated with long-term abuse ceased, although health did not then return to pre-abusive relationship levels. At the time of the interviews, all women had left their abusive relationships, but many continued to feel helpless or feared their partners' retaliation.

Does Predictability of Abuse Lead to More or Less Distress?

Three somewhat contradictory theories have been offered to explain the relationship between predictability of abuse and psychological distress. One theory suggests that women who can predict the occurrence of abuse will be more prepared and able to protect themselves, feel more in control, and thus suffer less psychological distress. Some research evidence suggests that when laboratory subjects could anticipate a noxious stimulus or could control when a noxious stimulus occurred, their stress reactions were not as severe as when they could not predict or anticipate these events (Dohrenwend & Dohrenwend, 1982).

A second theory suggests that when women anticipate stress, they become aroused earlier, remain vigilant longer, feel helpless to control their situations, and thus suffer more psychological distress. Seligman (1975) originally conceptualized this process as learned helplessness, and Lenore Walker further developed and applied the idea to battering relationships. Follingstad's research (Follingstad, Brennan, et al., 1991) supported this theory with findings that a woman's ability to predict the timing of abuse contributed significantly to the increased number of psychological symptoms reported. Those who could predict violence experienced more symptoms. The women victims usually used emotional abuse by their partners as a predictor of imminent physical violence. Long-term abuse also predicted more symptoms than short-term, and those with more severe abuse sustained more injuries requiring medical treatment. The bulk of this evidence on abused women suggests that more distress occurs when violence is predictable. Another theory suggests, however, that it may not be the predictability, but rather intermittency.

A third theory uses the concept of "intermittency" to describe the variable pattern of some abuse histories. Dutton and Painter (1993) found that predictability did not contribute to the psychological consequences associated with battered woman syndrome. They found that almost one half of the variation in their outcome measure of trauma symptoms was attributable instead to relationship variables. These included severity of the abuse, domination in the relationship, as well as the intermittency of psychological and physical abuse. *Intermittency* means that extreme positive and extreme negative behaviors occurred within a short period of time. The researchers found that these behaviors did not need to be cyclical or predictable to have a negative effect. Given these somewhat contradictory theories, more research is needed to provide a complete understanding.

Does Social Support Buffer Psychological Distress?

Theoretically, social support provides some buffer to the effects of violence on psychological outcomes. Social support can come from families, social services, or other sources of help. Bowker (1983a) found that almost any support or help source could aid women in "beating wife-beating." Social support also may play a role in actually reducing the amount and frequency of abuse. Families and agencies provide support that may lead to short-term reductions of abuse, but shelters and women's groups provide more of the necessary social support over the long term (Donato & Bowker, 1984).

Traditional norms tend to support both family privacy and the sanctity of the marriage even when serious problems exist and thus can lead to an absence of, or less social support for, battered women. Research has found that more traditional, less assertive, more isolated and restricted women and those with fewer economic alternatives to their marriages sought help less and were more severely battered (Follingstad, Wright, et al., 1991; Frieze, Knoble, Zomnir, & Washburn, 1980). Overall, women with the least social support sought help less, remained for longer periods of time in abusive relationships, and experienced both more severe abuse and more symptoms. These findings support a causal relationship between violence and psychological disorder and the buffering effect of social support.

Social support can be modified to meet some of the needs of battered women. In an experimental study of 141 women from a shelter sample, one project was designed to make existing sources of social support more alert to, and effective at, meeting the needs of battered women. In the longitudinal assessment, the 71 women who were assigned to the program and received help from trained advocates who provided empathy and helped generate support from other community resources had significantly more close friends (one measure of social support) at 10 weeks than did those in the control group (Tan, Basta, Sullivan, & Davidson, 1995).

Intense analyses of life histories of clinical patients with acute and chronic violent trauma histories also indicate long-term effects of lack of support (Herman, 1992). Histories of abuse, along with an absence of support, led to alterations in victims' perceptions of themselves and of their chances of escaping victimization.

How Does Partner Violence
Affect Self-Esteem?

Researchers have consistently reported low self-esteem and feelings of powerlessness among battered women (Aguilar & Nightengale, 1994; Cascardi & O'Leary, 1992; Mitchell & Hodson, 1983; Orava et al., 1996; Walker, 1984). Very early research even suggested that those with low self-esteem attracted batterers as partners (Shainess, 1977). But, a meta-analysis of risk markers for women's abuse provided no direct evidence that the women's low self-esteem contributed to future abuse. In fact, the only characteristic of women that consistently distinguished battered women from others in this meta-analysis was that the battered women were more likely to have witnessed violence in the family of origin (Hotaling & Sugarman, 1986).

Most early research asserted that the low self-esteem reported among battered women resulted from battering, rather than preceded or contributed to it (Walker, 1984), but the research here is limited because of its cross-sectional methodology. Questions remain about the processes that contribute to the association between witnessing parental violence and later victimization (Kaufman Kantor & Asdigian, in press). It may not be low self-esteem that leads to partnering with a batterer, but some form of matching based on familiarity. In other words, personality similarities may exist among married couples (O'Leary & Murphy, 1992). Much more research is needed on this possible relationship.

Research also needs to clarify the types of control or abuse that most likely affect self-esteem. Using standardized measures of self-esteem (the Rosenberg Self-Esteem Scale; Rosenberg, 1965), researchers have found that battered women have significantly lower self-esteem index scores than nonbattered women and that low self-esteem is particularly associated with emotionally controlling abuse (Aguilar & Nightengale, 1994). Among four types of abuse (physical abuse, emotional/controlling abuse, sexual/emotional abuse, and miscellaneous abuse), only the emotional/controlling abuse was significantly related to women's lowered self-esteem. These findings suggest that the controlling nature of abuse leads to feelings of powerlessness and hopelessness even more than the physical abuse does.

Low self-esteem and feelings of powerlessness and hopelessness contribute to depression and the difficulty that some battered women have leaving a relationship. Coping with being the victim of partner violence influences one's view of the self, one's sense of invulnerability, and other perceptions of the world. Women do sometimes blame themselves in response to the question, Why did this happen to me? Behavioral self-blame may lead women to action that protects them, whereas characterological self-blame suggests very little personal control (Janoff-Bulman, 1983). Characterological self-blame is most likely to be associated with depression.

Recent research has found self-blame associated with depressive symptomatology; however, only 12% of women in Cascardi's sample blamed themselves for their partner's violence (Cascardi & O'Leary, 1992). Media attention and public service information on partner violence and battered women stressing that women are not to blame for the violence may have reduced this problem of self-blame for some women battered today. In a sample of 70 women who had experienced partner violence, women currently living with their partners were more likely to self-blame, and women no longer living with partners reported changing their assessments from self-blame to partner-blame (Andrews & Brewin, 1990). Thus, blame can be modified through social awareness programs or direct intervention. This may ultimately help battered women seek help for victimization and reduce depression and other psychological and socially negative consequences of partner violence.

How Does Partner Violence
Affect Substance Abuse?

Alcohol and other substance abuse have long been correlated with partner violence and are often assumed to be causal (Kaufman Kantor, in press; Kaufman Kantor & Asdigian, in press; Zubretsky & Digirolamo, 1994). Alcohol abuse discriminates between men who are violent and not violent to partners (Hotaling & Sugarman, 1986). But other factors are associated with alcohol use that correlate with violence, including low income, history of arrests, and other drug use (Bennett, Tolman, Rogalski, & Srinivasaraghavan, 1994). Some of these factors may be outcomes of the interaction of violence and substance abuse.

Alcohol and other substance abuse could be consequences of being victimized. Some women may use alcohol and other drugs to soothe the effects of physical and psychological abuse. Stark and Flitcraft (1988) argue that female alcoholism may result from the adverse life events and psychological stress associated with partner violence. They found that the rate of alcoholism among battered women was 16%, compared with 1% for nonbattered women, and that 74% of alcoholism cases emerged after the onset of abuse (Stark et al., 1981). They also found a nine times greater risk of drug abuse after battering and psychological abuse. Other research compared substance abuse among two battered women's samples (a shelter sample and a community sample) with substance abuse in a normative population. In the battered samples, 23% and 44% of women reported alcohol abuse, compared with 4% for the normative population, and 10% and 25% of women in the battered samples reported drug abuse, compared with 4% for the normative population (Gleason, 1993). These figures cannot be used as authoritative findings on the rate of alcohol and other drug abuse among battered women without further research by using standard measures, but clearly substance abuse is related to partner violence. It remains unclear whether the abuse follows, coexists with, or predates the violence. These studies also did not control for partners' substance abuse. This is particularly critical because women's substance abuse may be highly correlated with their partners' substance abuse.

One alternative view of the relationship between partner violence and substance abuse is that the alcohol or other drug problems may predate and contribute to the violence, rather than be a result of attempts to cope with stress. The alcohol use of the batterer may also have contributed both to the violence and to the women's alcohol or other drug problems (Kaufman Kantor & Asdigian, in press). Thus, understanding alcohol abuse as an outcome of partner violence requires considering the partner's substance abuse history, as well as the violence perpetrated.

Are Women Revictimized by Service Providers?

When battered women seek help with personal or psychiatric problems, they may encounter revictimization in the form of bias against women with mental health problems. Women may be encouraged, on the basis of traditional ideology, to bear up and return home; they may be considered masochistic; they may be labeled hysterics or worse; and they may be considered the source of their own problems.

Victims of partner violence may also be revictimized by race and class prejudices and differential treatment. The pivotal point at which services begin is the initial police response and possible arrest. Contextual and demographic factors influence the outcome at this point. The race of the victim and of the offender appears to influence police outcomes. In one study, black women were more likely than white women to report victimizations, and black men who assaulted black female partners were more likely to face arrest than white men who assaulted white female partners (Bachman & Coker, 1995). (These and other problems of revictimization and issues related to treatment are discussed in Chapter 7.)

What Are Clinical Levels
of Depression Among Victims?

Women victims of partner violence report many psychological symptoms, but what percentage of those victims suffer clinical levels of depression? Researchers have reported largely similar results in different studies of battered women. A 1970s study of 31 battered women relied on a self-report depression scale (CES-D) and found that 80% of women had at least moderate depressive symptoms and that 20% had symptom levels comparable to those of hospitalized patients (Rounsaville & Weissman, 1978). When the researchers used a standard American Psychological Association diagnostic assessment, they found that 52% had notable symptoms of depression. But being a victim of abuse was not necessarily predictive of a psychiatric diagnosis. In the same research, 29% were found to have no psychiatric diagnosis. In another study, Sato and Heiby (1992) found that 47% of their sample of battered women scored 50 or more on the SDS—the recommended cutoff for clinical levels of depression. Gleason (1993) found major depression rates of 63% and 81% in two samples of battered women, compared with 7% in the normative population. Other studies of clinical populations report similar rates. In Cascardi and O'Leary's (1992) research, the mean scores on the Beck Depression Inventory (BDI) for women (but not men) in aggressive (mostly reciprocal) relationships met criteria for moderate levels of depressive symptoms. Another study comparing abused women with a control group by using the BDI found that 33% of abused women scored 30 and over, indicating severe levels of depression (Orava et al., 1996).

Together, these studies suggest that clinical depression likely characterizes at least one half of battered women populations, but perhaps one quarter do not present with a psychiatric diagnosis as an outcome of partner violence. These varying patterns of response may be related to length and severity of abuse, prior experiences of violence, and other factors in the immediate or larger social context. Several studies confirm that depression scores rise with increases in frequency and severity of abuse (Cascardi & O'Leary, 1992; Gelles & Harrop, 1989; Kemp, Rawlings, & Green, 1991; Orava et al., 1996).

Increasingly, research assesses battered women's symptoms by using instruments to measure PTSD (Astin, Lawrence, & Foy, 1993; Houskamp & Foy, 1991; Kemp, Green, Hovanitz, & Rawlings, 1995; Kemp et al., 1991; Saunders, 1994b; Vitanza, Vogel, & Marshall, 1995; Vitanza, Rowe, Hobdy, & Marshall, 1990; West, Fernandez, Hillard, Schoof, & Parks, 1990). PTSD is quite prevalent in clinical populations of battered women (Astin et al., 1993; Gleason, 1993; Houskamp & Foy, 1991; Kemp et al., 1991; Saunders, 1994b). In one study, for example, approximately 60% of battered women seeking help in two different settings met diagnostic criteria for PTSD (Saunders, 1994b). In this same study, most of the women (60%) reported symptoms lasting 6 months, and although most reported symptoms coincident with abuse, 16% reported a delayed onset of symptoms. Another study using the Structured Clinical Interview for *DSM-III-R* indicated that 45% of a sample of battered women met the full criteria for PTSD and that symptoms varied by level of exposure to violence, with 60%

of the high-level group and 14% of the low-level group meeting criteria (Houskamp & Foy, 1991). These robust findings indicate that many battered women suffer PTSD and certainly would benefit from clinical treatment.

How Common Is Suicidal Ideation Among Battered Women?

It is not surprising, given these well-documented levels of major depression among battered women, that they think about, attempt, or actually commit suicide. This outcome is most likely to occur when the women are overwhelmed with feelings of helplessness, have little support, and fear seeking help from police, medical, or other social services. One report indicates that 10% of a sample of battered women attempted suicide and that one half of that group tried more than once (Stark & Flitcraft, 1988). This study also reported that 26% of all female suicide attempts coming to the attention of hospitals are associated with battering and that a large majority of those who attempt suicide had been seen before for battering injuries. Pagelow (1984) and Gayford (1975) both found that 50% of their samples of battered women had contemplated suicide, and Pagelow reported that 23% of her sample had actually attempted suicide. Suicidal behavior is consistent with the context of domestic assaults, particularly assaults against women, which include increasing isolation and not being able to discuss victimization experiences with others (Gelles, 1974; Straus et al., 1980). Furthermore, suicide attempts may increase with the frequency and severity of battering (Straus & Gelles, 1987).

The overall picture that may lead to suicide includes the following:

- An accelerating pattern of battering
- Attempts to seek help from others
- Retaliatory violence in some cases
- Increasing isolation
- Negative self-esteem
- An increase in physical illnesses and somatic symptoms
- Increasing negative attitudes toward the husband
- Decreasing love and realistic hope for changing the violence
- Increasing attempts to leave, seek help, and change
- Feeling that there is no other escape but suicide

All of these can occur simultaneously or in any order. The research on suicide attempts among battered women is limited but generally supports a theory of escalating violence, threats, lack of help and support, and eventually complete hopelessness. More research is needed to examine these processes.

What Are Some Limitations of Research on Psychological Impact?

As noted earlier, research on psychological consequences of partner violence has varied in quality of measurement, samples studied, and representativeness. A limited amount of information is available on outcomes of different levels, types, and intensity of violence and on males as victims. This research has also been limited by the lack of multivariate analyses needed to account for the contribution of partner violence and other factors to the psychological outcomes of interest. Research has evolved considerably over the last two decades, but further advancements are needed.

Most research on the psychological impact of partner violence focuses on women as victims and the psychological impairments that women suffer as a consequence of the abuse. More research is needed on consequences for male victims. There is also a need for research on how victims cope, how they do escape, how others can help facilitate change in these relationships to buffer stress, women's strengths and resilience in the face of battering, and most important, how to prevent violence or protect victims early on so that the psychological consequences are reduced or eliminated.

Overall, the best research designs to answer the remaining questions will be prospective, longitudinal studies of both women and men. These studies will also need to consider more carefully the social and demographic factors identified in this review as they may also contribute to the variation in psychological outcomes of partner violence.

Social Consequences of Intimate Violence

The consequences of partner violence include more than just the psychological symptoms of victims, horrendous and important as they are. Intimate violence harms other family members both directly and indirectly. Children suffer as a result of their parents' violence (see Chapter 3 for details). Partner violence often precipitates marital dissolution and may seriously diminish the quality of family life for victims and the entire family system. Less research exists on the social consequences than on the psychological outcomes of partner violence. But what does exist indicates the need for more attention to this area. Case studies suggest that when partner violence occurs, the whole complex of related persons suffers worry, fears, and often extreme stress. Other possible negative social consequences include decreased economic productivity and educational achievement, additional use of community service resources, deterioration in community norms and values, and more negative attitudes toward men and women and male-female relationships in general.

Does Partner Violence Lead to Marital Dissolution?

Not surprisingly, evidence indicates that marital relationships that include violence suffer more negative feelings and less satisfaction. In a study of nonaggressive, mildly aggressive, and severely aggressive clinical couples, the discordant/aggressive couples rated their relationships more negatively (Langhinrichsen-Rohling, Smutzler, & Vivian, 1994). Despite low marital satisfaction, many physically abused women are committed to staying married (Bauserman & Arias, 1992). Thus, a complicated relationship exists between partner violence and marital dissolution. Women may not divorce violent partners because of psychological entrapment.

Scant research exists on the link between partner violence and divorce. Many battered women seek to leave marital relationships and divorce their partners, but follow-up research from shelter populations also indicates that approximately one half of battered women who have used shelters return to their partners (Giles-Sims, 1983; Pagelow, 1984; Walker, 1979). Thus, battering does not strongly predict divorce, but those who get divorced often mention that violence was an important factor in the dissolution. Early research reported that between 20% of middle-class subjects and 40% of working-class divorcing couples mentioned violence as a major problem leading to dissolution (Levinger, 1966). Thus, violence is a risk marker for divorce, but divorce is also a social consequence of the violence.

More recent reports have focused on the violence that follows battered women's decisions to separate or divorce. Mahoney (1991) refers to violence during this period of time as "separation assault" and calls for much more research on this type of partner violence. Assault during separation often results from retaliation attempts or jealousy. Most women who are killed by partners have been killed during separations (Browne, 1987). These data suggest that those going through a divorce have realistic fears of retaliation and need protection.

What Are the Productivity and Medical Costs of Partner Violence?

Abused women are often economically dependent, and keeping them dependent maintains power and control. Leaving battering relationships may require, or is at least easier when victims attain, financial self-sufficiency. Thus, work productivity and stability that suffer as a consequence of violence make becoming economically independent more difficult. Research on battered women identifies negative effects on employment status (Shepard & Pence, 1988). Shepard and Pence (1988) found that although many of the battered women in their sample were employed, the women's absenteeism was high and performance was hindered by a history of abuse. Clearly, this represents costs not only to the abused victims but also to employers.

Partner violence also leads to substantial medical costs. Analyses of National Crime Victimization Survey data reported an estimated $1.3 billion in annual medical costs because of adult domestic assaults (in 1993 dollars; Miller et al., 1996). Straus (1986) estimated that family homicides cost $1.7 billion annually. Costs of lost workdays tend to be assessed with medical costs, and estimates of medical costs and lost work productivity as a result of domestic violence run $5–10 billion (Meyer, 1992). The Bureau of National Affairs estimates costs of $3–5 billion from health care premiums and lost work. Given that much partner violence is hidden and total economic costs are undiscoverable, the true economic consequences can only be roughly estimated but likely will exceed these estimates. Inflation of medical and other related costs also continues to escalate sharply the costs of partner violence.

What Are the Criminal Justice Costs of Partner Violence?

Intimate partner violence puts an enormous burden on police and the larger criminal justice system. One study of 911 emergency calls found that 22% were domestic disturbance calls (Baker, Cahn, & Sands, 1989). All police departments respond to a large number of these calls, escalating the immediate costs. The National Institute of Justice reports that the costs of domestic crimes against adults account for almost 15% of total crime costs—$67 billion per year (Miller et al., 1996).

In addition to direct costs of police intervention, apprehension, and protection, courts devote much of their scarce resources to giving protection orders, prosecuting assailants, following up perpetrators, trying to protect victims, and housing the most serious offenders. In these cost-conscious times, this represents a serious social problem. The tragedy is that research indicates these costs could be eliminated through appropriate social changes and prevention efforts.

What Is the Intergenerational Impact of Partner Violence?

In the long run, intimate partner violence is related to violent patterns in the next generation and perhaps in the contemporary community. Witnessing physical violence between one's parents is highly correlated with severe aggression in one's own partner relationships (Hotaling & Sugarman, 1986; Kalmuss, 1984), creating a cycle of violence that may continue for generations. Most research in this area, however, has focused on viewing violence as a risk marker for partner violence, rather than as an outcome of it, but it is important to remember that it is both a risk marker and an outcome. If violence continues without punishment, others will likely choose this alternative as well.

Implications for Responding to the Problem

Research findings have implications for responding to the problem of partner violence. To reduce the negative consequences, the first priority has to be safety and protection for the victims and other family members. Cessation of partner violence is also possible and needs to be addressed in any program development (Aldarondo, 1996). All mental and physical health workers need training to help them identify victims, make accurate diagnostic assessments, provide opportunities for battered partners to disclose their victimization experiences safely, and provide appropriate referrals and services. (Primary prevention and more details of intervention strategies are addressed in Chapter 7.) Only a brief overview of ways to intervene to lessen or eliminate the negative consequences of partner violence is presented here.

Identification and Diagnosis

Only a small percentage of battered women are identified by physicians when seeking health care. In one study, during a 2-month period, all adult women seeking health care from a family practice were asked to complete anonymous questionnaires about physical assault. Of 374 participants, 23% reported assaults by their partners in the last year, but only 6 participants had ever been asked by their physicians about abuse (Hamberger, 1994; Hamberger, Saunders, & Hovey, 1992). Although battered women seek medical care—both general care and care for injuries—only a small proportion are identified by physicians as battered. Because physicians often provide the only services that battered women receive, lack of attention to the battering precludes referrals and treatment.

For many reasons, both victims and assailants may deny the existence of the problem. Many victims deny or hide the problem out of shame, fear of reprisal, beliefs that nothing will change, and concern for their own financial and domestic well-being and that of their children. Both men and women involved in partner assault often seek to keep their problems secret for many reasons. Social norms suggest that family problems are private affairs. Victims and perpetrators experience shame in revealing their problems. Both partners can be concerned about the possible negative consequences for their careers. In addition, norms in the general society support violence against women. Therefore, women victims often feel helpless and lack self-esteem or enough confidence to reveal the violence and seek help.

Service providers need to be trained to identify domestic violence, to name it as a problem of relationships rather than just of a particular injury, and to indicate to victims that this problem needs to be diagnosed and addressed fully because it is a threat to her or his physical and mental health. It is illegal and not the victim's fault; victims also need to know that many others are in this same situation. Identifying the problem becomes the first step in confronting and changing it. Identification serves both the service provider and the victims. Historically, domestic violence has been ignored, disguised, and even found relatively acceptable. Service providers must confront and change these attitudes and behaviors in the context of all helping relationships and supervisory activities.

Referral and Provision of Services

Despite widespread domestic violence and its major role in women's health, the medical community often fails to identify victims of partner violence when they come for primary medical services (Burge, 1989; Hamberger et al., 1992). Even in the emergency room, suspicious stories go unquestioned, and women are often not asked about a history of violence and are not given proper referrals. Often, medical facilities extend services for the physical injuries that women receive and then discharge them without making any arrangements for their safety (Kurz, 1987). Victims then return to the abusive relationships in which they sustained the original injuries. A physician's reluctance to acknowledge the source of a victim's injuries can lead to increased isolation and considerable frustration. Disconfirmation of the abuse also contributes to further escalation and stabilization of violence patterns (Giles-Sims, 1983).

Historically, therapeutic services have emphasized adjustment, particularly for women, and have led women to identify as helpless victims (Hansen et al., 1991; Walker, 1979). Newer strategies emphasize first working through the victimizing experience and then empowerment of the victim (Orava et al., 1996; Walker, 1994). To prevent physical and psychological injuries, these services must be readily available and without negative consequences. These interventions must also address the violence within a partnership pattern of dominance and control of resources and persons. For victims to fully appreciate benefits from services, resources and appropriate alternatives must be available for protecting themselves and their children from either threat or further abuse. The sooner in the violence cycle the better, and the more definite the response, the less likely violence will recur.

Qualitative research with samples of battered women also indicates the importance of services given by providers who can identify with the victims or in self-help groups of victims sharing similar experiences (Bowker, 1983a; Donato & Bowker, 1984; Walker, 1994). It is also important that service providers consider racial and cultural fit. Research suggests the importance of a bridging relationship of support with a friend, counselor, or other service provider in attempts either to change a relationship or to successfully end a battering relationship (Hamberger & Hastings, 1988b). Services usually include both a buddy system and advocates that may have been in similar past situations. Advocates help victims get psychiatric or social work counseling or both, legal services, shelter protection, and other forms of support and relocation help (Tan et al., 1995).

Counseling services also need to explore, evaluate, and adapt models of couples therapy for those who wish to continue their relationships. As is noted in Chapter 7, encouraging women to remain in battering relationships is an extremely controversial subject. Some women may never be able to be protected while they remain in their couple relationships. Others may face the possibility of changing patterns of violence. Thus, a thorough evaluation of these factors is needed, and only some clients can be successfully treated in couples therapy. Couples treatment, for those who are appropriately evaluated and referred, could educate couples about the dynamics of violence relationships and train both members of a couple to change their individual behaviors and their interactional communication. They can also be taught alternatives for expressing anger or frustration without resorting to violence.

Forensic Investigations

Some partner violence does lead to more serious consequences, including death from suicide or murder. Therefore, service providers likely will be involved with the criminal justice system at least occasionally. Thus, records need to be kept, investigations need to be thorough, and officers need to become familiar with patterns of violence that lead to murder and suicide and to build files that could be used in court in case a prosecution or defense includes the abuse history.

Social Policy Agenda

The significant physical, psychological, and social consequences of partner violence clearly indicate a need for social policy directives aimed to prevent these traumas in the future. Social policy must continue to reduce the inequities between men's and women's lives. Women suffer most of the negative physical and psychological consequences associated with partner violence. They are more likely to be injured, killed, and psychologically damaged. If women live in partner relationships that are inequitable and experience the negative consequences of lower power positions in the larger society (lower opportunities, lower incomes, and more negative valuations), their victimization will continue. Basic norms and values of society have changed toward more equitable relationships, but the availability of those advantages do not extend across all individuals or groups. More work needs to be done.

Social service providers can make service administrators aware of the critical areas of need. Keeping records of services provided and documenting partner violence reported or not reported can provide evidence of the need for resources and services. First, service providers must prioritize the prevention and elimination of violence, and second, assign enough resources to this problem to adequately address prevention, identification, diagnoses, and services. From the top to the bottom of any organization, programs and regulations must be evaluated as to how they protect and provide safety to victims.

Conclusions

Victims of partner violence suffer both social and psychological consequences. Their losses include safety and security, love and caring from partners, self-esteem, psychological and physical health, work, status and support systems, and confidence and faith in the future (Varvaro, 1991). All persons and organizations concerned about these losses need to mobilize in response to this problem. The following list offers a summary of recommendations for reducing consequences associated with intimate partner violence:

1. The first priority is to identify and protect victims.

2. Diagnostic assessments must always include a set of questions to assess partner violence.

3. Time, patience, and persistence are needed to allow victims to disclose their secrets and to cope with the trauma and psychological consequences. A safe and private space and a supportive, culturally, and gender-appropriate interviewer are advised.

4. Personnel trained in violence issues must educate, train, and consult with health and mental health service providers to ensure appropriate referral and treatment.

5. All health and mental health service providers must educate themselves about male-female violence, its nature and effects, and the complex societal factors that prevent or facilitate disclosure, help seeking, and change in family systems.

6. More research is needed that addresses the limitations noted in this review, particularly psychological issues related to victims. In the past, psychological research has tended to focus on the perpetrator, rather than on the outcomes for victims or the possible role that victims' psychological processes have on outcomes and social costs of partner violence.

7. Research directed toward prevention of secondary victimization or amelioration of symptoms is also needed. For example, social support and ways to improve self-esteem deserve more attention.

Continued progress in building family strengths and in enhancing the quality of family life requires that these recommendations be implemented to the fullest extent possible.

CHAPTER  THREE

Children Exposed to
Partner Violence

JANIS WOLAK

DAVID FINKELHOR

Partner violence is often described as unseen because it usually occurs in the privacy of a home. But violent homes often include children, and these children do see the violence (Fantuzzo, Boruch, Beriama, Atkins, & Marcus, 1997; Hilton, 1992; Holden & Ritchie, 1991; Jaffe, Wolfe, & Wilson, 1990). Children hear their parents, the adults they love and depend on, screaming in anger, pleading in fear, and sobbing in pain. They hear fists hitting bodies, objects thrown and shattered, and people thrown against walls and knocked to floors. They may see blood, bruises, and weapons. Some children witness domestic rapes and even murder (Eth & Pynoos, 1994; Pynoos & Nader, 1988). These children often show signs of trauma, but partner violence has even broader implications because family relationships have such a profound influence on development (Aldwin, 1994; Davies, 1991; Hartup, 1989).

This chapter describes current knowledge about how partner violence affects children and the different ways children respond to, and cope with, violence in their homes, focusing on developmental differences. It covers approaches to assessing and treating child witnesses to partner violence.

73

Defining the Problem

Childhood exposure to partner violence, as we define it here, occurs
when children see or hear physical assaults between their parents or
observe its effects. Most of the literature focuses on violence in two-
parent families, but "parents" should be broadly construed to include
stepparents or cohabiting or other intimates or even dating partners
of a parent. When we refer to parents in this chapter, we do not mean
to exclude other family structures, such as single-parent families. No
type of family is immune from this kind of violence.

Much of the research on child observers of partner violence has
been based on data from battered women in shelters and thus tends
to involve children who have seen their mothers victimized severely—often and chronically. Other patterns of violence can occur
but are not as well documented in the literature. The assault victim
can be someone besides the mother: a stepmother, live-in partner, or
dating partner of the child's father. In some cases, the mother may be
a perpetrator of assault, and the victim the child's father, stepfather,
or live-in or dating partner of the child's mother (Stets & Straus,
1990). The violence in a child's home may be entirely one sided, or
both parents may use it to varying degrees. Children may see their
mothers use violence in self-defense or see their parents trade blows
(Stets & Straus, 1990).

Other situations also differ from typical shelter cases. Many children are exposed to less severe violence in homes in which parents
occasionally or routinely slap, shove, and throw things at each other.
Some children see severe violence but live in homes in which the
mothers do not flee or incidents are not reported to police or other
agencies (Straus & Gelles, 1990a). The violence that children observe
can vary in its onset and duration. Children may live with parents
who have been married and violent for many years, or violence may
suddenly erupt over money problems or other stressful events. Violence may set in as a marriage disintegrates and either ceases or per-
sists after parents are divorced or separated. Or, children living with
a single parent with no history of partner violence may suddenly
witness attacks on their parent by a new stepparent or dating partner.

Although children may be exposed to different degrees of violence
under a variety of circumstances, the unique and salient characteristic of this exposure is that children observe violence done by or

against their parents or both. These children may grow up fundamentally confused about the meanings of love, violence, and intimacy. The parent-child relationship on which a child relies for nurture, security, and guidance is often distorted as children attempt to cope with viewing their parents as victims or perpetrators of violence or both. The partner violence that children observe occurs within their core relationships, and its significance for the children lies in that fact (Aldwin, 1994; Davies, 1991; Hartup, 1989).

<hr>

Scope of the Problem

<hr>

Researchers are beginning to establish how many children witness partner violence. Estimates are primarily based on a few surveys asking adults to recall childhood experiences. This research suggests that substantial numbers of children are exposed to adult violence in their homes as they grow up.

Incidence of Child Exposure
to Partner Violence

Four surveys asking adults about childhood memories suggest that between 11% and 20% of adults remember seeing violent partner incidents when they were young (Henning, Leitenberg, Coffey, Turner, & Bennett, 1996; J. L. Jasinski, personal communication, June 19, 1996; Straus et al., 1980; Straus & Smith, 1990a). More than 10% of adults surveyed recalled their mothers or fathers hitting each other in the two representative National Family Violence Surveys conducted in 1975 and 1985. In the 1975 survey, 11% of those responding recalled at least one occasion of violence, with 13% reporting their fathers hitting their mothers, and 9% their mothers hitting their fathers. In the 1985 survey, 13% of adults remembered violent incidents between their parents (Straus, 1992; Straus et al., 1980; Straus & Smith, 1990a).

Sixteen percent of those surveyed in the 1992 National Alcohol and Family Violence Survey remembered their parents hitting or throwing things at each other. People were asked to recall incidents that happened when they were teenagers: 7% recalled their fathers as the perpetrator, 4% remembered their mothers hitting and throwing things, and 5% recalled both parents being violent (J. L. Jasinski, personal communication, June 19, 1996).

In a fourth survey, in which 617 women responded to a mail questionnaire in a small New England city, 20% remembered violence in their homes when they were age 15 or younger (Henning et al., 1996), 8% reported that their fathers attacked their mothers, 6% reported their mothers as the assailants, and 6% reported violence by both parents.

At least one study asked children directly about observing partner violence. The 1991 National Child Victimization Prevention Study, a telephone survey of 2,000 children ages 10 through 16, asked children, "Have you ever seen any of the adults in your household hit one another?" Seven percent of children surveyed answered yes. When children were asked who did the hitting, 3.4% identified their fathers or stepfathers, 1.5% identified their mothers or stepmothers, and the remainder identified other adult relatives, mostly siblings. Children were not asked who was hit. Three percent of children surveyed had seen such violence in the past year (D. Finkelhor, personal communication, June 19, 1996).

Although these surveys provide the best figures we have, it remains difficult to know precisely how many children see violence in their homes. People surveyed about such matters may forget experiences or remember incorrectly or be unwilling to disclose painful or embarrassing events. At best, survey figures give a range in which the true rate for childhood exposure to partner violence exists. The 5% rate of exposure to parental violence found in the National Youth Prevention Study underestimates true rates because these survey participants had not finished their childhoods. The rates between 11% and 16% found by the three national surveys of adults may also be low because some people forgot violent incidents or failed to disclose them for other reasons. Also, these surveys each asked only one question about violent behavior by parents. The Henning mail survey, which found that 20% of adult women saw violence between their parents, asked several detailed questions about types and severity of violence, but the sample in this study was based on a local survey of women only, and only 617 of the 6,000 in the sample returned questionnaires.

Researchers estimate that between 20% and 28% of couples who are dating, cohabiting, or married experience at least one violent incident during the course of their relationships (see Chapter 1). Assuming that rates of violence for parents equal rates for couples in general, these figures are fairly consistent with a range of 11% to 20%

for how many children witness assaults. The estimates for violence over the course of a relationship include couples who admit to occasional and relatively mild incidents like slaps and shoves that a child might not notice, as well as couples who engage in frequent or severe violence or both, which would be harder for other household members to miss. This possibility might account for the discrepancy in rates for couple violence and child observation of violence.

None of this is to say that partner violence only affects children if they see it. As described later in this chapter, viewing violence between parents directly affects children in several ways, yet partner assault also has an indirect impact because it physically and psychologically affects parents, particularly mothers, in ways that are consequential for parent-child relationships.

Chronicity of Exposure to Partner Violence

Little is known about how many incidents children who witness violence observe and how often violence occurs. Straus (1992) reported that adults who recalled partner violence as they were growing up were aware of an *average of nine incidents* between their parents, with most people remembering at least four episodes. Kaufman Kantor and Jasinski (personal communication, June 19, 1996) found that, of people who remembered their parents hitting and throwing things, 60% reported more than one violent incident. In the National Youth Prevention Study, one half of children who had seen partner violence had seen it more than once (D. Finkelhor, personal communication, June 19, 1996). Although multiple incidents seem more prevalent than single ones, it is likely that children are more aware of, and more likely to remember, violence when it happens more than once.

Severity of Violence That Children Witness

Henning et al. (1996) asked women about the severity of violent behaviors they recalled between their parents. About one third of women who grew up with partner violence (7% of all women surveyed) had seen their fathers kick or bite their mothers or hit them with fists. Six percent of all women surveyed had seen their fathers beat up their mothers, 3% had witnessed choking and threats with weapons, and 1% had seen their fathers use knives or guns. Somewhat smaller numbers of women had seen their mothers engage in

severe violence. One percent of children in the National Youth Prevention Study (11% of those who reported witnessing violence) had
seen violence so severe that the victim required hospitalization
(D. Finkelhor, personal communication, June 19, 1996), but researchers
did not ask more specific questions about the types of violence.

Some parents may try to protect their children from violent marital fights, but people who work with children of women who have
sought refuge in shelters note: "[W]e find that almost all (children)
can describe detailed accounts of violent behavior that their mother
or father never realized they had witnessed" (Jaffe et al., 1990, p. 20).
Most children in shelters have witnessed acts of severe violence
(Giles-Sims, 1983; Hilton, 1992; Holden & Ritchie, 1991). McCloskey,
Figueredo, and Koss (1995), studying children from violent families,
some of whom lived at home and some of whom lived in shelters,
found that almost one half had witnessed potentially lethal violence
such as choking.

Exposure to Sexual Violence

Although growing numbers of researchers have become interested
in children's exposure to partner violence, few have broached the
topic of exposure to domestic sexual assault even though substantial
percentages of women who are assaulted by their partners also suffer
rape (see Chapter 4). In one study of 115 women from a battered
women's shelter who had been sexually abused as well as physically
assaulted, 18% reported that their children had witnessed sexual attacks (Campbell & Alford, 1989). The small body of research into
marital rape recounts many instances of children seeing or hearing
their mothers raped and sexually abused (Finkelhor & Yllö, 1985;
Russell, 1990).

Different Ways Children Are
Exposed to Partner Violence

When we speak of children being "aware" of or "exposed" to violence,
it implies that children are passive observers. This does not mean
children are at a distance from what they see. One researcher who
reviewed police reports of partner assaults noted the disturbing con-
texts for children who were witnesses:

They sat crying and frightened and watched what was going on, or
they ran into the adjoining room and put their hands over their ears.
A seven-year-old girl . . . fainted from fear. A seven-month baby girl
lay in her crib in the living room when an explosive fight broke out.
It ended with the mother getting beaten and landing on top of the little
girl. A four-year-old girl sat weeping in her mother's lap as the father
threatened with a knife. (Hyden, 1994, p. 123)

Sometimes children are more than observers; they can be participants in the battles of their parents in varying degrees:

The children were still in the kitchen during all the squabbling. When
they saw the knife being waved like a sword, they both started to
scream and run for the door. . . . He yelled, "I'm going to cut you all
into tiny little pieces." (Roy, 1988, p. 174)

A seven-year-old girl witnessed how her father was trying to choke her
mother. The girl forced her way in between her parents, and begged
and pleaded for her father to spare her mother. (Hyden, 1994, pp. 123-
124)

Another woman told of her 3-year-old son coming to defend her, saying: "No, Daddy, no!" And he came behind his father and started hitting him. (Hoff, 1990, p. 204)

Some children are targets of attack, along with their mothers, as
in this mother's account:

He got me down and started kicking me. . . . He kicked me three times
in the head. . . . He grabbed Amy by the neck and broke Bobby's arm.
(Hoff, 1990, p. 34)

Children are also witnesses to sexual abuse:

Then he . . . forced himself into me from behind . . . the whole time
he had the knife against my leg. . . . I thought he was going to kill me.
. . . And the whole time I could see Anna (their preschooler) standing
in the kitchen. (Hyden, 1994, pp. 113-114)

It is easy to see from these accounts how children can become
overwhelmed by witnessing violent, emotion-laden scenes between
their parents. Children may react intensely to these frightening adult
displays, and their reactions may include acute fear for their own and

their parents' safety. Many children have difficulty coping with the feelings of fear, anger, and pain aroused by the violence they witness in their homes (Roseby & Johnston, 1995; Rosenberg & Rossman, 1990).

Symptoms of Children
Exposed to Partner Violence

Children who observe partner violence cannot be described as having one particular pattern of response to their experience (see Table 3.1). A recent summary of 29 studies of children who have witnessed partner assaults (Kolbo, Blakely, & Engleman, 1996) reports harm in several areas of functioning: behavioral, emotional, social, cognitive, and physical.

Behavioral problems include aggression, cruelty to animals, tantrums, "acting out," immaturity, truancy, delinquency, and attention deficit disorder/hyperactivity (Ascione, in press; Davies, 1991; Dodge, Pettit, & Bates, 1994; Graham-Bermann, 1996c; Hershorn & Rosenbaum, 1985; Hughes & Barad, 1983; Jouriles, Murphy, & O'Leary, 1989; McCloskey et al., 1995; Sternberg et al., 1993). Common emotional problems are anxiety, anger, depression, withdrawal, and low self-esteem (Carlson, 1990; Davis & Carlson, 1987; Graham-Bermann, 1996c; Hughes, 1988; Jaffe, Wolfe, Wilson, & Zak, 1986). Social problems are poor social skills, peer rejection, and an inability to empathize with others (Graham-Bermann, 1996c; Strassberg & Dodge, 1992). Cognitive difficulties generally include language lag, developmental delays, and poor school performance (Kerouac, Taggart, Lescop, & Fortin, 1986; Wildin, Williamson, & Wilson, 1991). Physical problems include failure to thrive, difficulty sleeping and eating, regressive behaviors, poor motor skills, and psychosomatic symptoms such as eczema and bed wetting (Copping, 1996; Jaffe et al., 1990; Layzer, Goodson, & Delange, 1986).

Most of the research cited used various standardized instruments that measure psychological and other problems. Researchers compared the scores of children exposed to partner violence with normed scores or with scores of control groups. Most, but not all, of this body of research found that children who witness violence are signifi-

TABLE 3.1 Symptoms of Children Exposed to Partner Violence

Behavioral	*Emotional*
Aggression	Anxiety
Tantrums	Depression
Acting out	Withdrawal
Immaturity	Low self-esteem
Truancy	Anger
Delinquency	
Physical	*Cognitive*
Failure to thrive	Poor academic performance
Sleeplessness	Language lag
Regressive behaviors	
Eating disorders	
Poor motor skills	
Psychosomatic symptoms	
Rejection by peers	

NOTE: Researchers are uncertain whether these types of problems are attributable to exposure to partner violence alone or to the cumulative effect of exposure and other problems prevalent in violent homes.

cantly more likely to have problems in one or more of the five areas cited than children who do not.

These findings do not imply that every child who witnesses partner violence, even frequent and severe violence, will have problems. Many children are able to cope successfully with disturbing events. Moreover, this body of research is relatively recent, and its findings are limited by methodological and other difficulties detailed later in this chapter. At this point, researchers are uncertain whether the problems of these children are attributable to exposure to partner violence alone or to the cumulative effect of exposure and other difficulties prevalent in violent homes.

Why Exposure to Partner Violence Harms Children

Researchers believe that partner violence damages children developmentally in several ways. A model of these influences is described by Jaffe and his colleagues (1990), who theorize that children are affected by partner violence both directly and also indirectly through the impact the violence has on their parents. Direct effects include physical danger to the child, emotional and behavioral problems stemming from attempts to cope with violence, and the learning of aggressive behavioral patterns. Indirect effects ensue from maternal physical and psychological ill health resulting from the stress of being abused, exposure to paternal anger and irritability, and inconsistent or overly harsh parental disciplinary practices by parents who may be particularly distracted and irritable.

Direct Influences

Physical Danger

Some children are in physical danger because of the violence in their homes (Jaffe et al., 1990). Proximity to an assault can imperil a child who is nearby when objects are thrown, weapons used, or people shoved and hit. A child may be injured while being held in his or her mother's arms, fleeing, or trying to intervene in an assault. Some children become targets of assault.

Exposure to physical danger is also associated with post-traumatic stress disorder (PTSD) and related symptoms. *PTSD* is a specific psychiatric disturbance caused by exposure to an extreme stressor that results in the involuntary reexperiencing of the event (in the form of intrusive recollections or dreams), a residue of heightened physiological arousal (as in difficulty falling asleep, irritability, and exaggerated startle responses), and a pattern of avoidant behavior (feelings of detachment or estrangement and emotional constriction; see *DSM-IV* for exact criteria for diagnosis). Exposure to violence seems to trigger PTSD in children more consistently than other stressors (McNally, 1993). Studies have found that 100% of children who witnessed parental homicide (Malmquist, 1986) or who witnessed a mother's violent sexual assault by strangers (Pynoos & Nader, 1988) qualified for the diagnosis of PTSD. Current theory about PTSD views it as resulting from overwhelming levels of fear and helplessness, particularly combined with perceptions that one is going to be killed or seriously injured, so it is easy to see how PTSD could be triggered by exposure to partner violence. It is not clear, however, how many children who witness less serious forms of partner violence may suffer from PTSD. In one study of 64 7- to 12-year-old children whose mothers had been assaulted by partners in the past year, 13% were suffering from clinically diagnosable PTSD, and the majority of children exhibited some PTSD symptomatology: 52% experienced intrusive, unwanted memories of traumatic events; 19% exhibited traumatic avoidance; and 42% suffered from traumatic arousal symptoms (Graham-Bermann, 1996d).

Emotional and Behavioral Problems

Some children from violent homes exhibit symptoms of emotional and behavioral problems that appear to be attributable to the violence they witness (Jaffe et al., 1990). These children are fearful because they are subjected to frightening domestic scenes. They are anxious because they are worried about their safety and the safety of other family members. They are listless from sleepless nights, sad from seeing a parent victimized, angry at one or both of their parents, and depressed because the situation seems hopeless.

Some coping mechanisms that children use to deal with partner violence may cause them trouble. Fearful children may alienate parents, teachers, and day care providers by being aggressive or clingy and dependent (Davies, 1991; Holden & Ritchie, 1991). Some children isolate themselves from peers to keep the family secret of partner violence hidden (Jaffe et al., 1990). Adolescents may run away from home (Carlson, 1990) or anesthetize themselves with alcohol or other drugs.

Aggressive Behavioral Patterns

Considerable evidence suggests that children whose parents are violent at home are more aggressive, both at home and in other settings, than children whose parents are not violent (Davis & Carlson, 1987; Dodge et al., 1994; Holden & Ritchie, 1991; Thornberry, 1994). One simple and widely accepted explanation of this, called *social learning theory*, proposes that children with aggressive parents learn to be aggressive by imitating their parents' behaviors (Bandura, 1973). When parents use violence to exert control, to deal with problems, and to settle conflicts, children come to see aggression as a powerful and appropriate tool for interpersonal relations. Children may identify with parents who use violence. Also, children from violent homes may not have the opportunity to learn negotiation and other peaceful methods of conflict resolution.

Indirect Influence

Disciplinary Practices

Some researchers have explored the association between the quality of marital relationships and the quality of parenting skills, finding that parents in violent conflict with each other may tend to have qualities that can interfere with healthy child development, including irritability, harsh disciplinary practices, fewer positive interactions with their children, and more inconsistency in child rearing (Belsky, 1984; Holden & Ritchie, 1991). Holden and Ritchie (1991) note that inconsistency may be a particular problem in these families for two reasons: (a) Parents may disagree more about child rearing and may communicate poorly, and (b) mothers may respond to their children one way when they are alone with them and a different way when fathers are present. Parents coping with their own violent relationships may be unable to provide consistent supervision and guidance to their children (Holden & Ritchie, 1991; Jaffe et al., 1990). Parents may fail to teach their children how to control aggression and may even unwittingly reinforce aggressive tendencies by ignoring them or by backing down from confrontations over violent acts (Patterson, 1982; Patterson, DeBaryshe, & Ramsey, 1989).

Maternal Stress

For children, the risk of harm comes not only from exposure to frightening and emotional scenes involving parents but also from the toll on parents' abilities to maintain close and positive parent-child relationships. Most children turn to their mothers for help in coping with problems. When the problem is partner violence, however, a mother's life may be so disrupted by the stress of her own victimization that she is unable to respond to her child's concerns and fears.

Several studies have found that high levels of maternal stress, particularly stress related to parenting, are associated with emotional and behavioral problems in children living in battered women's shelters (Graham-Bermann, 1996b; Holden & Ritchie, 1991; Wolfe, Jaffe, Wilson, & Zak, 1985). Mothers may be physically injured, in poor health, and overwhelmed with anxiety and depression, as well as dealing with stresses from money problems, unemployment, divorce, and homelessness (Jaffe et al., 1990). At least one study, however, has found that, in violent homes, mothers' mental health problems are not causally related to children's mental health and that most of the variance in children's mental health scores can be attributed to the violence in the home, rather than to maternal distress (McCloskey et al., 1995).

Paternal Characteristics

It seems apparent that children who witness assaults between their parents would be affected by their fathers' actions, but data allowing for the assessment of paternal behavior are rarely gathered in partner violence research (Sternberg, in press). One exception is Holden and Ritchie (1991), who interviewed battered mothers about their husbands' child-rearing behaviors. They found that paternal "irritability" was one of two significant predictors of behavioral problems in children of battered women. (The other significant factor was maternal stress.) They also found that, compared with fathers in a control group, fathers in violent families did less child care, were angry at their children more often, were less affectionate, and were less likely to reason with their children and more likely to spank them. At least one other study found that paternal irritability predicted antisocial behavior in boys (Patterson & Dishion, 1988).

Hartup (1989), reviewing the research on fathers, notes that "father-child attachments show many of the same qualities that mother-child attachments do" (p. 122). Where a mother is the primary caretaker, Hartup speculates, the father's support of maternal care giving, or lack of support, will have important implications for a child. Disagreements about child rearing are rife between parents in violent families (Salzinger, Feldman, Hammer, & Rosario, 1992; Straus et al., 1980). If Hartup is right, in violent families in which mothers are the primary caretakers and fathers are disengaged from child rearing, paternal challenges to a mother's parenting ability may weaken and damage mother-child relationships. Some tenuous support for this idea comes from a study of Israeli children (Sternberg et al., 1994), which looked at children's perceptions of fathers and mothers, comparing four groups: (a) children who were abused, (b) children who witnessed partner violence, (c) children who witnessed such violence and were abused, and (d) a comparison group. Although children from both abused groups viewed a perpetrating parent, whether father or mother, more negatively than children from the comparison group, children who witnessed partner violence but were not abused did not view their violent fathers more negatively. They did, however, have more negative perceptions of victimized mothers. (Children from all four groups were similar in the number of positive traits they assigned to their parents.) The impact of paternal behavior on children exposed to partner violence is an important area for future research.

Factors Determining the Extent of the Impact of Partner Violence

Although the above mechanisms help explain why exposure to partner violence can result in trauma and symptomatic behavior, it is not possible to generalize about the form or magnitude of harm to an individual child. Each child will have a different experience. Several factors are particularly likely to determine how a child perceives, responds to, and copes with observing parental violence and how any harm is manifested: (a) the age and developmental level of the child, (b) the nature and severity of the violence witnessed, (c) the family context of the violence, (d) the nature of social interventions, and (e) the cumulative stress factors acting on the child.

Age and Developmental Level

Children's levels of understanding and coping abilities differ with age, and the impact of exposure to violence cannot be assessed without considering a child's developmental level (Davies, 1991; Jaffe et al., 1990; Roseby & Johnston, 1995; Rosenberg & Rossman, 1990).

Infants Through 5-Year-Old Children. Children in this age-group may be disproportionally exposed to partner violence and particularly vulnerable to it (Copping, 1996; Fantuzzo et al., 1997).

Infants are cognizant of the emotional states of others at an early age (Cummings, Zahn-Waxler, & Radke-Yarrow, 1981), and they may be disturbed by the anger and turmoil of a violent household. More-over, babies require sensitive, responsive caretakers, and mothers who are suffering in violent relationships may be too injured or under too much stress to respond to their infants' distress or to give them the intense physical care they need. As a result, some infants from violent homes may show signs of health problems and neglect. They may be underweight, have problems eating and sleeping, cry incon-solably, and be unresponsive to adults (Jaffe et al., 1990; Layzer et al., 1986). Also, infants are fragile and at risk of being injured in violent homes.

Toddlers and preschool children still rely heavily on their care-takers to help them control emotions and behavior. Children of this age may become increasingly aware of, and disturbed by, the chaotic atmosphere generated by partner violence. They lack the resources to cope with confusing and frightening events on their own and are particularly dependent on caretakers for explanations and reassur-ance (Davies, 1991; Jaffe et al., 1990). Because they are too immature to regulate their own behavioral and emotional responses without help, they tend to show signs of behavioral and emotional problems if their mothers are too depressed or otherwise incapacitated to pro-vide responsive care (Davies, 1991; Graham-Bermann, 1996b). As they get older, they also begin to think about and try to understand the things that go on around them. Young children who have observed violent domestic scenes need to talk about their experiences with adults who can help them explain and clarify what they have seen. If the children cannot do this, they may try to express themselves by acting out (Davies, 1991).

Children between the ages of 2 and 5 who have been exposed to partner violence often behave aggressively (Graham-Bermann, 1996c), possibly "to ward off imagined aggression" (Davies, 1991, p. 521). Children may also become excessively demanding, talkative, and physically active (Copping, 1996). Boys may exhibit these "external-izing" behaviors more often than girls (Copping, 1996; Cummings, Pelligrini, Notarius, & Cummings, 1989; Davies, 1991). Children of this age may also become whiny and clingy, have trouble sleeping, regress in behaviors such as toilet training, be anxious or sad or both, and have trouble interacting with peers and adults (Davies, 1991; Graham-Bermann, 1996c; Jaffe et al., 1990). Some researchers believe that preschool children are especially likely to feel responsible for violence between their parents because of their developmentally

appropriate egocentrism and inability to view things from the perspectives of others (Jaffe et al., 1990; Roseby & Johnston, 1995).

Six- Through Twelve-Year-Old Children. School-age children usually have more resources to cope with exposure to violence. They
have more control over their emotions and more sophisticated cognitive skills, including more realistic understandings of events. They
develop problem-solving and reasoning skills, and their social circles
broaden to include friends and adults outside their families (Aldwin,
1994). They are still very oriented within their families, however, and
tend to see their parents as role models (Jaffe et al., 1990). Because
of this, they may feel particularly confused and conflicted about partner violence. For instance, they may admire a powerful father but also
fear him, or love and worry about a victimized mother but feel angry
at her for appearing weak. Boys may feel particularly ambivalent
about their fathers (Hughes, 1982).

As children get older, they tend to blame themselves less for parental conflict (Jaffe et al., 1990; Jenkins, Smith, & Graham, 1989).
This does not mean, however, that they stay out of it. Jenkins et al.
(1989) found that whereas only 24% of 9- to 12-year-olds blamed
themselves for their parents' quarrels, 71% intervened in various
ways, trying to stop the disputes. Children of this age also worry
about the vulnerability of their mothers and siblings (Graham-
Bermann, 1996a).

Behavioral problems resulting from exposure to violence may become apparent as children enter school and start interacting with
peers and teachers. Aggressive behavior is often a particular concern
(Davis & Carlson, 1987; Hughes & Barad, 1983; Jaffe, Wilson, & Wolfe,
1988), but children may also act out, have conduct problems, and be
emotionally needy, fearful, and anxious (Davis & Carlson, 1987;
Hershorn & Rosenbaum, 1985; Jaffe et al., 1986; Jouriles et al., 1989;
Rosenbaum & O'Leary, 1981a; Sternberg et al., 1993). They may have
academic problems (Kerouac et al., 1986), have difficulties with peers
(Strassberg & Dodge, 1992), and suffer from sadness, depression, and
low self-esteem (Davis & Carlson, 1987; Hughes, 1988; Jaffe et al.,
1986). Isolation may also be a problem. In some cases, children are
ashamed of their homes and concerned about keeping the violence a
secret. In other cases, children may be isolated by a domineering
father who seeks to control the family by limiting access to outsiders
(Jaffe et al., 1990).

Adolescents. By adolescence, most children are able to understand the perspectives of others, come to independent conclusions about events, and appreciate what they can and cannot control (Aldwin, 1994). Adolescents are more able to view partner violence as their parents' problem and to turn to friends and adults outside their families for support. They may be less fearful and anxious about the situation than younger children and less likely to feel responsible for violent events (Jaffe et al., 1990).

Some teenagers, however, will have lived with partner violence for many years and may show evidence of long-term effects. Children who have grown up with violence are more prone than other teens to delinquency and violent behavior (Dodge et al., 1994; Thornberry, 1994). These teens may assault peers, siblings, and parents. Some teens may use alcohol and other drugs to escape from their problems, or they may escape literally by running away. Suicide is also a concern with troubled adolescents, particularly those who are withdrawn and depressed (Carlson, 1990; Hollis, 1996; Spirito, Overholster, & Stark, 1989). Although some adolescents from violent homes find ways to escape, others stay at home and assume parenting duties for younger children in the household. These adolescents bear heavy burdens of responsibility (Jaffe et al., 1990).

Gender Differences

Some researchers have considered whether gender differences contribute to the extent or types of problems exhibited by children who witness partner violence. Some studies indicate that boys from battered women's shelters or other clinical populations are more likely than girls to behave aggressively or to exhibit conduct problems (Davis & Carlson, 1987; Hughes & Barad, 1983; Jaffe et al., 1990; Jouriles & LeCompte, 1991) or that girls have more problems with depression, anxiety, and other internalizing behaviors (Davis & Carlson, 1987; Holden & Ritchie, 1991; Jaffe et al., 1990). Other studies finding various problems have not reported significant differences between boys and girls (Cummings et al., 1989; Fantuzzo et al., 1991; Hughes, 1988; Hughes, Parkinson, & Vargo, 1989; Jaffe et al., 1988). One study found that girls who witnessed violence, were abused, or both had more problems with aggression and other externalizing problems than boys and were also more depressed (Sternberg et al., 1993).

The evidence here is inconclusive for several reasons. Studies that find boys have more problems with aggression may simply be reflecting a trend in the general population where boys exhibit more aggression outside the home than girls (Dodge et al., 1994). Moreover, most of these studies are based on mothers' reports, and some evidence suggests that women who are victims of partner violence rate their sons as more aggressive than other observers would rate them (Hughes & Barad, 1983). Also, these studies use small groups of children, and when the groups are divided by gender, they become even smaller, reducing the statistical reliability of the results. Clearly, this is another area where more research needs to be done.

Nature and Severity of the Violence Witnessed

Besides developmental stage, another factor that can influence the impact of witnessing partner violence is the nature and severity of what is seen. Scant research has been conducted on this topic within the field of partner violence, but an extensive literature describes what characteristics of other kinds of violence are more likely to affect a child seriously. It is clear that the greater and more threatening the violence, the more likely it is to have an impact.

Research with crime victims demonstrates that people who are injured or who believe that they could be seriously injured or killed are more likely to experience later traumatic stress symptoms (Kilpatrick, Edmunds, & Seymour, 1992). In studies of PTSD in children, being physically close to an act of violence, hearing screams or cries for help, being closely related to the victim, and seeing bloody wounds or serious injury tend to correlate with amount of trauma, along with duration of the episode, number and nature of threats, and degree of brutality of the act witnessed (Pynoos, Steinberg, & Wraith, 1995). The trauma literature has also made an important distinction between exposure to single traumatic events and multiple or chronic traumatic events (Terr, 1990). Chronic exposures tend to produce more devastating and difficult-to-treat problems. Thus, we would expect that children exposed to multiple, ongoing episodes of partner violence over an extended period of time would be more affected than those who witnessed isolated episodes.

Family Context of the Violence

Partner violence rarely takes place in the context of an otherwise happy or stress-free family. In addition to marital conflict are other major stressors, such as poverty, unemployment, mental or physical illness, alcohol abuse, and entanglements with the legal or criminal justice system. Moreover, other violence may occur, particularly directed toward the children (Jaffe et al., 1990). These factors can affect the impact of exposure to partner violence.

Marital Conflict. In trying to understand the impact of exposure to partner violence, one important theoretical question is the extent to which it can be distinguished from the effects of exposure to marital conflict without violence. Research into the effects of observing partner violence has produced findings that are consistent with a body of research that looks at how overt parental hostility affects the emotional and behavioral development of children. When children who live in "discordant homes," where parents are overtly hostile but the hostility stops short of violence, are compared with children from harmonious homes, they tend to have the *same sorts of problems* as children from violent homes (Grych & Fincham, 1990). Children from discordant homes are more psychologically disturbed when parental quarrels are frequent and severe (Grych & Fincham, 1990; Jenkins et al., 1989).

Researchers have tried to determine whether children who are exposed to actual violence are somehow different from children who are exposed to parents' verbal hostility with no violence. Evidence suggests that children who witness partner violence are at greater risk of adjustment problems than children whose parents are simply angry and hostile but not violent (Fantuzzo et al., 1991; Jouriles et al., 1989). Some studies, however, have found no differences between discordant homes and violent homes (Hershorn & Rosenbaum, 1985), and some studies have found only weak differences (Hughes, 1988; Hughes et al., 1989; Sternberg et al., 1993). These studies do find that children from both groups have significantly more problems than do children from nonviolent, harmonious homes.

Taken together, these studies suggest that pervasive conflict that takes the form of overt verbal hostility *or* violence harms children by causing stress, impairing effective parent-child relationships, and training children to be aggressive (Grych & Fincham, 1990). Overall, children from violent homes appear to be at greater risk for showing clinical-level behavioral and emotional problems, but it is likely that some symptoms are caused by the conflict and not necessarily the violence.

Child Maltreatment. In understanding the impact of witnessing partner violence, another fact to keep in mind is that many of these children are not just witnesses to violence, but victims themselves. Children exposed to adult partner violence are at high risk for being physically abused (Kenning, Merchant, & Tomkins, 1991; McCloskey et al., 1995). In a national sample of the population in 1985, 22% of husbands who had hit their wives in the previous year had also physically abused their children, compared with 8% of husbands in other families (Straus & Smith, 1990a). Similarly, 23% of women who had hit their husbands had also physically abused a child in the previous year (Straus & Smith, 1990a).

Even higher rates of physical child abuse are found among children subjected to partner violence. One review notes that researchers have consistently found that 25% to 45% of children of women in shelters have been physically abused (Hotaling, Straus, & Lincoln, 1989). A survey of several shelter populations found that more than one half of the children in residence were abused or neglected, frequently both. The physical abuse was often severe: 5% of these children had been hospitalized for injuries caused by physical abuse, and 8% had been identified as sexually abused (Layzer et al., 1986). A study that included children living in shelters and children living at home found that children in 10% of families studied had been sexually abused (McCloskey et al., 1995).

In addition, the issue of emotional maltreatment is important. One could argue that, by definition, children exposed to partner violence experience emotional maltreatment. But even independent of this, it is very likely that children in violent homes have been yelled at, threatened, manipulated, or triangled into the parental conflict—other forms of emotional abuse separate from the witnessing.

At least three studies have attempted to compare children who have been exposed to partner violence and children who have been abused, with inconclusive results. One small study found that abused children had more behavioral and emotional problems, but the differences between the two groups were not reliable (Hughes et al.,

1989). A second study found the same number of problems in the two groups (Sternberg et al., 1993). A third study measuring the relative effects of being abused and witnessing violence found that physical abuse wielded the most powerful effect on a child's behavior but that witnessing partner violence added to that effect (Salzinger et al., 1992).

Again, it must be recognized that some effects seen in children who witness partner violence are probably a result of the physical and emotional maltreatment they have additionally suffered and that these effects may be difficult to distinguish from the witnessing itself. On the basis of available research, it also seems plausible that when physical and emotional maltreatment are present in addition to partner violence, one would expect more severe difficulties for a child.

Nature of Social Interventions

Many children who live with partner violence become involved with social service and governmental agencies that attempt to intervene in the situation (Jaffe et al., 1990). These agencies are usually focused on the adult parties to the violence and are often not cognizant of, or equipped to deal with, the special needs of children. Two of the most common agencies are battered women's shelters and the criminal justice system.

Battered Women's Shelters. When mothers escape from violent relationships by fleeing with their children to shelters, the flight and the shelter residence are distressful in themselves. Children find themselves abruptly severed from their homes, toys and belongings, pets, and daily routines. These families are often in hiding, with children cut off from the supports of school, close friends, and most relatives. Children may miss their fathers, resent the move, and press their mothers to return home (Jaffe et al., 1990).

Many children in shelters score in the clinical range for behavioral and other problems measured with standardized instruments such as the Child Behavior Checklist (Achenbach & Edelbrock, 1984). In one study, 70% had clinical-level behavioral problems and 53% appeared to be clinically depressed (Davis & Carlson, 1987), although the extent to which these symptoms can be attributed to shelter residence is unclear. One study that investigated children who were exposed to violence and compared children living in shelters with children living at home found higher internalizing behaviors in shelter residents.

The children in shelters were sadder and more withdrawn and depressed than the children at home (Fantuzzo et al., 1991). These children may also be more anxious (Hughes et al., 1989).

Shelter stays are often short, and many problems exhibited by children in shelters may be temporary reactions to family disruption. Problem behaviors may decrease over time during shelter residence (Copping, 1996), and behavioral and emotional problems may decrease for most children living with their mothers in nonviolent homes, within 6 months after leaving the shelter (Wolfe et al., 1986). Because these children tend to have many family problems, it is difficult to isolate the effects of shelter residence. Many battered women's shelters have become sensitive to children's needs and have instituted special programs to assist children during their stay (Jaffe et al., 1990).

Criminal Justice System. When police, prosecutors, and criminal courts become involved in partner violence, this increases the potential for additional negative effects on children. In addition to the upsetting exposure to violence, children may now have to deal with the embarrassment of public disclosure, the fears and confusion engendered by the presence of police and the legal system, the disruption of routine, and the possible conflict of loyalties. For example, when police arrive at a home, the children are often afraid that they will be accused of a crime. Police are sometimes not adept at handling children and their fears, and in the confusion surrounding arrest, children can be very disturbed, not understanding what is happening, and may get separated from parents.

Police and prosecutors will often want to interview the children, and the children may have to repeat their stories on many occasions (Whitcomb, Shapiro, & Stellwagen, 1985). Children may experience a crisis of loyalty, not wanting to be responsible for putting their parents in jail. They may also fear retribution by the offending parents, and so they may lie, change their stories, forget details, and end up suffering the ire and frustration of investigators.

Most research on children's involvement in the legal system has been done in regard to child sexual abuse and relatively little in regard to partner violence cases. Sexual abuse cases are similar in some of the stresses they impose on children (crisis of loyalty, police investigation, public exposure), although they do differ in that a child him- or herself has been the direct victim and is the primary witness in legal actions, which certainly adds to the stressfulness. Children rarely have to testify in cases of partner violence.

Cumulative Stress Factors

As can be seen from reviewing all these potential contributing factors, it is difficult for researchers to isolate exposure to partner violence from other stressful factors in a child's life. Children who live with violent parents may be particularly prone to experience cumulative stresses. They generally grow up in discordant homes and suffer high rates of abuse. Their parents are likely to move frequently, to have problems with alcohol, and to get divorced (Spaccarelli, Sandler, & Roosa, 1994). In extreme cases, these children are forced to flee their homes for a shelter and to cope with the intrusions of child protective services, police, and criminal justice agencies. Witnessing partner violence is often part of a "cumulative stressor" chain of events (Jaffe et al., 1990), meaning that children with more than one serious difficulty in their lives are more likely to show signs of harm from exposure to violence, maltreatment, and other problems than children who have only one serious problem. The number of stress factors may be even more important than the exact type of stress factor in determining whether a child is harmed (Rutter, 1985). Ultimately, specific effects are probably associated with specific stressors, and generalized stress effects are associated with the number of stressors and magnitude of the total stress burden. But the important point is that witnessing partner violence must be seen in this total context.

Protective Factors

Despite the harmful influence of violence and abuse on children's lives, many children who live in difficult circumstances do not show signs of great disturbance. This is possible because protective factors in these children's lives buffer them against the harmful impact of the violence. Studies tend to divide protective factors into three categories: (a) the characteristics of the child, (b) the quality of family support, and (c) the quality of extrafamily support. Children who are adaptable, are particularly intelligent, have unusual talents or strong

interests, or have other internal resources tend to overcome adversi-
ties. The style with which children tend to attribute causes to bad
events can also be a protective factor, particularly if they can avoid
pessimism and self-blame. Children who have strong, supportive relationships with some significant adults also tend to fare well. Other
protective factors include support from peers and teachers, success
in school, and athletics (Herrenkohl, Herrenkohl, & Egolf, 1994;
Mrazek & Mrazek, 1987; Rutter, 1985).

Two studies indicate that family support may not be as effective
a protective factor for children exposed to partner violence.
McCloskey et al. (1995) found that children from violent families
who reported supportive family relationships were not shielded from
the mental health effects of witnessing violence. Kolbo (1996) found
that boys exposed to partner violence who reported high levels of
support scored significantly higher in self-worth than did boys who
lacked support, but that level of support did not make a difference in
the self-worth scores of girls in the study (the source of support was
not specified). Other protective factors have not been studied in this
context.

Long-Term Effects

Although some problems that children develop in response to exposure to partner violence constitute immediate reactions to difficult
situations, the risk is that these children will develop chronic behavioral and psychological problems that could mark their lives into
adulthood. One area of concern is the association between witnessing
partner violence as a child and behaving aggressively as an adult.
Adults who recall partner violence in their homes when they were
young are more likely to use violence against their spouses, to be
abusive with their children, and to commit violent crimes outside
their homes than adults who grew up in nonviolent homes (Straus,
1992). Among married couples, both men and women exposed to
partner violence as children are about three times more likely to hit
their own spouses (Straus et al., 1980). Moreover, adults who witnessed severe violence are much more likely to perpetrate severe violence than those who witnessed milder violence or no violence. In
the National Family Violence Survey, 20% of men who remembered

witnessing extreme violence between their parents severely abused their wives, compared with 2% of men who never observed partner violence (Straus et al., 1980).

The idea that children brought up in violent homes may be more likely to become perpetrators or victims of partner violence than children raised in nonviolent homes has been characterized as the "intergenerational transmission" of violence, wherein aggressive or victimizing family patterns are passed from parent to child. Although much, but not all, research in this area supports this idea, intergenerational transmission is certainly not an inevitable process, and much remains to be learned about the mechanisms by which such family patterns may be passed from parent to child (see Chapter 2 for a more detailed discussion).

Some evidence also suggests an association between exposure to partner violence as a child and enduring psychological problems as an adult. Studies have found that college students who observed parental violence were more anxious than those who did not, experienced more trauma-related symptoms, and had lower self-esteem and that the women were more depressed and more aggressive (Forsstrom-Cohen & Rosenbaum, 1985; Silvern et al., 1995). Another study comparing women who recalled violence between their parents with women who did not reports that the former showed more symptoms of psychological distress and lower levels of social competence (Henning et al., 1996). The women in this study who were exposed to violence also reported more physical child abuse by parents, more verbal conflict between parents, and less caring and support; these findings make it difficult to attribute their problems to any one source. Another study found that adults who witnessed partner violence as teenagers had more symptoms of stress and depression and more alcohol and other drug problems than other adults (Straus, 1992).

Limitations of the Research

The body of research concerning children exposed to violence is relatively recent, and much of it is limited in some respects. In a 1989 review of 29 studies, Fantuzzo and Lindquist (1989) pointed out many of the shortcomings in this literature:

- The existence of partner violence is usually determined solely on the mother's report, or it is assumed because the mother is living in a battered women's shelter. The types and severity of partner violence and its frequency are seldom reported.

- The details of a child's exposure to violence, including type of violence, severity, frequency, and recency, are rarely noted. The child's exposure is sometimes assumed, rather than actually determined.

- The existence of important relevant factors is often not assessed, including basic demographic information such as socioeconomic status, race, unemployment, family structure, and age of parents, as well as family factors known to affect children adversely, such as substance abuse by parents, paternal or maternal physical and mental health, pathology and stress, parenting ability, and stability of the home environment.

- Data on children are usually gathered from a single source and often from the mother despite evidence that mothers in battered women's shelters may assess their children's behavior differently from other observers or the children themselves (Hughes & Barad, 1983; Sternberg et al., 1993).

- Child variables such as age, gender, and intellectual functioning are not always carefully assessed. Older adolescents are rarely studied. Wide age ranges are grouped together without consideration for developmental differences.

- Many of the children participating in these studies are from battered women's shelters, and some of their problems may be attributable to the family disruptions they have undergone, rather than to the violence they have seen.

- Child abuse and neglect are often not assessed despite the high risk in this population of children.

- No longitudinal studies and virtually no follow-up studies have been conducted.

Research is also lacking on the effects of a child's relationship to the perpetrator or the victim of partner violence or both. Although the most frequent scenario may be mother as primary caretaker *and* victim of violence, this is not always the case. Mothers can be assailants, and violence can be mutual. Children may perceive violence perpetrated by a caretaker quite differently from the way they view violent attacks against a caretaker, and perpetrators of violence may be more or less responsive to the needs of their children than are victims of violence.

The closeness of a child's relationship with the perpetrator is also an unexplored factor. When a mother is the victim of violence, her child's relationship to the perpetrator may range from that of a barely known new dating partner to that of an involved father with whom the child has complicated intimate ties. If the assailant is a father who is also a close caretaker, the situation for the child may be particularly convoluted.

This is a relatively new area of research, and despite these weaknesses, its quality has steadily improved. It is difficult to conduct this kind of research. It is difficult to locate children who have been exposed to partner violence in the general population, and women's advocates and social service and medical practitioners who know of and work with these children may be reluctant to participate in research. Parents may distrust the research process or believe that participating is burdensome. Once a research project is started, the instability in the lives of these children presents obstacles to data gathering and to follow-up. The need to expand this research is compelling, however, given the large percentage of children who may be affected by partner violence.

Responding to the Problem

Responding to children caught up in partner violence is a complex challenge. Concentrating attention and resources on these children requires special efforts because, frequently, neither they nor their parents request assistance or attend to the children's crisis, and the urgent situation between the adults is often the overwhelming and compelling focus of those trying to intervene. To ensure that the children are a priority, wherever possible, professionals should be available who can devote their full attention to the situation of these children. It has been demonstrated that children have fewer symptoms when a trained professional is available to advocate for them (Rossman, 1994).

It should be kept in mind that child victims of partner violence come to professional attention in a variety of ways: in crisis situations because of police or shelter intervention in a violent episode between the parents; when the parents seek counseling in a noncrisis situation and the violence is disclosed; or when a child discloses parental violence in the course of some professional contact concerning the child at school, in a mental health setting, or during the course of a child welfare investigation.

Some have raised questions about the utility of intervening on behalf of a child witness when the parents are not ready to admit to

TABLE 3.2 Guidelines for Practitioners

Guidelines for Crisis Intervention

Conduct lethality assessment
Formulate safety plan
Train children in security procedures
Report child abuse if situation warrants
Provide crisis counseling

Guidelines for Noncrisis Situations and General Practice

Screen children for partner violence
Assess children who have been exposed
Recognize possible need for child abuse report
Assign independent worker to children
Consider crisis intervention needs
Be developmentally and culturally appropriate
Coordinate with other professionals
Encourage healthy parenting practices
Be aware of child custody issues
Promote parent education that teaches about the impact of exposure to
partner violence

or deal with their own situation (Gentry & Eaddy, 1982, cited in Jaffe et al., 1990), but it is generally believed that interventions can be helpful. Several authors have conceptualized the intervention in three phases: (a) crisis intervention and initial assessment, (b) short-term therapy, and (c) long-term therapy.

Crisis Intervention

In a crisis situation wherein police have been called or a mother is fleeing her home, crucial, special issues (see Table 3.2) must be attended to (Rossman, 1994).

The safety of the children must be ensured. So, as a first priority, a "lethality assessment" is required to determine where the children should be residing and with whom. Even if it is clear that the family cannot remain together, family members may meet at court hearings, at relatives' homes, during exchanges of the children for visitation, and so forth, and the potential for violence at these times should be assessed. A good assessment requires that information be obtained from all family members, as well as close associates, and from professional evaluations of the violent adults.

A safety plan must be formulated for the children concerning what to do in case violence recurs. For children old enough to take action on their own, this plan should include a rehearsal of how to tell whether the situation is approaching dangerousness, how to get out of a dangerous situation (e.g., where to go in the home, or where to hide, whom they can call, secret ways of communicating what is happening), and places in the neighborhood or surrounding area that may be safe.

For families in shelters or other locations where they are hiding from a violent parent, the children must be trained in how to protect secrecy. Children need to learn how to avoid divulging their location to friends or relatives, how to make sure the abuser cannot use caller ID to trace the family, and how to take other precautions.

A child abuse report may be necessary. Most states require professionals who are aware that a child has been attacked or seriously endangered by a parent or caretaker to make a report to child protective services. In some states, exposure to parental violence is itself evidence of child endangerment. In all states, a report should be made if there are any signs that violence or threats have been directed at the child. A report would likewise be required if evidence suggests that the family violence has created an environment in which children's basic needs for food, supervision, and other care have not been met.

Children who have just witnessed something very frightening or disturbing, such as a serious assault, or who have just suffered a traumatic dislocation, such as fleeing home, need the benefit of a crisis interview with a professional trained in crisis counseling with the children. (A detailed description of this interview is available in Arroyo & Eth, 1995, and Rosenberg & Rossman, 1990.) The goal of such an interview is to forestall some typical post-traumatic symptoms, such as intrusive imagery, by giving the child a chance to recount the traumatic events, to correct any misattributions of self-blame, and to develop initial strategies for managing overwhelming feelings.

Noncrisis Situations

Although sometimes children's contacts with professionals will come as a result of a crisis created by an acute violence episode, frequently a situation of partner violence exposure will occur outside a crisis situation. Because more and more professionals are following the recommended practice to screen for possible partner violence in all child, marital, and family assessment situations, they are turning up an increasingly large number of exposed children.

When disclosure of violence exposure comes through contact with a child's parents, the parents should be asked in detail about the circumstances of exposure and their assessment of its impact on the child. Parents are frequently unable to assess impact on children accurately, however. An independent interview with the child is required in order to make that assessment (Jaffe et al., 1990).

The discovery of violence can also come through contact with the child, who may disclose it to a school guidance counselor or to a pediatrician in a routine visit. These situations are a challenge to handle because of the competing needs to protect the child's confidentiality and the safety of the child and possibly other household members. Thus, the practitioner receiving the disclosure must explore the situation with the child to know whether the child is in danger of retaliation, what kinds of dangers other household members face, and whether the child is comfortable with any practitioner communications with either parent. Adding to the dilemma, depending on the age of the child, practitioners in many states cannot provide counseling to a child without parental permission. Moreover, children who have been abused and threatened are subject to mandatory child abuse reports, whatever the wishes of the child. Thus, although the goal is generally to get support and counseling for the child and assistance to the family, the route to these outcomes may be complicated, depending on the details of the situation.

Assessment

A thorough assessment should be made of a child who has been exposed to partner violence; screening protocols suited to the child's developmental level should be used. During this assessment, practitioners need to establish a respectful, understanding relationship with the child and not press prematurely for disclosures before adequate trust is established.

Particularly for a preschool child, assessment requires observation of the child alone, with the mother, and even in the whole family context at home or in the clinic. Starting with preschoolers and up through adolescents, clinical interviews with children are possible.

These interviews are often greatly facilitated by the use of drawings, art materials, and other forms of creative, nonverbal expression.

The information that needs to be elicited during the clinical interview includes the kinds of violence to which the child has been exposed; whether the child him- or herself has been the target of violence; the identity of all individuals who may be violent in the child's environment, including sibling and peer violence; and the nature of any physical punishment the child may have been receiving. It is important to explore whether the child is concerned about his or her own safety or about the safety of a parent or other family member. If violence has been directed toward the child, a medical examination is likely warranted to check on the child's health and to establish any evidence of child abuse. As in the case of a crisis evaluation, an assessment of whether the child is at risk for abuse or neglect and whether he or she is receiving adequate parental care must be made.

Assessments are generally facilitated by the use of some structured instruments and assessment protocols. One assessment for exposure to violence, though not specifically marital violence, is the Survey of Children's Exposure to Community Violence (Martinez & Richters, 1993). The Conflict Tactics Scale (Straus, 1979; Straus & Gelles, 1990b) can be used for a specific inventory of partner violence, but so far it has been primarily developed as a research tool, rather than as a clinical instrument, particularly in regard to child interviews.

A good instrument is important for assessing the various kinds of symptoms and problem areas that a child may be manifesting. The Child Behavior Checklist (Achenbach & Edelbrock, 1984) has forms both for parental administration and for child self-administration. Sources for several other instruments are listed in the appendix at the end of this chapter.

General Case Management Issues

Cases involving children exposed to marital violence often entail some difficult case management issues that professionals need to anticipate and plan for. One common problem is unwillingness to accept treatment or intervention. Parents may prohibit help for their child because they are afraid of further disclosures of family violence or because of general hostility toward "meddling outsiders." The control tactic in some violent families is for the abuser to try to isolate the family. Children themselves may decline help, seeing it as stigmatizing in some way or focused on an area of their lives they would rather deny than deal with.

Another common case management problem is the involvement of other agencies and professionals. These cases frequently come to one's attention through police, courts, or shelter agencies that continue to be involved with the family. The case may entail a child abuse report or an ongoing child welfare investigation. Criminal actions may have occurred about which the child must testify. The parents may have their own therapists and attorneys who are actively involved in the problem. These entanglements can create rapid developments in the case—a court order, a child protection finding, a police interview, the calling of a family therapy meeting—to which the professional working with the child must respond. Good liaison with other involved parties is important (Ammerman & Hersen, 1990).

An important concern is that other agencies and other professionals may have different priorities and different points of view that do not necessarily mesh well with the therapeutic needs of the child. Thus, police and courts may not be willing to take the child's needs into consideration in deciding how to conduct investigations or how to pursue charges. Other professionals may hold blaming attitudes toward the perpetrator or victim parent that do not correspond to the child's view. Ideologically oriented agencies may have agendas for the child that are not the child's own.

Unfortunately, in some communities, tensions and unresolved conflicts exist between partner violence professionals and child protection agencies. Partner violence professionals have sometimes been concerned that child protection agencies, lacking sufficient awareness about, and sympathy for, the situation of battered women, were overly hasty to remove children from their mother's care. Child protection agencies, for their part, have been concerned that overidentification with mothers has kept partner violence professionals from recognizing children who were in such danger that they needed separate child welfare intervention, apart from partner violence services. Fortunately, an increasing number of communities have developed collaborative protocols among these groups of practitioners.

Child therapists should be prepared for parents to have strong and often contradictory views about what should be done for the child. Some of these views may result from displaced anger as parents vent ire at each other or the system or the therapist. Parents should not be allowed to dictate treatment, but child therapists are in a more diffi-cult situation than those with adult clients because parents can de-cide to terminate treatment.

Custody Issues

One challenging case management dilemma concerns issues of child custody. Violent relationships often end in divorce, which then leaves important questions to be resolved about custody and visita-tion rights of parents. Delicate assessments and resolutions must be made to ensure the welfare of the children—who need parental con-tact but also safety, security, and healthy parenting—while at the same time protecting adults who may have been victims of partner violence. Among the complex factors that must be weighed in cus-tody decisions are the legitimate questions about the future safety of the children while in the custody of a parent who has exhibited vio-lent behavior; the fact that violence can sometimes escalate or inten-sify, rather than diminish, after a separation or divorce; and the reality that custody arrangements frequently necessitate contact between parents, which can conceivably put them at risk for additional assault or harassment.

These issues have challenged family courts, which have not al-ways had good information about partner violence and its conse-quences on children. In the past, some courts completely ignored the matter of partner violence in custody decision making, on the pre-sumption that the roles as spouse and parent were distinct and that violence in one role did not presuppose it in another. But research has clearly suggested some interrelationship (see Saunders, 1994a, for a review of this research). The question begging for more research concerns in what circumstances partner violence is or is not a risk factor for violence and abuse toward children and whether and under what circumstances other negative effects accrue for children from continued frequent association with parents who have committed partner violence.

Another factor that needs sensitive assessment concerns the situ-ations of the victims of partner violence in the course of custody decision making. Because courts often carefully examine the material and psychological resources that parents will bring to their parenting, victims of partner violence can appear at a disadvantage because they may be suffering from the psychological effects of their abuse, and possible homelessness and financial instability related to their need to leave the home in a precipitous fashion. Moreover, custody arrangements determined by courts often entail the need to exchange children and to communicate about the details of the children's needs and living arrangements. Sometimes these needs can set up victims for additional harassment and possibly violence from their violent partners.

Thus, the need is for those who work with children who have witnessed partner violence to be familiar with the many sensitive and difficult issues that custody decisions can pose for children and parents. These professionals must be prepared for the rancor and intensity with which these issues can be battled—including the possibility of exaggerated or false claims on all sides and attempts to triangulate children into the conflict. They should be aware of and anticipate the impact these disputes may have on children. They also need to recognize that they may be called on to make assessments that will play an important role in court decision making.

Specialized agencies and professionals now provide assistance in this process. For example, at visitation centers, children can be with parents under supervised conditions, or ex-partners can meet to exchange children or negotiate child management issues. Those who may have contact with child witnesses to partner violence should be familiar with these resources.

Treatment Issues

Although all children exposed to partner violence need to be assessed, not all children need treatment or can necessarily benefit from it, although many can. It is important to assess this before referring for or starting a course of treatment. Children who are not symptomatic, who have good coping abilities and support systems, who have not been exposed to lengthy or highly disturbing violent episodes, or who are not particularly interested in therapy may not be appropriate for therapy. Such children can be given some brief prophylactic information that may facilitate their getting help if they should begin to experience difficulties.

Decisions about type of treatment and length of treatment should be based on an assessment of the child's problems, the child's developmental level, and the family context. Sometimes the clinician does not have enough information at the outset and may wish to set a course of treatment that will be reassessed at a later point.

Short-term treatment may be sufficient for a child suffering from traumatic stress and adjustment problems, but not more deeply rooted behavioral problems. These more readily treated problems tend to involve anxiety and fears, feelings of self-blame, hopelessness and discouragement, anger, and revenge fantasies.

One component of short-term work with children, especially those who have witnessed disturbing scenes, is *trauma processing.* This involves getting the child to describe, often with the assistance of drawings and play activities, all the details of the traumatic event and the emotions that were evoked. The goal is to help the child begin to master and gain some ability to manage the strong feelings and images evoked by the experience (Terr, 1990, cited in Rossman, 1994). Trauma processing can be done in play therapy or in mother-child dyad situations for younger children and in individual or group therapy for older children and adolescents. Some children will need time before they are ready to deal with the traumatic events in the therapeutic setting.

Another component of short-term work involves reduction of feelings of responsibility and self-blame. Steps must be taken to lessen the children's sense of responsibility by making clear to them that their own behavior or qualities are not the basic source of the violence or conflict and that, as children, they are not capable of stopping the violence or protecting their parents on their own.

A child's developmental level will be an important consideration in the form that treatment will take. Infants primarily require a reestablishment of a safe and secure environment where a caretaker can deal reliably and responsively with infant needs for food, sleep, and physical contact. Therapy with toddlers and preschoolers is largely organized around play activities. For school-age children and adolescents, group settings can be a particularly effective form of treatment. School-age children and adolescents often have acute feelings of isolation and stigma resulting from their family situation that is readily dealt with in groups of children from similar violent families. Peled and Davis (1995) describe a short-term group approach to working with 8- to 13-year-olds in a model that is widely accepted as a way of working with children exposed to partner violence (Jaffe et al., 1990). Some preliminary evaluation studies of these support groups have been done (Grusznski, Brink, & Edleson, 1988; Peled & Edelson, 1992;

Wagar & Rodway, 1995). These groups seem to work best with children exposed to less severe levels of violence who have mild to moderate, but not severe, adjustment problems.

Short-term treatment of adolescents has some additional challenges that may not be present for younger children. As a result of
neglect, resentful feelings toward violent parents, and socialization
to violent modes of conflict resolution, adolescents from violent families may be engaged in a variety of acting-out behaviors. One therapeutic goal for such adolescents is to help parents reestablish appropriate limits, boundaries, and discipline (Harway & Hansen, 1994).
To this end, resources intended to ease the stress on the parent, such
as gaining safety from the abusive partner so that the mother may
attend to the child, may very much help the child. Such parents need
specific help in how to set clear and appropriate limits without getting into protracted conflicts with the child that may resemble conflicts with the partner. They also need help learning effective nonviolent disciplinary practices. This is particularly challenging because
parents, out of guilt for their neglect and responsibility for exposing
the child to violence, as well as fear that the child may develop the
patterns of the violent partner, may easily overreact in their attempts
to deal with adolescent acting out.

A difficult issue that may confront therapists who work with child
witnesses concerns the advisability of whole family treatment sessions including the violent partner. Although child therapists can
often see many valuable reasons for such sessions, this form of treatment has been controversial among those who work with partner
violence (issues in the debate are discussed in more detail in Chapter
7). In general, it is important for the child therapist who sees some
possible benefit from a whole family session to accept the lead from,
and the judgment of, those professionals who may be working with
parents. Similarly, a therapist who is working with a child and who
sees a family session as contraindicated for the child should not allow
the child to be pressured into participation. The situation is more
difficult in families with episodes of partner violence, wherein the
parents are not themselves in treatment. In such a situation, a child's
therapist would want to convene a family session only after ascer-
taining that there is no risk of provoking violence or retaliation from
an abuser, that the session is desired by all parties, and that the child
feels safe and capable of coping with the situation (Rossman, 1994).
It may be important in such a situation to ensure that multiple pro-

fessionals are present—one who can take responsibility for the parents and their reactions, and one who is available to respond to the child.

Long-Term Treatment

Long-term treatment is possibly indicated for children who manifest problems of serious depression, suicidality, or self-injury, as well as for children with conduct disorders and aggressive behavior. These problems probably stem from more than the witnessing of partner violence and may arise from an environment of chronic conflict, emotional deprivation, and actual abuse and neglect of the child. Good resources concerning the treatment of such children are available, but it is beyond the scope of this chapter to review this literature.

Implications

1. Questions about possible exposure to parental and partner violence should be asked of all children being assessed or treated for other problems of a mental health, academic, or social nature (e.g., delinquency, sexual abuse, depression, academic difficulties).

2. All children exposed to parental partner violence should be given a detailed assessment to determine the nature and impact of their exposure.

3. In encounters with children who have been exposed to partner violence, the possibility of physical and emotional abuse of the child needs to be recognized, along with the potential responsibility for a report to the mandated child abuse and neglect reporting agency. All professionals need to be trained in such assessments and procedures.

4. All children involved in partner violence crisis situations should have a professional working with them independently who is able to assess them and act on their behalf.

5. Agencies and professionals should develop and be trained in protocols for providing crisis intervention with child witnesses that take into consideration their needs for safety, confidentiality, and post-traumatic counseling.

6. Work with child witnesses should take into account developmental level and cultural differences in parenting and family practices.

7. Professionals working with child witnesses need to coordinate and collaborate energetically with a variety of other professionals involved in these cases, such as shelter workers, police, prosecutors, attorneys, judges, and parents' therapists.

8. Partner violence implies some disruption of, or compromise to, parenting abilities and resources, and therefore work with adult victims and perpetrators of partner violence needs to focus on developing and maintaining healthy parenting practices.

9. Professionals working with violent partners and their children should be familiar with the difficult custody issues posed by separation and divorce in such families. Services that provide visitation centers and facilitate exchange of children and communication about child custody issues are needed.

10. Parent education programs for new parents and others in the community should include material alerting parents to the impact on children of witnessing violence; this is a way of trying to discourage violence from occurring, but also a way of encouraging parents to better protect and get help for children who do get exposed.

General Implications for Public Policy

The widespread prevalence of partner violence and its clear association with negative impacts on children contain an important message for public policy: Screening for exposure should take place much more consistently and universally than is currently the case in every environment where children are screened for problems, including pediatric visits, school counseling programs, emergency rooms, and child welfare investigations. This means that agencies and professionals who screen for spousal abuse should make sure they inquire about children's exposure (Jaffe et al., 1990). Likewise, it means that agencies and professionals who screen for child abuse should also look for exposure to partner violence.

Moreover, the realization that children can be traumatized by violence from a variety of possible sources suggests that screening should be as broad as possible and not limited to one or two narrow forms of violence or abuse. In addition to child abuse and parental violence, children are traumatized by exposure to peer and sibling violence, encounter violence at the hands of nonfamily caretakers, and in some communities witness a great deal of violence in their streets and neighborhoods. Discussions are available on the wide range of children's violence exposure (Finkelhor & Dziuba-Leatherman, 1994), and protocols exist for screening systematically for such exposure (Martinez & Richters, 1993).

Conclusion

Research and practice concerning child witnesses of partner violence are still in the beginning phases and have yet to achieve the maturity of work that has been done with adult victims. A great deal is now recognized, however, and the clear message is that practitioners need to make concern about such children a central aspect of interventions. One of the most serious challenges is learning how to integrate this concern in a natural and organic way into the work with adult victims and perpetrators. The result is certain to be a major advance in the mitigation of suffering caused by partner violence and a stronger bulwark against its transmission onto future generations.

APPENDIX

Sources for
Assessment Instruments

Achenbach, T. M., & Edelbrock, C. S. (1984). *Child Behavior Checklist.* Burlington: University of Vermont.

Briere, J. (in press). *Professional manual for the Trauma Symptom Checklist for Children (TSCC).* Odessa, FL: Psychological Assessment Resources.

Nader, K. O., Dudley, D. B., & Kriegler, J. (1994). *Clinician-Administered PTSD Scale, Child and Adolescent Version (CAPS-C).* Rockville, MD: National Center for PTSD.

Pynoos, R. S., & Eth, S. (1986). Witness to violence: The child interview. *Journal of the American Academy of Child Psychiatry, 25,* 306-319.

Shaffer, D. (1992). *Diagnostic Interview Schedule for Children.* Rockville, MD: National Institute for Mental Health.

CHAPTER FOUR

Sexual Assault in Marriage

Prevalence, Consequences, and Treatment of Wife Rape

PATRICIA MAHONEY

LINDA M. WILLIAMS

In addition to physical assault of intimate partners, an area worthy of separate study is sexual violence in marriage. The prevalence, dynamics, consequences, and treatment of wife rape are the focus of this chapter.

Forcible rape is recognized as a crime across the United States. When a male stranger attacks a woman at night, kidnaps her or breaks into her home, and then forces her at gunpoint to submit to sexual acts (what Williams, 1984, calls the "classic rape"), the violation is easy to recognize and name. Although many women experience such assaults, this scenario does not describe the typical rape experience. In reality, rape is most likely to be perpetrated by a man known to the victim; rape by an intimate partner is more common than rape by a stranger (Bachman & Saltzman, 1995; Finkelhor & Yllö, 1985; Randall & Haskell, 1995; Russell, 1990), and women who are or have been married are more likely to be raped by their husbands than by strangers (Russell, 1990). Despite these data, many people continue to hold inaccurate beliefs about the nature of rape in U.S. society, when and to whom it happens, and its impact on the victims.

Stereotypes and misunderstandings are common in discussions of wife rape. *Wife rape* is still generally regarded as a contradiction in terms; the common notion of rape is not one that includes a marital context. In fact, a marital rape exemption legally shielded husbands from being charged with the rape of their wives, and this exemption was not successfully challenged until the late 1970s (see "Wife Rape and the Law," this chapter). The long-standing tradition of failing to recognize wife rape as a problem reflects cultural beliefs about men, women, and sexuality that have interfered with the acknowledgment of, and societal response to, wife rape. Such beliefs are embedded in such notions as a woman's sexuality is a commodity that can be owned by her father or husband, what happens between husband and wife in the bedroom is a private matter, a man is entitled to sexual relations with his wife, and a wife should consensually engage in sex with her husband, thus making rape "unnecessary." Although such notions may appear to be outdated, their influence on current attitudes and laws is evident, as noted throughout this chapter.

This chapter reviews the available literature and discusses the definition and prevalence of wife rape. Then it reviews the dynamics of wife rape and some typologies that are helpful in framing a discussion. It examines the consequences of wife rape on wives, husbands, and children. The chapter concludes with a discussion of treatment and assessment issues, policy implications, and directions for future research.

Wife rape, as we shall see, is not rare; it is just rarely discussed. It is noteworthy that this topic has been relatively neglected, receiving scant attention in both the domestic abuse and rape literatures. The social science research and the discussions of wife rape in the literature are primarily descriptive and have, for the most part, not attained the sophistication of research on partner violence involving physical assault. Much of the discussion in the literature today is still focused (as is the beginning of this chapter) on defining the problem, examining its prevalence, and legitimating societal concern about its occurrence.

One reason for the lack of development in the thinking and research on wife rape may be that it is unclear where this issue "fits"; separate fields of research on spousal violence and on sexual assault have developed with their own separate theories, methodologies, and research agendas. These differing literatures have left many issues relevant to wife rape unexamined and many questions unanswered.

Is sexual assault of a spouse best understood when viewed as one of many forms of domestic violence and abuse, or should discussion of wife rape be considered within the context of theories of sexual violence? Does the husband who rapes his wife have motivations and characteristics similar to those of a stranger-rapist? Should husband-rapists receive the same treatment as stranger-rapists under the law? Zimring (1989) asks, "[I]s the same core moral wrong present in sexual predations within marriage as in forcible rape by strangers?" (p. 559). These are controversial issues for which no consensus currently exists.

Research and policy recommendations on wife rape represent a minor focus of the literature on domestic violence or on rape in general, notwithstanding the convincing evidence that wife rape is frequent and damaging. Two of the best studies that have investigated the prevalence of wife rape in representative samples of women (Finkelhor & Yllö, 1985; Russell, 1990) have found that between 10% and 14% of ever-married or cohabiting women have been raped at least once by their partners.

The short- and long-term impacts of rape have been well documented (Goodman et al., 1993; Kilpatrick & Resnick, 1993; Resick, 1993; Weaver & Clum, 1995) and continue to be the focus of considerable research. Although myths about the nature of sexual assault in marriage may lead people to believe that such experiences are less traumatic than stranger rape, these myths are adequately dispelled by recent research. Victims of wife rape develop psychiatric disorders similar to (or more severe than) those developed by stranger rape victims (see below). Survivors of wife rape describe a deep, personal violation of trust as well as body:

> When a stranger does it, he doesn't know me, I don't know him. He's not doing it to me as a person, personally. With your husband, it becomes personal. You say, this man knows me. He knows my feelings. He knows me intimately, and then to do this to me—it's such a personal abuse. (Finkelhor & Yllö, 1985, p. 118)

> I mean you can compartmentalize it as stranger rape—you were at the wrong place at the wrong time. You can manage to get over it differently. But here you're at home with your husband, and you don't expect that. I was under constant terror (from then on) even if he didn't do it. (Bergen, 1996, p. 43)

Many victims of wife rape also suffer severe physical injuries and endure multiple rapes throughout their marriages. As Finkelhor and Yllö (1983) note, a woman who is raped by a stranger lives with a memory of a horrible attack; a woman who is raped by her husband lives with her rapist.

This long-neglected issue deserves the attention of all professionals who come into contact with families, and because of the higher rate of rape in marriages in which physical violence occurs (Hanneke, Shields, & McCall, 1986), those who work with battered women must give this issue additional attention. This chapter focuses on the rape of women by husbands and intimate, cohabiting partners. Sexual assault of men by their female partners is believed to occur much less frequently and with less severe consequences (see Struckman-Johnson & Struckman-Johnson, 1994, for further review of this topic). Sexual assault in dating or homosexual relationships or both, though similar in some respects to wife rape, is outside the scope of this chapter.

Definition of Wife Rape

One difficulty in addressing the issue of wife rape, as is the case with rape in general, is defining what behaviors should be considered "rape." At its most basic definition, *rape* is forced sexual contact, yet what constitutes "force" and what sexual acts are included must be defined. This review focuses on *marital rape* defined as any unwanted sexual penetration (vaginal, anal, or oral) or contact with the genitals that is the result of actual or threatened physical force or when the women is unable to give affirmative consent (see also Bergen, 1996; Pagelow, 1984). This also includes sexual exploitation involving sexual contact, such as when a husband coerces a wife to engage in sexual acts with someone else. We have endeavored to review studies to find relevant information about such experiences perpetrated by men in marital or cohabiting intimate relationships. Although it may appear that research on "wife rape" should, by definition, include only legally married couples, most studies have not limited themselves in this way. Many have included cohabiting couples, suggesting that the relevant relationship dynamics of long-term cohabiting couples are similar to those of legally married couples. In addition, because such experiences may occur during a separation period or after divorce, the relationship of ex-wife to ex-husband is relevant to our review. In this chapter, we include information on the incidence and dynamics of sexual assault in long-term intimate relationships and generally exclude or limit our discussion of sexual assault that occurs in the context of short-term intimate relationships and dating relationships.

The way we define wife rape in this chapter does not always parallel the available research on which we have drawn to examine this problem. In theory-driven research, the problem to be studied is defined by examining the theoretically relevant social constructs. But as we have noted, scant research has directly targeted this issue, and definitional problems have plagued research on both partner violence and sexual assault. These definitional problems are compounded in a review that crosses both fields. Some studies that we have reviewed only include completed penile-vaginal intercourse in the definition of rape, whereas others include not only completed but also attempted acts or include oral and anal intercourse, objects inserted into the vagina, or touching of sexual organs. In addition, what constitutes "force" (or coercion) is complicated by the problem of defining force in the context of an ongoing relationship. Typically, studies of sexual assault, on the one hand, require physical force or the direct threat of physical force for the assault to be considered rape. Studies focused on the experiences of battered women, on the other hand, may more broadly define coercion to include more temporally distal acts or coercion stemming from past experiences with violence perpetrated by the husband when his wishes were not accommodated. Further complicating the definitional issues, some studies of prevalence have considered sexual assaults in all intimate relationships, including dating couples.

When summarizing information across this diverse group of studies, the terms *wife rape* or *marital sexual assault* or both will be used to refer to any of the acts outlined above in our definition of wife rape. When referring to a specific study, the terms and definitions used in that study will be used when appropriate.

Wife Rape and the Law[1]

In the United States, no husband had been successfully convicted for the rape of his wife until the late 1970s. The marital rape exemption, which precluded a state from charging a husband with the crime of rape of his wife, was the presumed common law in the United States until this time. The most frequently cited source of this exemption was 17th-century British Chief Justice Matthew Hale, who wrote that husbands could not be guilty of a rape of a wife because "by their mutual matrimonial consent and contract the wife hath given up herself in this kind unto her husband, which she cannot retract" (as cited in Drucker, 1979). It has been noted in several high court decisions that Hale's words were not delivered in the context of a court decision nor was any authority cited and that, therefore, they should not have been considered precedent for common law. Some criminal law authorities in the United States, however, accepted these words to imply a common law, whereas others have questioned Hale's authority, as well as the constitutionality of such a statement (Drucker, 1979). In addition, legislators have enacted in their own states laws that have created a marital rape exemption in the penal codes for those states. Although the origins of the exemption may appear to be "ancient history" rooted in the outdated concept of wives as the property of their husbands, the exemption has had a long life, thriving through the "sexual revolution" of the 1960s and 1970s without change. In fact, the 1980 Model Penal Code extended this exemption to all persons living together as "man and wife" (as cited in Estrich, 1987). As recently as the early 1980s (Jeffords & Dull, 1982), an opinion poll of 1,300 Texas residents found that only 35% were in favor of Texas having a law that permits a wife to accuse her husband of rape.

The arguments for keeping the exemption have included (a) to keep the marital relationship private, (b) to protect husbands from vindictive wives, (c) because it is nearly impossible to prove, and (d) because a charge of rape would discourage reconciliation between husband and wife. These issues were addressed during one of the landmark cases of marital rape in the 1980s. In *People v. Liberta*, a husband raped and sodomized his wife in front of their 2-year-old son while the man was living apart from her under a court order. The trial court ruled that the court order had rendered him "not married," and thus the husband was found guilty of rape (as cited in Augustine, 1990–1991). The husband appealed the ruling, claiming that the court order did not declare him "not married" and that, therefore, he should retain the exemption. In addition, he claimed that this exemption was unconstitutional because it did not offer all men the same protection from prosecution. In 1984, New York's highest court not only upheld his conviction but also struck down the exemption as an unconstitutional denial of equal protection *for married women* (*People v. Liberta*, 64

N.Y., 2d 152 [1984], as cited in Augustine, 1990–1991). (For a further discussion of wife rape court cases, see "Appendix I: Husbands Accused of Wife Rape in the United States, Selected Cases" in Russell, 1990.)

During this ruling, the court made clear the following "responses" to the issues outlined above: (a) Marital privacy is meant to provide privacy of acts that both husband and wife find agreeable—it is not meant to shield abuse; (b) labeling all wives potentially vindictive is a poor stereotype not supported by any evidence; (c) many crimes without witnesses are difficult to prove, yet this is no reason for making a crime "unprosecutable"; and (d) making rape in marriage a crime does not make marriage more difficult—rather, it is rape that would make marriage more difficult (Center for Constitutional Rights, 1990). (For a further discussion of these issues, see Center for Constitutional Rights, 1990; Drucker, 1979; Freeman, 1985; Ryan, 1996.)

According to the National Clearinghouse on Marital and Date Rape, as of March 1996, only 17 states and the District of Columbia have completely abolished the marital rape exemption (the exemption is also abolished on all federal lands).[2] In 33 states, some exemptions remain in certain circumstances—for example, typically, when the husband has not used force because the wife was either temporarily or permanently, mentally or physically, impaired or disabled. These marital privileges are extended to unmarried cohabitants in 5 states and to dating partners in 1 state (Delaware). Under at least one section of the sexual offense codes (usually those code sections regarding force), however, marital rape *is* a crime in all 50 states. Each state has its own sexual offense codes, and professionals working with marital sexual assault survivors must familiarize themselves with the codes in their states to provide accurate information regarding legal rights.

Only a very small percentage of wife rape cases ever make it to trial, and those that have gone to trial have been cases in which a great deal of additional physical force or violence has taken place. Many barriers exist for the wife rape victim who wishes to prosecute. She must overcome her own fears and mixed feelings, including fear of retaliation; fear of a negative reaction from friends, family, or the legal system; concern for how she will support her children without her husband; and even concern for the rapist, with whom she has shared a marriage and family. She must then overcome potential negative reactions of police and prosecutors, who may decide that there is not enough evidence for prosecution. Many victims of rape are likely to "destroy evidence" unwittingly by immediately showering or douching after the rape and by delaying the report (Estrich, 1987). Because victims of intimate sexual assaults are less likely to recognize the assault as a crime (see "Barriers to Assessment," this chapter), they will be less likely to consider "collecting evidence" in the aftermath of a sexual assault. As Estrich (1987) notes, pursuing a rape complaint under the best of circumstances is difficult; doing so when one's friends or family, the police, the prosecutor, and possibly the jury are not convinced that the act is a crime may be more than most women can endure.

It is important to end this very brief review of legal issues with two important pieces of information. The first is that even if no criminal prosecution or an acquittal has taken place, wives who have been raped by husbands may sue their husbands in civil court for financial compensation for injury and suffering and for medical and other costs (Laura X, National Clearinghouse on Marital and Date Rape, personal communication, November 3, 1996; Lehrman, 1996). The second important piece of information also comes from the Clearinghouse, as cited in Russell (1990): Of the 118 wife rape cases prosecuted during 1978–1985, 104 resulted in convictions. This is a prosecution rate of 88%, a rate considerably higher than that for nonmarital rape cases. This is most likely because those selected cases that have made it to trial have been particularly brutal in nature. Many other cases were likely to have been diverted from trial by women's own self-doubts or fears or by the decision-making of representatives of the legal system that the cases were not serious or not "prosecutable." These high conviction rates should be noted by those working with wife rape survivors as advocates, police, and prosecutors; wife rape survivors should not be discouraged on the basis of the erroneous belief that convictions are unlikely.

Prevalence and Incidence of Sexual Assault in Marriage

Prevalence Rates Based on General Population or Community Studies

When we examine the best national data providing estimates of the prevalence of partner violence (Kaufman Kantor et al., 1994; Straus & Gelles, 1990a), we find that these studies did not include questions designed to estimate the prevalence of marital sexual assault. The best information on sexual victimization experiences comes from two national surveys: the National Crime Victimization Survey (NCVS; Bachman & Saltzman, 1995) and Rape in America (Kilpatrick, Edmunds, & Seymour, 1992). Unfortunately, reports from these studies do not present information that permits direct calculation of the rate of sexual assault of wives, although further analyses of these data sets are possible in the future. In addition, Mahoney (1997) notes that reports of sexual assaults by husbands/ex-husbands gathered by the NCVS may not be representative of most marital sexual assault experiences.

Other studies of sexual assault contain methodological problems or limitations in the way the data were reported that make it difficult to arrive at estimates of the prevalence and incidence of wife rape. For example, some studies have reported rates of rape for which wife rape is grouped together with incestuous rape (Koss, Dinero, Seibel, & Cox, 1988). Others group data on wife rape with information on boyfriends and lovers (Bachman & Saltzman, 1994; Ullman & Siegel, 1993). Other studies have methodological limitations, such as using only one question to ask about sexual assault experiences, asking questions in nonprivate settings, or using male interviewers (Sorenson, Stein, Siegel, Golding, & Burnam, 1987; Ullman & Siegel, 1993).

Two studies based on interviews with community samples of women have assessed and reported data on the prevalence of wife rape. One of these studies (Russell, 1990) reported rates of wife rape for adult women in general and also calculated rates for the "ever-married women." This calculation is important because those who were never married have no risk of wife rape. Russell (1990) interviewed a randomly selected representative community sample of 930 San Francisco women and found that 8% were survivors of wife rape. When calculated on the basis of only those in the sample who had been married at some time in their lives, the prevalence of wife rape was 14%.[3] In the second study that provides some basis for estimating the rate of sexual assault of wives, Finkelhor and Yllö (1985) interviewed 323 Boston mothers and found that 10% of these ever-married or ever-cohabited women were survivors of wife or partner rape. In terms of estimating lifetime prevalence of wife rape, it is important to note that most of the women in both of these samples were under the age of 40 and would continue to be at risk for rape in marriage for many more years. It should be noted, however, that although we know little about the relationship between age and wife rape, it is likely that, as is the case with other partner violence (Straus et al., 1980), the rates of wife rape will decrease with age. Our best estimate based on these studies is that 1 in 10 to 1 in 7 married women will experience a rape by a husband.

Rape by Intimates as a Proportion of All Rapes

Some studies that have examined rape by intimates as a percentage of the total number of rapes reported per year have found that rape by intimate partners accounts for over one quarter of all rapes. Randall and Haskall (1995), who interviewed a random sample of 420 women in Toronto, found that 30% of adult rape cases were committed by husbands, common-law partners, or boyfriends and that 12% were committed by strangers (the remaining cases involved perpetrators who were dates or other acquaintances, e.g., coworkers, neighbors). They concluded that "women in intimate relationships with men are at higher risk for sexual assault than are women who are not in intimate relationships with men" (p. 24). Ullman and Siegel (1993) found that 28% of adult (16+ years of age) survivors of sexual assault were assaulted by intimates, and George, Winfield, and Blazer (1992) found that 29% of all sexual assaults of adult women were perpetrated by husbands or lovers.

Kilpatrick and colleagues (1992) reported that one out of every eight adult women in the United States had experienced at least one forcible rape in her lifetime. Many of the women experienced multiple rapes. Nine percent of the rapes experienced by the women were committed by husbands and ex-husbands; another 10% were committed by boyfriends and ex-boyfriends. In their estimate of the proportion of rapes that involves husbands or boyfriends, the Kilpatrick et al. study arrived at a lower figure (19%) because this rate is calculated on the basis of all rapes reported, including those experienced during childhood.

Wife Rape Among Battered Women

Some studies that have gathered data on the sexual assault of women by their husbands or intimate partners have relied on convenience samples, including women seeking help for "relationship problems" and battered women seeking help, living in shelters, or who have answered advertisements. Although such studies clearly do not allow generalization to the total population of married women, they do provide insight into the prevalence of sexual assault among battered women and women experiencing other difficulties in their heterosexual relationships. (For a thorough review of studies of wife rape in these special populations, see Hanneke & Shields, 1985, and Pagelow, 1988.)

The incidence of sexual assault reported by battered or help-seeking women is much higher than that found in the general population. Of women seeking relationship maintenance, counseling, or assistance, between 20% and 30% have reported at least one forced sexual assault by a partner (Campbell, 1989b; Yegidis, 1988). The incidence of sexual assault among battered women has been assessed by many studies, most of which report that at least 50%, and as many as 70% (Pence & Paymar, 1993), of all battered women have been sexually assaulted by their partners. This is a rate five to seven times higher than that reported by ever-married women. It should be kept in mind, however, that these samples are composed of women who have sought help or who were residing in battered women's shelters. It is unlikely that these samples are representative of all battered women. Women living in shelters or those seeking help are likely to be those women who have experienced the most severe abuse. It could be argued, however, that many of the most severely abused women do not seek help because of fear of the abusers and that, thus, the rate of rape of battered women in shelters may not be an overestimate of the rate of sexual violence for all battered women. Moreover, as Russell (1990) noted, the most severe abuse cases, those in which the husbands kill the wives, will not be included in these samples. In 1992, at least 1,414 women were killed by intimates[4] (Uniform Crime Reports, 1992, as reported in Bachman & Saltzman, 1995).

Barriers to Assessment, the Invisible Victim, and the Underreporting of the Prevalence of Wife Rape

Our ability to gauge the prevalence and incidence of wife rape is likely to be seriously limited by underreporting and cultural factors that conspire to keep the wife rape victim invisible. What would prevent wives from reporting forced or violent sex or both? The answers to this question highlight some of the complex issues facing researchers and practitioners in this field.

Rape is one of the most underreported crimes in the United States (Bachman & Saltzman, 1995; Kilpatrick et al., 1992). In a recent study of women's lives that used a large, nationally representative sample (Kilpatrick et al., 1992), only 16% of all rapes disclosed to the interviewer had been reported to the police. Rape victims may also be reluctant to discuss their experiences with researchers. In one study, only one half of a sample of acquaintance rape victims who had reported the rapes to the police disclosed the rapes to an interviewer (Curtis, 1976).

Considerable evidence suggests that victims of wife rape would be less willing than victims of stranger rape to discuss their experiences with either friends or formal service providers. Koss et al. (1988), for example, found that only 3.2% of women who were raped by people they knew reported the incidents to police, compared with 28.6% of women who were raped by strangers. Ullman and Siegel (1993), using a large nationally representative sample, found that women assaulted by strangers were more likely than women assaulted by nonstrangers to talk with a friend, relative, or professional helper. In her study of rape victims, Williams (1984) concluded, "Of all the factors that influence a victim's decision to report, the relationship between the victim and the rapist appears to be the most important" (p. 464). Browne (1987), in her study of women who killed their partners, noted that "women were more reluctant to talk about their partners' sexual assaults than about any other type of abuse" (p. 101). This reluctance and discomfort in talking about sexual assault experiences have also been noted by Finkelhor and Yllö (1985), Hanneke and Shields (1985), Russell (1990), and Bergen (1996).

Factors that contribute to the underreporting of wife rape and women's reluctance to discuss these experiences include the following:

1. *Loyalty to husband/privacy of family:* One woman in the Russell (1990) study wrote (on a postinterview questionnaire), "I felt I was betraying my husband by answering truthfully" (p. 215). Women realize that discussing such experiences will cast their husbands in a negative light. Issues of loyalty and keeping the family secret are typical in battering relationships.

2. *Unwillingness to accept their own victimization:* It is emotionally painful to acknowledge that one is being betrayed by the person one depends on for love and support. For many women who lack the economic resources, social support, or job skills that would enable

them to leave their relationships, acknowledging rape by a partner would only add to an already painful situation. Both dependent and independent women sexually assaulted by their partners may minimize their experiences in order to make their lives bearable (Campbell et al., 1995).

3. *Reluctance to label the experience "rape":* A common theme found in studies of wife rape is the women's avoidance of the words *rape* or *sexual assault* when discussing experiences of forced sex by husbands or intimate partners (Bergen, 1996; Finkelhor & Yllö, 1985; Koss et al., 1988; Russell, 1990; Williams, 1984). One woman interviewed by Finkelhor and Yllö (1985) was physically assaulted (punched in the face) by her husband routinely, and her husband demanded sex three times a day. If she did not comply, he would hit her, demean her verbally, or throw her out of the house. He forced her to have sex four times in front of their child. One day, he threatened to "rip out her vagina" with a pair of pliers. The woman recounted these experiences to the interviewer, yet when asked whether she had ever been raped, she replied, "No." A woman who was routinely beaten and choked during intercourse to the point where she would lose consciousness said that she had never been raped because she always submitted to sex out of fear (Pagelow, 1988). (For further case study examples, see Bergen, 1996; Browne, 1987; Finkelhor & Yllö, 1985; and Russell, 1990.)

Both Browne (1987) and Pagelow (1981b) have documented, in their studies of battered women, that the sexual assaults experienced by the women often included severe physical battering and often resulted in injury. Pagelow noted that, because of the severe physical battering during the sexual assault, many of the victims did not define the act as "sexual" and instead labeled it a "battering incident." Other factors that may influence the tendency of wives to avoid applying the label of rape to such incidents include (but are not limited to) perceptions about a woman's role in marriage, uncertainty regarding what constitutes normal sexual relations, ambiguity regarding what constitutes "force," feelings of guilt and responsibility for the abuse, and having no words to describe their experience.

As discussed by Bergen (1996), many wife rape survivors do not have a word to describe what happens to them. Although they recognize their experiences as being unwanted and harmful, they, like most other people, do not conceptualize the term *rape* within a marital context. Williams (1984) suggests that the more an incident fits the "classic rape" scenario (stranger-perpetrated, in a dark public place), the more likely rape victims are to label the incident a rape: "The classic rape provides the victim with the evidence she needs to convince both herself and others that she was indeed a true rape victim" (p. 464). Bergen found that, among battered women, many survivors of multiple rapes only defined a particular experience as rape when it resembled the classic rape in some way (e.g., the woman was abducted). Many women in the Bergen study only began redefining their experiences as rape after reading battered women's literature, seeing shows on battered women, or speaking with a service provider.

Not only battered women have ambiguous notions regarding what constitutes forced sex. Sullivan and Mosher (1990) used guided imagery to depict a rape or consensual sex scene. Men were asked, "Was this woman raped?" and, "Did she consent to having sex?" Fourteen of the men who received the rape scenario (for 10 of these men, the depiction was of a marital rape) denied that the woman was raped, yet only 3 of these men said that the woman consented, indicating that, for some people, a gray area exists between consensual sex and rape. This study and others (Cahoon & Edmonds, 1992; Cahoon, Edmonds, Spaulding, & Dickens, 1995; Hattery Freetly & Kane, 1995; Monson, Byrd, & Langhinrichsen-Rohling, 1996) have found that people tend to perceive a woman as more responsible for, and less harmed by, forced sex when the offender is her husband, rather than a stranger.

4. *Misunderstandings about a woman's role in marriage and marital responsibilities:* That the term *wifely duty* refers to sexual relations is linguistic evidence that the belief that women engage in sexual relations as one of the chores of marriage has a strong influence in our culture. Many wife rape survivors have expressed the belief that they are obligated by their marriage vows to submit to all sexual acts and that, therefore, these acts are not considered rape regardless of the nature of the sexual experience, as demonstrated by the following quotes.

> He was the husband and I was the wife and it was my responsibility to satisfy him. (Finkelhor & Yllö, 1985, p. 51)

> Every time we had sex it was unwanted, but I knew I had to do it because I was his wife. (Russell, 1990, p. 79)

Similar to women who are physically abused by their husbands, women who are raped by their husbands often accept responsibility for the attacks, blaming themselves for doing or saying something that they should have known would make the husbands lash out at them. Some women believe that they are wrong or frigid for not wanting sex.

> If I refuse he will go to other women. Then it would be my fault and a sin. Whether I like it or not I have to give in. (Russell, 1990, p. 83)

> I told him to f*** off . . . and he sat up on my torso and forced his penis into my mouth. I bit it, so he got off of me immediately, saying that if I expected to keep the marriage together I would have to cooperate sexually. (Russell, 1990, p. 153)

5. *Sexual inexperience and uncertainty about what constitutes "normal" and "forced" sexual relations:* Many women who are sexually assaulted in marriage have not had much experience with other sexual partners, or their other sexual partners have also been abusive. Some women believe that violent sex is a "normal" or inevitable part of marriage. As one wife rape survivor said, "You just have to make the best of it. . . . Who knows what the next one would be like" (Russell, 1990, p. 214). Wife rape survivors report that their husbands have called them frigid or sexually inadequate for not "enjoying" forced sex; or, the wives are told that it is their duty. Women with little sexual experience or knowledge or both are more likely to believe that forced sex in marriage is normal and thus not "real rape."

> I guess some of our problems came from the fact that I never knew much about sex, and I never enjoyed having him touch me that way. Maybe some of it came from the fact that the first time I ever had sex was when he raped me—I was so ignorant! (Pagelow, 1984, p. 431)

The survivors themselves are not the only people uncertain how to distinguish normal from forced sex. Researchers in the field of intimate sexual assault have still not adequately answered this issue, and it remains a problematic aspect of doing such research. Although forced sexual penetration against another's will is always rape, other behaviors, such as fondling of the breasts or genitals, may be normal in one context (e.g., when intended and perceived by both parties as an invitation to consensual sex) yet abusive in another (e.g., when it has, in the past, been the precursor to rape). This discussion should make clear that the field of intimate sexual assault is still in need of considerable fine tuning of its basic concepts. The addition of behaviorally specific terminology has increased the accuracy with which we are able to gauge sexual assault experiences, especially when such experiences have involved force. Future work, however, must pay attention to the relationship between meaning and behavior and endeavor to develop methods for assessing a wider range of experiences within the normal sex—forced sex continuum.

"Use or threat of force" is a complicated issue in the study of wife rape. A woman's prior history of being dominated, intimidated, or battered in a relationship may be the threat of force she experiences, although the offender may not use physical or even verbal threats immediately prior to or during a sexual assault. One half of the 115 battered women in the Campbell and Alford (1989) study were threatened with beatings for refusing sex. For 15 of these women, the threats involved weapons. Many women who in the past have suffered beatings because they refused to engage in sex with their husbands later submit to sex to avoid beatings or to minimize their physical injuries (Finkelhor & Yllö, 1985; Pagelow, 1981b; Russell, 1990). Many wife rape survivors believe that because they choose to give in rather than fight, the experience is not rape even if they have made very clear their desire not to engage in sex.

> I live in an apartment where you go up the steps to get in, and do you know how many times I've been dragged up the stairs? Get away? It just doesn't happen. So I learned quick, and then I never fought back or anything because it would just prolong the agony. It's over quicker if I just give in. (Bergen, 1996, p. 28)

It is apparent from this discussion that each incident of wife rape may not include actual physical or verbal threats and therefore may not be reported by a woman in response to questions about physically forced sexual contact.

Women who have been sexually assaulted in marriage may remain invisible because they fear the negative responses or judgment of others or because they are embarrassed or ashamed. This reaction may be fostered by the societal response to victims of sexual assault (Weis & Borges, 1973), which, especially in cases in which the victims knew the offenders, continues to be one in which the victim is considered blameworthy for either precipitating the attack or not fighting back vigorously enough (Estrich, 1987).

Although we consider the Russell (1990) and Finkelhor and Yllö (1985) studies to be the best estimates of the overall prevalence of wife rape, indicating that at least 1 out of every 10 married women will be raped by a husband or cohabiting boyfriend in her lifetime, it is likely that practitioners who work with battered women will find that these women are much more likely to have experienced such assaults (Campbell, 1989b; Pence & Paymar, 1993). The rest of this chapter is focused on exploring the dynamics of sexual assault in marriage and assessment and treatment issues.

Characteristics and Dynamics of Wife Rape

A myriad of possible problems in sexual functioning may occur in couple and family relationships. Sex may be unpleasant, unfulfilling, or unwanted by either or both partners. Sexual infidelities and dysfunctions in either partner may trouble a marriage. Here, however, we focus on partner violence, and in this chapter we examine the problem of sexual assault in marriages and cohabiting relationships—that is, sexual contact by force or threat of force.

Most evidence about the dynamics of wife rape comes from the accounts of battered wives recruited into research studies from shelters or clinics. Their reports may not be representative of wives who are raped but not battered or wives who do not seek any source of help. Despite these limitations, these accounts are the best source of knowledge available. This section reviews the characteristics and dynamics of wife rape, as well as a typology of wife rape.

Characteristics of Wife Rape

Force. One woman in the Russell (1990) study, when discussing force in her sexual relationship with her husband, said, "He never used force except to hold me down" (p. 50). As this quote illustrates, defining *force* is a complicated issue in the study of wife rape because a woman's history of being dominated, intimidated, or battered in a relationship may shape her beliefs regarding what her options are in any sexual encounter with her husband. Four types of coercion in wife rape have been identified by Finkelhor and Yllö (1985) and are useful here: (a) social coercion, (b) interpersonal coercion, (c) threat of physical force, and (d) physical force. The literature suggests that wife rape survivors may experience a combination of these types of coercion and that the nature of the coercion may change over the course of the relationship, as with the type of assault.

Social coercion is enforced by societal messages regarding appropriate sex roles for men and women within marriage. For example, survivors of wife rape have said that they believed it was their "wifely duty" to submit to sexual relations regardless of their own desires (Bergen, 1996; Finkelhor & Yllö, 1985; Russell, 1990). Such beliefs may be reinforced by religious, family, or other cultural norms and are further reinforced when women who attempt to discuss sexual assaults with friends or service providers are rebuffed, not taken seriously, discouraged from taking action, or blamed for the assault.

Interpersonal coercion includes threats by husbands that are not of a physical nature—for example, threats to leave the relationship or withhold money. It is important not to minimize the impact of such threats. Many women are economically, as well as emotionally, dependent on their husbands and rely on them for their own and their children's sustenance. If a husband threatens, "You have sex now, or I'll get sex elsewhere. I'll leave you" (as cited in Russell, 1990, p. 112), this is a real and potentially terrifying threat. In fact, Russell found that although 70% of wife rape survivors she interviewed said they were "extremely upset" by threats of a physical nature, a larger proportion of the women (83%) were "extremely upset" by threats to leave or "not love her." Thus, even women who are economically self-sufficient may submit to having sex against their will even when it involves painful or humiliating acts, rather than risk losing their husbands and the dissolution of their marriages or families.

Threats of physical force range from minor threats (e.g., telling the woman it will hurt more if she resists) to death threats to her or her children. These threats may be bolstered by a woman's past battering experiences. Battered women know what they risk if they refuse the sexual advances of their batterers. Actual physical coercion may also be used and may include a range of severity from relatively minor (e.g., slaps, shoves) to severe (e.g., punching, burning, tying up, using a weapon, homicide) physical assault. Current data on the

TABLE 4.1 Characteristics of Marital/Partner Sexual Assaults:
Selected Results From Four Studies (Percentage of
Sample Who Experienced Each Type of Sexual Assault)

Study	Vaginal	Oral	Anal	Objects	Beating	Raped > Once
Finkelhor and Yllo (1985) (N = 50)	94	20	32	n.a.	40	72
Russell (1990) (N = 74)	82	7.[1]	7.[1]	n.a.	35	69
Campbell and Alford (1989) (N = 115)	83	n.a.	53	29	44	n.a.
Bergen (1996) (N = 40)	57	33	40	n.a.	"often"	83

NOTE: n.a. = no data available.

1 Russell (1990) reported the figure 7% for oral and anal assaults combined. This number was
duplicated in this table in both categories for readability.

use of physical violence during sexual assaults come primarily from
anecdotal accounts. Force and fear are common, however, as indicated by one study. Riggs, Kilpatrick, and Resnick (1992) examined
the experiences of women who reported wife rape only (with no
physical assaults) in comparison with women who had experienced
stranger rape. The researchers found that the proportion of women
in each group who feared they would die during the assault was
nearly equal (36% and 40%, respectively). This finding indicates a
high level of violence or fear of violence experienced during forced
sex experiences of marital rape victims.

Sexual Acts Perpetrated. As can be seen in Table 4.1, in four major
studies of the characteristics of marital rape, the majority of survivors
reported that they had experienced forced vaginal intercourse, and
nearly one half of them had been beaten immediately preceding or
during the sexual contact. From one quarter to one third of women
reported forced anal or oral intercourse.

In Campbell and Alford's (1989) study of 115 battered women who
had experienced marital sexual assaults, some of the women also reported being forced to engage in sex with other women, sex with
animals, prostitution, and public exposure. Five percent of women
reported that their children were also forced by the husbands to engage in the sexual act, and 18% of women reported that their children

witnessed sexual assaults. Such reports are not rare and are also described by women in the Finkelhor and Yllö (1985) and Russell (1990) studies. Ullman and Siegel (1993) found that, when compared with stranger-perpetrated attacks, sexual assaults by intimates are more likely to result in completed sex acts (78% vs. 49%). Another study (Peacock, 1995) found that wife rape survivors were more likely than acquaintance rape survivors to have experienced unwanted oral and anal intercourse.

Timing and Duration of the Assaults. The pattern of when and under what circumstances sexual assaults against a wife or cohabiting partner occur has not been well documented in the literature. Case studies and interviews indicate that rape may occur in the absence of prior physical abuse when a marriage is deteriorating, after long periods with no sexual contact, when the husband is suspicious of sexual infidelity, or when the husband is intoxicated. These factors may also precipitate sexual assault in marriages in which physical assaults have occurred. In these relationships, sexual assaults may occur in the course of batterings or separate from battering incidents.

The majority of survivors of wife rape report enjoying consensual sexual relationships with their husbands at some time before or after the rapes or both (Browne, 1987; Finkelhor & Yllö, 1985; Walker, 1989). It is clear from such reports that wife rape is not "caused" by lack of sexual relations in marriage; forced sex in marriage, like forced sex by nonspouse perpetrators, appears to be more about force than about sex.

A disturbing finding about the timing and nature of wife rape is the large number of cases that have come to the attention of practitioners in which the rape occurred either during the woman's illness or immediately after her discharge from a hospital. Campbell and Alford (1989) found that one half of their sample of wife rape survivors had been forced to have sex when ill and that almost one half were forced immediately after discharge from the hospital, most often after childbirth. One third of Bergen's (1996) sample of wife rape survivors who sought services from rape crisis centers or battered women's shelters reported an increase in physical and sexual violence during pregnancy. Campbell (1989b) also found that raped and battered women were more likely than battered-only women to have been battered during pregnancy.

Several women in both the Finkelhor and Yllö (1985) and Bergen (1996) samples were forced to have sex after they had been given doctors' orders not to, including one woman whose physician-husband forced her to have oral and anal sex after returning from the hospital following the cesarean section birth of their child. Bergen speculates that the husband's perceived challenge to his authority increases the risk of rape; to reestablish himself as the decision maker, he disregards both his wife's wishes and the doctor's orders.

Case studies indicate that there is an increased risk for sexual assault just preceding, during, or after a separation or divorce. Bergen (1996) found that 20% of women in her sample were sexually assaulted during this time period; Finkelhor and Yllö (1985) found that two thirds of women in their sample experienced sexual assaults in the waning days of their relationships (either before or after separation). Russell (1990) reported that 8% of wife rape survivors experienced sexual assault by their husbands while separated and that 7% were assaulted just prior to separation. In sum, a considerable number of women across various studies report that wife rape occurred during a separation/divorce period. The victims as well as the researchers speculate that, during these times, a husband may use rape to express anger at the loss of his wife or to express some form of dominance and power over his wife in an attempt to hold on to something he knows he is losing or, alternatively, because he "has nothing to lose."

Studies consistently report that most wife rape survivors have experienced multiple rapes during a relationship. In Finkelhor and Yllö's (1985) sample, one half of women were raped 20 or more times; for some, it was so frequent that "they lost count." Two thirds of the Russell (1990) sample were victims of multiple rapes, with one third experiencing more than 20 rapes. The Koss and associates (1988) study found that over one half of women assaulted by spouses or other family members reported 5 or more rapes by the same perpetrators. Riggs and associates (1992) found that although no stranger rape victims reported multiple attacks by the same offenders, 64% of wife rape victims did. Browne (1987) found that women who had killed their husbands were more likely to have been raped more than 20 times, when compared with a battered control group, indicating a possible link between high frequency of rape and homicide potential. In her analysis of NCVS reports during 1992 to 1994, Mahoney (1997) found that victims of husband- or ex-husband-perpetrated sexual attacks were more than 10 times as likely as victims of stranger- or acquaintance-perpetrated sexual attacks to have experienced multiple sexual attacks.

Some wife rape survivors reported that rape episodes lasted for many hours, during which time they were repeatedly raped and brutalized. Such reports of rapes of long duration usually involved husbands who were drunk, were on drugs, or had a history of being severely abusive (Browne, 1987; Pence & Paymar, 1993; Russell, 1990).

It is not surprising that women raped in marriage tend to be raped more frequently than women raped by strangers, because these women live with their rapists. In such marriages, they have no place in which they can feel safe from revictimization.

Characteristics of the Offender

We have not found any large, representative study of husband-rapists, nor has any study focused on the characteristics of husbands who have raped their wives. What we know about the characteristics of the husband-rapist typically comes from reports by wives who have sought shelter from their battering and sexually assaultive husbands. Although much of this information is not highly sensitive (e.g., income, age at marriage), some important factors (e.g., alcohol abuse history, attitudes toward violence) are subject to either bias or misinformation when reported by the wife and should be viewed with caution. Further research with multiple measures is clearly needed in this area.

In Russell's (1990) study of one of the largest community samples, the husband-rapists were reported to be from all ethnic groups and of varying ages, social classes, and educational backgrounds. Some studies with shelter and service-seeking samples have reported that husbands who rape as well as batter their wives are more violent (exhibit more severe and more frequent battering) than batterers who have not raped their wives (Bowker, 1983b; Campbell, 1989b; Frieze, 1983; Monson et al., 1996). The husband who rapes his wife is characterized as domineering and is reported to be more accepting of wife abuse (Campbell, 1989b). It is reported that he believes it is the husband's right to have sex whenever it pleases him (Campbell & Alford, 1989), as is illustrated in this quote from a husband, as told by a wife rape survivor in Bergen's (1996) study: "That's my body—my ass, my tits, my body. You gave that to me when you married me and that belongs to me" (p. 20). Frieze (1983) found that women reported the batterer/rapist was more likely than the batterer/nonrapist to be jealous of his wife and children and was more likely to be violent in other ways, including toward people outside the home. Spousal abuse in the family of origin and sexual dysfunction have been reported to be associated with husbands who committed wife rape (Bowker, 1983b; Rosenbaum & O'Leary, 1981b).

Reports from a batterer group discussion of attitudes about sexuality reveal that many batterers hold stereotypical, male-dominant attitudes about sexuality:

> . . . we're supposed to be the aggressor. You know, in the animal world, the male chases the female. No difference. (Pence & Paymar, 1993, p. 137)

> . . . the whole thing is kind of a game. She knows it, and I know it. (Pence & Paymar, 1993, p. 137)

> . . . sometimes women say no and they're just playing hard to get. (Pence & Paymar, 1993, p. 137)

Pence and Paymar (1993), in their treatment manual for batterers, note that men in abuser groups often express their beliefs that sex is their right in marriage and that they may perceive a woman's refusal of sex as unfair or as a control tactic. Some men see women as attempting to control the relationship by withholding sex, and thus the men justify their use of force to regain control. A husband-rapist told Finkelhor and Yllö (1985), "[S]ince a woman's ultimate weapon is sex, a man's ultimate weapon has to be his strength" (p. 68). We do not know how the opinions of these batterer-rapists differ from those of nonbatterer-rapists because these beliefs have also been found to be prevalent in the general population (see Burt, 1980; Finkelhor & Yllö, 1985; and Malamuth, Heavey, & Linz, 1993, for reviews of rape myths).

Such beliefs preclude the notion that a woman may refuse sexual advances because she actually does not want to have sex, for whatever reason (e.g., illness, fatigue). Each refusal of sex, whether it be while the woman is ill or immediately following a fight, is perceived by such men as a control tactic and an attempt to manipulate, rather than as an expression of a woman's true wishes. Under this belief system, women are perceived, not as human beings with their own desires and feelings, but rather as manipulators, and thus rape is viewed as justified.

Alcohol and the Husband-Rapist

The relationship between alcohol and wife rape is complex, and the available data are contradictory and unclear. Alcohol may decrease inhibitions or excuse the sexually assaultive behavior of husbands (Barnard, 1989). This may increase the rate of wife rape by alcohol-abusing men and may also decrease the reporting of this behavior if intoxication provides an excuse that the wife accepts. It is not surprising, then, that some studies have found no relationship between alcohol abuse and wife rape (Bowker, 1983b), whereas others have found that husbands who raped their wives were more likely than battering, nonrapist husbands to have had a drinking problem (Frieze, 1983). Nearly one quarter of women in Russell's (1990) study responded that the husband-rapist was drinking at the time of the rape, and about an equal number were described as habitual drinkers. Again, these studies were based on the wives' reports. Because many wives may be unwilling to report their own or their husbands' drinking (or may be in denial about it), this could contribute to the inconsistencies in findings.

Because of the limitations of current research, our picture of the husband-rapist is not based on representative studies, and this may be confusing to the practitioner. Some of the literature paints a picture of the husband-rapist as a severely dominant and possessive patriarch who may abuse alcohol; yet, this picture is based on nonrandom samples and is usually based on reports by intimate family members who are victims of abuse. The husband-rapist may behave differently in public than when in a one-on-one interaction with his spouse and thus may not be so obvious to outsiders, including practitioners. As Finkelhor and Yllö (1985) noted from their interviews with three husband-rapists, these men appeared very normal. Of one man, they wrote: "He was, in fact, such a nice, average guy that after meeting him it was much easier to say with conviction that almost any husband can be a rapist" (p. 70). Practitioners need to be aware that husband-rapists need not fit the stereotype often painted of them.

Why Do Men Rape Their Wives?

We have not found studies that examine the motivations of the husband-rapist. It is unclear how similar the motivations of husband-rapists are to those of stranger-rapists. When women were asked their opinions about why their husbands committed sexual assaults, issues of power, control, dominance, and humiliation were commonly reported (Frieze, 1983). Many women also indicated that their husbands believed in a wife's obligation to consent to sex on her husband's expression of desire (Campbell & Alford, 1989).

These themes are also present in the narratives of three husband-rapists who were interviewed by Finkelhor and Yllö (1985). On the basis of the stories of these men, each was classified as having raped his wife by using "force only." None of the men were chronic batterers, all were middle class, and all talked about conflicts that were "typical" of normal relationships. Thus, although these men were not the batterer-rapists described by most women from shelter samples, the themes of dominance, control, and humiliation were present in their stories:

> You could say, I suppose, that I raped her. But I was reduced to a situation in the marriage where it was absolutely the only power I had over her. (Finkelhor & Yllö, 1985, p. 66)

> I was damn sure I didn't want any more children, but I remember just being angry enough that I decided, "I'm going to take the risk anyway." (Finkelhor & Yllö, 1985, p. 73)

> I guess I was angry at her. It was a way of getting even. (Finkelhor & Yllö, 1985, p. 80)

All the men described feelings of emasculation and powerlessness in their relationships. Each expressed feeling that he was not appreciated by his wife for the hard work he put into earning income or other relationship tasks. Sex was seen as an entitlement by some, and forced sex was used as a weapon—"one of the only ways I could best her" (Finkelhor & Yllö, 1985, p. 65). These men had trouble managing the anger in their lives and used sexual assaults against their wives as an outlet.

Each man also expressed at least one common rape myth (see Burt, 1980): that his wife sometimes enjoyed being forced; that she wasn't really hurt; and that if his wife "really wanted to," she could have defended against the attack. Husbands may be unwilling to admit to the harm they cause their wives during forced sexual experiences. This is clear in a case study from Russell (1990), in which a husband held down his wife as she struggled, and he ignored her pleas to stop during an anal rape, all the while saying, "Tell me if I'm *really* hurting you" (p. 138).

In the absence of studies based on representative samples of men who have raped their wives, we do not know how closely these descriptions of the men's thoughts and feelings reflect the thoughts of the "average" husband-rapist. The fact that the same issues emerge in several studies indicates that these themes are central to this discussion. It is likely that one reason men rape their wives is that it is a relatively risk-free act. Because of the complex factors outlined earlier, many women do not discuss their forced sex experiences, even among friends. Wife rape remains a crime with little or no risk of being found out and little or no risk of consequences even when the crime is reported. Until the secrecy and leniency with which this issue is now handled change, there is little incentive for husband-rapists to refrain from raping their wives.

Typologies of Wife Rape

Some researchers have found it useful to summarize these characteristics and to consider possible typologies of wife rape (Bergen, 1996; Finkelhor & Yllö, 1985; Russell, 1990). In the sexual assault literature, typologies of rape have described the dynamics of rape and have been used to understand the etiology of the rapist's behaviors, to develop treatment strategies, and to predict treatment outcomes (Groth, 1979; Prentky & Knight, 1991; Prentky, Knight, & Rosenberg, 1988). Groth (1979) conceptualized three types of rape and rapists: *Anger rape* is perpetrated as a means of retaliation and humiliation and to hurt the victim. *Power rape* is motivated by desire to assert dominance and control. *Sadistic rape* is motivated by fetishistic sexual fantasies and sexual deviance. Attempts have even been made recently to develop typologies of batterers (Gondolf, 1988b; Holtzworth-Munroe & Stuart, 1994; Saunders, 1992; Snyder & Fruchtman, 1981).

On the basis of their interviews with 50 women who had been raped by their partners, Finkelhor and Yllö (1985) developed a typology of wife rape. *Battering rape* occurs in the context of a relationship in which there is also much physical battering and verbal abuse. Physical battering often accompanies the sexual assault. The husband-rapist is frequently angry, may be belligerent to his wife, and may have an alcohol or other drug problem. In such relationships, the sexual violence is but one of many types of violence perpetrated

TABLE 4.2 Distribution of Cases From Two Studies on a Typology of Wife Rape (Percentage Distributions)

Type	Bergen (1996) (N = 40)	Finkelhor & Yllö (1985) (N = 50)
Force only	25	40
Battering	33	48
Sadistic	5	6
Mixed	37	6

by the husband. Hurting, debasing, and humiliating victims are the ways anger is expressed by these rapists, and the men may use far more actual force than would be necessary to overpower their partners. This type of wife rape is similar to Groth's (1979) anger rape. *Nonbattering* (or force-only) *rape* occurs in relationships that do not have much additional physical violence and in which the arguments typically are focused on sexual issues. Even though the motivation of the husband-rapists in these cases may not be to inflict pain or humiliate, these may be the consequences for the victims. Assertion of dominance and control over sex is the primary motivation for these attacks, and they are similar to Groth's power rape. *Obsessive rape* involves bizarre obsessions of the husband. The men in this group may be heavily involved in pornography, may be fetishistic or sadistic, and may demand that their wives perform deviant, unusual, or painful sexual acts. This is comparable to Groth's sadistic rape.

Bergen (1996) applied Finkelhor and Yllö's typology (1985) to the accounts of 40 women in her convenience sample of individuals who had experienced marital rape and had sought services at a rape crisis center or battered women's shelter. The breakdown of her cases according to the Finkelhor-Yllö typology is presented in Table 4.2 and compared with Finkelhor and Yllö's findings.

Bergen (1996) reports more "mixed"-type cases than Finkelhor and Yllö (1985). This point suggests, and the researchers themselves acknowledge, that it is likely that other types of wife rape are not covered by this typology. As is frequently the case with typologies derived in this way, researchers later find that cases often do not clearly fit into one category or another or that others have difficulty classifying new cases. A further complication is that sexual assaults in marriage, like other aspects of marital relationships, undoubtedly

change over time. The changes in the relationship over time, particularly in the marriages with force-only marital rape (nonbattering relationships), has not been well described in the literature; actually,
very little is known about this type of wife rape. In Browne's (1987)
sample of battered women who killed their batterers, a frequent pattern was for sexual assaults to begin as force-only rapes and later to
become battering rapes. Browne also noted that sexual assaults on
women who killed their partners had often become more brutal and
bizarre over time. Generalizations cannot be made from these more
extreme cases in Browne's sample. A detailed study of a large representative sample of wife rape cases would help us to understand better the pattern of relationships in couples in which wife rape occurs
and to develop more useful typologies of wife rape. As the existing
typologies are developed and refined, they need to be used in further
research, and the implications for practice need to be hypothesized
and tested.

Some researchers have suggested that wife rape is a distinct "syndrome" (Bowker, 1983b), although scant evidence has been found to
support what sets this syndrome apart from severe battering. Others
(Browne, 1987) have argued that wife rape should be considered
within the scope of severe abuse. In her study of women who killed
their partners, Browne (1987) noted that when the women were asked
to describe the worst battering incident, it often involved a sexual
assault.

There is as yet no consensus regarding where the issue of wife
rape fits—whether it should be considered a type of battering or a
form of rape or both. It is clear, though, that wife rape is reported
much more frequently among samples of battered women. Hanneke
et al. (1986) provide a review of studies of wife rape, with a focus on
the difference in prevalence between battered and nonbattered populations. As suggested by Russell (1990), it may be helpful to consider
different types of abuse in marriage: battered only, battered and sexually abused, and sexually abused only.

Characteristics of the Victims of Wife Rape

As mentioned above, wife rape appears to be much more common
in battering than nonbattering relationships, occurring in an estimated one half of all battering relationships. Thus, characteristics
associated with battered women would be relevant to many wife rape

survivors (see Chapter 1). Not all battered women are raped in marriage, however; in addition, research on rape in marriage has documented a small but consistent number of women who report rape in marriages in which there are no physical assaults (rates typically range between 1% and 5% of samples, depending on the type of sample; see Hanneke et al., 1986, for a review of these studies and their rates). Practitioners may wonder whether characteristics distinguish the raped and battered women from the battered-only or raped-only women.

Research that would allow exploration of these issues is too scant and contradictory to allow for a clear answer to these questions. There is no known research on the differences between raped-only (nonbattered) wives and nonvictimized wives. Researchers in this field have noted that a focus on the characteristics of the victim is unwarranted. Because it is not the victims who are committing the assaults, it is not surprising that the victims do not share identifying characteristics. As Russell (1990) suggests, demographics may have less influence on whether a woman experiences wife rape than on how she responds to the rape (e.g., if she stays, if she gets help).

Women who are battered and raped in marriage are more likely than battered-only women to leave or consider leaving their marriages (Bowker, 1983b; Frieze, 1983), although because wife rape is also associated with severe physical assaults, it is unclear whether the sexual nature of the assaults or the severity of the assaults in general are more closely related to a woman's decision to leave. Russell (1990) found that women who were the primary breadwinners at the time of their husbands' first rape were more likely than others to "take effective action" (either leave the relationship or other action) that put an end to the rape, a finding consistent with other research indicating that financial insecurity is one barrier to a woman's leaving an abusive relationship.

Consequences of Wife Rape

Effects on the Victim: Physical Outcomes

Kilpatrick, Best, Saunders, and Veronen (1988), using a nationally representative sample to study rape in the United States, found that women assaulted by husbands and boyfriends were actually more likely to sustain physical injuries. Campbell and Alford (1989), who interviewed 115 raped/battered women, found that 72% experienced painful intercourse and that 63% had vaginal pain as a result of sexual assaults by their husbands. Other problems that respondents attributed to sexual assaults included vaginal bleeding (37%), anal bleeding (30%), leaking of urine (32%), miscarriages and stillbirths (20%), and unwanted pregnancies (18%). Eby, Campbell, Sullivan, and Davidson (1995) found that, among 110 battered women, 38% reported pelvic pain and 21% reported painful intercourse in the 6 months prior to the interview.

Most women who are raped in marriage also experience severe forms of physical abuse (Bergen, 1996; Campbell & Alford, 1989; Eby et al., 1995). Campbell and Alford (1989) found that one half of the women had been forced to have sex when ill and that almost one half were coerced immediately after discharge from a hospital, often after childbirth. Nearly one half of the women had been hit, kicked, or burned during sex. Bergen (1996) noted that common injuries of severely battered and raped women included black eyes, broken bones, blood clots in their heads, and knife wounds. Rape often followed physical assaults (Bergen, 1996; Campbell & Alford, 1989; Russell, 1990).

McFarlane et al. (1992) found that abused women were twice as likely as nonabused women to delay prenatal care until the third trimester. The study authors speculated that this rate may be higher for women who became pregnant as the result of rapes, although no research attention has focused on wife rape and pregnancy. Given the strong link between prenatal care and positive birth outcomes, the relationship among rape, pregnancy, and prenatal care deserves attention (Campbell et al., 1995).

Effects on the Victim: Psychological Outcomes

Psychological consequences of rape include anxiety, depression, lack of sleep, eating disorders, lack of interest in sex, fear of men, other social phobias, substance abuse, suicidal ideation, and posttraumatic stress disorder (PTSD) (Goodman et al., 1993; Kilpatrick et al., 1988). No evidence suggests that victims of wife rape are less likely to experience these outcomes relative to victims of stranger rape. To the contrary, considerable evidence suggests that the psychological consequences for wife rape victims are more severe. For example, Kilpatrick and colleagues (1985) found that suicidal ideation and nervous breakdown rates were higher among victims who had experienced completed rape, compared with victims of attempted rape and other crime victims. Studies have shown that sexual assaults between intimates are more likely to result in completed rape than are assaults by strangers (Ullman & Siegel, 1993).

Rape victims who experience high levels of stress and have few coping resources are at higher risk for negative psychological outcomes (Goodman et al., 1993). As noted by Browne (1993), "[S]ome researchers suggest that PTSD is most likely to develop when traumatic events occur in an environment previously deemed safe" (p. 1081). A wife rape victim experiences the violation of her body in a place (her home) and by a person previously "deemed safe." Living with a person who has sexually assaulted her, she may have no place in which she feels safe from future assaults. Such an experience may cause her to "cease believing that she is secure in the world, that the world has order and meaning, and that she is a worthy person" (Goodman et al., 1993).

The limited research that has focused on wife rape survivors has found that the consequences of wife rape are severe and long-lasting. Among raped/battered women, frequency and duration of wife rape is associated with more severe and long-term impacts (Frieze, 1983; Russell, 1990). Koss and colleagues (1988) found that "women raped by husbands or family members, particularly when compared with women raped by nonromantic acquaintances or casual dates, gave more severe ratings of their anger and depression and of the offender's aggression" (p. 14). Ullman and Siegel (1993) found that sexual distress was highest for assaults by intimates. Finkelhor and Yllö (1985) noted that the survivors expressed betrayal, anger, humiliation, and guilt.

Women who were both raped and battered by their partners scored significantly lower than battered-only women on body image and self-esteem scales (Campbell, 1989b). Not surprisingly, they reported being unhappy in their sexual relationships (Frieze, 1983). In one study, no significant differences were found between raped/battered and battered-only women on measures of depression, self-care agency, self-blame, control in the relationship, predictions that the relationship would improve, valuing of the wife-mother role for women, feeling alone in their situation, or their own tolerance of men hitting women. No differences have been found in physical symptoms of stress and perceived health status (Campbell, 1989b).

A common misconception regarding wife rape is that forced sex between a husband and a wife should be less traumatic for the victim because she has previously engaged in consensual intercourse with her husband. Kilpatrick and associates (1988), however, found no differences by victim-offender relationship in the way victims "subjectively judged the danger of the attack." The study authors concluded that "common assumptions about women assaulted by strangers having a more difficult time adjusting to the event than women raped by husbands and boyfriends appear to be incorrect" (p. 343). The same conclusion was drawn by Riggs and colleagues (1992), who also found reports that similar percentages of marital rape victims and stranger rape victims feared they would die during the assaults (36% and 40%, respectively).

Moss, Frank, and Anderson (1990) found that married rape victims with poor partner support reported high levels of psychological symptoms. It is expected that husband-rapists would not be very supportive of their wives' recovery—indeed, would hamper it—indicating more negative psychological outcomes for wife rape victims.

A forced sexual experience with a stranger is traumatic because of unfamiliarity with the offender's intentions, in addition to threat of potential diseases. Unfamiliarity with the rapist, however, is not the sole cause of distress for rape victims. Violation of a woman's body and her perception of living in a safe and just environment can contribute to negative outcomes following a rape. For a woman raped by her husband, we can expect such violations not only to be more deeply felt but also to continue to be a part of her life if she continues to live with the rapist.

Effects on the Offender

So little is known about the experience of the husband-rapist that it is only possible to speculate on how wife rape affects his life. His behavior and the force he uses to have sex against his wife's wishes may lead to the loss of intimacy between himself and his wife and to the disintegration and loss of his family. Although the husband-rapist may also experience negative psychological outcomes from the abuse he inflicts, he may not have other means of managing his anger and thus may continue to create an unstable home environment in which he is feared and even hated by his family.

Effects on Children

Personal accounts of wife rape indicate that children often witness sexual assaults or overhear struggles and screams during rapes. As noted earlier, some studies reveal that a small percentage of children are also forced to participate in sexual acts (Campbell & Alford, 1989). Unfortunately, aside from the finding that raped/battered women are more violent to their own children than battered-only women are (Frieze, 1983), almost nothing has been written about the effects of marital rape on children. Children are often aware of the conflicts between their parents even when the parents believe otherwise (see Chapter 3). We know that children who witness physical abuse between parents are more likely to be involved in physically abusive relationships as adults. It may be that children who witness sexual assaults between their parents will be more likely to be involved in sexually assaultive relationships as adults. Further research on these relationships is needed.

Effects on Family

Scant research has focused on characteristics of the relationship between husbands and wives when wife rape occurs. A myriad of marital problems are likely (Hanneke & Shields, 1985). Bowker (1983b) examined the family characteristics of social isolation and social embeddedness and found that neither characteristic was associated with rape in families in which battering had also occurred. Bowker did find that marriages in which rape had occurred were more likely to have more continuous disagreement over finances, friends, children, drinking, drugs, and marital violence. Wife rape creates an environment in which the woman and her children may feel a constant threat. Women have reported coping mechanisms such as never sleeping in the bedroom and avoiding forced sex by going to bed only after the husband has dozed off. The family environment in which wife rape occurs thus appears to be one of inequality, fear, constant threat, and a sense of loss of loving relationships (Browne, 1993; Finkelhor & Yllö, 1985). This is likely to have a significant impact on all family relationships and functioning in many domains. Several studies have reported that raped/battered women are more likely to be considering leaving their husbands and to have left their husbands at least once (Bergen, 1996; Bowker, 1983b; Frieze, 1983; Russell, 1990).

Screening and Assessment

Various researchers have suggested that wife rape should be screened for in families with alcoholic husbands (Barnard, 1989), batterer husbands (Pence & Paymar, 1993), or a great deal of conflict and value dissimilarity between husband and wife (Bowker, 1983b). Medical professionals must screen for sexual assault when women report other related health problems (Campbell, 1989b), especially in the case of pelvic pain or vaginal or rectal bleeding. One frequently stressed recommendation coming out of the wife rape literature is the need for assessment of the sexual history of all women coming to the attention of medical and mental health professionals. Sexual assault by a partner is not a topic that survivors of wife rape will want to discuss spontaneously. Direct, sensitive assessments will be necessary. To be most effective, assessments must avoid labels such as "rape" or "sexual assault" and must include more than one behaviorally specific question. Concerned professionals might ask about "unwanted sexual activity" or contacts including sexual intercourse and sexual touching. They might ask about sex that was uncomfortable, painful, or unwanted or threats or force used by a partner to achieve sexual contact (see Appendix A, this chapter).

Follow-up questions should ask about what sexual act or acts occurred, the relationship to the person with whom it occurred, the frequency with which it occurred, and whether unwanted sexual contacts are still occurring. Appropriate referrals should be made for counseling, shelter, protection, or legal assistance. Women should be advised of the dangers of staying in their relationships, encouraged to seek counseling, and informed of their legal rights. Men who come to the attention of medical or mental health professionals should also be asked about their sexual histories. If men report that they have forced sexual contact on their partners, they should also be referred to counseling and informed of the seriousness of their behavior.

Medical and family services settings should display information regarding sexual assault in marriage prominently in both waiting room areas and in private rooms, facilitating the reading of such material in private and encouraging individuals to talk with someone about experiences with sexual assault. Posters proclaiming slogans such as "If it's against your will, it's against the law, even in marriage" should be displayed with telephone numbers of hotlines or counselors. Media campaigns should routinely address a woman's right to live in a home safe from both physical and sexual assault.

Routinely asking women about forced sexual experiences and providing clear information about their rights in marriage may encourage more women to recognize that they are not required by their marriage vows to engage in unwanted sexual experiences. Routinely asking men about the same thing sends a message that forced sex in intimate relationships is unacceptable and against the law; asking also gives them an opportunity to discuss these experiences and to get help. These recommendations necessitate providing education and training to service providers and developing resources such as manuals for service providers to consult when advising clients where they may seek counseling or legal help.

Special Issue: Separation and Divorce

Women who seek legal advice or counseling for separation or divorce must be informed of the increased risk of sexual assault during this time if they have a history of past abuse (Finkelhor & Yllö, 1985). They should be advised against meeting their husbands in places that put them at risk, including in their own homes.

Special Issue: Medical Concerns

Women who are in need of medical rest or who have been advised to abstain from sex for medical reasons, especially those who have experienced prior battering or marital problems, should be asked questions to assess the safety of their home situations. If a woman discloses that she is unsure of her safety at home, the health care professional should consider whether the risk of sexual assault warrants sending the woman to a shelter, keeping her in the hospital an extra day, or providing other assistance to reduce the risk of assault (clearly, contacting the husband in such a case would be inappropriate and may increase the risk of assault).

Treatment Issues

Although many researchers suggest that counseling is indicated for the victim, the offender, and the children, few treatment models have been developed that specifically address the issues surrounding wife rape. As noted in Bergen's (1996) extensive study of rape and domestic violence service providers, wife rape remains outside the scope of many agencies. Because the issue has been addressed so infrequently, professionals in all sectors remain uninformed about the causes and consequences of wife rape and how to respond to disclosure by either the victim or the offender of forced sex in marriage.

The Victim

Raped wives need different types of support than battered-only wives (Bowker, 1983b) or raped women (Hanneke & Shields, 1985; Kilpatrick et al., 1992; Resnick, Kilpatrick, Walsh, & Veronen, 1991). Of utmost importance in responding to a disclosure of forced marital sex is validating the woman's experience and assisting her in finding safety and any medical care she may need. Simply referring her to a rape crisis hotline or battered women's hotline is not adequate. People who staff these hotlines are often not prepared to respond to wife rape survivors (Bergen, 1996). Many women will struggle to overcome fear and feelings of guilt before discussing such experiences and may not choose to disclose the experience to another service provider if they have been "brushed off" by a service provider the first time they reached out for help.

As with the battered woman, priority must be given to ensuring physical safety for the victim of wife rape and her children. To approach her treatment with crisis intervention strategies similar to those used for victims of rape by strangers or nonfamily members would be inappropriate. Her relationship with the offender may be ongoing and must be addressed. The wife rape victim is similar to the battered woman in her need for naming the violence, taking the responsibility for the violence off herself, and acknowledging the loss of her hopes for a happy marriage (Weingourt, 1985). Bergen (1996) noted that, as with battered-only women, naming the violence and getting support from a service provider were central to a woman's being able to leave the relationship. In addition, the victim of wife rape may also need counseling specific to sexuality and body image issues. She needs to be able to discuss the sexual victimization, as well as the physical abuse.

Medical Needs

Kilpatrick and colleagues (1992) reported that only 17% of rape cases in the United States resulted in medical exams following the assaults. It is less likely that victims of sexual assault by intimate partners will seek medical attention. When Mahoney (1997) examined the seeking of medical care by perpetrator relationship, she found that women who were sexually attacked by husbands/ex-husbands sought medical care significantly less than women who were sexually attacked by strangers (8% vs. 27%, respectively). In all cases of known or suspected wife rape, the women should be given thorough rape exams with careful documentation (Campbell & Alford, 1989). The women should be encouraged by police and others to have forensic evidence collected because this information will be vital in the event of prosecution.

Legal Needs

Many women are unaware that forced sex within marriage is a crime. Unfortunately, most service providers are also unfamiliar with the state laws regarding wife rape. A woman must be told that her husband can be prosecuted for raping her and that she can sue her husband in civil court for pain and suffering (Lehrman, 1996). Legal teams working with sexually assaulted women must be trained on these legal issues (see Appendix B for legal resources).

The Offender

Some people have suggested that, when working with batterers or alcoholic men, one should assume until proved otherwise that the man has forced or coerced sex with his partner (Barnard, 1989; Pence & Paymar, 1993). Although this is an extreme position, at a minimum men with a history of partner violence or substance abuse problems should be asked about their attitudes toward sex and, by using behaviorally specific questions in a nonthreatening way, be asked about their sexual behaviors to assess past sexual violence and current danger to spouses. This information should be used in treatment planning. If sexual assaults are reported, the wives/partners should be contacted and offered confidential counseling and other appropriate assistance.

We do not know the extent to which the husband-rapist differs from the rapist or the batterer. Although treatment protocols have not been clearly described for this type of offender and no evaluations of treatments have been conducted, it appears wise to recommend that treatment models for dealing with husband-rapists be sensitive to issues that have been addressed by both batterer treatment and sex offender treatment programs. One treatment program for men who batter, the Duluth Model (Pence & Paymar, 1993; see Chapter 7), includes a unit on sexual respect that addresses many issues relevant to wife rape. In addition, Johnson (1992) and Knopp (1994) have discussed sexuality in the context of wife and date rape; the practitioner may find these useful (see Appendix B for ordering information).

Discussions in this unit on sexual respect center around the distinctions between consensual intercourse, coercive intercourse, and rape. Sexuality is discussed as it relates to using (a) intimidation, emotional abuse, and isolation; (b) minimizing, denying, and blaming; and (c) children, male privilege, economic abuse, and coercion and threats. Pence and Paymar (1993) note that men in the groups will resent any assertion that their behavior could be construed as rape and will attempt to justify their behavior and place the responsibility for their behavior on their wives. The authors assert that the clinician must challenge all attempts at avoiding responsibility for forced sex and minimize lewd jokes and "locker room behavior." Practitioners in batterer treatment groups and marital counseling programs alike may wish to consult the Duluth Model for a more thorough review of the unit. This unit could serve as a basis for the development of a comprehensive treatment program for husband-rapists.

Kalichman and colleagues (1993) note that sexually coercive men may be deliberately manipulative and insincere in their sexual relations. The authors suggest focusing on the development of empathy, changing negative attitudes toward women, and engaging the men in relationship values clarification. Programs for sex offenders have also begun to emphasize deficits in empathy and approaches to treatment designed to increase ability to take the perspective of, and to empathize with, the victim (Marshall, 1989).

The materials discussed in this section offer a psychoeducational approach to counseling the husband-rapist. Such approaches have not been evaluated and are considered an introduction to working with men who sexually assault their partners. It should be assumed that such men will also need additional counseling to understand and change their sexually assaultive behavior.

The Children

No known treatment programs have been designed for use with children of wife rape survivors or perpetrators. It is recommended that, in addition to the treatments suggested for children who witness physical violence between their parents, such children receive age-appropriate counseling on sexual issues.

Special Issue: Keeping the Family Together
Versus Separation

A critical issue for counselors working with all abusive relationships is that of knowing when it is best to work toward keeping a family together and when it is best to counsel the family for separation. Some professionals suggest that the family must be treated as a whole and be taught how to express anger and love in acceptable ways (Barnard, 1989). Many others, however, suggest that, when dealing with sexual assault in families, at least temporary separation is essential. Bowker (1993) suggests that families in which wife rape has occurred have so much hostility, distrust, and pain that the better course of action seems to be to counsel the family members for divorce. Realistically, however, many women will want to try to salvage their relationships. Finkelhor and Yllö (1985) and Bergen (1996) noted that some women were able to stop the sexual assaults from recurring but only when they retaliated immediately (after the first incident) with threats or physical resistance that was severe and believable. It appears that a husband must believe that his wife will go through with leaving or prosecuting him in order for him to stop.

No available literature allows for a clear recommendation regarding this issue. Practitioners are encouraged to discuss such issues in in-service trainings. Topics that need to be addressed in this context include (but are not limited to) the following:

- How do we determine *and value* the survivor's wishes?
- What are the survivor's reasons for choosing a particular option (e.g., is she wanting to stay because she needs the financial income from the husband)?
- Are children involved, and how will they be affected?
- Is the offender willing to get counseling?

The Professionals

The most frequent recommendation of wife rape researchers is that professionals receive education about wife rape and training about how to respond to disclosures of spousal sexual assaults and how to ensure the woman's future safety. This includes education regarding the prevalence, dynamics, and consequences of wife rape for emergency room personnel, family practitioners, OB-GYNs, pediatricians, psychiatrists, family lawyers, therapists and counselors, police, and religious service providers (Kilpatrick et al., 1992; Yllö & LeClerc, 1988).

Practitioners must attend to the needs of survivors of wife rape for safe, private environments and sympathetic persons in order to feel comfortable discussing a part of their lives they may not have discussed with anyone else. Practitioners must learn to facilitate disclosure (Hanneke & Shields, 1985) and to respond in a supportive manner, letting the women know that they are not alone and that it is all right to feel hurt, angry, betrayed, or confused (Yllö & LeClerc, 1988).

Frequently, researchers have suggested that practitioners and service providers need to confront their own biases surrounding marital sexual assault (Barnard, 1989; Hanneke & Shields, 1985; Prescott & Letko, 1977; Weingourt, 1985) and to work toward understanding the dynamics of wife rape. If a service provider believes common marital rape myths (e.g., that the woman must be frigid, that she probably was not hurt, that she would have left if the rapes had been really bad), she or he will not be able to help survivors effectively. Counselors must also recognize that if they are uncomfortable discussing sexual issues, this may make disclosure a negative experience for survivors. Counselors who are uncomfortable discussing sexual issues should seek training designed to reduce this discomfort and improve their ability to establish rapport with survivors.

Counseling wife rape victims is difficult because the women may still love the offenders and desire continued relationships with them.

Because of transference issues, counseling may be especially difficult for a survivor if the counselor is male. Because many women have been told in their relationships that they should defer to men, it may be difficult for a male therapist to empower a wife rape survivor (Weingourt, 1985).

It should also be noted that, at least in the anecdotal accounts of battered women, husband-rapists have been described as very violent individuals. Professionals must remember, when working with this population, that they must take precautions (e.g., have a secure working environment) to keep themselves and their clients safe.

Policy Issues

1. Wife rape as an issue must be "claimed" by the domestic violence field. Those working in this field must make the identification and treatment of wife rape part of their mission. All research agendas and policy development related to the physical abuse of wives must also address the sexual abuse of wives.

2. Domestic violence services must be expanded to include wife rape survivors. Monies should be appropriated specifically for this population. Shelter and counseling services must be made available to women who have experienced sexual assaults in marriage and their children. All batterer treatment programs should include units on sexual issues.

3. Wife rape must also be claimed as a health issue by health care providers, mental health practitioners, and health educators. Health care providers must routinely include sexual histories in their intake process and must be trained to identify health problems that may result from sexual assaults by intimates. Mental health providers must also routinely ask for sexual histories during the intake process. Health education must include a sexual health component in which force, pressure, and manipulation to obtain sex are specifically addressed as both wrong and unhealthy. Pamphlets and posters about intimate sexual assault should be available in all health care waiting rooms.

In addition, given the large number of battered women who report being sexually assaulted after medical rest orders, this issue deserves immediate attention from health care professionals. Some of the women have had to return to the hospital to replace stitches and to treat aggravated wounds. It may be necessary for hospitals to allow women who risk assault at home to have a longer stay in the hospital.

4. Monies should be allocated for the development and distribution of pamphlets and posters about wife rape/intimate sexual assault. This information should be displayed and made available to the public via health care providers and social workers in public and private places and should be available in as many languages as possible.

5. Husband-rapists must be treated with the same severity as other rapists by all law enforcement personnel and courts. Policies must be created to ensure that such cases are not dismissed or treated as less serious. For example, bail should be set at the same level as it is for other rapists; the rapist should not be released on his own recognizance. All marital rape exemptions must be completely abolished because they unconstitutionally deny some women legal protection from sexual assaults.

6. Further steps must be taken to end women's economic dependency on men. These steps include providing reliable, quality day care at low cost; making child support payment evasion as serious as tax evasion, with the same serious consequences; and providing training and skill-building programs for mothers who have been out of the workforce while raising their children.

Recommendations

All Practitioners

A resource listing of agencies or counselors or both who work with survivors of intimate sexual assault must be compiled and distributed; appropriate referrals should be made when intimate sexual assault is expected.

If a woman discloses sexual assault to you, take her disclosure seriously and make a referral to an agency that can help her emotionally or legally or both. Do not minimize her experience or simply tell her to leave the relationship. Respond in a supportive manner.

If a man discloses sexually assaulting his wife or partner to you, advise him that such sexual assaults are crimes and are destructive to his partner and his relationship. Refer him to an agency that can help him stop the abuse. Be aware of what interventions you are able to make on behalf of his partner on the basis of such a disclosure.

Social Workers/Counselors

Familiarize yourself with the complicated relationship dynamics surrounding wife rape. When working with a wife rape survivor, if you are in a domestic violence setting, do not minimize her sexual assaults. If you are in a rape crisis setting, do not attempt to treat her relationship to her rapist as you would a stranger or acquaintance rape victim. Be knowledgeable about where she may get legal counseling specific to wife rape victims.

Conduct in-service trainings on how to discuss sexual issues with clients. Discuss your own potential biases and countertransference issues regarding wife rape survivors.

Display brochures with the term *wife rape* in public and private rooms.

Sexual assault histories should be asked of both men and women as part of routine health histories.

Religious Workers

Religious workers must recognize the harm being done by wife rape and take a stand against it. "Religious leaders who are well informed can begin to disrupt this pattern before the effects disable the woman and destroy her relationship with her clergy and her faith in the church as an institution" (Yllö & LeClerc, 1988, p. 57).

Health Care Providers

Sexual assault histories should be asked of both men and women as part of routine health histories.

Resource listings of agencies or counselors or both who work with survivors of intimate sexual assault must be maintained and appropriate referrals made when intimate sexual assault is suspected.

Display brochures with the term *wife rape* in public and private rooms.

Health Education Workers

Healthy sexual communication and healthy sexuality should become standard components of health education classes for adolescents and adults.

Recommendations for Research

We recommend that, in future research on wife rape, rape be specifically and operationally defined and prevalence data be presented for each of the definitional criteria assessed. For example, studies would be most useful if they reported the number of cases involving each of the following: sexual penetration, sexual contact without penetration, and sexual exploitation. For the best use to be made of study data, researchers should report prevalence data for each level of force and for different types of victim-offender relationships (e.g., husband-wife, ex-husband-wife, cohabiting partners, dating but not cohabiting partners).

It is time for the field to embark on a large, case-controlled, longitudinal study of a representative sample of wife rape victims and offenders, supplemented by a longitudinal study of a randomly selected representative community sample of couples. Such a study should be designed to measure the prevalence, precursors, and consequences of marital rape. Case studies of husband-rapists are needed to refine the typologies of wife rape, to inform our understanding of the etiology of sexually assaultive behaviors in intimate relationships, and to develop and test hypotheses for prevention and treatment.

More research needs to be done on what types of mental health, sexual, and body image counseling are needed and appropriate for survivors of sexual assaults in marriage.

Research attention must be paid to children in marriages in which the husbands sexually assault the wives. Because no research has focused on children in sexually assaultive marriages, research that is retrospective, prospective, quantitative, or qualitative is equally needed.

Conclusion

When rape occurs in a marriage, it is typically a chronic problem that results in severe psychological and physical outcomes for the wife. Although scant direct research has been conducted in this field, considerable evidence suggests that homes in which wife rape is occurring are homes in which anxiety and distrust are common emotions for wives, husbands, and their children. Wife rape creates an unstable home environment for all family members. It is of utmost importance to recognize the damage being done by wife rape and to implement research, programs, and policies that will stop wife rape before it starts.

APPENDIX A

Assessment Tools

The following questions were constructed by using recommendations from articles reviewed for this chapter. These questions have not been systematically evaluated. Attempts were made to draw on the scant knowledge in this field to offer some preliminary guidelines. A consistent recommendation is that rapport be established with a client before asking questions with sexual content. Persons asking questions containing sexual content should first receive training in how best to discuss sexual histories and negative sexual experiences in a nonthreatening, nonjudgmental, and supportive manner.

The suggestions below are offered as examples of nonthreatening questions and are written so that they may be used with either males or females in intimate relationships. The questions are designed to facilitate disclosure—that is, to get a person to talk about negative sexual experiences in a nonthreatening manner. People conducting the interviews will need to decide *before* using such questions what they will do in the event someone discloses being either the victim or the perpetrator of forced or coerced sex. Before using such questions, interviewers must know the answers to the following questions:

- What kinds of answers would lead you to believe that an intervention is warranted?
- What kind of intervention are you prepared to make?
- What further questions would you need to ask?
- What resources or information do you have to offer?

To inquire about sexual assaults and not be prepared to offer resources and assistance would be irresponsible. Practitioners must be prepared for disclosure. Even though men are typically the perpetra-

158

tors of forced sex, some men may disclose feeling pressured by their partners to have sex. Such disclosures must also be taken seriously. Sexual disagreements of any type may indicate deep problems in the marital relationship that warrant attention. The goal of these questions is to get people talking in order to identify persons in sexually abusive relationships.

As mentioned earlier, to facilitate disclosure it is recommended that more than one question be used. Below are examples of such introductory and follow-up questions. We are not suggesting that all of these questions be asked in one instrument; rather, we are offering a variety of questions, some of which may be more or less appropriate, given a particular context.

Sample questions and prompts:

- Have you ever had any unwanted sexual experiences with your partner? What happened?
- Are these types of experiences still happening? Have you ever spoken with anyone about these experiences? What happened?
- Have you ever experienced painful intercourse? Did you see a physician about these experiences? Were you able to figure out why intercourse was painful?
- Do you and your partner ever have disagreements about sex; for example, when or how often to have sex? Does one of you want to have sex more frequently than the other? How do you resolve this when it happens? Do you think that you and your partner enjoy your sexual relationship about equally?
- Are there times when sex between you and your partner is unpleasant for either one of you? What happens?
- Has your partner ever forced or pressured you into doing sexual things that you weren't comfortable with—for example, using objects during sex, posing for photographs, or not using birth control when you wanted to? Has your partner ever said sexually degrading things to you?
- Have you ever had sexual intercourse with a partner when you didn't want to? Was any force or pressure involved? What happened?
- Do you feel that you can talk with your partner openly about your sexual relationship? Do you respect your partner when he or she doesn't want to have sex and you do? Does your partner respect you when you don't want to have sex but he or she does?

APPENDIX B

Resources

National Clearinghouse on Marital and Date Rape

Director: Laura X

2325 Oak Street
Berkeley, CA 94708
(510) 524–1582

The National Clearinghouse on Marital and Date Rape is a business that provides rape prevention education through speakers and consultation (via telephone or in person) and by publication. Since 1978, the clearinghouse has served as the headquarters for changing laws, policies, customs, and attitudes surrounding intimate violence. Access to Clearinghouse services: $30/year, organizations; $15/year, individuals; plus $7.50/15 minutes telephone consultation and document searches. Information packet, including a state law chart on marital, cohabitant, and date rape: $10.00.

National Organization for Women (NOW)
Legal Defense and Education Fund

99 Hudson Street, 12th Floor
New York, NY 10013
(212) 925–6635

To order *The Status of Marital Rape Exemption Statutes in the United States, February 1996*, send a check for $25.00 to the NOW LDEF address above. No telephone orders are possible.

Center for Constitutional Rights

666 Broadway, 7th Floor
New York, NY 10012
(212) 614–6464

The pamphlet *Stopping Sexual Assault in Marriage/Suppression Del Ataque Sexual En El Matrimonio* is published by the CCR.

Safer Society Press

Box 340
Brandon, VT 05733–0340
(802) 247–3132

Specializing in sexual abuse prevention and treatment publications, publications include *When Your Wife Says NO* by F. H. Knopp and *Man-to-Man: When Your Partner Says NO* by S. A. Johnson. Call or write for a catalog with current prices.

Recommended Reading

General

Bergen, R. K. (1996). *Wife rape: Understanding the response of survivors and service providers.* Thousand Oaks, CA: Sage.
Finkelhor, D., & Yllö, K. (1985). *License to rape: Sexual abuse of wives.* New York: Holt, Rinehart & Winston.
Russell, D. E. H. (1990). *Rape in marriage.* Indianapolis: Indiana University Press.

For Counselors/Social Workers

Center for Constitutional Rights. (1990). *Stopping sexual assault in marriage/Suppression del ataque sexual en el matrimonio.* New York: Author. (See ordering information in Appendix A.)
Johnson, S. A. (1992). *Man-to-man: When your partner says NO: Pressured sex and date rape.* Brandon, VT: Safer Society Press. (See ordering information in Appendix A.)
Knopp, F. H. (1994). *When your wife says NO: Forced sex in marriage.* Brandon, VT: Safer Society Press. (See ordering information in Appendix A.)
Pence, E., & Paymar, M. (1993). *Education groups for men who batter: The Duluth Model. Theme six: Sexual respect.* New York: Springer.

For Religious Workers/Counselors

Fortune, M. M. (1996). *Violence against women and children: A Christian theological sourcebook.* New York: Continuum.

Yllö, K., & LeClerc, D. (1988). Marital rape. In A. L. Horton & J. A. Williamson (Eds.), *Abuse and religion: When praying isn't enough* (pp. 48-57). Lexington, MA: Lexington.

Legal Issues

Center for Constitutional Rights. (1990). *Stopping sexual assault in marriage/Suppression del ataque sexual en el matrimonio.* New York: Author. (See ordering information in Appendix A.)

Drucker, D. (1979). The common law does not support a marital exemption for forcible rape. *Women's Rights Law Reporter, 5*(2-3).

Lehrman, F. L. (1996). *Domestic violence practice and procedure.* Deerfield, IL: Clark, Boardman, & Callaghan. (See chapter on marital rape.)

Russell, D. E. H. (1990). *Rape in marriage.* Indianapolis: Indiana University Press. (See Appendix II: State-by-State Information on Marital Rape Exemption Laws.)

Ryan, R. M. (1996). The sex right: A legal history of the marital rape exemption. *Law and Social Inquiry, 20*(4), 941-999.

Notes

---

1. The authors thank Laura X at the National Clearinghouse on Marital and Date Rape for considerable feedback on a draft of this section.

2. A 1-page reference guide to wife rape laws by state is available from the National Clearinghouse on Marital and Date Rape; a comprehensive guide to the laws by state is available from NOW LDEF. See Appendix B for information.

3. Only husband and ex-husband perpetrators are included in Russell's figures; cohabiting partners are not.

4. For one quarter of the female victim homicide cases, the victim-offender relationship was not identified.

CHAPTER FIVE

Leaving a Second Closet

Outing Partner Violence in Same-Sex Couples

CAROLYN M. WEST

Researchers have been investigating partner violence for more than 20 years (Straus et al., 1980). Yet, there is a discernible absence of research on violence among same-sex couples. Information on lesbian battering, for example, did not emerge until approximately 12 years ago (Lobel, 1986), and the analyses of gay male intimate violence is even more recent (Island & Letellier, 1991). Within the last few years, some journals have devoted special issues to same-sex partner violence (Renzetti & Miley, 1996), and several second editions of self-help books have incorporated chapters on lesbian battering (e.g., NiCarthy, Merriam, & Coffman, 1994; White, 1994). Although more empirical studies have been conducted on same-sex partner violence (e.g., Renzetti, 1992), much of the material concerning gay and lesbian battering continues to appear in the forms of occasional articles in lesbian and gay newspapers (Shomer, 1997), anecdotal accounts (Lobel, 1986), and unpublished empirical reports (Gardner, 1989).

The dearth of research makes it difficult to obtain an accurate estimate of same-sex partner violence. The available literature, however, indicates that partner violence among gays and lesbians appears to be as prevalent as it is among heterosexuals (Renzetti, 1997). Furthermore, violent couples of all sexual orientations may share

163

some similarities; for example, sexual assaults may accompany battering (Campbell & Alford, 1989; Waterman, Dawson, & Bologna,
1989). Despite the similarities, intimate violence may not always be
the same across sexual orientations. Because of the marginalized status
of gay men and lesbians, the experience of battering may take different
forms in same-sex couples (Hart, 1986). In addition, effective therapeutic intervention requires awareness and sensitivity to the particular
stressors and difficulties faced by this population, such as discrimination based on sexual orientation (Morrow & Hawxhurst, 1989).

On the basis of national sexuality surveys, approximately 10% of
the population identifies their sexual orientation as gay or lesbian
(Gebhard, 1997; Janus & Janus, 1993). As more attention is focused
on the concerns of homosexuals, both community activists and researchers agree that it is time to "out" partner violence in same-sex
couples (Island & Letellier, 1991; Lobel, 1986). *Outing,* or revealing
an individual's sexual orientation without his or her consent, can be
a negative experience (Wallace, 1996). In contrast, the "coming out"
process, in which a person publicly declares his or her sexual orientation, can signal acceptance and liberation (Miranda & Storms,
1989). With regard to partner violence, the latter form of outing is
referred to in this chapter.

The purpose of this chapter is to discuss the emerging literature
on same-sex partner violence. First, a brief description of the challenges and types of discrimination faced by this population is presented. Second, the incidence rates and distinct forms that gay and
lesbian battering might assume are discussed. Next, correlates of partner violence and research limitations are highlighted. Finally, treatment implications and recommendations for policy are suggested.

Description of the Population

Gay men and lesbians have experienced and continue to endure
stereotyping, harassment, and discrimination in employment, housing, and public accommodations. This intolerance so permeates
every aspect of society that members of this group can lose jobs or
custody of their children, often without legal recourse. In some instances, gays and lesbians have lost the support of their families and
friends (Almeida, Woods, Messino, Font, & Heer, 1994). As a result of

prejudice, some homosexuals may develop a negative self-image, which may in turn contribute to substance abuse and suicide attempts, particularly among individuals who lack a positive gay identity (Arey, 1995; D'Augelli & Dark, 1995).

Although media attention to gay and lesbian issues has increased, public opinion remains negative. For example, in a 1993 New York Times/CBS News Poll of 1,154 adults, 55% believed that homosexual relationships between adults were morally wrong (*New York Times,* 1993). *Homophobia,* or the irrational fear and hatred of lesbians and gay men (Weinberg, 1972), also may culminate in criminal victimization, commonly referred to as *hate crimes* or *bias crimes* (Klinger, 1995). In a recent survey of 157 lesbians, gays, and bisexuals, for example, 41% reported being the target of physical assaults, verbal harassment, threats, and vandalism of their property as a result of their sexual orientation (Herek, Gillis, Cogan, & Glunt, 1997).

Researchers have found that, despite unfair treatment, many lesbians and gay men were satisfied with their sexual orientation and intimate relationships (Isay, 1989; Miranda & Storms, 1989; Peplau, 1991). In addition, many are actively engaged in a civil rights movement dedicated to educating the larger society about lesbian/gay issues and changing unfair legal and employment practices. A thriving gay community also offers support in the forms of crisis hotlines, churches, social groups, community centers, and bookstores (Arey, 1995; Butke, 1995).

Incidence of Same-Sex Partner Violence

Violence among homosexual couples has not been well documented for several reasons. Societal institutions have not recognized same-sex partnerships as legitimate. For example, the law often limits the definition of partner violence to male-female couples. As a consequence, same-sex partner violence is not counted in police reports and other official statistics (Hart, 1986; Island & Letellier, 1991). Lack of resources and education concerning gay and lesbian battering has also prevented service providers from recognizing and conducting research on this form of aggression (Island & Letellier, 1991; Renzetti, 1996).

Furthermore, within the gay community there is pressure against revealing partner assaults. Researchers, activists, and often victims fear that discussing battering will reinforce negative societal stereotypes (that lesbian/gay relationships are dysfunctional or unhealthy; Elliot, 1996; Hart, 1986). In addition, after battling more visible forms of prejudice, such as hate crimes and discriminatory laws, little time and energy has been left for many activists to conduct research on intimate violence (Byrne, 1996).

How Much Violence Exists in Same-Sex Relationships?

Lesbian Partner Violence. Estimates of partner violence in lesbian relationships have varied widely. In a survey of lesbian sexual practices, Loulan (1987) found that 17% of 1,566 lesbians surveyed had experienced "adult abuse" by a female partner. Substantial rates of partner violence were discovered by other researchers as well. Approximately one third of 284 lesbians surveyed by Lockhart, White, Causby, and Isaac (1994) reported being physically abused by partners, as measured by the Conflict Tactics Scale (CTS; Straus, 1979); and Coleman (1990) categorized 46% of 90 lesbian couples she interviewed as violent. Higher percentages of battering were reported when women were queried about violence in previous relationships in comparison with current partnerships. Using a sample of 36 lesbian undergraduates, Bologna, Waterman, and Dawson (1987) found that 40% were victims in their current or most recent relationships and that 64% were victimized by previous partners. Respondents also reported substantial rates of inflicting physical aggression in current (54%) and past (56%) relationships as measured by the CTS. Bologna et al.'s results should be interpreted with caution, however. Not only are these findings based on a small sample, but the researchers also asked respondents to participate in a study on "conflict resolution tactics," a method of solicitation that might have attracted more respondents who were willing to reveal partner violence.

When the definition of aggression was broadened to include psychological and sexual abuse in addition to physical violence, even more respondents reported victimization. In a sample of 1,099 lesbians surveyed at a music festival, one half of the respondents reported a combination of physical, psychological, and sexual abuse (Lie &

Gentlewarrier, 1991). Similarly, in a sample of lesbians surveyed through the mailing lists of lesbian organizations in Arizona, researchers found that, when all forms of aggression were considered, 50% were victimized (Lie, Schilit, Bush, Montagne, & Reyes, 1991; Schilit, Lie, Bush, Montagne, & Reyes, 1991).

Gay Partner Violence. Few researchers have attempted to estimate the amount of gay male partner violence. Using a very small sample of 34 gay male undergraduates, Bologna and colleagues (1987) found that 18% were victims and 14% were perpetrators of violence in their current relationships. An even higher percentage of respondents sustained (44%) or inflicted (25%) violence in previous relationships.

In the absence of reliable prevalence studies, other means have been used to approximate the number of violent gay male partnerships. For example, researchers at the Seattle Counseling Service for Sexual Minorities predicted that 30,000 gay men have been battered in that city alone (Farley, 1992). Island and Letellier (1991) believe that 500,000 gay males are battered annually; they based their estimate on a 10% to 20% rate of battering among the 9.5 million adult gay males who are believed to be in intimate relationships (64%). Given the difficulties of calculating the number of gay relationships and the amount of partner violence experienced by couples regardless of sexual orientation, there is no way of knowing the accuracy of these estimates.

Does Partner Violence Differ by Sexual Orientation?

Several studies have compared rates of partner violence by sexual orientation. The results, however, have been mixed. Bologna and associates (1987) found that a higher percentage of lesbians, compared with gay men, reported being victims and aggressors in both current and past relationships. Several other studies found that partner violence did not differ by sexual orientation. For example, Gardner (1989) used the CTS (Straus, 1979) to assess physical aggression in a sample of 43 lesbian, 43 heterosexual, and 39 gay male couples. The results revealed that lesbian couples reported the highest rate of physical violence (48%), followed by gay (38%) and heterosexual couples (28%). These differences were not significant, however. Similarly, Brand and Kidd (1986) compared the reported frequency of physical aggression experienced by 75 self-identified heterosexual women and 55 lesbians. The authors found that the percentage of lesbians who were physically abused by female partners in *committed* relationships was comparable to the frequency of heterosexual women who were abused by male partners in committed relationships (25% vs. 27%, respectively). When *dating* relationships were considered, however, heterosexual women were significantly more likely to be physically abused by male dates than lesbians were to be abused by female dates (19% vs. 5%, respectively).

Mixed findings have been reported when researchers have compared partner violence rates among self-identified lesbians with a history of intimate relationships with both men and women. Loulan (1987), for example, found that almost twice as many lesbians reported being abused by male partners as female partners (30% vs. 17%, respectively). In contrast, Lie and colleagues (1991) found that more lesbians reported being physically victimized in previous relationships by women (45%) than men (32%).

In conclusion, it is difficult to obtain an accurate estimate of partner violence in same-sex relationships, particularly among gay men. This difficulty may be partially a result of the small sample sizes in many studies (e.g., Bologna et al., 1987; Gardner, 1989), as well as the different measures used to assess partner violence across studies. Although some researchers have used standardized measures of intimate violence (Bologna et al., 1987; Lockhart et al., 1994), such as the CTS (Straus, 1979), other researchers have simply asked, "If you are currently in a lesbian relationship, is it abusive?" (Schilit, Lie, & Montagne, 1990). Despite the limited research, battering appears to be as prevalent among gays and lesbians as among heterosexuals. More research needs to be conducted, however, before conclusions can be drawn about whether couples are at greater risk on the basis of their sexual orientation.

Types of Same-Sex Partner Violence

What Forms Does Lesbian and Gay Battering Take?

Lesbian battering has been defined by Hart (1986) as a "pattern of violence (or) coercive behaviors whereby a lesbian seeks to control the thoughts, beliefs, or conduct of her intimate partner or to punish the intimate for resisting the perpetrator's control" (p. 174). *Gay male partner violence* has been characterized as "any unwanted physical force, psychological abuse, or material or property destruction inflicted by one man on another" (Island & Letellier, 1991, p. 28). Regardless of the definition, partner violence among same-sex couples generally takes the same forms as abuse in heterosexual relationships (Morrow & Hawxhurst, 1989). In a sample of 100 lesbian victims of partner violence, for example, Renzetti (1989) found that pushing and shoving (75%), being hit with a fist (65%), and having an object thrown at them (44%) were the most frequently reported forms of victimization. A similar pattern of lesbian abuse was discovered by Lockhart and colleagues (1994). The same study also revealed that between 4% and 12% of respondents experienced severe aggression, including beatings and assaults with weapons. Furthermore, on the basis of both clinical (Farley, 1996; Island & Letellier, 1991; Margolies & Leeder, 1995) and empirical samples (Renzetti, 1992), same-sex partner violence tends to occur multiple times and to increase in severity over time. Again, this pattern of violence frequently occurs in heterosexual relationships as well (e.g., Walker, 1979).

Although many similarities are found between same-sex and heterosexual partner violence, several important differences exist. For example, aggressors may use homophobic control (Hart, 1986), the HIV (human immunodeficiency virus) positive status of themselves or their partners (Letellier, 1996), or the myth of "mutual battering" (Renzetti, 1992) to control their victims. Each form of aggression is discussed below.

Homophobic Control. According to Hart (1986), homophobic control includes such actions as the following:

> Threatening to tell family, friends, employer, police, church, community, etc. that the victim is a lesbian . . .; telling the victim she deserves all that she gets because she is a lesbian; assuring her that no one would believe she has been violated because lesbians are not violent; reminding her that she has no options because the homophobic world will not help her. (p. 189)

This form of abuse appears to be a common occurrence in violent same-sex relationships. For example, in Renzetti's (1992) survey of 100 victims of lesbian battering, 21% indicated that their partners had "threatened to bring her out"—that is, to reveal one's sexual orientation without permission. Several victims in this study responded to this form of abuse by quitting their jobs. Their rationale was that quitting was preferable to being terminated as a result of being "outed" (Renzetti, 1996). Thus, homophobic control appears to be an effective form of dominance in some battering relationships.

HIV Status. Although AIDS (acquired immunodeficiency syndrome) and HIV are not solely a problem of the gay community, this population has been disproportionately affected by this health crisis in the United States. According to the Centers for Disease Control and Prevention (1993), gay and bisexual men account for 58% of AIDS cases in the United States. A considerable number of gay men must contend with both HIV infection and partner abuse. For example, 30% of battered gay and bisexual men served by the San Francisco Gay Men's Domestic Violence Project were also HIV positive (cited in Letellier, 1996). Although HIV does not cause battering (Island & Letellier, 1991; Letellier, 1994), Letellier (1996) cites numerous examples of ways this infection can further complicate intimate violence. Specifically, if a batterer is HIV positive, he may threaten to infect his victim or use his failing health to make the victim feel guilty about leaving the abusive situation. He may also use his poor health to manipulate others into believing that he is not the aggressor in the conflict. As a result, both friends and legal authorities may be less likely to intervene. Alternatively, if the victim has been infected with HIV, the batterer may threaten to withhold medical care or to reveal the victim's HIV-positive status, which may result in discrimination and the loss of income or insurance benefits. In addition, the internalization of societal animosity toward both gay men and people living with AIDS, in conjunction with the lack of financial resources and fear of losing a caregiver, may further hamper a victim's ability to leave a violent relationship.

Mutual Battering. In same-sex relationships, researchers and clinicians cannot rely on gender to determine the roles (victim vs. aggressor) played by each partner in a battering incident. As a result, intimate violence among same-sex couples has often been perceived as an "equal fight" or mutual battering (Island & Letellier, 1991; Renzetti, 1992). At first glance, empirical studies appear to support the existence of mutual violence in same-sex relationships. For example, Lie and associates (1991) found that 39% of respondents who had been both aggressors and victims of lesbian battering labeled their violence as mutual abuse. However, many lesbian respondents—

between 30% (Lie et al., 1991) and 64% (Renzetti, 1992)—have also characterized their aggressive behavior as self-defensive.

Researchers assert that gay (Island & Letellier, 1991) and lesbian (Hart, 1986; Renzetti, 1997) batterers use the myth of mutual batter-ing to further control and victimize their partners. Specifically, ag-gressors may claim mutual abuse to deny responsibility for their vio-lent behavior. If a victim retaliates or takes self-defensive actions, the batterer may use this to further justify his or her behavior. For exam-ple, a perpetrator may claim that "she hit me too" as a reason for her continued abuse. A victim, regardless of her motivation for the use of aggression, may feel guilty for using violence against a partner and as a result may perceive herself as an equal combatant (Farley, 1992; Hart, 1986; Island & Letellier, 1991; Leeder, 1988). Letellier (1994) further argues that, because of the social stigma associated with male victimization, male victims might be encouraged to "take it like a man." As a consequence, men may label themselves as equal partici-pants in the violence, rather than as victims.

In conclusion, aggression among same-sex couples generally takes the same forms (physical, sexual, and psychological abuse) as it does in heterosexual relationships. Despite the many similarities in types of aggression inflicted and sustained, however, there are some impor-tant differences. Batterers may use homophobic control (Hart, 1986), the HIV-positive status of themselves or their partners (Letellier, 1994), and the illusion of mutual battering to further victimize their partners (Renzetti, 1992). Future research should focus on the dynamics of these forms of violence. Specifically, more information is needed concerning the prevalence and variety of forms that homophobic con-trol might assume (Renzetti, 1992) and the effect of HIV on battering (Letellier, 1996). Because gay men may be even more reluctant to label themselves as victims, their perceptions of mutual battering warrant particular attention (Letellier, 1994).

Correlates of Same-Sex Partner Violence

What Are Some Correlates of Same-Sex Partner Violence?

One unique variable specific to gays and lesbians, *internalized homophobia,* defined as the acceptance of negative societal attitudes toward homosexuals (Pharr, 1986), has been examined as a potential

contributor to partner violence in same-sex couples (Renzetti, 1997).
Specifically, researchers argue that societal discrimination fosters internalized homophobia, which in turn may contribute to low self-
esteem, feelings of powerlessness, denial of group membership, and
difficulty establishing committed, trusting, intimate relationships
(Letellier, 1994; Margolies, Becker, & Jackson-Brewer, 1987). These
negative feelings may then be acted out in the form of partner violence (Byrne, 1996; Hart, 1986). As an example of internalized homophobia, Letellier (1994) cited a case of a gay batterer who shouted at
his victim after an attack: "You might as well get used to it. This is
how gay relationships are" (p. 100). Although it certainly seems plausible that internalized homophobia may play a role in same-sex partner violence, this theory awaits further empirical investigation.

The majority of factors that appear to contribute to same-sex partner violence have been shown to be predictors of heterosexual battering as well. In particular, the bulk of empirical research has investigated the intergenerational transmission of violence (Schilit et al.,
1991), alcohol abuse (Schilit et al., 1990), conflicts around dependency and autonomy, and imbalances of power (Lockhart et al., 1994) as
correlates of same-sex battering. Although these risk factors are discussed separately in the following section, they are often interrelated;
that is, they may occur in conjunction to increase the probability of
intimate violence among gay and lesbian couples (e.g., Farley, 1996;
Renzetti, 1997).

Violence in the Family of Origin. The intergenerational transmission of violence theory proposes that individuals exposed to violence
in their families of origin, either as witnesses or as victims, are at
increased risk of experiencing aggression in adult relationships
(O'Leary, 1988). Regardless of sexual orientation of respondents, researchers have found mixed results (Renzetti, 1992; Straus et al.,
1980). In some studies, no association was reported between violence
in the family of origin and lesbian battering (Coleman, 1990; Kelly &
Warshafsky, 1987; Renzetti, 1992). In contrast, other investigators
have discovered significant correlations between both witnessing
family violence and experiencing various forms of childhood victimization, including physical, sexual, and verbal abuse, and being an
aggressor and victim of lesbian battering (Lie et al., 1991; Lockhart
et al., 1994; Schilit et al., 1991). An association between a prior history of family abuse and intimate violence has been discovered in

clinical samples of gay and lesbian batterers as well (Farley, 1996; Margolies & Leeder, 1995).

Evidence both supports and refutes the belief that abuse is transmitted intergenerationally. Methodological differences, such as the many ways violence in the family of origin has been measured, may contribute to these contradictory findings. Conversely, the attributions made about witnessing or experiencing abuse in childhood, such as the belief that childhood victimization inevitably leads to partner violence, may affect adult behavior (Gelles & Cornell, 1990). For example, like heterosexual victims, lesbians may attribute battering to the violent upbringing of their partners (Renzetti, 1992).

Substance Abuse. Drinking has been linked to intimate violence among heterosexual couples (e.g., Kaufman Kantor & Straus, 1987). Similarly, a connection has been found between alcohol use and battering in lesbian partnerships (Coleman, 1990; Kelly & Warshafsky, 1987; Schilit et al., 1990). In addition, substance abuse has been associated with sustaining injuries in violent lesbian relationships; for example, in a sample of 125 lesbians and 27 bisexual women, Perry (1995) discovered positive correlations between frequency of alcohol use and being physically injured by both a previous and current partner, and frequency of marijuana use was associated with being injured by a past partner.

These results should be interpreted with caution, however. Many of these findings are based on very small samples; for example, several studies based their results on fewer than 42 violent respondents (Coleman, 1990; Schilit et al., 1990). Furthermore, the association between substance abuse and lesbian battering has been assessed by using such questions as "Were you or your partner ever under the influence of drugs or alcohol at the time of the battering incident?" (Renzetti, 1992). This type of question is not sufficient to differentiate patterns and levels of alcohol consumption. This is a research limitation because different types of drinking patterns—for example, binge drinking—have been linked to wife assaults (e.g., Kaufman Kantor & Straus, 1987). With the available methodology used to measure alcohol abuse among same-sex couples, however, it is not possible to access links between different types of drinking behavior and partner violence.

Although substance abuse may occur in conjunction with partner violence, it does not *cause* violence in either heterosexual (Kaufman

Kantor & Straus, 1987) or same-sex relationships (Island & Letellier, 1991). In fact, battering can and often does occur in the absence of alcohol use (Margolies & Leeder, 1995); for example, one third of Renzetti's (1992) sample was not under the influence of alcohol during the violence. Therefore, it is imperative that multiple factors, which act in conjunction with or mediate the association between substance abuse and battering, be investigated. For instance, Renzetti (1992) discovered that dependency of the batterer on her partner was highly correlated with alcohol use. On the basis of qualitative analysis of interviews with 10 lesbians, Diamond and Wilsnack (1978) made a similar association between alcohol use and dependency. Thus, this area warrants further discussion.

Dependency and Autonomy Conflicts. Although male batterers have been found to be very dependent on their female victims (e.g., Walker, 1989), it has been argued that additional factors may influence how dependency is experienced in lesbian partnerships. Women continue to be socialized to define themselves in relation to significant others and to place a high value on intimacy (Chodorow, 1978). Thus, when two women are romantically involved, it may be even more difficult for them to establish a sense of independence and autonomy in their relationship. In addition, lesbians, like gay men, may develop a greater attachment to their partners in response to the lack of social validation and support for their relationships that they receive from the larger society (McCandlish, 1982; Renzetti, 1992). A sense of intimacy and closeness may also act as a buffer against discrimination. Among some lesbian couples, however, high levels of intimacy can create a sense of "fusion" (Lindenbaum, 1985) or "merging" (Pearlman, 1989), which may make it difficult for each partner to have a sense of independence and separate identity in the relationship. As a result, having a different opinion or initiating social activities without the partner might be perceived as rejection, which in turns leads to conflict and possibly physical violence (Margolies & Leeder, 1995).

Although Coleman (1990) found no correlation between relationship interdependency and partner violence among lesbian couples, other researchers have discovered that conflicts around dependency and autonomy were related to lesbian battering (e.g., Renzetti, 1992). For instance, Lockhart and associates (1994) found that, when compared with their nonvictimized counterparts, respondents who reported severe levels of physical abuse perceived that their partners had a high need for social fusion, as measured by such beliefs as couples need to do everything together and the use of communication techniques that include mind reading. Severely victimized respondents in this study also reported more conflict around issues of independence and autonomy, such as a partner's emotional and financial dependency, a partner socializing without the respondent, and a respondent's intimate involvement with other people. Similarly, in her sample of lesbian victims, Renzetti (1992) assessed dependency and autonomy with such items as "My partner and I have a separate set of friends." Her results revealed that batterers who were very dependent on their partners, as well as victims who desired more independence, reported a greater frequency of abuse and more types of abuse, such as shoving, pushing, and choking.

The association between dependency and autonomy requires further investigation. For example, the extent to which dependency issues reflect borderline or narcissistic personality disorders should be considered (Coleman, 1994). Dependency issues may also be related to concern around power and control. For instance, it has been argued that some gay men might avoid relationship dependency for fear of losing power and control (Farley, 1992). Thus, it is also important to consider the role of power imbalances in same-sex battering.

Power Imbalances. Among heterosexual couples, power imbalances have often been associated with partner violence (Coleman & Straus, 1990; Straus et al., 1980). The link between the imbalance of power and battering is less clear among same-sex couples (e.g., Bologna et al., 1987). This inconsistency may be partially a result of how power imbalances are defined across studies. When indicators of social status, such as income, were used as predictors of partner violence, the findings have been contradictory. For example, Kelly and Warshafsky (1987) found no significant correlations between partner violence and indicators of status as measured by income, education, race, religion, and age. In contrast, Renzetti (1992) found that as differences in social class and intelligence became a source of conflict between the partners, the severity and frequency of some forms of violence increased. In particular, social class and intellectual differences between partners were associated with batterers hitting, choking, and pushing their partners. It is not clear, however, whether the victim or the batterer was the partner with the higher social class or greater intellectual ability. Renzetti (1992) concluded that the cumulative effects of differences in status and resources between partners should be taken into consideration; that is, social class differences between partners may not necessarily result in abuse—for example, if the older, more educated partner makes more money. In contrast, if the younger or less educated partner has more economic resources relative to the older, more educated partner, such a relationship may experience a greater likelihood of conflict concerning the balance of power.

Results were more consistent when division of labor between the partners was considered to be a form of power. In several studies, lesbians who assumed primary responsibility for household duties, such as cooking and managing the finances, were more likely to be abused (Kelly & Warshafsky, 1987; Renzetti, 1992). Similarly, Lockhart and associates (1994) found evidence to support the link between power imbalances and victimization in lesbian relationships. Specifically, respondents who sustained severe aggression reported more conflicts around housekeeping and cooking duties, when compared with nonvictims and those who sustained mild forms of violence. On the basis of the research, however, it is not clear whether these divisions in household duties existed before the abuse. It could also be that the victims assumed domestic chores in an attempt to appease the abusers (Renzetti, 1992). These speculations await further empirical investigation.

In conclusion, intergenerational transmission (Schilit et al., 1991), alcohol abuse (Schilit et al., 1990), conflicts around dependency and autonomy, and imbalances of power (Lockhart et al., 1994) have been linked to partner violence among same-sex couples. Although these risk factors may occur independently, they are often interrelated and occur in conjunction, which may increase the probability of violence in both heterosexual and same-sex partnerships (Renzetti, 1997). Many of these results need to be replicated, however, before firm conclusions can be made about the roles these risk factors play in gay and lesbian battering.

Research Limitations

What Are Some Research Limitations?

The majority of published empirical studies on same-sex violence have surveyed young, white, educated, middle-class respondents who were members of lesbian organizations (Lie et al., 1991; Schilit et al., 1991) or attending social events that attracted large groups of lesbians (Lie & Gentlewarrier, 1991; Loulan, 1987). In addition, most participants were openly lesbian. For example, among the 152 lesbians and bisexual women surveyed by Perry (1995), 63% classified their sexual orientation disclosure as being "out." Because of nonrandom sampling procedures and self-selection factors, knowledge of partner violence among gay men (Island & Letellier, 1991) and homosexuals who are "closeted" (not open about their sexual orientation), working class (Almeida et al., 1994), or ethnic minorities (Kanuha, 1990; Mendez, 1996; Waldron, 1996) is limited.

Another major research limitation is the dearth of theoretical models that address partner violence among homosexuals. Mainstream gender-based theories have attributed battering to rigid adherence to patriarchal values (Hamberger & Hastings, 1988a) or to traditional feminine sex role stereotypes (Walker, 1979). Although some researchers have argued that same-sex partner violence is the result of gay and lesbian couples acting out traditional heterosexual masculine and feminine gender roles (e.g., Walker, 1979), other investigators have not found evidence of "gender role playing" by gay and lesbian couples (Hart, 1986; Renzetti, 1992). Therefore, a theory that associates battering with traditional gender roles appears to be of limited use in explaining assaults among gay and lesbian couples. A related argument is that sexism and male dominance contribute to intimate violence among heterosexual couples (e.g., Yllö & Straus, 1990). Again, such a theory does not take into account the role of internalized homophobia or relationship dynamics in which power differences are not based on gender. To better understand the dynamics of same-sex partner violence, Letellier (1994) suggests that researchers should consider gender-neutral theories, which focus on "power imbalances, both on the societal and interpersonal levels, and on the psychological characteristics of individual perpetrators" (p. 104).

To summarize, it is difficult to obtain an accurate estimate of partner violence, particularly among gay male couples. On the basis of the limited research, same-sex couples appear to be equally likely as their heterosexual counterparts to experience violence. Many similarities are found in the types of violence experienced by heterosexual and homosexual couples. Important differences are also found, however, including the use of homophobic control (Hart, 1986), HIV-positive status (Letellier, 1996), and the myth of mutual battering

(Renzetti, 1997). Although internalized homophobia has been proposed as one possible contributor to partner violence in same-sex relationships (Renzetti, 1997), the correlates of partner violence tend to be the same regardless of sexual orientation. In particular, gay and lesbian partner violence has been empirically linked to violence in the family of origin (Schilit et al., 1990), alcohol abuse (Schilit et al., 1990), conflicts around autonomy, and power imbalances (Lockhart et al., 1994).

Therapeutic Implications

It is important to focus on the role of the therapist in the treatment of violent same-sex couples. It is not safe for some gays and lesbians to reveal their sexual orientation to relatives and friends. Consequently, therapists may be one of the few sources of help that victims and batterers have left to consult (Renzetti, 1989). The mental health profession, however, has a long history of discrimination against gay men and lesbians (Arey, 1995; D'Augelli & Dark, 1995). For therapeutic intervention to be effective, service providers need greater awareness of the strengths in the gay and lesbian community, as well as the challenges faced by this population (Morrow & Hawxhurst, 1989). Therefore, the following section focuses on barriers to help seeking, hallmarks of an appropriate assessment, and treatment recommendations specific to same-sex couples.

What Barriers Impede Help Seeking?

Scant research has examined the extent and nature of help-seeking efforts made by battered gay men (Island & Letellier, 1991) and lesbians (Lie & Gentlewarrier, 1991; Renzetti, 1989). In a sample of more than 1,000 lesbians, Lie and Gentlewarrier (1991) asked respondents to indicate what resources they "would be likely to use after an abuse, assuming these were available and accessible to you either as a survivor or a perpetrator." Regardless of their victim or perpetrator status, approximately two thirds of the sample reported that they would not use any of the resources listed in this study, such as support groups and battered women's shelters. Similarly, Renzetti (1989) also found low rates of help seeking from formal sources among the

100 battered lesbians in her sample. Although 58 sought help from counselors, fewer than 20 sought help from legal authorities, religious leaders, shelters, or physicians. On the basis of anecdotal reports, Island and Letellier (1991) found that gay male victims also were reluctant to seek help from legal and social service agencies. Taken together, these studies point to a pattern of service underuse.

Feelings of shame and fear of retaliation may preclude victims of both heterosexual (Pagelow, 1981a) and same-sex partner violence from seeking help (Renzetti, 1989). Concerns around revealing one's sexual orientation to service providers, relatives, and friends may further impede the help-seeking efforts of gay men and lesbians (Farley, 1992). Real and perceived homophobia and discriminatory practices, however, are the most widely cited reasons by some gays and lesbians for the underuse of mainstream community services (Lie & Gentlewarrier, 1991; Renzetti, 1992). Homophobia impedes help-seeking efforts because it

> helps to create the opportunity for abuse without consequences by isolating the victims and preventing them access to resources such as their family, appropriate social services, and the criminal justice and legal systems. As a result, battered lesbians and gay men are unlikely to seek assistance, and even if they do, are not likely to be helped. (Merrill, 1996, p. 17)

Empirical research supports this speculation. For example, among the battered lesbians who sought help in Renzetti's (1989) study, many reported that service providers refused to help, excused or denied the seriousness of the violence, or characterized the battering as mutual abuse. Battered gay men also have encountered similar responses when seeking help from professionals (Island & Letellier, 1991).

According to Renzetti (1996), the fear that professionals will be unresponsive to same-sex partner violence is not unfounded. On the basis of surveys with 544 service providers listed in the 1991 National Directory of Domestic Violence Programs, only 10% of the programs had intervention and outreach efforts specifically designed for lesbians (e.g., advertisements in lesbian and gay newspapers, support groups for battered lesbians). In addition, fewer than one half of the programs addressed lesbian battering when they trained their staff and volunteers. Despite the limited services offered by these agencies, only 32% of service providers planned to expand their services to battered lesbians.

What Are the Hallmarks
of an Appropriate Assessment?

An appropriate assessment should include the same demographic and background information that would be gathered from any client or couple, such as family and personal history of mental illness (Farley, 1996; Klinger, 1995), violence in the family of origin (Farley, 1992), and substance abuse (Schilit et al., 1990). Therapists also should explore the following areas that are relevant to gay men and lesbians:

Unique Forms of Violence. In addition to assessing the history, duration, and course of partner violence (Hamberger, 1996), professionals should be prepared to explore the presence of homophobic control (e.g., threats to reveal the victim's sexual orientation; Hart, 1986). The HIV-positive status of the batterer or victim can play a role in battering as well; for example, a batterer may threaten to withhold medicine or to reveal the victim's illness (Letellier, 1996).

Influence of Homophobia. Farley (1992) recommends that, because homophobia so adversely influences the lives of gays and lesbians, professionals should explore the extent to which societal homophobia is internalized by both victims and aggressors, the degree to which both partners are closeted regarding their sexual orientation, and each individual's acceptance of his or her sexual orientation.

Role of Each Partner. Rather than assume that both parties are mutually abusive, service providers should explore the roles played by each partner in the abuse. On the basis of clinical observations with 64 lesbian victims and perpetrators, Marrujo and Kreger (1996) found that three roles emerged: (a) primary aggressors (27%), (b) primary victims (39%), and (c) participants (34%). Although participants did not initiate the aggression, they engaged in "fighting back" or a "repeated pattern of physical and/or emotional aggression in response to the partner's aggressive act" (p. 28). Furthermore, participants did not appear to be interested in disengaging from the conflict once it started. In contrast, primary victims desired to end the conflict and secure their personal safety. Following the violent episode, primary aggressors often expressed victimization (e.g., "She [her partner] did X to me"), and participants expressed retaliatory anger (e.g., "I wasn't going to let her get away with it") (p. 31), whereas primary victims expressed feelings of confusion. Although more research is needed to confirm the existence of these different roles in violent same-sex couples, these findings suggest that practitioners need to take a closer look at the roles that lesbians and gay men play in abusive relationships.

Prior Exposure to Violence. The effects of partner violence may be exacerbated by prior exposure to violence, such as hate crimes (Herek et al., 1997). Consequently, an assessment should include experiences with these forms of violence as well.

What Are Specific Treatment Recommendations?

Scant research has focused on specific strategies for the treatment of violence among same-sex couples (e.g., Leeder, 1988; Margolies & Leeder, 1995; Morrow & Hawxhurst, 1989). The research indicates that selecting the appropriate treatment modality is important. Generally, violent same-sex couples have access to fewer sources of help (Renzetti, 1989). Therefore, the treatment modality for same-sex couples is based on the resources available. For example, in large urban areas, group therapy might be an option; in rural settings, which typically have smaller lesbian and gay communities, individual and couples therapy might be the only treatment alternatives (Margolies & Leeder, 1995).

Despite the limited treatment options available for same-sex couples, the intervention strategies are generally the same regardless of sexual orientation. For example, victims of homosexual partner violence may need practical assistance, such as financial support and help with finding shelter, as well as emotional support and validation of their victimization (Island & Letellier, 1991; Renzetti, 1989). In therapy, victims may need to explore self-esteem issues and their reasons for staying in abusive relationships (e.g., fear of AIDS, small pool of potential partners, lack of support from family and friends; Farley, 1992; Island & Letellier, 1991; Margolies & Leeder, 1995).

For gay and lesbian batterers, the initial sessions should focus on assessment and establishing rapport. Once trust is established, therapists may need to focus on anger management, assertiveness training, and communication skills. At the later stages of therapy, batterers can be confronted about the consequences of their violent behavior. It is also recommended that therapists confront and set limits in a supportive manner so that clients do not terminate therapy prematurely (Leeder, 1988).

Group therapy may be effective with victims and aggressors of same-sex partner violence as well. For victims, groups can reduce feelings of isolation, facilitate a sense of empowerment, and provide a safe place to share their stories (Island & Letellier, 1991). For batterers, groups can counteract the social isolation common in battering relationships. An additional benefit of a group format is the establishment of a peer group that can confront the abuser about his or her violent behavior. Because of societal homophobia, however, it is not recommended that gay and heterosexual batterers be in the same groups (Farley, 1992; Klinger, 1995; Leeder, 1988; Margolies & Leeder, 1995).

Other treatment modalities have been proposed for violent same-sex couples. In particular, some clinicians argue that couples counseling can be helpful once the safety of the victim is ensured and both parties have worked out their individual problems (Leeder, 1988, 1994; Margolies & Leeder, 1995). Others contend, however, that couple treatment is contraindicated because it compromises the safety of the victim (Farley, 1992; Island & Letellier, 1991; Klinger, 1995). Similar opposition has been raised about mediation as a conflict resolution strategy (Renzetti, 1989) and the community treatment model, which involves the identification of friends and relatives who would be available to intervene and consult with the violent couple (Leeder, 1988, 1994). Specifically, these forms of intervention may minimize the power imbalances in the relationship, therefore creating the illusion that both parties are equally responsible for the abuse.

Regardless of the modality used to treat violent same-sex couples, the literature stresses the importance of service providers being aware of their own biased attitudes and myths concerning homosexuals. Effective therapeutic intervention requires validating same-sex relationships and understanding how self-hatred and homophobia influence gay and lesbian couples. Professionals should educate themselves about the unique challenges faced by this population and the resources available in the homosexual community. With this knowledge, service providers can strive to eliminate discriminatory practices in their agencies (Island & Letellier, 1991; Klinger, 1995; Lobel, 1986; Renzetti, 1996).

In summary, violent same-sex couples desire assistance despite the barriers that impede their help-seeking efforts (Renzetti, 1989). When treatment is sought, therapists should take into account the unique forms that violence may take in same-sex relationships, the influence of homophobia, the role played by each partner in the violence, and prior exposure to violence. Service providers also should strive to be sensitive to the unique challenges faced by this population.

Policy Recommendations

Based on the literature, the following recommendations are made:

1. Identifying the problem is the first step to motivating the gay and lesbian community and service providers to recognize and confront same-sex battering (Lobel, 1986). This entails such actions as broadening the language in partner violence laws to ensure that victims are equally protected regardless of gender and sexual orientation (Island & Letellier, 1991). Defining the problem also involves conducting more empirical research on the prevalence and incidence of same-sex partner violence, characteristics of the violence, and contributing factors (Hamberger, 1996).

2. Extensive training is needed for service providers in law enforcement, social service agencies, and the medical and mental health professions. Professionals may need to address homophobia and discrimination against gays and lesbians in their agencies and to develop written and spoken language that is inclusive of same-sex relationships (Hamberger, 1996; Renzetti, 1996).

3. Massive intervention efforts should be directed toward the gay and lesbian community. These intervention strategies could include newspaper advertisements, telephone books that specifically list services for same-sex partner violence, and flyers posted at parades and conferences with a larger presence of gays and lesbians (Island & Letellier, 1991). A special effort should be made to reach gay men and lesbians of color through outreaching to communities of color, advertising services for victims and batterers in different languages, and recruiting ethnically diverse staff and volunteers (Mendez, 1996; Waldron, 1996).

4. Finally, factors that contribute to same-sex partner violence must be addressed, such as substance abuse, violence in the family of origin, and discrimination against gays and lesbians.

CHAPTER SIX

Lifting the "Political Gag Order"

Breaking the Silence Around Partner Violence in Ethnic Minority Families

CAROLYN M. WEST

A fter more than two decades of research, it is clear that partner violence is a serious social problem that affects many segments of society (Straus et al., 1980). Despite the increased focus on batter-ing, investigators are just beginning to explore the complexities of partner violence among ethnic minorities. This void in the literature has existed for several reasons. First, some researchers have taken a "color blind" approach to examining partner violence; that is, it has been assumed that the dynamics of battering were similar regardless of ethnicity (Fontes, in press). Although violent families of all ethnic backgrounds may share some similarities (e.g., high rates of marital

---

The terms *ethnic minorities* and *people of color* are used to refer collectively to the four ethnic groups discussed in this chapter (African Americans, Latinos, Asian Americans, and American Indians). Also, the terms *African American* and *Anglo American* are used interchangeably with *black* and *white*, respectively. Where possible, the ethnic group is identified (e.g., Mexican American, Chinese American). The terminology used to refer to racial groups may vary on the basis of regional, political, and personal preference. The author acknowledges the limitations of the terminology used in this chapter.

dissatisfaction), a color-blind perspective disregards the ways race/ ethnicity shapes the experience and interpretation of violence (O'Keefe, 1994). Alternatively, other researchers have considered violence to be a problem primarily of poor, ethnic minorities. As a consequence, research findings have been presented without consideration for factors that might act as mediators between ethnicity and partner violence (e.g., level of acculturation) or structural inequalities (e.g., social class) that may account for higher rates of partner violence among ethnic minorities (Asbury, 1993; Cazenave & Straus, 1990; Jasinski, 1996). Furthermore, failure to consider historic and sociocultural factors that influence minority partner violence may result in stereotypes, unfair public policies, and ineffective intervention efforts (Fontes, in press).

Information on ethnic minority partner violence is also lacking because some members of the ethnic minority community have imposed a "political gag order" concerning battering (Crenshaw, 1994). Specifically, some community members fear that research findings will be misinterpreted or used to reinforce negative societal stereotypes about minorities. Mistrust of authorities has led some community leaders and activists to deny the problem of partner violence or to resist the release of data indicating that minorities are more aggressive (Crenshaw, 1994; Eng, 1995; Ho, 1990).

Ethnic minorities are projected to constitute approximately 50% of the U.S. population by 2050 (U.S. Bureau of the Census, 1991). Therefore, researchers can no longer afford to maintain the silence around partner violence in this group. This chapter reviews research in this area.

Although the term *ethnic minority* may encompass many groups, this chapter focuses on the four largest groups in the United States: African Americans, Latinos, Asian Americans, and American Indians. First, a brief description of each group is presented. Second, the literature on partner violence among these groups is reviewed. Specifically, ethnic differences, demographic and cultural factors that potentially contribute to higher rates of partner violence among ethnic minorities, and limitations of the research are addressed. Third, therapeutic implications, including barriers to help seeking, hallmarks of culturally appropriate assessments, and culture-specific treatment recommendations are discussed. Finally, recommendations for policy are suggested.

Description of the Populations

The purpose of this section is to describe briefly the four ethnic groups discussed in this chapter. An emphasis is placed on conditions associated with increased levels of partner violence, including demographic characteristics (e.g., youthfulness, poverty), and important historic events (e.g., forced migration). Cultural strengths, which may act as buffers against violence, also are highlighted (Asbury, 1993; Cazenave & Straus, 1990). The reader is reminded that conclusions cannot be drawn about individuals totally on the basis of ethnic group membership.

African Americans

African or black Americans make up approximately 12% of the U.S. population and constitute its largest racial minority. Although largely descendants of tribes along the west coast of Africa, many also have American Indian and European ancestry. Unlike other immigrants, African Americans entered the United States via the slave trade. Their 200-year history of enslavement was characterized by forced separation of families, beatings, and loss of language and culture. Following slavery, discrimination took the form of de facto segregation (Greene, 1994; Hammond & Yung, 1994). Substantial societal gains have been made; nevertheless, black people have not achieved economic, employment, and educational parity with Anglo Americans. For example, one in three African Americans currently lives in poverty (U.S. Bureau of the Census, 1992). Despite social and economic injustices, African American families have developed cultural strengths and coping strategies, including adaptability of family roles; strong kinship bonds; emphasis on work, education, and achievement; religious values; and a humanistic belief system that stresses concern for others and spontaneous interactions (Allen, 1986; Greene, 1994).

Latino Americans

Latinos represent approximately 22.4 million people, or about 9% of the U.S. population. They are projected to be one of the largest minority groups by the turn of the century (U.S. Bureau of the Census,

1991). Mexicans, Puerto Ricans, and Cubans constitute the three largest Latino ethnic groups living in the U.S. mainland. They differ substantially in terms of immigration history and number of generations in the United States. Mexican Americans have been in the United States for 150 years and account for 60% of the Latino population. The original population did not enter the United States as immigrants; rather, they were conquered during the Mexican American War. As a result of the acquisition of their land during the Spanish American War, Puerto Ricans share a similar history of domination. Nevertheless, large waves of Puerto Rican migration to the United States began only 45 years ago. This group came primarily to escape high unemployment rates. Today, Puerto Ricans account for 15% of Latinos. Finally, Cubans, the most recent immigrants, make up 5% of the Latino population. The "first wave" of Cuban immigrants were predominately white, educated professionals who arrived in Florida between 1959 and 1965. As political refugees, the Cubans received economic assistance from the federal government. By the 1980s, U.S. immigration laws were stricter and the economy was declining. Consequently, subsequent waves of nonwhite, less educated Cuban immigrants were met with hostility (Ginorio, Gutierrez, & Cause, 1995; Portes & Truelove, 1987).

These differing migration histories contribute to demographic variations between ethnic groups. For example, Cuban Americans are older than Latinos as a group (median age 40 vs. 26, respectively; U.S. Bureau of the Census, 1993). They also tend to be more economically advantaged. For example, in one nationally representative sample, Cuban American families were more likely than Puerto Rican and Mexican American families to report two incomes and employment in managerial or professional occupations. Despite the economic success of some Cubans, Latino families are two to five times more likely than Anglo families to live in poverty (Jasinski, 1996; Kaufman Kantor et al., 1994). Nonetheless, Latinos maintain strong social support networks and multigenerational families characterized by loyalty and honor (Ginorio et al., 1995).

Asian Americans

Asian/Pacific Island Americans represent 2.9% (7.27 million) of the U.S. population. Three predominant Asian groups reside in the United States. The first group can trace its origins to mainland Asiatic culture (Chinese, Vietnamese, Japanese, and Koreans); the second group came from Southeast Asia (Filipinos, Indonesians, Malaysians, Cambodians, and Laotians); and the third group, Pacific Islanders (Hawaiians, Samoans, and Guamanians), are considered "natives" rather than immigrants (Okamura, Heras, & Wong-Kerberg, 1995; Trask, 1990).

The experience of Asian American groups differs greatly by immigration and generational status. Immigrant-descendent families, such as Chinese, Japanese, and Korean Americans, can trace four or more generations in the United States. In general, these groups are highly acculturated; that is, they have adopted the norms and behaviors of U.S. society. Immigrant American families, in which the parents are foreign born and the children are American born, sometimes experience cultural and generational conflicts as they attempt to manage both traditional and new norms and values. Despite this challenge, these families are often able to pool their resources and achieve relatively high levels of educational and economic success (Okamura et al., 1995). Because of the prosperity of these two-family constellations, Asians have been dubbed "model minorities." This stereotype minimizes the poverty that exists among Asian Americans, which is almost twice the rate for Anglos, with recently arrived immigrant/ refugee families being most impoverished (U.S. Bureau of the Census, 1993). Their economic instability is often coupled with other difficulties, such as language barriers, lack of education, unsafe neighborhoods, and anti-Asian violence. Despite their diverse backgrounds, as a group Asians emphasize family loyalty, responsibility, respect, and cooperation (Chen & True, 1994; Stevenson, 1992).

American Indians

The indigenous native peoples of North America are referred to as American Indians. The 2 million American Indians in the United States, which represent more than 500 different tribes, account for 0.8% of the U.S. population. Because of increased willingness to acknowledge Indian ancestry, interracial marriages, and high birth rates, this population has grown by almost 600,000 in the last decade. Almost every tribe was subjected to forced removal from ancestral homelands, brutal colonization, confinement to reservations, and pressure to assimilate into European American society. Currently, one third live on federal reservations; the remainder live in either rural or urban settings. Migration between the two locations is common (LaFromboise, Berman, & Sohi, 1994; U.S. Bureau of the Census, 1991).

As a consequence of the high unemployment rate—over 80% in some communities—American Indians experience substantial rates of poverty (Bachman, 1992; Indian Health Service, 1989; LaFromboise et al., 1994; LaFromboise, Choney, James, & Running Wolf, 1995). Death at an early age is also common. More than one third of all American Indian deaths involve people under age 45—three times the rate of the general population. This high death rate, primarily because of suicide, homicide, and accidents, may account for the youthfulness of this population (median age 22.6 years). The prevalence of alcoholism, which is 3.8 times higher for American Indians than for other ethnic groups (Asbury, 1993), is a major contributor to many of these deaths. For example, alcohol is a factor in 90% of American Indian suicides (Johnson, 1994). Despite great adversity, many American Indian families, such as in the Hopi of Northern Arizona, maintain traditional values and customs, including reverence to elders, cooperation, and group cohesion (Wasinger, 1993).

In conclusion, a great deal of cultural, linguistic, historic, and geographic diversity exists both between and within ethnic minority groups. As a group, however, they are disproportionately more likely than Anglo Americans to be youthful and impoverished. Nevertheless, these groups have developed cultural strengths (e.g., cooperation) and strong kinship bonds, which may reduce the likelihood of battering (Cazenave & Straus, 1990).

Incidence of Partner Violence

Ethnic differences and prevalence rates of partner assault are best estimated by using large national probability samples (Hampton, Gelles, & Harrop, 1989), such as the First (Straus et al., 1980) and Second National Family Violence Surveys (Straus & Gelles, 1986), which are composed of national probability samples of 2,143 and 6,002 households, respectively. Clinical and convenience samples can provide valuable information as well. Thus, this chapter reviews studies that use a variety of samples. The majority of the literature focuses on African Americans and Latinos. Although the absence of research on Asian Americans and American Indians is discernible, the research in these areas is discussed when available. Demographic contributors to violence, such as social class, age, and husband's occupational and employment status, are considered. In addition, cultural factors, including level of acculturation, alcohol abuse, and normative approval of violence, are other risk markers addressed. Finally, limitations of the research are discussed.

Are Ethnic Minorities More Violent Than Anglo Americans?

African Americans. Researchers have found contradictory results in rates of partner violence among African Americans when nonrepresentative samples were used. Using case records of partner violence victims, Fagan et al. (1983) found that white batterers, compared with their black counterparts, were more violent toward both family members and nonfamily members. In contrast, a multiethnic (black, Mexican American, white) community sample of Texas residents revealed that black women were three times more likely than Anglo women to beat or be beaten by a partner (Neff, Holamon, & Schluter, 1995). Other studies have not found ethnic differences in rates of partner assault in samples of battered women who were incarcerated (Roundtree, Parker, Edwards, & Teddlie, 1982) or residents of a women's shelter (O'Keefe, 1994).

Large national probability studies, however, have consistently revealed a higher rate of partner violence among African Americans, compared with Anglo Americans. For example, in the First National Family Violence Survey (Straus et al., 1980), the overall rate of black husband-to-wife abuse was four times higher than white husband-to-wife abuse (113 vs. 30 per 1,000, respectively). The same study revealed that African American wives were twice as likely as Anglo wives to engage in severe acts of violence against their husbands (76 vs. 41 per 1,000, respectively). A decade later, a similar pattern of racial differences emerged in the Second National Family Violence Survey (Hampton & Gelles, 1994; Straus & Gelles, 1986). When Hampton and associates (1989) compared violence rates from these two national studies, battering of black wives decreased by almost half (42%). Despite this decline, African Americans were still found to be more violent than their Anglo counterparts.

National probability studies have been criticized for excluding family constellations with high representations of ethnic minorities, such as single-parent families and families with children under age 3 (Kanuha, 1994). When these family types were included in the National Survey of Families and Households, however, racial differences remained. African Americans were almost twice as likely as Anglos to report physical violence toward their partners (e.g., hitting, shoving, throwing objects; Sorenson, Upchurch, & Shen, 1996).

Latino Americans. Researchers using community (Neff et al., 1995), clinical (Mirande & Perez, 1987), and shelter samples (Torres, 1991) have found no differences in rates of partner assaults between Mexican Americans and Anglos. National probability studies, however, have revealed contradictory results. Latinos in the Second Family Violence Survey reported a higher rate of partner abuse than Anglo couples (23% vs. 15%, respectively; Straus & Smith, 1990b), whereas Sorenson and colleagues (1996) discovered that Latinos were less violent than Anglos, as measured by a modified version of the Conflict Tactics Scale (Straus, 1979).

These discrepant findings can be attributed to two major research limitations. By regarding Latinos as a homogenous group and by limiting studies to English-speaking participants, important ethnic group differences are often obscured. Kaufman Kantor and colleagues (1994) avoided these problems by conducting face-to-face bilingual (Spanish-English) interviews with a national probability sample, including an oversample of Latinos. Large ethnic group differences emerged, with Puerto Rican husbands (20.4%) being approximately 2 times more likely than Anglo husbands (9.9%) and 10 times more likely than Cuban husbands (2.5%) to assault their wives.

Asian Americans. To date, no nationally representative studies of Asian American partner violence have been conducted (Sorenson et al., 1996). Instead, much of the research has relied on case histories (Eng, 1995), clinical samples (Chan, 1987), anecdotal reports (Lai, 1986), and newspaper accounts (Chin, 1994). Consequently, estimates of wife assault have varied widely. For instance, one study that used focus groups composed of 6 to 10 Chinese women estimated that between 20% and 30% of Chinese husbands hit their wives (Ho, 1990). In another study, Song (1986) found that 60% of her nonrandom sample of 150 immigrant Korean women were battered. Although it is not possible to draw conclusions about ethnic differences on the basis of these limited studies, interviews with victims (Ho, 1990) and community leaders (Huisman, 1996) indicate that battering is a serious problem in this ethnic group as well.

American Indians. No accurate lifetime prevalence rates of partner violence within or between American Indian groups are known (Chester, Robin, Koss, Lopez, & Goldman, 1994). Estimates of battering have ranged from 50% (Wolk, 1982) to 80% (Chapin, 1990). Many of these findings, however, are based on anecdotal reports (e.g., Allen, 1986) and samples as small as 20 respondents (Verlarde-Castillo, 1992). Using the Second National Family Violence Survey (Straus & Gelles, 1990a), Bachman (1992) found that American Indian couples were significantly more violent than their Anglo counterparts (7.2 vs. 5.3 per 100 couples). The relatively small number of American Indian families surveyed ($N = 204$) and the failure to assess tribal affiliation, however, make it difficult to draw conclusions about ethnic differences.

To summarize, research using nonrepresentative samples, such as shelter residents, has found no racial differences in rates of partner violence among African American, Latino, and Anglo battered women (Gondolf, Fisher, & McFerron, 1988). Some community samples (Neff et al., 1995) and several large nationally representative samples have indicated that African Americans (Sorenson et al., 1996; Straus & Gelles, 1986) and American Indians (Bachman, 1992) reported higher rates of partner violence than Anglo Americans. Findings for Latino Americans are contradictory, with national studies finding both higher (Straus & Smith, 1990b) and lower rates of physical violence (Sorenson et al., 1996) for Latinos, compared with Anglos. The failure to consider ethnic group differences in much of the research on Latino Americans may account for these conflicting findings. When Latino ethnic group differences were considered, Puerto Rican husbands reported the highest rate of wife assault, and Cuban husbands reported the lowest rate in one study (Kaufman Kantor et al., 1994). No accurate estimates of Asian American partner assaults have been made, although evidence from focus groups and community activists suggests that violence is also a concern in this population (Ho, 1990; Huisman, 1996).

What Factors Contribute to These Ethnic Group Differences?

Are ethnic minorities more violent? This question is far too simplistic. A structural explanation is necessary for understanding the higher rates of partner violence in these populations; that is, ethnic minorities are disadvantaged in a society in which race and ethnicity determine access to economic resources. Lack of opportunities and societal inequalities create stress, which in turn may increase the risk of violence (Gelles & Straus, 1988; Jasinski, 1996). Economic marginalization also shapes the culture of the family. For example, less acculturated individuals are likely to be economically marginalized because they lack access to education and job opportunities. Poverty also increases the probability of drinking to excess and endorsing more approving attitudes toward violence (Hampton et al., 1989; Kaufman Kantor et al., 1994; Kaufman Kantor & Straus, 1987). Stated in another way, ethnic minorities are not inherently more violent than Anglo Americans; rather, they are more likely than Anglos to be over-represented in demographic categories that are at greater risk for physical violence. In many instances, racial differences in rates of partner violence disappear when age, social class, and husband's occupational and employment status are taken into account (Straus et al., 1980). The remaining ethnic differences can often be explained by level of acculturation, alcohol abuse, and the normative approval of violence (Cazenave & Straus, 1990; Kaufman Kantor et al., 1994). The following section reviews the research in these areas.

Demographic Factors

Age. Younger age—specifically, being under age 30—is highly correlated with partner violence (Straus & Gelles, 1990a). Research based on the Second National Family Violence Survey has consistently found that younger white (Suitor et al., 1990), African American (Hampton & Gelles, 1994), and American Indian couples (Bachman, 1992) were more violent than their older counterparts. The same pattern appears to be present in Asian American couples. Both anecdotal accounts (Yoshihama, Parekh, & Boyington, 1991) and empirical studies (Lane & Gwartney-Gibbs, 1985) have documented dating aggression among Asian American young adults.

When racial differences were examined, Straus and Smith (1990b) found that Latino couples did not have a higher probability of partner violence than Anglos when age was considered; that is, youthfulness, rather than ethnicity, accounted for the differences in rates of battering between Latinos and Anglos. Given the youthfulness of ethnic minority groups, the association between younger age and partner violence is likely to exist for African Americans and American Indians as well.

Social Class. Ethnic differences in rates of partner violence often disappear when social class is taken into account. Using the First National Family Violence Survey (Straus et al., 1980), Cazenave and Straus (1990) found that African Americans experienced *less* partner violence than Anglos in three out of four income categories (the two highest and the lowest income group). Higher rates of partner assaults were only reported by African American respondents in the $6,000 to $11,999 income range. However, 40% of black respondents in this sample were in this income category. Similarly, in the Second National Family Violence Survey, Straus and Smith (1990b) found that lower income and urban residence accounted for the differences in rates of partner violence between Latinos and Anglo Americans.

Although income and partner violence were not correlated among American Indians in one national study, a significant association was found between these two variables for the entire sample. Given that a higher percentage of American Indians was represented in the lower income levels, the link between social class and assault may still exist (Bachman, 1992). Poverty also has been linked to partner violence among Asian focus group participants, with Chinese Americans attributing wife battering to the poor, rural, less educated members of their community (Ho, 1990).

Husband's Occupational and Employment Status. Nationally representative studies have revealed a link between husband's occupational and employment status and partner violence. Specifically, African American men employed in blue-collar occupations reported more violence than their black professional counterparts (13% vs. 7%, respectively; Cazenave & Straus, 1990). Additionally, black families in which the husbands were unemployed reported higher rates of wife assault than black families with employed husbands (Hampton & Gelles, 1994). A similar association is expected to exist for

American Indians. Although Bachman (1992) did not empirically test this link, more American Indian than Anglo couples were employed in blue-collar occupations, a group that reported significantly higher rates of partner abuse. Media accounts and interviews have associated wife battering with limited employment opportunities among Chinese immigrant husbands as well (Chin, 1994). There is no way of knowing, however, what other factors may be acting in conjunction with husband's unemployment to account for these finding. Like the aforementioned demographic factors, when employment status was taken into consideration, racial differences disappeared. For example, one study found that husband's unemployment, rather than ethnicity, was the strongest predictor of partner violence when Latinos and Anglos were compared (Kaufman Kantor et al., 1994).

Cultural Factors

In some instances, even when social class and occupational status were considered, the rate of partner violence continued to be higher for African Americans than for Anglo Americans (e.g. Neff, et al., 1995). For instance, in a community sample, more middle-class African American women (46%) were battered than their middle-class Anglo counterparts (27%; Lockhart, 1987). Similarly, results from a national study revealed that controlling for husband's occupation did not always eliminate racial differences. In this study, African American men employed in white-collar occupations were still more abusive than Anglo professionals (7% vs. 3%, respectively; Cazenave & Straus, 1990). Given the previous discussion of demographic risk markers, these findings seem contrary to expectation. Cazenave and Straus (1990) concluded that "there are some effects of racial oppression which are independent of income and may cause marital stress and tensions that may erupt in violence" (p. 336). Therefore, escaping poverty may not totally eliminate the risk of partner violence for ethnic minorities because their higher economic status is often precarious and potentially lost with slight economic changes. This financial uncertainty may lead to stress, which in turn may contribute to battering (Lockhart, 1987). Empirical research supports this association. For example, Bachman (1992) found that as *stress,* defined as nervousness and the inability to cope, increased, the probability of American Indian couple violence escalated. Wife assault also has been empirically linked to alcohol abuse and normative approval of violence.

Stressors such as poverty and lack of job opportunities place ethnic minorities at greater risk for heavy drinking and possibly greater tolerance of violence. These factors, along with level of acculturation, interact to contribute to increased levels of wife abuse among ethnic minorities (Kaufman Kantor, 1990; Kaufman Kantor et al., 1994). The influence of acculturation, alcohol abuse, and normative approval of violence on partner violence rates are discussed below.

Level of Acculturation. Defined as the extent to which immigrant groups take on the norms and behavioral patterns of the host society (Gordon, 1964), level of acculturation has been investigated as a contributor to wife assaults. Results have been contradictory, with both high (Jasinski, 1996) and low levels of acculturation (Okamura et al., 1995) being linked to partner violence. Other studies have found no association between acculturation and partner violence (e.g., Perilla, Bakeman, & Norris, 1994).

High Acculturation as a Predictor of Violence. The majority of the empirical research conducted on acculturation has focused on Latino Americans. In one study, a greater level of acculturation, as measured by comfort with the English language, was associated with increased levels of partner violence. When economic factors were considered, however, such as poverty and husband's employment status, English language preference was no longer a significant predictor of wife assault (Jasinski, 1996). When country of origin was used as a measure of acculturation, which is highly correlated with English preference, important ethnic group differences were revealed. Specifically, Kaufman Kantor et al. (1994) found that being born in the United States was associated with increased risk for wife assault among Mexican American and Puerto Rican American husbands. A study conducted by Sorenson and Telles (1991) revealed a similar pattern among Latinos in a Los Angeles community sample, with Mexican Americans who were born in the United States reporting higher rates of hitting or throwing things at their partners (30.9%) than both Mexican Americans who were born in Mexico and Anglos (20% vs. 21.6%, respectively).

Level of acculturation as it relates to black partner violence has not been investigated empirically. However, researchers have hypothesized a link between *racial identity,* defined as cultural pride and commitment to the black community, and intimate assaults. In particular, African Americans with lower racial identity are expected to be more violent (Myers, 1990; Oliver, 1989). In Taylor and Zhang's (1990) interviews of 96 black couples, maritally distressed spouses scored lower than nondistressed couples on black cultural identity. Although physical abuse was not measured directly, partner violence and marital distress have been theoretically and empirically linked (e.g., Miller, Lefcourt, Holmes, Ware, & Saleh, 1986).

Authors assert that intimate violence toward American Indian women can be traced to the introduction of alcohol, Christianity, and the European hierarchal family structure into Indian cultures (e.g., Allen, 1986). Research that establishes the link between increased abuse as a result of modernization and acculturation, however, has yet to be conducted (Chester et al., 1994).

What accounts for these findings? One explanation suggests that as Latinos become more Americanized, the American Dream of greater economic and educational opportunities also may be desired. When discrimination blocks these efforts, feelings of frustration and hostility could potentially be acted out in the form of wife assault (Jasinski, 1996). This may hold true for other ethnic groups as well. Additionally, as ethnic minorities become more acculturated, cultural values and family strengths (e.g., communalism, religiosity, fear of community disapproval) may be relinquished. Consequently, social controls, which might have curtailed partner violence, are no longer in place (Kaufman Kantor et al., 1994).

Low Acculturation as a Predictor of Violence. Evidence also suggests that less acculturated members of ethnic groups are more violent. For example, Jasinski (1996) found that, among Puerto Ricans, partner violence was associated with being born outside the United States. She hypothesized that, in their efforts to assimilate, non-U.S.-born Latinos may experience conflict between their culture of origin and Anglo culture. They also may experience economic marginalization because of language and educational barriers. The stress associated with making this adjustment may lead to violence.

Similar conclusions have been drawn for Asian Americans. According to anecdotal research (Dunwoody, 1982; Lai, 1986; Rimonte, 1989), case studies (Eng, 1995; Okamura et al., 1995), and legal accounts (Anderson, 1993; Jang, Lee, & Morello-Frosch, 1990), Asian immigrants and refugee families experience more partner violence than their U.S.-born counterparts. Cultural isolation, coupled with the lack of educational and job opportunities, limited English-speaking skills, and poverty, are hypothesized to contribute to the increased risk of violence (Chen & True, 1994). Asian women who enter the United States illegally or through "mail order" marriages are also potentially more vulnerable to victimization. Substantial documentation of abuse, in the form of affidavits from police, medical personnel, and social service agencies, may be required from these immigrant women in order to receive assistance. Without proof, which is difficult in obtain in most cases, victims risk deportation by fleeing their violent husbands (Anderson, 1993).[1]

The ethnic groups under investigation, the myriad of ways acculturation has been defined, and the failure to consider the confounding effects of socioeconomic status may partially account for these conflicting results (Kaufman Kantor et al., 1994). As Jasinski (1996) asserts, however, under particular circumstances both high *and* low acculturation could be associated with partner violence:

> On the one hand, more acculturated individuals (as measured by language preference and generational status) may be faced with the strain of being led to believe that hard work will result in success while experiencing first hand the effects of discrimination and prejudice. (p. 191)

Alternatively, a "lack of integration into the economic structure of the U.S. could interfere with chances for upward mobility and create economic stresses which could increase the risk for spousal violence" (p. 107). More empirical research needs to be conducted before the association between acculturation and violence can be understood. Future investigations should include other dimensions of acculturation, such as feelings of cultural marginality and discrimination from the dominant Anglo society (Portes, 1984).

Alcohol Abuse. The linkage between drinking and wife beating is not a problem solely of poor, ethnic minorities. Kaufman Kantor and Straus (1987) found that, regardless of race, wife battering was seven times greater among binge drinking, blue-collar men who approved of wife slapping. Social isolation, economic marginalization, and a host of other stressors place segments of the African American, Latino (Kaufman Kantor, 1990), and American Indian (Asbury, 1993) communities at increased risk for heavy drinking, therefore making them more susceptible to alcohol-related wife assaults (Hampton, 1987). Research using the 1985 National Family Violence Survey (Kaufman Kantor, 1990) has linked high-volume drinking by Latino men to increased rates of partner violence. Specifically, Latinas with binge-drinking husbands were more than 10 times more likely to be assaulted than those with low-to moderate-drinking husbands. When ethnic group differences were investigated in the 1992 National Alcohol and Family Violence Survey, heavy-drinking Puerto Rican husbands were five times more likely than their nondrinking counterparts to hit their wives (Kaufman Kantor, in press). Similarly, the husband's heavy drinking was also found to be associated with partner violence among African Americans (Kaufman Kantor, 1990) and American Indians (Bachman, 1992). Researchers have not yet explored the linkage between drinking and Asian American violence.

Normative Approval of Violence. The endorsement of cultural norms sanctioning partner assaults, often measured by the item "Are there situations that you can imagine in which you would approve of a husband slapping his wife?" (Owens & Straus, 1975), has been linked to increased levels of partner violence. Using data from the First National Family Violence Survey, Straus and colleagues (1980) found that African Americans, when compared with whites, were more approving of both husband and wife slapping. It has been hypothesized, however, that economic inequalities contribute to more approving attitudes toward intimate violence. According to Oliver (1989), when traditional wage earner roles are unavailable, working-class black men take on alternative roles, which often emphasize physical violence and the sexual exploitation of women. Because black women have historically contributed economically to the household, they may be less tolerant of violence. Consequently, conflict may erupt in these relationships (Hampton et al., 1989; Ucko, 1994). Some empirical evidence supports the theory that social class accounts for the higher percentage of normative approval of violence by African Africans. Cazenave and Straus (1990) found that, when income and occupational status were taken into consideration, differences in approval of violence between blacks and whites disappeared.

The male-dominated Latino family structure and *machismo,* a cultural script characterized by sexual prowess and aggression, have been theoretically linked to more approving attitudes toward violence (Perilla et al., 1994; Zambrano, 1985). When tested empirically, studies have revealed that the endorsement of violent norms, regardless of ethnicity and income level, more than doubled the odds of husband-to-wife assault. Latino couples, however, were not significantly more male-dominated or accepting of violence than Anglo American couples (Jasinski, 1996; Kaufman Kantor et al., 1994).

Similarly, hierarchal family structures and rigid gender roles that emphasize male dominance and female submissiveness have been theoretically linked to battering among Asians (Ho, 1990; Rimonte, 1989). Results from focus group interviews imply ethnic group differences in cultural approval of violence. For example, on the basis of statements such as "Physical abuse of a wife once in a while is OK," Ho (1990) concluded that the Vietnamese, Khmer, and Laotians were more tolerant of abuse than the Chinese.

In conclusion, level of acculturation, alcohol abuse, and normative approval of violence do not occur in isolation (Perilla et al., 1994). Future research should consider factors that mediate the aforementioned variables and partner violence, such as work stress (Jasinski, Asdigian, & Kaufman Kantor, in press), relationship quality, and depression (Julian & McKenry, 1993).

What Are the Research Limitations?

Much of the information about ethnic minority partner violence is derived from anecdotal accounts, self-report surveys, incidence reports from public sources (e.g., FBI Uniform Crime Reports), and survey-based research. Although these sources provide valuable information, they can be biased in important ways. Anecdotal accounts, such as those collected by battered women's programs, provide excellent first-person accounts. They are often subjective, however, and based on small samples (Burns, 1986; White, 1984; Zambrano, 1985). Furthermore, they often represent the most severe cases of battering. Although self-administered surveys are more objective, most have failed to include illiterate participants and samples that are diverse enough to examine racial/ethnic differences. Despite the larger, more diverse samples used in government-sponsored reports, they frequently rely on public sources that are overwhelmingly used by minorities and the poor, such as the police and community health clinics (Kanuha, 1994). Large national probability studies have corrected these problems by including more representative samples and by oversampling African Americans (e.g., Straus & Gelles, 1986) and Latinos (e.g.,

Kaufman Kantor et al., 1994). Nevertheless, many have failed to include Asians, American Indians, and other groups with high representations of ethnic minorities, such as single-parent families, cohabiting couples, and families with children under age 3. Furthermore, the reliance on telephone interviews has resulted in an underrepresentation of non-English-speaking participants (Asbury, 1987; Lockhart, 1987).

The existing research is limited in other important ways as well. In particular, "ethnic lumping" has been a problem (Fontes, in press). In one type of ethnic lumping, for example, research on Latino Americans often assumes that Mexican Americans represent the experience of other Latino groups. A second type of ethnic lumping entails collapsing diverse ethnic groups—for instance, Japanese, Chinese, and Koreans—into one "Asian" group without consideration for their diverse experiences. Finally, much of the research is race comparative and relies on psychometric rating scales that are rarely normed by using diverse populations (Sorenson et al., 1996).

In summary, at first glance, partner violence appears to be more prevalent among African Americans, American Indians, and some Latino ethnic groups than among Anglos. On closer inspection, these ethnic differences often disappear when age, social class, and husband's employment status are taken into account. When ethnic differences remain, they may be explained by level of acculturation, binge drinking, and normative approval of violence. Despite the growing knowledge of violence in these groups, more empirical research needs to be conducted, particularly with Asian Americans and American Indians. Future research should compare violent ethnic minorities with their nonviolent counterparts. Also, research needs to be culturally sensitive, which includes using the participants' preferred languages, having minority researchers help design and conduct studies, and incorporating measures of acculturation and racial identity (Fontes, in press; Root, 1996; Sorenson et al., 1996).

Therapeutic Implications

The available data on ethnic minority partner violence need to be used in developing culturally appropriate and effective intervention strategies. This chapter takes the position that "success of the therapy depends less on the identity into which therapists are born than on their skills, knowledge, cultural competency, and genuine comfort with people of diverse cultures" (Fontes, 1995, p. 261). With this said, the following section focuses on three therapeutic issues: (a) obstacles that impede help seeking by battered women, (b) hallmarks of a culturally appropriate assessment, and (c) culture-specific treatment recommendations.

What Barriers Impede Help Seeking?

Scant empirical research has examined the extent and nature of help-seeking efforts by battered minority women. Research using both national probability (West, Jasinski, & Kaufman Kantor, 1997) and shelter samples (Gondolf et al., 1988; O'Keefe, 1994) revealed that Latinas reported receiving less help from family, friends, clergy, and social service agencies than black and Anglo women. Taken together, these findings point to a pattern of service underuse. According to the Latino mental health literature, cultural and institutional barriers, rather than lack of desire for services, impede minority help-seeking efforts (Rodriguez & O'Donnell, 1995). Community activists further argue that stereotypes concerning ethnic minority partner violence act as an additional obstacle (Richie & Kanuha, 1993). The following sections review the research on each of these barriers.

Cultural Barriers. Cultural barriers to help seeking consist of "subcultural values and beliefs that predispose those who identify with them to avoid use of specialty mental health" (Rodriguez & O'Donnell, 1995, p. 170). These barriers may take different forms for various ethnic groups. African Americans' strong religious beliefs that emphasize faith and prayers (Abney & Priest, 1995); Puerto Ricans' *cultural fatalism,* or belief that certain negative life events happen regardless of efforts to prevent them (Comas-Diaz, 1995); Asians' fear of dishonor and "losing face" (Ho, 1990); and American Indians' emphasis on endurance of misfortune may contribute to reluctance by assaulted women to seek assistance (LaFromboise et al., 1994). This is not to imply that some cultural beliefs are necessarily maladaptive. In fact, these tenets may have helped minority families survive great adversity. They become cultural barriers when they impede help seeking through formal or informal avenues. The extent to which cultural beliefs inhibit help seeking is governed by a combination of acculturation level, language skills, educational attainment, and socioeconomic status. For example, greater acculturated, educated, and second- and third-generation Latina and Asian battered women may be more familiar with, and accepting of, mental health services (Kanuha, 1994).

Institutional Barriers. Institutional barriers are characteristics of the agency delivery system that make it difficult for ethnic minorities to gain access to services (Rodriguez & O'Donnell, 1995). For instance, agencies may lack translators and bicultural/bilingual professionals, reading material in the client's native language, or ethnically sensitive treatment programs. Other structural barriers include rules against treating non-English-speaking or immigrant clients, geographic distance from minority communities, prohibitive fee structures, and inflexible or inconvenient hours of operation (Bachman, 1992; Chester et al., 1994; Comas-Diaz, 1995; Eng, 1995; Fontes, 1995; Williams, 1992). A political ideology that is contrary to community beliefs may present a challenge to help seeking as well. For example, shelters that discourage the involvement of men of color or agencies that attribute battering solely to sexism, rather than consider other forms of oppression such as racism and class privilege, may be perceived as unlikely sources of help (Crenshaw, 1994). Williams (1994) found evidence of the aforementioned institutional barriers in a national survey of 142 domestic partner violence treatment programs. In particular, program coordinators admitted that more than one half (55%) of the agencies were located in Anglo neighborhoods, 15% did not provide training on ethnic minority issues, 70% did not have manuals or literature concerning culturally sensitive practice methods, and 61% did not have bilingual counselors. When these institutional barriers were removed, community agencies reported an increase in ethnic minority clients (Rimonte, 1989).

Racial Stereotypes. Racial stereotypes have been hypothesized to pose barriers to help seeking for numerous reasons. Specifically, if legal and social service agency workers characterize people of color as inherently violent, they may view intervention efforts as futile (Hawkins, 1987). Stereotypes may also lead professionals to underestimate the impact of abuse on minority women or to overestimate the ability of these women to cope (Brice-Baker, 1994). Ammons (1995) concluded that images of black women as "either very strong or somehow inherently bad, but never weak or passive" (p. 1007) have contributed to battered black women receiving less help from the criminal justice system.

Furthermore, the internalization of stereotypes (e.g., black women as "emasculating matriarchs," Latinas as "hot-blooded") may contribute to some women of color not perceiving themselves as victims or in less need of help (Brice-Baker, 1994; Rasche, 1988). The fear of reinforcing stereotypes, coupled with community and family loyalty, may encourage other women to hide their abuse. For example, one battered Korean American woman feared that her coworkers would believe that "there was something wrong with Korean people" if they learned of her abuse (Richie & Kanuha, 1993 p. 291).

What Are the Hallmarks of a Culturally Appropriate Assessment?

A culturally appropriate assessment should include the same demographic and background information that would be gathered from any other client or family (e.g., history of substance abuse, mental illness). Therapists should also explore the following areas relevant to minorities (Abney & Priest, 1995; Chan & Leong, 1994; Comas-Diaz, 1995; LaFromboise et al., 1994; Okamura et al., 1995):

Race/Ethnicity. Ethnic identities of all family members should be carefully assessed. It would be a mistake to assume that every visibly black client identifies as African American. These clients may identify as West Indian or African-Caribbean. Among Asians, the father may be Chinese, the mother Laotian, and the children might define themselves as Chinese-Laotian Americans. The ethnic identity of Latinos and American Indians should also be considered. It is best to ask the client how he or she identifies.

Economic Status. Objective measures of economic status should be obtained (e.g., amount and source of income, ability to meet basic needs). Subjective measures should be considered as well. For example, how is the family's economic status perceived in comparison with others in the neighborhood or the extended family?

Family Structure. Clarifying boundaries and family roles (e.g., wage earner, child caretaker) will provide information about family power structure. Additional information about the family support network can be gathered by asking questions about, for example, the location and amount of contact with relatives and economic support provided to or obtained from family members.

Level of Acculturation. Information about acculturation can be gathered from language preference and immigration history:

- Several languages may be spoken or comprehended. Therapists should carefully assess preferred language among ethnic groups. For example, which language does the client prefer to speak at work and home? Awareness of language nuances is important as well; that is, *battering* may have a different meaning, depending on the language. Therapists should make sure that communication is clear.
- Premigration and postmigration history of the family will give clues about significant stressors. Important areas to explore include loss of property and homeland or significant people (through death and separation); changes in status (e.g., inability to obtain employment); and effects of culture shock and displacement.

Prior Exposure to Violence. Personal history of incest and child physical abuse (Lujan, DeBruyn, May, & Bird, 1989; West & Williams, 1997) should be assessed. It is also important to evaluate family history of trauma (e.g., lynchings, war atrocities) for several reasons:

- Prior exposure to violence, such as living in high-crime areas, may heighten the effects of a trauma, including partner violence (Allen, 1996).
- Interviews about partner violence may trigger memories of traumatic historic events (e.g., a Cambodian being interviewed about wife assault may remember the interrogations she faced in resettlement camps; Fontes, in press).
- Second and third generations may minimize partner abuse when they compare it with previous family and historic traumas (Yoshihama et al., 1991).

Suicide Potentiality. Battered Asian American (Crites, 1990) and black women (Stark & Flitcraft, 1995) are at increased risk for suicide attempts. It is wise to conduct a suicide assessment with clients from all ethnic backgrounds.

Cultural Coping Strategies. Therapists should assess family strengths, as well as past and current family coping strategies. These could include family rituals or religious practices, such as visiting healers (Comas-Diaz, 1995) or sweat lodges (Williams & Ellison, 1996).

What Are Culture-Specific Treatment Recommendations?

An effective treatment program must take into account the specific culture, beliefs, and traditions of the treated population. For example, an "Afrocentric perspective" may be more appropriate for African Americans (a worldview framed by African American historic traditions of racial pride and respect for family and community; Abney & Priest, 1995, pp. 13-20; Campbell, 1993).

Although many treatment recommendations for ethnic populations are based on clinical and anecdotal accounts (Eng, 1995; Ho, 1990; White, 1994; Zambrano, 1985), they may be beneficial for some minority clients. The following sections review these recommendations:

Treatment of Female Victims

Determining the appropriate therapeutic format is important. An ethnic minority woman who perceives someone outside her community as more objective and able to maintain confidentiality may prefer an ethnically different therapist, whereas other minority women may believe that only a person of similar ethnic background can understand their issues. These women may prefer community resources (White, 1994).

Support groups can reduce the level of isolation and provide social support if a woman experiences community ostracism. Shame and fear of bringing humiliation on the family, however, may make this a less effective milieu for some ethnic groups, such as Southeast Asians (Kanuha, 1987). The fear of reinforcing stereotypes about minority men or concerns about revealing family or community affairs to outsiders may make racially mixed groups uncomfortable for some Latinas (Zambrano, 1985) or black women (White, 1994). Mental health professionals should discuss these concerns in detail with clients before deciding on the appropriate therapeutic format.

With any client, establishing rapport is important. Providing legal and employment information for undocumented women without directly inquiring about the clients' immigration status is one method of building trust (Zambrano, 1985). Depending on the level of acculturation and assimilation, indirect questioning, use of metaphor, or third-party references may be more effective; for example, some Asian women respond better when asked about ways to help a fictitious friend who has been victimized (Huisman, 1996; Kanuha, 1987). Less acculturated or immigrant women may need more advocacy and help negotiating the system. They may prefer a hierarchal relationship, with the therapist being very directive, rather than asking open-ended questions (Franco, 1996; Rimonte, 1989). It is recommended that therapists take their lead from the clients.

Therapists are encouraged to discuss discrimination when appropriate. This discussion can be facilitated by pointing out the similarities and differences between institutional and individual abuse. For instance, it might be beneficial to explore ways the client experienced domination, isolation, and threats as a woman, minority, and victim of partner violence (Crites, 1990; NiCarthy, 1982). Addressing cultural barriers that impede help seeking might also be advantageous. One goal is to reframe cultural beliefs in a way that empowers battered women. For example, the therapist can reassure the client that revealing the abuse and seeking help are not a "loss of face" or betrayal to the ethnic community and that, instead, they can be acts of courage and means of improving the family and community (Dao, 1988; Dunwoody, 1982; Ho, 1990). Ultimately, therapists should respect a woman's right to choose which aspects of her culture to embrace, rather than force her to adhere to dominant cultural expectations.

Therapists are also encouraged to provide a welcoming environment for ethnic minority clients and their children. A visible display of books, artwork, and toys depicting characters of different racial backgrounds can convey openness (Coley & Beckett, 1988). If shelter services are necessary, culturally sensitive accommodation should be sought (e.g., those with bilingual counselors, ethnic foods, and hair care products; Sorenson et al., 1996). Cultural resources also can be used if the woman prefers. Some programs for American Indian battered women are now integrating traditional herbs, foods, meditation, and ceremonies to complement psychoeducational therapy (Kanuha, 1994). Additional options include consulting with extended family members, community elders, or healers (Ho, 1990). Translators have been recommended as well. If possible, children should not be asked to function in this role. Therapists should be aware of confidentiality and power dynamics if the translator is an influential community member (Huisman, 1996). Whatever help sources are used, they should be supportive, knowledgeable about partner violence, and willing to adhere to the client's self-determination.

Treatment of Male Batterers

Much of the research on male batterers is theoretical and addresses the treatment of African American men (Dennis, Key, Kirk, & Smith, 1995; Williams, 1992; Williams & Becker, 1994). Many therapeutic goals for abusive black men are similar to those for Anglo men: (a) preventing violence by focusing on conflict resolution, (b) developing interpersonal skills, and (c) improving poor communication (Campbell, 1993; Dennis et al., 1995).

Several recommendations, however, are made for culturally sensitive practice. First, treatment tactics that label black abusers as devoid of positive personal or social characteristics or that require clients to view themselves as "sick" should be avoided. African American men are likely to resist these strategies because they perceive them as punitive. Instead, the focus should be the client's capacity for change and his responsibility to participate in the treatment process. Therapists also must be prepared to discuss racism and other forms of discrimination while continuing to challenge the batterer to be accountable for his behavior (Williams, 1992).

Group therapy can be a particularly effective treatment modality for black batterers. Racially homogeneous groups are effective because they create an increased level of trust by group members. Black batterers often experience a greater identification with themes discussed in the group (e.g., experience with personal and institutional racism). The group environment is also consistent with black men's help-seeking patterns of confiding in community members. Mixed-race groups can be effective as well if therapists create a trusting environment. This entails resisting "color blindness" or attempts to respond to all clients as ethnically similar. In addition, it means a willingness to discuss the impact of racism within the group and to challenge racist comments if they occur. To be safe, it might be beneficial for groups to have at least two men of color (Williams & Becker, 1994).

In summary, despite stereotypes about ethnic minority partner violence and cultural and institutional barriers, these groups seek help from both formal and informal sources. When assistance is sought, a culturally appropriate assessment that takes into account race, level of acculturation, economic status, and prior exposure to violence should be conducted. Effective therapeutic intervention requires culturally appropriate and ethnically sensitive treatment.

Policy Recommendations

Based on the literature, the following policy recommendations are given (Franco, 1996; Jasinski, 1996; Williams & Becker, 1994):

1. Improved research on ethnic minority populations is required. Specifically, more information is needed on prevalence and incidence of partner violence, nature and characteristics of abuse, and contributing factors. In addition, more research should be conducted on ethnic group differences as well as generational status, gender, age, and socioeconomic differences in partner violence.

2. Future research efforts should focus on culturally appropriate education concerning partner violence. Information can be disseminated through word of mouth, community leaders, religious institutions, ethnic events, and English-as-a-second-language classes. Community hotlines can also be established for victims and batterers who are reluctant to be identified.

3. "Culturally competent" shelters and counseling services should be established. This entails networking with the minority community, using outside consultants with expertise in minority issues, and employing at least one bilingual counselor.

4. Most important, factors that contribute to minority partner violence, including poverty and lack of educational opportunities, must be addressed.

Note

1. Although the Violence Against Women Act (VAWA), signed by President Bill Clinton in September 1994, provides greater protection for battered immigrants, it is still too early to tell whether they are benefitting from its passage. The reader is referred to the following resources for a more detailed discussion of legal matters faced by battered women: Anderson, 1993; Franco, 1996; Huisman, 1996; Jang et al., 1990; Narayan, 1995; and Orloff, Jang, & Klein, 1995.

CHAPTER SEVEN

Partner Violence

Prevention and Intervention

SHERRY L. HAMBY

T his chapter provides a review of the literature on prevention and
intervention of partner violence. It is divided into three main
sections. The first focuses on *prevention,* or efforts to reduce the numbers of individuals who become violent. The second concentrates on
interventions, which are responses to violence that has already occurred. The final section focuses on *training and personal issues* that
should be addressed by all individuals who work with violent individuals and their victims.

Primary and Secondary Prevention of Partner Violence

Purpose of Prevention Review

This section on prevention has three purposes: (a) defining prevention and how it applies to partner violence, (b) describing the
scope of current partner violence prevention efforts, and (c) evaluating whether they work. Most prevention efforts involve complex,
multifaceted programs. This section attempts to provide some flavor
of the main programs. For in-depth descriptions of programs, the
reader will want to consult the manuals and publications of the spon-

soring organizations. In-person training programs are the best preparation for providers who wish to conduct such programs themselves, and many programs offer such training.

What Is Prevention?

Prevention means *addressing a problem before it starts.* Prevention efforts are usually classified into three main categories: primary, secondary, and tertiary. *Primary prevention* refers to educational or other programs that are offered to everyone in a community or social group. A good example of a primary prevention program is childhood immunization. Immunizing everyone for polio, measles, and similar diseases ensures that epidemics of these diseases are prevented. In the United States, the goal is 100% immunization even though only a relatively small percentage of the population would develop these diseases even if no immunizations were given. The emphasis is on the safety of the whole community. In the case of programs such as immunization, prevention is also very cost-effective because it costs much less to immunize than it would to treat the thousands of people who would otherwise get these serious illnesses.

Secondary prevention involves identifying a high-risk sample of the population and providing extra services to only that segment. Once again, the services are provided before any problems arise. A good example of a secondary prevention program is Head Start. Head Start identifies preschool children who are likely to develop problems in school and provides these children with special preschool programs that emphasize school readiness. Head Start uses social services, pediatric clinics, community centers, and other providers to identify the at-risk children. The goal is to provide assistance to these children before they begin to fail at school. Secondary prevention is a good option when at-risk groups can be reliably identified and either the costs of prevention are too high to provide the additional services to the whole community or some risk is involved in receiving the additional services (flu shots are an example of the latter).

Tertiary prevention focuses on people who already have the identified problem and tries to stop future occurrences or relapses. Thus, tertiary prevention means the same thing that most people mean by intervention or treatment. The lines between these three kinds of prevention are often not razor sharp. For example, an educational program may have the dual effects of reducing society's tolerance for partner violence (primary prevention) and telling victims how to get help and protect themselves (intervention). *Intervention* is the term used throughout this chapter to describe efforts aimed at helping domestically violent individuals and their victims—all those who already have the problem of violence in their lives—lead nonviolent and safe lives. These programs are discussed in the intervention section. In most fields of psychology, when people speak of prevention, they usually mean either primary or secondary prevention. These kinds of programs are the focus of this section on prevention.

Prevention and intervention programs of all kinds can focus on two kinds of factors that are important in understanding a problem: risk factors and protective factors (Bogenschneider, 1996). *Risk factors* are behaviors or conditions that increase the chances of having a problem; *protective factors* are behaviors or conditions that decrease the chances of having a problem or, if it occurs, decrease the chances of having a bad outcome. Historically, most programs have emphasized risk factors, but an increasing number are focusing on protective factors (Bogenschneider, 1996).

What Does It Mean to Prevent Partner Violence?

Using these terms, prevention means working with *nondomestically violent* individuals in ways that will help them stay nonviolent. Sometimes these individuals already have spouses or partners, but sometimes programs are aimed at people before they get into relationships. Some programs are targeted at entire communities (e.g., public service announcements), and some are targeted at high-risk populations. Some prevention programs focus on risk factors, such as increasing public awareness about the harmful effects of partner violence and trying to change attitudes that accept or promote violence. Other programs focus on protective factors, such as providing skills and information about healthy relationships to students in junior high and high schools and teaching newly engaged or married couples nonviolent conflict resolution skills.

Current Partner Violence Prevention Strategies

In general, the number of prevention programs has increased considerably in recent years, and many communities and organizations have developed programs and curricula. Most of these programs are still quite new. Unfortunately, many of the curricula have not been published, and accessibility is often poor. Evaluations of these programs are even less commonly available.

Community-Level Strategies

Reducing Societal Tolerance for Partner Violence. Many professionals who work in the field of partner violence advocate for changing attitudes that are essentially tolerant of partner violence, especially by working with community institutions such as religious organizations, workplaces, schools, and the media (Jackson & Garvin, 1995; Koss et al., 1994; Tifft, 1993). They cite studies, such as the one conducted by Peterson and Pfost (1989), that indicate exposure to certain media, such as violent rock videos, can increase adversarial sexual beliefs and other attitudes thought to be associated with partner violence. Organizations such as the Family Violence Prevention Fund prepare posters, public service announcements, and similar materials for these purposes. Every state and the District of Columbia have coalitions against partner violence. Many of them concentrate on providing services and resources to victims, but many also focus on increasing public awareness of the problem, lobby for more community attention to the problem, and generally try to reduce tolerance of aggression in intimate relationships. These latter goals all have preventive effects in that they try to decrease the prevalence of risk factors. The Pennsylvania Coalition Against Partner Violence, for instance, recommends 15 citizen action steps to help end partner violence. Several of these focus on community-level prevention strategies, which are quoted below:

- Cultivate a respectful attitude toward women in your family and at your workplace. Avoid behaviors that demean or control women.
- When you are angry at your partner or children, respond without hurting or humiliating them. Model a nonviolent, respectful response to resolving conflicts in your family.
- Develop a women's safety campaign in your workplace, neighborhood, school, or house of worship. Build a consensus among your colleagues and neighbors that abusive behavior and language are unacceptable.
- Bring together your local partner violence program staff, parents, teachers, students, and school administrators to start a discussion about developing a school-based curriculum on dating and family violence.

- Ask your local partner violence program about important pending legislation. Urge your local, state, and federal elected officials to support partner violence legislation and increased funding for services and prevention. Ask candidates to identify their platform for ending partner violence. Hold them accountable for their commitments.
- Write to music and movie companies, video game producers, and television stations to speak out about violence against women.
- In your involvement with religious and civic organization, encourage projects that raise consciousness about partner violence. Ask your local day care center, substance abuse prevention program, and teen pregnancy prevention program to include support for battered women and their children in their efforts.

Some authors (e.g., Paymar, 1993) believe that formerly violent men should also get involved in these kinds of community efforts by joining antiviolence organizations, putting the topic of violence on the agenda of community organizations, and lobbying for tougher laws. For some men, going public with their stories can be a particularly powerful means of educating others (Paymar, 1993).

Making Structural and Economic Changes. Many advocates for the primary prevention of family violence argue that structural and economic changes in society are needed (Campbell, 1991; Dobash & Dobash, 1992; Hackler, 1991; Tifft, 1993). Hackler (1991) advocates broad-based economic programs that reduce family strain. He cites the Canadian Family Allowance, which is provided to all mothers of young children (rich and poor), as a model program that can help markedly reduce the incidence of family violence. Anthropological data indicate that societies that both culturally sanction partner violence and provide women with the most economic, political, and social resources are generally the least violent (Campbell, 1991; Levinson, 1989). Some authors (Campbell, 1991; Tifft, 1993) argue that hierarchical forms of social organization, especially intrafamilial organization, need to be avoided if partner violence is to be prevented. Also, the value of all individuals needs to be preserved regardless of gender or other characteristics (Tifft, 1993).

Other social factors have been identified as causes of violence that need to be addressed. Exploitation of individuals through labor practices, social customs, feminization of poverty, and other global and societal structural elements contribute directly to the occurrence of partner violence. So does tolerance of other violent behaviors, especially other family violence, such as corporal punishment (Tifft, 1993). One study has, in fact, shown an association between childhood corporal punishment and later spousal assault (Straus & Yodanis, 1995). Some shelters have implemented programs aimed at preventing the intergenerational transmission of violence by targeting parenting skills and by offering counseling to children (Hughes, 1982).

Reframing Partner Violence as a Human Rights Violation. One recent approach to changing societal attitudes and structural supports for domestic violence has been to link partner violence with human rights violations (Copelon, 1994; Fitzpatrick, 1994; Roth, 1994; Stark & Flitcraft, 1995). The authors of these approaches focus on three aspects of partner violence that are similar to other human rights violations. First, some extreme forms of partner violence involve behaviors that could be described as torture, including the element of captivity (Copelon, 1994). Second, the political effects of domestic violence, especially the ongoing subordination of women, are compared with those of torture. Finally, these authors argue that, contrary to common perceptions, there are reasons to implicate the state as a blameworthy agent because of its implicit or, in some countries, explicit tolerance of partner violence that essentially produces a situation of public legitimation.

One primary focus of these efforts is to increase the international consensus that partner violence is harmful and illegitimate, with a long-term goal of increasing the number of societal resources devoted to the problem (Copelon, 1994). Many who advocate for the reclassification of partner violence as a human rights violation want international organizations, such as the United Nations, to draft and implement declarations that acknowledge the status of partner violence as a human rights violation (Fitzpatrick, 1994). Many of these advocacy efforts include other forms of violence as well, such as genital mutilation and rape. Recently, the first indictment of rape as a war crime was handed down by the Bosnian war crimes tribunal, indicating that this movement may be meeting with some success.

Family and Individual-Level Strategies

Programs for Couples. A longitudinal study has suggested that couples who are psychologically aggressive (but not physically violent) prior to marriage are at increased risk for violence in the early months of marriage (Murphy & O'Leary, 1989). Other cross-sectional research has also suggested that severe psychological aggression is a marker for physical violence (Hamby, Straus, & Sugarman, 1997).

These kinds of findings lend support to the idea that teaching communication and conflict resolution skills early in a relationship can help prevent future violence (and other marital problems). This is a major focus of many programs that promote violence prevention by trying to create conditions that facilitate healthier relationships. Thus, these programs are examples of approaches that focus on protective factors more than on risk factors. One of the best known of these programs is the Prevention and Relationship Enhancement Program (PREP), developed by Howard Markman and his colleagues (Markman, Renick, Floyd, Stanley, & Clements, 1993). PREP, like most relationship training and enhancement programs, does not expressly address partner violence. Rather, PREP uses cognitive-behavioral techniques to teach such skills as active listening, expressive speaking, and problem solving. Consultants are available to provide immediate feedback to participating couples as they complete the exercises. Couples practice the skills during a relatively short-term program that is typically offered either as a weekend workshop or a 5- to 6-week course (Renick, Blumberg, & Markman, 1992). In contrast with marital therapy, PREP focuses on the future of the relationship, not directly on current problems.

Programs for Teens. Numerous programs try to educate teens about violent behavior in the hopes that they will not become perpetrators or victims of intimate violence (Jaffe, Sudermann, Reitzel, & Killip, 1992; Jones, 1991; Kaufman Kantor & Jasinski, 1995; Powell, 1991; Sousa, 1991). Most of these are school-based programs that target junior high or high school students. Recently, however, calls have been made to expand these programs into elementary schools (Koss et al., 1994). Of course, some teens will already be engaging in violence at the time any schoolwide program is initiated, but the major thrust of these programs is primary prevention.

Most of these programs have several elements in common: (a) defining violence and violent relationships and dispelling myths about violence; (b) examining societal messages about gender roles, power, and violence; and (c) brainstorming about techniques to prevent violence from emerging in the students' lives and communities. Role playing is a technique adopted by some programs (Sousa, 1991). Some suggest that peer counseling is a particularly effective means of reaching teens (Powell, 1991; Sousa, 1991). Others incorporate speakers from community agencies and formerly battered women (Jaffe et al., 1992). Some programs, such as the Minnesota School Curriculum Project (Jones, 1991), focus on training teachers rather than students so that the teachers can go back to their schools and reach greater numbers of children than would be possible by one program alone. Some programs (Jaffe et al., 1992; Kaufman Kantor & Jasinski, 1995) involve parents and administrators as well to develop a long-term prevention plan.

Does Prevention of Partner Violence Work?

Evaluation of Attitude and Social Change Programs. Few studies have evaluated the results of the specific efforts to change attitudes about partner violence at the community level or the efforts to change social structures. One study of the effects of televised public service announcements in a Texas community (Davis, 1996) found an 11.8% increase in all hotline calls after adjusting for a concurrent decrease in hotline staff. Referrals from the television station increased even more dramatically. Well-publicized incidents, such as the battering that Nicole Brown Simpson experienced, are also often associated with an increase in hotline calls (Jones, 1995), but no formal studies have examined this phenomenon. A study of a media campaign on general crime prevention did show specific increases in public awareness from the campaign (Sacco & Trotman, 1990). Public awareness of child abuse appears to be increasing in the United States (Straus & Gelles, 1986), and it is likely that this is true for domestic violence as well. Two Canadian studies have shown an increase in awareness over time (Sacco & Trotman, 1990). Current attitudes in the United States appear to show intolerance of partner violence, but it is less clear whether attitudes about domestic violence at the societal level affect how victims perceive their own situations (Hamby & Gray-Little, 1996).

Evaluation of Couples Programs. Few evaluations of the effects of couples programs on partner violence have been conducted. Markman and colleagues (1993) conducted a good outcome study of PREP that included a control group and a group that declined the intervention, as well as the group that actually received the intervention. All were followed over several years. Only the 3-, 4-, and 5-year follow-ups included measures of violence (initial levels of violence were not assessed). At all these years, rates of violence were lowest for couples receiving the intervention, although only significantly lower in comparison with couples in the control group. Other benefits of PREP, such as improved communication between spouses, were also found. A study of the efficacy of PREP with at-risk couples that have already experienced "destructive conflict" (secondary prevention) is underway (Holtzworth-Munroe, Markman, O'Leary, & Neidig, 1995).

Evaluation of Programs for Teens. A few evaluation studies of teen programs have been completed. A Canadian study reported the most promising results to date (Lavoie, Vezina, Piche, & Boivin, 1995). The researchers reported improvement in both knowledge and attitudes for brief programs of two to four 1-hour sessions. One evaluation of a 5-day program (Jones, 1991) reported success in increasing knowledge about partner violence among junior high and high school students but not in changing attitudes (e.g., "It is never OK to slap the person you are in a relationship with"). In an evaluation of another 5-day program, Kaufman Kantor and Jasinski (1995) found that all students, including both those who did and who did not receive the program, improved somewhat in knowledge, attitudes, and behaviors by the time of the 1-year follow-up, suggesting at least some maturational effects. The program itself did not appear to have consistent results across the evaluation measures. Jaffe and associates (1992), in an evaluation of a shorter (½ to 1-day) program, found similarly mixed results in follow-ups that took place between 1 and 6 weeks after the program. In the Jaffe et al. study, some attitude and knowledge measures did change in the desired direction after the program, but some also changed in the undesired direction, especially among males. This finding is sometimes called a "backlash" effect of educational programs. The results of the above studies are not more conclusive, however, because none used standardized questionnaires to measure knowledge or attitudes about partner violence. Most of these interventions were also quite short, and it is not clear whether longer programs would have greater or more consistent impact.

Summary of Prevention Review

Recent years have seen a large increase in prevention programs for both adolescents and adults. Although a "gold standard" still has not been established for such programs, many incorporate similar elements that focus on identifying abusive behavior and trying to decrease tolerance for violence. Some programs, such as PREP (Markman et al., 1993), focus on protective factors more than on risk factors, and early results suggest that this focus may be a very promising avenue. Future prevention efforts may increasingly focus on teaching healthy relationship skills in addition to, or possibly even to the exclusion of, warning people about the dangers of abusive relationships.

Interventions for Partner Violence

Purpose of Intervention Review

This section on intervention has three purposes: (a) defining interventions that are targeted toward partner violence, (b) describing the scope of current partner violence intervention efforts, and (c) evaluating whether they work. Because there is generally more literature on perpetrator interventions than on victim interventions, perpetrator interventions are discussed first in each section.

The descriptions of various approaches attempt to communicate the main thrust of each. It is important to emphasize, however, that obtaining expertise in partner violence intervention requires specialized education. For in-depth descriptions of programs, consult the manuals and publications of the developers. In-person training programs are the best preparation for providers who wish to conduct such programs themselves, and many programs offer such training.

What Is Intervention?

Intervention, in contrast with primary or secondary prevention, means *trying to eliminate or improve an existing problem and trying to stop future occurrences or relapses.* In cases of partner violence, this usually means helping people lead nonviolent and safe lives. For mental health providers, responding to partner violence is more complicated than responding to many psychological problems. Why?

Because partner violence is also a crime; this means both perpetrators and victims are involved (in contrast with, for example, depression or schizophrenia, neither of which inherently involve victims and perpetrators or even multiple individuals). It is also possible that one person can be both perpetrator and victim in some circumstances (discussed in more detail below). The criminal status of partner violence also means that the legal system is often involved and that a major concern of many interventions is *not* therapeutic change, but rather social control and safety. The term *intervention* is used throughout this chapter to refer to more conventional mental health approaches to partner violence and also to legal and other approaches that focus on social control. As with prevention efforts, these approaches may incorporate interventions targeted at either decreasing risk factors or increasing protective factors.

Historical Overview

Female victims of partner violence were the primary focus of attention when partner violence gained wide recognition as a social problem in the 1970s. Early inquiries into this problem tended to derive from either grassroots shelter movements (Pizzey, 1974) or traditional psychiatric viewpoints. Among the latter, several early papers achieved notoriety for emphasizing the provocative and masochistic behavior of victims (Gabbard, 1981; Gayford, 1976; Snell, Rosenwald, & Robey, 1964). A particularly egregious example (Gayford, 1976) classified victims into types such as "Tortured Tina," "Fanny the Flirt," and "Go-Go Gloria." Thorough critical evaluations of these approaches (Caplan, 1985; Hilberman, 1980; Pagelow, 1981b) contributed, in part, to a subsequent move away from an often harmful focus on victim behavior to a focus on social control.

Because of this increased emphasis on social control, interventions for perpetrators of partner violence have grown exponentially in the last 15 years. The first program specifically designed for batterers did not open its doors until 1977 (Adams, 1994), but changes in the laws of most states have made them a fixture of many large legal jurisdictions. Several hundred programs specifically for batterers now exist (Edleson & Tolman, 1992). Most states now also have pro-arrest laws (Adams, 1994) that have resulted in large increases in the use of arrest and other legal interventions. Couples therapy is also still a common intervention. The effectiveness of these programs is controversial, as is the appropriate balance between social control and therapeutic interventions.

An unfortunate by-product of this trend toward social control is that services for victims have developed more slowly in recent years than those for batterers. Services for victims have not changed dramatically in the last 20 years; they still tend to be organized around community-based shelters that emphasize ensuring the immediate safety of victims. Many also provide legal advocacy and social services. On the one hand, interventions for victims aimed at ameliorating the aftereffects of trauma exist but are not as coordinated or as widely available as batterers programs and shelters. On the other hand, interventions for batterers have been in a period of rapid development and change for the last 10 to 15 years. One reason for this discrepancy is that evaluating the psychological status of victims, even for the purpose of evaluating outcome or facilitating recovery, is still controversial. Many professionals believe that "psychologizing" the problem of violence should be avoided (Bowker, 1993; Common Purpose, 1996; Rosewater, 1988); they believe that mental health approaches excessively pathologize victims. Others, however, believe that psychological outcomes are an important consequence of violence and need to be addressed (Walker, 1993).

Community-Based Services

Community members who are motivated to respond to partner violence are often prompted by a desire to make their communities less violent. They may be more likely than mental health providers to see partner violence as stemming from societal problems and therefore in need of a societal, or at least a communitywide, response. As one might expect, virtually all community-based services focus primarily on social control of perpetrators and safety for victims and other community members. Batterers programs, shelters, and police and judicial responses are the main types of community services. Individual psychopathology or relationship skills deficits are rarely the focus of community services. Historically, there has been considerable animosity between community advocates and mental health professionals because of these differences in the focus of interventions.

Batterers Programs: Single-Gender Group Intervention

Most current programs that specifically address partner violence are groups designed for male batterers. Most clients are court-ordered into these groups, and the programs typically maintain close contact with probation and parole officers. In one study, over two thirds of all members were court-ordered, and some programs reported that 100% of members were court-referred (Finn, 1987). In fact, the original impetus for many of these groups was a twin desire to increase the safety of women who remained with perpetrators and to provide a more acceptable sentencing option for judges, which would make arrests and convictions of batterers more likely (Bodnarchuk, Kropp, Ogloff, Hart, & Dutton, 1995). One study did find that district attorneys and probation officers in California had generally favorable attitudes toward diversion to batterers programs (Kaci & Tarrant, 1988). Members are often simultaneously in substance abuse treatment as well.

Men in batterers programs are a relatively dangerous population: One study estimated that, on the basis of norms from the National Family Violence Surveys conducted by Straus and Gelles, their clients fell into the most violent 1% of the U.S. population (Bodnarchuk et al., 1995). Programs do not limit themselves, however, to addressing severely violent perpetrators, and few, if any, programs change their interventions to address different levels of violence. The primary goals of virtually all batterers groups are (a) ensuring the female partners' safety, (b) altering attitudes toward violence, (c) increasing perpetrators' sense of personal responsibility, and (d) learning nonviolent alternatives to past behaviors (Edleson & Tolman, 1992). Some authors, however, believe that these goals place unrealistic demands on perpetrators (e.g., Jennings, 1990). Psychoeducational techniques are commonly used in these groups. Some authors believe that the achievement of these goals follows a developmental path that begins with denial and proceeds only slowly to acceptance and behavior change (Adams, 1989; Gondolf, 1987a). The major models currently in use are described briefly below. In general, all the programs begin with an analysis of risk factors that promote violence and use educational techniques to try to reduce those risk factors.

Approaches That Focus on Power and Control (e.g., Duluth and Emerge Programs). Several group treatments for batterers have developed out of the shelter movement and focus primarily on power and control issues. According to a 1990 report, about one fifth of a sample of batterers programs were using this model (Gondolf, 1990). Although there are differences between models, they all share a similar analysis of male violence against women. In these models, physical violence and other forms of abuse are seen to be intentional methods of maintaining control in the relationship (Adams, Bancroft, German, & Sousa, 1992; Common Purpose, 1996; Pence & Paymar, 1993), and the male batterer is seen to be completely responsible for the violence and abuse. Using violence is seen to be a part of an agenda to control the relationship, and men are often described as being quite skilled in their use of violence and other coercive and intimidating tactics. Changes in the batterer's personality, in the relationship, or regarding other issues are explicitly *not* a focus of these programs. Thus, some programs have moved away from the term *treatment* to the term *intervention* (Common Purpose, 1996). Such distinctions do affect how the programs are conducted and evaluated. For example, re-arrest might be a setback from a treatment perspective but a successful safety intervention. Another consequence of these programs' analysis of male violence is that they do not condone couples therapy or individual psychological treatment when violence against women is involved.

In all of these groups, admitting to controlling and abusive behaviors without using denial, minimization, or victim blaming is an important goal. *Denial* is the most primitive of these three defenses because the perpetrator refuses to admit that he was violent. Phrases such as "Somehow she fell" or "I never laid a hand on her" are common examples of denial. *Minimization* involves making the event sound trivial or harmless, such as "I just grabbed her," "It didn't really hurt," and similar pronouncements. *Victim blaming* involves making it sound as if the victim's behavior was so provocative that violence was the only possible response—for example, "She just kept going on and on, digging at me constantly" or "She hit me first." Two primary goals of these programs are getting men to admit to what they have done and to recognize that they always have a choice about how they will respond. Confrontation is often used in an effort to change these defenses, although some providers who focus on power and control issues use less confrontational strategies, such as storytelling, to get the message across (Sakai, 1991).

In addition to discussion around these themes, several techniques are taught to help prevent future violence; this practice is generally known as *safety planning.* "Watching for cues" involves becoming aware of bodily responses, emotions, and situations associated with violence and breaking the chain of events before violence occurs. Changing "self-talk" from negative (e.g., "I'll make her pay if she doesn't stop") to positive (e.g., "This isn't worth going to jail") is another goal. Additionally, "time-outs," when mutually agreed upon by both the batterer and his partner, are brief (usually 20–30 minute) cooldown periods followed by a calmer discussion of the disagreement.

Progress in keeping violence-free is monitored, in part, by batterers' self-reports and police records but also by partner contact. Batterers must consent to partner contact. What women say is kept confidential if they ask for that, again in the interest of promoting safety. Partner contact is also used as a means of ensuring that partners are not hearing distorted messages about the content of the group from batterers (e.g., "They told me I should just take off if I am feeling violent," which is not how time-outs are supposed to occur).

Approaches That Focus on Anger Management. Sonkin and Durphy (1985) were among the first to develop programs that emphasize anger management. The underlying philosophy of the anger management model is that violent individuals have problems with anger in that they dwell on anger, easily escalate during confrontations, and spend much time in an angry frame of mind. In 1990, about one quarter of a sample of batterers programs used this approach (Gondolf, 1990). Time-outs and positive self-talk were originally introduced in this curriculum and later adopted by other approaches (Common Purpose, 1996). An emphasis on addressing concurrent substance abuse problems is also common to both anger management and power and control approaches. In contrast with power and control approaches, however, this approach identifies skills deficits as a major problem for violent men. Thus, these programs are also likely to include teaching assertive communication skills, emotional expressiveness, and stress reduction and relaxation techniques (Hamberger & Hastings, 1988b; Sonkin & Durphy, 1985). Anger management approaches place less emphasis on the elements of control and coercion that are often present in battering, and at least one author has described power and control and anger management approaches as opposite ends of a continuum (Gondolf, 1990), in part, because power and control approaches focus more on societal-level risk factors, whereas anger management approaches focus more on individual-level impulse control problems.

Eclectic Approaches. Many programs are eclectic in nature and combine elements of both above approaches. In Gondolf's (1990) survey of 30 programs, over one half used some combination of communication, relaxation, assertiveness, self-talk, and responsibility skills. The approach used by Bodnarchuk and associates (1995) is a good example of an eclectic approach. These researchers use a cognitive-behavioral model that incorporates most elements of the anger management approach but that is augmented by confrontational exercises about gender attitudes and early socialization for the use of violence. Another eclectic approach, the ecological model (Edleson & Tolman, 1992), attends to personality factors in addition to those described above.

Do Batterers Programs Work?

To know whether batterers programs work, one must first decide what "work" means. Most studies have used a criterion of complete cessation of violence (Tolman & Edleson, 1995). Some focus on reducing violence, rather than eliminating it (e.g., Poynter, 1989), often because it is easier to demonstrate reducing versus eliminating violence. Some authors (Edleson, 1995; Tolman & Bennett, 1990) caution against focusing on reduction, however, because a perpetrator could reduce his violence and still be dangerous to his partner. A few studies have focused on psychological variables, such as anger and jealousy, and have not actually measured violence after treatment at all (Saunders & Hanusa, 1986).

Some providers have argued that greater attention needs to be paid to threats, other forms of psychological aggression (Rosenfeld, 1992; Tolman & Edleson, 1995), and sexual aggression. Few studies have incorporated such measures, however (Harrell, 1991, and Poynter, 1989, are exceptions). It has also been suggested that measures of increases in positive and caring behaviors of perpetrators and well-being of partners and children should be included as measures of outcome (Tolman & Edleson, 1995). Few studies have considered whether a decrease in some kinds of abusive behaviors, but increases in others, still qualifies as success (Gondolf, 1995). Some authors (Gondolf, 1987b) propose that true success would involve former perpetrators joining the social movement against partner violence. Anecdotal reports indicate that some former perpetrators have, in fact, done just that (Common Purpose, 1996).

The relevant time frame is also an important consideration (Gondolf, 1995). How long a period of nonviolence counts as success? Too short a period may not provide an accurate estimate, especially if the perpetrators are also being monitored by parole officers during that period. Too long a period may make follow-ups too difficult.

Treatment Attrition. Attrition, or dropout, rates are high in batterers programs despite the fact that most members are court-ordered to treatment. Attrition rates also complicate evaluations of success. Studies indicate that between 20% and 30% of men who begin short-term (12-week) treatment do not complete it (DeMaris, 1989; Saunders & Parker, 1989). A survey of 30 programs of varying lengths (Gondolf, 1990) found a wide range in completion rates, with one half of programs reporting completion rates of 50% or less. If attrition is documented from the first assessment, rather than from the first treatment session, noncompletion rates are even higher. A 32-week treatment program showed a 67% noncompletion rate among men who completed two intake sessions (Grusznski & Carrillo, 1988). A similar study that also documented attrition after the initial assessment (Cadsky, Hanson, Crawford, & Lalonde, 1996) found that 59% of those who completed the initial assessment never attended a single session and that 75% dropped out before the 10-week program was over. A more comprehensive study (Gondolf & Foster, 1991) actually looked at attrition rates beginning with initial telephone inquiries to a program, and found even more dismal results. In this study, of 200 initial telephone inquiries regarding the program, only 53 (27%) men showed for their initial assessment, only 27 (14%) ever went to a single counseling session, and only 2 (1%) completed the entire 32-session program.

Unemployment is the characteristic probably most consistently related to dropping out of treatment (Bodnarchuk et al., 1995; Cadsky et al., 1996; DeMaris, 1989; Grusznski & Carrillo, 1988; Hamberger & Hastings, 1988a; Saunders & Azar, 1989). Some studies indicate that voluntary attendees, especially those with college educations, stay in treatment longer (Cadsky et al., 1996; Gondolf & Foster, 1991; Saunders & Azar, 1989). Other research (Bodnarchuk et al., 1995; Grusznski & Carrillo, 1988) has found better attendance among college-educated men regardless of whether they were court-referred or voluntary.

Attrition rates are high, in part, because in many jurisdictions the courts do not impose penalties for nonattendance. For example, in one study (Harrell, 1991), the men who dropped out of treatment

(24% of those mandated) did not receive any penalties for failing to comply with the court orders because no cases were returned to court for noncompliance. Gondolf (1990) reported that 45% of surveyed programs said lack of court action for noncompliance with treatment was a problem.

These high attrition rates are important for evaluations of the success of batterers programs. It is clear that evaluations based on men who complete these programs are focusing on a very select group of men who probably differ from the general population of batterers in many ways, especially with regard to socioeconomic status (as measured by education and employment status). "Success" rates are likely to be inflated because follow-up is not done with treatment dropouts, who are probably the most likely to continue their violence. One study (Hamberger & Hastings, 1988a) found just that in a comparison of completers and dropouts from a 12-week anger management program. Recidivism at 1-year follow-up was 35% for program completers, which is similar to the estimates obtained in the above studies. Recidivism was markedly higher among dropouts, over one half of whom (55%) had been violent in the year following dropping out. Unfortunately, only police records were available for most dropouts, and this study only included men who had completed at least three intake sessions; both of these factors strongly suggest that true recidivism rates are even higher among treatment dropouts. On the positive side, levels of violence and anger did significantly decrease for the completers in this study.

A similar study (Edleson & Grusznski, 1989) produced more complicated results. The first group of men who were referred to a primarily power-and-control-based program did show lower recidivism rates for completers versus noncompleters. Among referrals from 3 years later, however, recidivism was the same among completers and noncompleters. The study authors hypothesized that the changing nature of the client population during that time accounted for the differences. By the time of the third cohort, fewer men who were referred to the program were employed or married, and many more had concurrent mental health or substance abuse problems.

What can be done about high attrition rates? Reducing or eliminating pregroup intakes is one suggestion to help decrease attrition (Cadsky et al., 1996; Gondolf & Fisher, 1988). Cadsky and colleagues (1996) suggest that providing more information about the purpose of the program and focusing quickly on useful interventions may also help decrease attrition. Hanson and Whitman (1995, cited in Cadsky et al., 1996) found that home visits after no-shows also helped decrease dropout rate. Many factors may influence treatment completion and success. Accurate evaluations of treatment success cannot be made until the violence of men who do not finish treatment is incorporated into the estimates.

Recidivism Estimates. True recidivism rates, or evidence of continuing violence, are difficult to estimate for some important reasons. The high attrition rates noted above are one. Even among those who complete treatment, many are not located for follow-up. The percentage of treatment completers who participated in follow-up is under 20% in some studies (DeMaris & Jackson, 1987; Faulkner, Stoltenberg, Cogen, Nolder, & Shooter, 1992). Batterers' reports of recidivism are often suspect because they may be motivated to lie about their violence in order to avoid probation or parole violations or other sanctions (Tolman & Bennett, 1990). Partners' reports, when available, may also be underestimates, especially if the partners fear retaliation by their batterers, are themselves in denial about the severity of the violence, or fear that reports will be made to child protective services.

In many studies of recidivism, another reason is especially important: No control or comparison group is used to help evaluate outcome. This means that one cannot tell whether the treatment itself is the true cause of any improvement. For example, most perpetrators in batterers programs have received other interventions in addition to group treatment. Many have been arrested and are now on probation, and any improvement in their behavior could be a result of legal interventions. Moreover, the partners of many of these men have left them, and any reduction in partner violence may be because of a lack of an available target. Some batterers are involved in divorce and custody proceedings and may be motivated to be nonviolent, at least in the short term, to make a good impression in family court. Others may be experiencing pressure from family members, workplaces, or the community to stop their violent behavior. Thus, the estimates from the following studies are probably best considered estimates of recidivism following multiple interventions for men who are most compliant with treatment recommendations. In other words, outcome studies with no control groups offer a fairly limited view of true treatment outcomes and probably present a picture that is biased in favor of making these treatments look more successful than they actually are.

Even under these circumstances, the results of these studies are only moderately favorable. One follow-up study of batterers who participated in a program that generally followed an anger management approach (DeMaris & Jackson, 1987) obtained only a 17% response rate, which by most survey standards would be considered extremely low. Even among those willing to participate in the study, 35% admitted to being violent since their last contact with the program. Given the extremely low response rate, however, it is likely that the actual recidivism rate was much higher. The study also looked at factors associated with recidivism. Not surprisingly, batterers living with their partners was associated with higher levels of violence. Current alcohol problems were also associated with higher recidivism.

Another study (Edleson & Syers, 1990) reported similar results among a group of men, most of whom had voluntarily entered group programs that were eclectic in nature. In this study, 39% of respondents were violent at 6-month follow-up (using batterers' reports and, when available, partners' reports). Rates of violence were actually somewhat higher among those who completed the 32-week group (46% violent) versus the 12-week group (35% violent) program at 6-month follow-up (Edleson & Syers, 1990), although this pattern had reversed by 18-month follow-up (Edleson & Syers, 1991). Terroristic threats were still being reported for over one half of the men receiving treatment. Unfortunately, only one third (33%) of the original sample was included in the study's 6-month follow-up. Participating in follow-up was associated with being better educated and having higher incomes, similar to the characteristics of program completers. Thus, unfortunately, it seems likely that this study also overestimated treatment success. One study (Rosenfeld, 1992) averaged together the estimates from several studies and found an average recidivism rate of 27% according to perpetrator reports and an average of 36% for the subset of studies that included victim reports.

Control Group Studies. A rigorous test of batterers programs would involve a randomized assignment to treatment and no-treatment conditions for a group of perpetrators that was otherwise relatively homogeneous. Unfortunately, such studies are rare, and ethical considerations make it unlikely that true no-treatment controls can be used (Rosenfeld, 1992). Some research, however, does compare batterers who completed treatment to batterers who did not receive or complete treatment for other reasons (e.g., perpetrators dropped out on

their own, different judges ordered different treatments). These studies have shown a wide range of results. Some studies have reported
very discouraging findings. One study of three programs used by the
courts in Baltimore, Maryland (Harrell, 1991), showed no changes in
attitudes or knowledge between treatment and control (no-treatment)
groups. Even worse, the treatment groups actually reported higher
levels of violence at follow-up than the control groups, on the basis
of both perpetrator and victim reports of violence.

A long-term (5-year) follow-up of police records compared completers, noncompleters (came for intake but did not complete program), rejections (those deemed by staff to be inappropriate for treatment), and no-shows (referred but never came for intake) on violent
arrests (Bodnarchuk et al., 1995). Arrests for wife assault were highest for noncompleters, but neither treatment completion nor whether
treatment was voluntary or mandatory significantly predicted later
rates of arrest. A very small subsample (fewer than 10% of the original
pool) was available for more detailed follow-up, and these men did
appear to be less violent at follow-up than prior to treatment, but such
results must be interpreted cautiously, given the sample size. Men
with borderline or antisocial personality symptoms appeared to benefit the least from treatment.

Other studies (e.g., Dutton, 1986) have reported more encouraging
results, showing a lower rate of arrest among treated than untreated
men. More recently, a United Kingdom study (Dobash, Dobash,
Cavanagh, & Lewis, 1996) reported a lower rate of recidivism among
men who received a batterers program in addition to criminal justice
interventions, compared with men who received criminal justice interventions only. Men were not randomly assigned to treatment, however, and study analyses indicated that men referred to treatment
were more likely to be older and employed, although equally violent,
compared with men in the criminal justice condition. The study
authors acknowledged the selection bias but did not statistically control for these differences when they compared outcome for the two
groups, even though they reported that these factors were associated
with recidivism. Thus, the study may most clearly add further support to the premise that employed men have better outcomes than
unemployed men. Palmer, Brown, and Barrera (1992), in one of the
only studies to use randomized assignment to treatment, also found
a lower arrest rate among treated men (10%) than among untreated
men (31%). It should be noted, however, that violence known to the

police is likely to be only a subset of all violence, as was demonstrated in the United Kingdom study (Dobash et al., 1996).

Critiques of Batterers Programs by Batterers Counselors. Programs that focus on power and control generally reflect the belief that anger management models do not sufficiently address the underlying motive for violence: control. Thus, anger management programs may reduce violence but not actually reduce other forms of coercive and abusive behavior (Common Purpose, 1996). At least one organization (Jackson & Garvin, 1995) has gone even further and advocated that time-outs, a mainstay of both anger management and power and control approaches, no longer be used by any program because so many perpetrators appear to use that as another means of exercising control. For example, many perpetrators simply leave without discussing it with their partners and often leave for extended periods of time. Often, they may leave their partners with the children so that the women cannot really take a time-out from their responsibilities.

Some shelter workers believe that enrolling men in batterers programs can falsely send a message of safety to their partners. One study (Gondolf, 1988a) found that counseling for the perpetrator was the strongest predictor that a woman would return to her partner. Some providers also believe that using programs as a diversion from conviction or serving jail time still sends the societal message that partner assault is not as serious as other forms of assault.

Finally, some providers have criticized existing batterers programs for not being sufficiently sensitive to cultural and ethnic issues. In one survey of 142 programs, one half made no accommodations for the needs of their minority clients (Williams & Becker, 1994). Williams (1992) has also written of the need for culturally sensitive treatment and for providers from all ethnic groups to examine issues of trust, racism, and cultural differences in responses to labels and treatment modalities (see Chapter 6).

Discharge Criteria. Because most men who attend these groups are ordered to do so by the courts, most programs use only attendance records as a criterion for discharge. It is clear that many men simply "put in their time" and do not actively participate in the programs. Recently, however, one program has developed a set of 10 discharge criteria to be evaluated when considering discharging a member (Gondolf, 1995). Although Gondolf (1995) notes that clinical judgment is far from infallible, these criteria do promise to improve somewhat over existing attendance-based requirements:

- Good attendance
- Nonviolence
- Sobriety
- Acceptance of problem with violence
- Using techniques taught in program
- Help seeking
- Appropriate group behavior
- Engaged in group
- Self-disclosure
- Using nonsexist and respectful language

Conclusions About Batterers Programs. Several reviews (Gondolf, 1997; Rosenfeld, 1992; Tolman & Bennett, 1990) have concluded that rates of violence of perpetrators who receive and complete treatment are not very different from those who do not. No decisive evidence indicates that one type of treatment is better than any other (Gondolf, 1997; Tolman & Bennett, 1990). These findings suggest that something other than the batterers programs are contributing to the cessation of violence among these perpetrators, and these factors remain largely unknown. Other research that uses community samples of less severely violent men has found high rates of cessation even without formal interventions (Aldarondo & Sugarman, 1996; Feld & Straus, 1990), and it is possible that this result may occur among more severely violent men as well (Tolman & Edleson, 1995).

Future batterers program evaluations need to define the following carefully: (a) the population that is evaluated, (b) the use of a control group, (c) the outcome or "success" measure, (d) the follow-up period, (e) the follow-up response rate, (f) the assessment of batterer accessibility to the victim, and (g) the presence of other interventions, including those adopted by victims (Gondolf, 1987b). Outcome studies also need to pay more attention to dangerousness assessment and cultural and minority issues and to how well the programs are implemented (Gondolf, 1997). Two ongoing multisite studies may improve our knowledge (Gondolf, 1997). In addition to a great need for more rigorously designed quantitative outcome studies, there is a need for qualitative research that explores in detail the types of changes involved in becoming nonviolent (Edleson, 1995).

All of the above involve raising the standards of batterers program evaluation to those commonly adopted in outcome studies of other forms of therapy and medical treatment. Gondolf (1997) suggests that batterers program evaluation should also incorporate some of the methodology and standards of community and educational assessment. One of these techniques, consumer-based assessment, involves determining how batterers programs might better meet the needs of both perpetrators and victims. For example, some battered women appear to want more relief from the abuse to help them make decisions about their future, rather than the heightened pressure that can arise from being in a relationship with a man who claims to be cured (Gondolf, 1997). A systems analysis that paid more attention to which component contributed to the outcome would also add to our understanding. Finally, social impact assessment could help identify what salutory effects the programs have on the community at large, perhaps by contributing to changes in public attitudes toward violence or improving other institutional responses (e.g., police may be more willing to arrest if they know some sanction is likely to actually follow).

Shelters: Housing and Support for Battered Women

The primary community service for victims is the offering of shelter for victims and their children. Shelters are usually homes in the community that provide short-term housing to battered women (and rarely, to men). Although the length of stay varies across shelters, few allow for stays of longer than 90 days. Most shelters are more than just "emergency hotels," however (Loseke, 1992). In addition to providing a safe haven, shelters often offer legal aid, assistance negotiating through social service agencies, community education, crisis hotlines, transportation, support groups for residents and nonresidents, and similar services (Gondolf & Fisher, 1988; Koss et al., 1994). They also teach safety planning, which involves preparing in advance to leave if the violence should become suddenly more severe or life-threatening. It should be noted that shelters are not universally available. Although more than 1,000 shelters are open in the United States (Adams, 1994), more than one half of all U.S. counties offer no formal services for battered women (Koss et al., 1994).

Safety Planning. In addition to being a commonly available intervention at shelters, safety planning is a feature of almost all interventions with victims (Dutton, 1992; Hart & Stuehling, 1992; Register, 1993; Walker, 1994). Increasing victims' safety is the primary goal of almost all interventions and is worth outlining in some detail because it is often the most pressing concern. Although some couples therapists accept a contractual promise of nonviolence on the part of the perpetrator as sufficient to ensure safety (Neidig & Friedman, 1984), safety planning has progressed to a relatively sophisticated technique tailored to both victims and perpetrators. The approach most commonly adopted with victims is outlined in this section.

Safety planning for victims involves developing a specific, prearranged plan for ensuring the safety of the victim and her children even in emergency situations (Hart & Stuehling, 1992). Usually twin emphases are placed on identifying escape routes and securing access to financial resources, personal records, and other essentials. Dutton (1992) also points out that training women to recognize the cues for impending danger is important. Common elements include the following (Hart & Stuehling, 1992):

- Practicing quick exits (using windows or fire escapes if necessary)
- Always keeping purse and car keys near door
- Hiding extra sets of keys and money
- Storing important documents in a safe place (e.g., bank deposit box)
- Keeping a suitcase packed and stored in a safe place at home or at a friend's home
- Teaching children how to call the police and fire departments
- Setting up a code word or signal for children or friends or both so they will know it is time to begin the safety plan
- Knowing a local partner violence hotline or shelter number

It is equally important *not* to include any plans that would actually increase the danger, such as many forms of fighting back (Dutton, 1992).

For women who have obtained restraining orders and are trying to ensure their safety in their own residences, Hart and Stuehling (1992) recommend the following:

- Changing locks
- Installing security systems
- Purchasing rope ladders
- Installing smoke detectors

- Informing local police about standing protection orders
- Making sure that teachers, neighbors, and friends know who has permission to pick up the children

Hart (1990b) has also outlined recommendations for developing safety plans for children who have unsupervised visits with batterers. These focus on the following:

- Providing information to children
- Allowing them to discuss their experiences
- Making sure they know they are not responsible for ensuring a successful visit

Hart also discusses some of the dilemmas in safety planning with children, such as identifying appropriate ages and weighing the benefits against a likely increase in fear on the part of children.

Do Shelters Work?

Clients' Perception of Services. Evaluation of the perceived adequacy of service provision has been quite limited, and scant work has been done in this area recently. One study (Donato & Bowker, 1984) reported that battered women found women's groups (shelters and other services tailored to the needs of women) somewhat more helpful than traditional social service agencies. In this study, women's groups most commonly offered modeling and testimony of members' own ways of dealing with the problem, along with direct services and material aid. Social service agencies most commonly offered focused talking or directing the woman in how to engage in problem solving.

Another older study of 1,000 women who were solicited through various media advertisements found that women's groups, which were usually part of a shelter program, were rated as the most helpful treatment in comparison with the clergy and with social services/counseling agencies (Bowker & Maurer, 1986). Women's groups were the least-used treatment option, however. Only about one fifth of the women had participated in women's group, compared with one third seeking out clergy and one half using social services/counseling agencies. Women with more previous separations and higher reports of their husbands' dominance found women's groups and social services/counseling agencies more effective than did other women.

Qualitative comments suggested that victim blaming was significantly more common among clergy and social services/counseling providers than in women's groups.

Leaving the Relationship. The main outcome that has been investigated for women who have sought shelter is whether they permanently leave their partners or return to their abusers after seeking shelter. Most studies find that a substantial portion of women, ranging from one quarter of all shelter residents to well over one half, return to their partners for at least some period of time (cf. Gondolf, 1988a; Strube, 1988, for reviews). Many professionals, however, emphasize that permanent separation is a process that can take a long time, especially for individuals who may lack financial or other resources (Dutton, 1992).

One study of women who had sought shelter (Gondolf & Fisher, 1988) found that obtaining legal assistance through shelters was significantly associated with leaving, although better economic status and the failure of the partner to get treatment were most predictive of leaving. Another program investigated whether providing post-shelter advocates increased the likelihood of women obtaining needed resources and reducing involvement with their partners (Sullivan, Tan, Basta, Rumptz, & Davidson, 1992). Ten weeks after their shelter stay, women who received advocates did report more success with obtaining resources and social support than did women who did not receive advocates. No significant differences between the advocates and no-advocates groups were found, however, in the percentage of women who returned to their partners, who had experienced postshelter physical abuse, or who had experienced postshelter psychological abuse, although the differences were in the expected directions. A 6-month follow-up produced similar results (Sullivan, Campbell, Angelique, Eby, & Davidson, 1994). A serious shortcoming of this study, however, was the use of undergraduates as advocates and the absence of any measures that assessed what the advocates actually did with their clients. Compliance of service providers with the intervention program is a basic element of program evaluation that is necessary to determine whether the absence of effects is a result of a genuine failure of the intervention or a failure to *implement* the intervention.

The emphasis on leaving the relationship is a major shortcoming of the literature on the effectiveness of community interventions and on the victims' responses to violence in general. Recent research (Hamby & Gray-Little, 1997) has suggested that self-protective responses increase as violence increases, even among a group of women who are still with their partners. Others have demonstrated that the persistence of help-seeking behaviors is associated with the success in obtaining needed economic support (Gondolf & Fisher, 1988). Unresponsive communities can contribute to women's inability to leave, and evaluation of community interventions should examine other factors. Even more important, substantial evidence supports the suggestion that leaving can increase the danger to women (Giles-Sims, 1983; Hart, 1996; Mahoney, 1991). It is also possible that overemphasis on leaving when a woman is not able or ready may lead to her terminating all contact with providers. Future research would benefit from the study of increases in all forms of self-protective behavior following community interventions and the effects of economic and legal assistance on protection.

Other Outcome Studies. A survey of women who had participated in 1 of 12 support groups in Canada revealed significant benefits of support group participation (Tutty, Bidgood, & Rothery, 1993). All the groups were conducted by female social workers and had a general focus on building self-esteem, making future plans, and providing education about gender socialization. A pretest-posttest design revealed improvement in several domains, including self-esteem and marital functioning, along with reports of reductions in stress, sustaining controlling behaviors, and sustaining abuse. Unfortunately, it is not known what other services women or their partners were receiving that may have contributed to the results. For example, it is not known whether reduction in abuse was accompanied by separation from their partners.

One study examined the impact of shelters on increased freedom from violence (Berk, Newton, & Berk, 1986). The study of women who had contact either with a shelter or the local prosecutor's office found that shelter stays alone were associated with a slight *increase* in violence at follow-up. The study authors hypothesized that this may be a result of retaliatory violence. Women who had *both* sought shelter and actively sought other forms of help experienced little new violence at follow-up. These results may be affected, however, by the relatively short follow-up period of 6 weeks. Most women (81%) did not experience any new violence between the two interviews.

Critiques of Services From Within the Shelter Movement. Most critiques from grassroots advocates have focused on the difficulties in extending the shelter movement to women from diverse ethnic, national, and religious backgrounds and to women in same-sex relationships (Koss et al., 1994; Timmins, 1995). Many women have reported that they find it difficult to integrate the ideology of shelters, which tend to be based on ideas that developed from Western forms of feminism, with their own cultural beliefs, religious values, and social and educational experiences. Hurdles encountered with this integration include difficulties becoming an accepted resource by all segments of a community, difficulties with beginning to provide resources in some communities, and difficulties with recruiting and training women from diverse backgrounds to be shelter workers and administrators (see Timmins, 1995, for a collection of essays on these topics).

Legal Interventions

Changes in Laws and Arrest Policies. Arrest policies have changed dramatically within the last 20 years, with all states enacting some kind of reform that has moved in the pro-arrest direction (Buzawa & Buzawa, 1996; Ford, Reichard, Goldsmith, & Regoli, 1996). Some mandate arrest, some have made probable cause determinations easier (e.g., in many jurisdictions, officers can arrest without a warrant even when they did not witness the assault), and some have instituted victimless prosecution so that victims need not confront their perpetrators directly for prosecution to proceed (Hart, 1989). Many jurisdictions have also made it easier to obtain civil restraining orders. Nonetheless, many states continue to prosecute domestic assault as a misdemeanor (Tolman & Edleson, 1995).

As is often the case, changes in attitudes sometimes come more slowly than changes in laws. In a review of victims' descriptions from the 1987 to 1992 National Crime Victimization Survey, Bachman and Coker (1995) found that police made an arrest in response to only 32% of calls. According to respondents in these surveys, arrests were more likely when the batterer had no prior criminal history, when the victim was not married to the batterer, when both parties were African American, and when the victim had been injured. One study (Ford, 1987) showed that victim-blaming attitudes and failure to perceive probable cause predicted individual differences in officers' tendency to arrest. A more recent study (Saunders, 1995) found that similar attitudes (beliefs that partner violence is sometimes justifiable and that women are in violent relationships for psychological reasons) were associated with a newly reported trend in arrest, that of arresting victims if there was any evidence of fighting back, even in self-defense. Some providers (cited in Saunders, 1995) found that mandatory arrest policies led to a doubling of the rate of arrests for victims after 1 year (from 13% to 25% of arrests). Many advocates report that victim-blaming attitudes and nonresponsiveness still occur in many police departments and courts, which can exacerbate the trauma that victims have already experienced (Hart, 1996).

Legal Outreach and Advocacy for Victims. Recently, some districts, often as part of a coordinated community action effort, have provided advocates that help victims navigate through the judicial process (Hart, 1996; Snyder, 1994). Advocates follow-up on calls to the police. They typically offer support, referrals, and a clear explanation of the legal options available. They also often accompany victims to court.

Do Legal Interventions Work?

Effects of Arrest on Batterers. One of the earliest studies on the effects of arrest (Sherman & Berk, 1984) reported very favorable outcomes for arrest. The researchers reported a study using randomized assignment of legally assaultive men to arrest, advice, and order to leave the scene (for 8 hours) conditions. They found that recidivism rates for arrested perpetrators were one half what they were for non-arrested men in the 6 months following initial police contact, using both police and victim reports to track offenses. Unfortunately, many later studies failed to replicate these positive findings (Tolman & Edleson, 1995), including a series of replications conducted by the National Institute of Justice (NIJ; Zorza, 1993). Some studies found no effects of arrest, some found a few deterrent effects, and some actually found escalation effects; most authors concluded that no definitive statement could be made about the effects of arrest (Garner, Fagan, & Maxwell, 1995; Tolman & Edleson, 1995). Unfortunately, major differences in these studies, even in the NIJ replications, make it difficult to draw conclusions. For example, one site of a replication experiment included any family-on-family violence, such as brother-on-brother, in the definition of "domestic violence," whereas other sites did not (Zorza, 1993). At least one study (Klein, 1996) reported similarly discouraging reports for restraining orders. Some studies found that those individuals with the least stake in the community, such as the unemployed and the unmarried, were most likely to have increased recidivism following arrest (Sherman, Smith, Schmidt, & Rogan, 1992). Several studies showed that arrest may be most effective for employed batterers (Zorza, 1993).

Schmidt and Sherman (1993) recently concluded that, in addition to differences in effects due to employment, arrests may decrease the risk of violence in the immediate short run but increase it in the long run. They proposed that police need some mechanism for handling chronic, repeat offenders, who comprise a high proportion of all calls, although the absolute number of individuals is small. They also advocate repealing mandatory arrest laws to increase police officers' discretion in cases in which arrest is likely to backfire. Other advocates examining the same data remain staunch defenders of mandatory arrest (Stark, 1993; Zorza, 1993). Most providers agree that enhanced risk assessment could help better inform such policy decisions and that arrest policies should be part of a coordinated community response to violence to maximize effectiveness. The lack of consistent findings for the effects of arrest may be a result, at least in part, of the continuing low rates of prosecution for partner violence cases (Tolman & Edleson, 1995), although one study did not find that prosecution affected recidivism (Ford, 1993), with the exception that women who retained the right to drop charges experienced less violence.

Victims' Perceptions of Helpfulness. One study (Hamilton & Coates, 1993) found that although police were among the most frequently contacted professionals, they were perceived as being among the least helpful. Crisis counselors were found to be the most helpful. Helpful responses generally included believing the victim's story and helping plan for safety. An older study (Bowker & Maurer, 1987) also found that police were found to be the least helpful of service providers. Another older study found that the responses of the criminal justice system to women varied to an unfortunate extent on which personnel were involved (Ford, 1983), but, one would hope, responses have improved since that study was conducted.

Effects of Restraining Orders on Victims. One recent study (Harrell & Smith, 1996) found that one quarter of women who had obtained restraining orders had been subjected to severe violence in the year following the establishment of the orders. Psychological abuse was experienced by over 50%, and 15% were stalked. Almost 10% were forced into having sex with the perpetrators. Most other studies on restraining orders and arrests have similarly focused on reabuse and also found mixed results regarding efficacy (cf. Berk, 1993; Buzawa & Buzawa, 1993; Stark, 1993). The Harrell and Smith (1996) study is unique in that it did examine other factors associated with the continuation of violence, some of which involved the adequacy of the legal response (other factors, such as the presence of children, also placed women at greater risk). Women who reported that judges did not include sufficient conditions in restraining orders (ROs) regarding matters such as visitation experienced more abuse (physical and psychological) than those who were satisfied with the specificity of the orders. If arrest occurred at the time of the incident that led to the RO, later severe violence was less likely. The helpfulness of the police at the time of the initial call was also associated with less severe violence at follow-up. This study also noted that women encountered many difficulties with the legal system and often did not know that they could ask for help or how to get it.

Utility of Legal Advocates for Victims. A Massachusetts jurisdiction saw a dramatic increase in the number of partner violence complaints remaining active for more than 30 days after they began providing legal advocates for victims (Snyder, 1994). During a 6-month period shortly before instituting the advocate program, almost all complaints (91%) were dropped in less than 30 days and 0% resulted in active restraining orders for more than a 30-day period. In contrast, in a 6-month period shortly *after* the district began providing advocates, only 36% of complaints were dropped and 64% resulted in active restraining orders. These changes occurred even though the overall number of complaints remained relatively constant throughout the study. These promising findings suggest that legal advocacy programs may have practical benefits for victims.

Coordinated Community Action Models

Many communities no longer see any single intervention as a stand-alone element that works independently (Hart, 1990a; Jackson & Garvin, 1995; Jackson, 1991; Pence & Paymar, 1993; Robertson, in press). Arising initially from the work of community advocates who were trying to stop violence against women, coordinated community action models (CCAMs) involve advocates reaching out to the justice system and other groups in the community, some of whom have not always had good relationships with each other. Many batterers intervention programs either implicitly or explicitly follow this model because they tend to coordinate their services very closely with those of the courts and those of shelters. Many batterers treatment programs were developed by individuals who were first involved with the shelter movement (Adams et al., 1992; Common Purpose, 1996; Pence & Paymar, 1993).

In addition to shelters, batterers programs, and the courts, coordinated community action programs now often also involve the health care system, educational systems, employers, clergy, the media, social services, and others who either provide services to victims and perpetrators or are in a position to influence public attitudes toward partner violence (Jackson & Garvin, 1995). Training and educating the professionals in all of these settings are often goals of coordinated community action programs (Hart, 1990a; Jackson & Garvin, 1995; Pence & Paymar, 1993; Robertson, in press). Technological advances can also be part of an improved community response. For example, one district in Britain included as part of its coordinated program the installation of a system so that victims could carry alarms to call the police more quickly and easily (Farrell, Buck, & Pease, 1993).

Do Coordinated Community Action Models Work?

Coordinated community action models are the most recent approach developed to address domestic violence, and hence few evaluations are currently available. Pence (1989) described positive perceptions of system responses among 65 battered women in Duluth, Minnesota, which developed the CCAM, but it is apparent that implementation of the model was variable across agencies, and few details are provided of the evaluation. Farrell et al. (1993) also reported positive qualitative data regarding the use of alarms as part of a more responsive community effort that included decreased police response time and improved access to victim services. More recently, Murphy, Musser, and Maton (1996) showed cumulative effects for each intervention that perpetrators received. These included successful prosecution, probation, and court-ordered counseling, and completion of treatment. Although each individual intervention produced only a modest effect, together they led to as much as 25% lower recidivism. Unfortunately, however, only a small percentage of the sample (4%) actually received all the interventions available in the community. The modest effects for any single intervention is consistent with the results reported for studies that examined only one treatment component and suggests that making a larger impact on domestic violence will require multiple services. I am not aware of any studies that also incorporate an investigation of the effects of services to victims, but it is possible that these may also have a cumulative effect on the reduction of violence.

Mental Health Treatments

Perpetrators

Individual Psychotherapy. Although it seems likely that many perpetrators continue to be treated within the context of individual psychotherapy (Thorne-Finch, 1992), virtually no writing has been done on this topic in the past 20 years (Edleson & Tolman, 1992). Many groups do offer individual counseling, however, as an adjunct to other forms of treatment (Edleson & Tolman, 1992).

Group Therapy. Most group interventions for perpetrators focus on safety issues and have an ongoing goal of changing societal attitudes toward violence and women. (These are reviewed under "Community-Based Services.") Some programs focus more on personal and relationship growth and thus have more in common with traditional mental health approaches. Perhaps the primary difference between the two approaches is that one sees perpetrators as victims (Waldo, 1987) and the other does not. Waldo (1987) describes a program that focuses on increasing ego strength, addressing dependency needs, and improving communication in abusers' relationships with their partners. Waldo asserts that arrest in itself is sufficient to motivate change, in tandem with a self-awareness and personal growth program such as the one described above.

Rachor (1995) describes a group approach that is based on reality therapy. It is similar to Waldo's program in that both the abusers and the abused are seen to be choosing their behaviors to get their needs met. One example is that both female victims and male perpetrators are equally encouraged to relinquish control over others. Partner violence is seen as a "human problem" and not a gender-based problem. Using this point of view, the program that Rachor describes integrated unrelated victims and perpetrators into the same group so that they could learn from each other. Few providers currently subscribe to the viewpoint of either Waldo or Rachor.

Do Mental Health Treatments for Perpetrators Work?

Individual Psychotherapy. Evaluations of individual psychotherapy for perpetrators of partner violence could not be located.

Group Therapy. Waldo (1987) reports lower recidivism rates for men who complete his 14-week treatment program that focuses on ego strength and relationship building, in comparison with those who do not participate in the program. His program, however, only accepts men who are voluntarily engaging in this treatment as a pretrial diversion and have no substance abuse problems or other problems that would interfere with their ability to comply with the treatment. Thus, this is a highly select group of men who are unlikely to be representative of all men arrested for battering. Rachor (1995) also reports low levels of violence (based on a single question) following treatment, but he presents no data on pretreatment violence with which to compare it. Further, 39% of females in his study reported continued harassment and 35% said they were still afraid of their partners. He quotes as evidence of success a court-ordered male who said he had "stopped getting down on myself" but still continued to insist that he was "falsely accused" and "did not really commit a violent act" (p. 32). This man would not be considered a treatment success according to most models of intervention.

Victims

Individual Psychotherapy. A de-emphasis on victim/survivor treatment has been one consequence of the controversy regarding the psychological status of those who have experienced partner violence. Mary Ann Dutton's (1992) and Lenore Walker's (1994) books on treating survivors of partner violence are two of the few to appear in recent years.

Dutton's (1992) book, *Empowering and Healing the Battered Woman,* is widely read and is considered by some (Koss et al., 1994) to be the standard in the field. In it, she describes a mental health treatment philosophy that focuses on three main goals: (a) protection, (b) enhanced choice making and problem solving, and (c) healing post-traumatic reactions. These goals are incorporated into a philosophical framework that emphasizes that a therapeutic stance involves accepting women's descriptions of their experiences, respecting the coping strategies women have used in the face of trauma (including denial, substance abuse, and others often considered to be pathological), communicating the benefits of disclosure, and appreciating the lifelong nature of the recovery process. Self-care for both client and therapist are also emphasized. Dutton relies primarily on cognitive-behavioral and supportive techniques.

Walker's approach (1994) also generally follows a trauma recovery model similarly grounded in feminist principles. The focus on empowerment, validation, and strengths is similar to that advocated by Dutton (1992). Cognitive-behavioral techniques to enhance decision making are also advocated by both authors. Both also emphasize safety. Walker's model differs from Dutton's primarily in its more explicit attention to the needs of children and a greater willingness to focus on intrapsychic problems of survivors. Walker also advocates using personality tests as part of the assessment process, in addition to obtaining a comprehensive history of the client and her experience of trauma.

Group Therapy. Most group therapy for battered women follows a support group model and is typically offered by professionals or paraprofessionals affiliated with shelters (these are discussed in the section on community interventions). Some groups, however, do take a more explicitly mental health approach. Cox and Stoltenberg (1991) describe a group treatment program that presented five modules using a cognitive-behavioral approach. One module, called the cognitive therapy module, focuses on self-concept and cognitive restructuring. Other modules focus on self-assertiveness and communication skills, problem solving, vocational counseling, and body awareness. Leventhal and Chang (1991) advocate for the use of dance/movement therapy with battered women and describe how changes in self-concept and interpersonal dynamics can be achieved by movement exercises that metaphorically explore concepts such as "reaching for what you want."

Walker (1994) notes that group therapy (including both treatment and support groups) can be very helpful in reducing the sense of isolation and ameliorating the shame and guilt that often accompany trauma. Group therapy can also provide a forum for practicing social skills and developing interpersonal trust. Group therapy can be problematic, however, because of problems with confidentiality, domination issues among group members, and a format that inherently limits the degree to which treatment can be tailored to an individual's specific needs. Walker also cautions against groups that mix trauma victims with individuals working on other problems and recommends that all groups for trauma victims be single-gender groups.

Do Mental Health Treatments for Victims Work?

Very few psychotherapy outcome studies focus on people who have sustained partner violence. Cox and Stoltenberg (1991) conducted one of the few outcome studies that also had the advantage of a control group. The treatment involved the cognitive-behavioral group intervention described above. Their study was limited, however, by an extremely small sample (fewer than 10 participants in each group). Findings on a variety of standardized measures yielded few differences, although some improvement in self-esteem was noted for both control and treatment groups and one of two treatment groups improved on anxiety and depression. The authors concluded that extratherapy variables, such as whether a woman remained committed to her partner, may have had important unexamined effects.

The long-term outcome for survivors of partner violence has received virtually no quantitative study although numerous books provide in-depth qualitative descriptions of the recovery process (Hoff, 1990; NiCarthy, 1987). Although these books suggest numerous avenues for further research, such as the role that establishing a new life can play in the development of increased self-esteem, it is not known how many victims fully recover from battering trauma or what that process typically entails.

Couples

Most conjoint therapy for violent couples follows a cognitive-behavioral framework that is similar in many respects to the anger management approach often adopted by batterers programs (Geffner, Mantooth, Franks, & Rao, 1989; Neidig & Friedman, 1984; Tolman & Bennett, 1990; Tolman & Edleson, 1995). It is also similar to many couples' therapy models in the focus on communication skills and cognitive restructuring and thus focuses on protective factors more than most other interventions do. In contrast with the philosophy of community-based interventions, some couples therapists believe that spousal abuse is best conceptualized as a process involving two victims (Geffner et al., 1989) although the goal of ending violence is also present. Many of these approaches involve either "no blame" or shared blame for the violence and are critical of any model that sets up a victim/victimizer dichotomy (Geffner et al., 1989; Lane & Russell, 1989).

Couples therapy for violence is a highly controversial treatment, in large part because of safety issues and implicit or explicit victim blaming. Critiques of the couples therapy approach (Bograd, 1984; Hansen & Goldenberg, 1993) focus primarily on the argument that a systemic framework involves allocating responsibility and blame among all parties, instead of locating the responsibility with the violent partner. Similarly, many authors believe that treatment assumes that power is, or at least can be, equally distributed in marital relationships, which is rarely the case when violence has occurred (Bograd, 1984; Walker, 1994). Conjoint therapy may also jeopardize the safety of the woman and make it impossible for her to speak freely without fear of repercussions. Conjoint treatment may explicitly or implicitly support the idea that remaining together is a viable and safe alternative when this cannot be ensured. In contrast with the emphasis on leaving the relationship in studies of shelters, one study (Sirles, Lipchik, & Kowalski, 1993) reported that 86% of couples planned to remain together following therapy; the authors interpreted this as a measure of treatment success.

Limited empirical evidence supports some of the concerns about couples therapy for violent couples. One study of 362 family therapists (Hansen et al., 1991) found that 40% of them, when asked to describe how they would treat a couple, did not focus on even extreme levels of violence presented in case vignettes. Only 10% focused on safety issues. Thus, although these findings may not generalize to actual clinical practices, it is clear that many family therapists do not readily identify problems related to treating violent couples.

Despite these concerns, some therapists (e.g., Edleson, 1995; Wylie, 1996) recommend the cautious use of couples therapy when the safety of victims can be ensured and the man has already success-fully participated in a batterers program for a period of several months. Edleson and Tolman (1992) outline several other specific criteria as well: no ongoing violence or psychological maltreatment, an acceptance of responsibility on the part of the perpetrator for the violence, and both partners' desire to remain together. Dutton (1988) adds an additional criterion: Perpetrators who have previously abused other victims are not good candidates for couples therapy. In contrast, many couples who have experienced violence in their rela-tionship may not have experienced extreme forms of aggression, and the violence may have been relatively infrequent. As the above guide-lines suggest, couples therapy may be more appropriate when the violence has been less severe. The appropriateness of couples therapy may also depend on the uses to which it is put. Ganley (1989) draws an important distinction between the *format* of a session and the *the-ory* guiding the session. She suggests that it may be possible to use couples sessions in a way that is not victim blaming. For example, she suggests that a couples session may be a good place for a batterer to acknowledge his use of violence to his partner.

Does Couples Therapy Work?

Fewer studies have been done evaluating couples therapy than have been done evaluating community services, but couples therapy is among the best researched of mental health services. Unfortu-nately, these studies are of generally much lower quality than those done on other interventions (Tolman & Edleson, 1995). Geffner and associates (1989) and Wylie (1996) both report very positive out-comes for couples treatment, but neither presented statistical analy-ses documenting whether significant change occurred, stated how many clients their results were based on, or examined other factors that might have contributed to the effects. Tolman and Edelson's re-view (1995) found this to be generally characteristic of couples ther-apy evaluations. No studies in their review included comparison groups of any kind, and recidivism rates ranged from a low of 13% to a high of 100% across several studies. Attrition is also a significant problem; at least one study lost almost one half of its clients to follow-up (Deschner & McNeil, 1986). The most optimistic of the studies on couples therapy tend to use reductions in violence versus cessation as their outcome measure, which makes it more difficult to compare them with other studies.

Summary of Intervention Review

A definitive treatment to stop the perpetration of violence and to ameliorate the suffering of victims has not been developed, and it is likely that one will not be forthcoming. High-quality evaluations of existing interventions are, unfortunately, rare. Nonetheless, the body of literature to date suggests that violence can be decreased at both societal and individual levels but that the degree of impact is modest. Batterers programs, arrests for assault, and social and economic services to victims may all have some salutory effect for at least some individuals. The development of CCAMs, which emphasize the need to offer all these services in tandem and in a consistent manner, is the best approach available because it has the potential to combine the small effects of individual strategies into a substantial effect.

Issues For Providers

Training Programs for Providers

Many people agree that inadequate responses from service providers help perpetuate the high rates of partner violence in our society. Not only may poor responses discourage victims from seeking help, but lack of documentation of injuries and other effects may impede efforts to prosecute perpetrators. One study on this topic found inconsistent documentation of issues related to violence in psychiatric evaluations (Gondolf, 1992). A lack of professional response to partner violence also helps maintain the implicit acceptance of partner violence at the community level. Many providers, such as physicians, nurses, and police, come into contact with many perpetrators and victims but often do not have specialized training in partner violence. In fact, the training of medical and police professionals emphasizes other intervention priorities and rarely includes specific training on partner violence (although this is slowly improving). Some professionals have attempted to increase awareness of partner violence and improve response to it in these disciplines

(Bekemeier, 1995; Easteal & Easteal, 1992). At least one physician, however, has gone on record as stating that helping to decrease partner violence is beyond the purview of health care (Fitzgerald, 1994), and one study found that many health care providers are reluctant to take on the added responsibility of addressing violence and have negative stereotypes about victims of partner violence (Kurz, 1987).

The training of those who provide preventive services is another important and very understudied area. Although some community psychologists are extensively trained in prevention, individuals who provide preventive services come from a wide variety of backgrounds, and there is no accepted standard of training for such professionals. Prevention specialists are not credentialed practitioners, and thus there is little community supervision of their work. Studies of the training or practice of those who work in prevention efforts could not be located, but this is an area of much-needed study.

Actual studies on the effects of training professionals of any type are, unfortunately, quite limited in number. One Australian study (Easteal & Easteal, 1992) found that only 10% of general practitioners had received any training in partner violence, most of which was quite limited. Of 25 different beliefs and practices they inquired about, only 3 were more common among those who had received training. Trained physicians were more likely, in contrast with those with no partner violence training, to agree that batterers should be imprisoned for assault, that physicians should report evidence of partner violence to police, and that victims should receive counseling as part of treatment. More rigorous outcome studies on the effects of such training have not been reported, but at least one such study is ongoing (Alpert, 1996, personal communication).

Basic Skills for Providers

Although most providers still do not receive training, some authors have made recommendations for basic skills that providers should possess. Most of these writings are aimed at individuals within the family violence field, so most do not include a review of basic knowledge about domestic violence, but of course that is an essential first step. The previous chapters in this volume all provide such a knowledge base. What follows are some additional considerations for anyone providing direct services or having direct contact with community members.

Screening and Risk Assessment. Screening is the most basic intervention skill that any provider should possess. Screening for partner violence is, unfortunately, still rather rare (Aldarondo & Straus, 1994) but critically important, especially because many victims do not present partner violence as their primary problem when they come into contact with service providers (especially those other than the police). The most important aspect of screening is simply *asking directly about partner violence.* Many interview formats for assessing partner abuse history are available (Lystad, Rice, & Kaplan, 1996; Walker, 1994). Some of the most important elements include assessing for injuries, the perpetrator's use of or access to weapons, the perpetrator's use of sexual aggression, the perpetrator's threats to kill the victim or other individuals, the risk to children, the suicide risk, and the existing safety plan (if any).

Many professionals are uncomfortable with asking about violence. Such discomfort is common and should be explored during the course of supervision or training. Clients, too, may be uncomfortable discussing violence, especially physical and sexual assault. Hamby et al. (1996) have documented that any evidence of severe psychological abuse, such as calling one's partner fat or ugly or destroying one's partner's belongings, are closely associated with physical assault, especially for male perpetrators. Evidence of such psychological abuse is a strong sign that violence should be assessed more carefully.

Practical Matters

Therapist and client safety must always be of paramount concern. Batterers may pose some risk to therapists, especially if the therapists have testified in court against them. Threats should be taken seriously and made known to relevant authorities. It is important that providers not engage in minimization themselves. Care should be taken not to publicize one's home telephone number and address, although it must also be recognized that such information can often be obtained despite precautions (Walker, 1994). Fees, after-hours telephone calls, vacations, and other matters should be addressed clearly and as early in therapy as possible. Records should be kept in a secure, locked place. It should also be borne in mind that these cases not uncommonly go to trial. Local laws about therapist confidentiality and confidentiality of records should be familiar to all providers.

Providers should also be familiar with other resources in the community. If a coordinated community action program is active in one's local community, efforts should be made to become a part of that cooperative effort. This will reduce the occurrence of overlap between and conflict among services.

Personal Issues

Two main issues are important to consider for anyone who works with victims of partner violence: (a) possible negative effects on service providers and (b) possible negative effects (e.g., from countertransference) on clients that arise from a lack of training or attention to personal responses to this work. No empirical research has studied the effects of working with victims of partner violence on therapists and other service providers, but research does suggest that vicarious traumatization does occur among professionals who work with childhood sexual abuse (Pearlman & MacIan, 1995), and it is likely that work with other trauma victims has similar effects. Vicarious traumatization usually involves evidence of post-traumatic stress disorder (PTSD) and other symptomatology among those who work with victims. Some authors (Dutton, 1992; Goodwin, 1993; Walker, 1994) have made recommendations for therapists to help alleviate vicarious traumatization, burnout, and other adverse effects. Self-care, addressing one's own victimization and abusive behavior, and exploring one's own attitudes and beliefs should be a part of all preparation for, and coping with, the stresses of trauma work.

Self-Care. Self-care can involve many strategies, including ongoing supervision, personal therapy, peer support, adequate time to process work experiences, and basic health and lifestyle issues, such as adequate rest and nutrition (Dutton, 1992). Regarding supervision, finding a supervisor who adopts a supervision model that one is comfortable with is important to consider (Goodwin, 1993). For example, one may want a supervisor who adopts a more collegial, less hierarchical professional stance. Another important component of self-care is *diversifying professional responsibilities* (Dutton, 1992). A full-time caseload of trauma victims will almost certainly lead to burnout. Diversification can include not only seeing clients with other treatment issues but also engaging in other forms of professional activity, such as research, teaching, consultation, administration, and program development. Some providers also believe that working politically to address the problem of family violence is a helpful coping strategy.

Personal Victimization and Perpetration Histories and Attitudes Toward Violence. Addressing one's own victimization or perpetration history is also a vital part of becoming a good provider. Many people have experienced some form of trauma in their past. At least for childhood sexual abuse, prevalence rates for trauma among mental health professionals are probably as high or higher than those found in the general population (Elliott & Guy, 1993; Gray-Little & Hamby, 1997), and this may extend to other forms of trauma. Rates are likely to be very high among staff at shelters, where having survived partner violence is often seen as a desirable experience for staff counselors and support group leaders, who are then able to model survival directly for clients. Notwithstanding possible positive benefits from having experiences similar to one's clients, potential difficulties must also be addressed. For example, it is important that providers not be too invested in a client following their own examples of recovery, not use treating others as a substitute for working on their own issues, avoid projecting their own experiences and feelings onto their clients, and not use treatment as an opportunity to gain control lacking in other relationships (Dutton, 1992; Walker, 1994).

Many people also have histories of violent or controlling behavior. Sometimes such people are specifically recruited to help intervene with other perpetrators after an extended period of nonviolence. Once again, though, potential difficulties must be addressed, most of which are similar to the transferential problems outlined above. Even providers who do not have a personal victimization or perpetration history need to examine issues of victim blaming, gender role attitudes, and tendencies to collude with clients' minimizing through the use of euphemisms (e.g., "an argument" or "a fight" instead of "a severe beating"). Finally, boundary issues are especially important for people who have been traumatized. Touching clients, for instance, can be more emotionally laden with traumatized clients (Walker, 1994).

Summary of Review of Issues for Providers

Providing services to individuals involved in domestic violence is substantially different from providing many other community and mental health services, and more specialized training needs to be offered. In particular, safety issues for both client and provider need to be addressed early in every contact. Working with perpetrators and victims of violence also often causes symptoms of secondary traumatization in providers, and providers need to be aware of this risk and ensure that they are receiving adequate support for their work. This is true for providers of all disciplines, including community advocates, police, mental health professionals, and health care professionals. Individuals involved in prevention efforts are even less likely to have formal training in how to provide such services, and more work needs to be done in this area as well.

Conclusions

In many respects, both prevention and intervention for partner violence are in their infancy. Shelters, the first service offered specifically for partner violence, originated only in the 1970s, and other programs have developed even more recently. Although many of these programs are well thought-out and take advantage of existing knowledge about the causes of partner violence, their success has been mixed. Perhaps the firmest conclusion that can be drawn is that even when considerable resources are spent and a variety of community institutions are involved, partner violence can still be quite an intractable problem. Providers in this field must be prepared to deal with a substantial number of individuals, both perpetrators and victims, who do not seem to change. Although it is generally the case that definitive outcome studies have not yet been done, some avenues for future services and service evaluation are suggested by this review.

Prevention

Prevention efforts are growing rapidly throughout the United States, especially those that focus on teenagers. Most, however, are still rather brief interventions, and their long-term impact has not been conclusively demonstrated. In particular, the effects of communitywide efforts are not well known because most studies of change at the community level have not looked at the effects of specific interventions. In the future, antiviolence programs for teens will probably become more fully integrated into the educational curriculum. Providers of such programs should also be aware, however, that some may cause a "backlash effect," or increase in violence, among a small percentage of participants. Offering relationship training skills to engaged or newly married couples, perhaps through institutions such as the military, churches, and community centers, is a promising avenue that has received only minimal application and study. In general, programs that focus on teaching protective factors, such as healthy relationship skills, may be more effective than programs that focus on warning about risk factors.

Intervention

Current efforts at social control of perpetrators may be meeting with some success. Over one half of perpetrators appear to cease their violent behavior during the 6-month to 1-year period following identification of the violence by law enforcement or other community agencies. It is not clear, however, what contributes to these results nor how much these results differ from the cessation of violence that occurs without intervention. Conclusive evaluations of individual change in perpetrators' behavior have not yet been done. Perhaps even more important, the impact on the community of changes in arrest and other intervention policies has essentially gone unstudied. It seems possible that effects on the community may have long-term deterrent effects that are not observed over the course of several months or even a few years. Thus, most providers and other partner violence professionals agree that such interventions need to be continued despite only modest evidence of their efficacy.

The study of services to victims is not well developed. Of the models that have been developed so far, the CCAMs, in particular, are promising avenues for improving the provision of services to victims in addition to perpetrators. Nonetheless, much more needs to be done to develop and evaluate services that are tailored to the needs of individuals who have sustained partner violence. It seems most likely that models based on helping individuals recover from trauma will be most applicable.

In the development of future interventions, one important area that has received little attention is the issue of matching individuals to treatment. Basic research on typologies of batterers is progressing, but these findings have yet to be incorporated into treatment models. It seems likely, for instance, that legal interventions will be most important for perpetrators who have extensive criminal histories. Similarly, couples who have experienced less severe forms of violence may be most suitable for couples therapy.

Training

Providers from a variety of backgrounds are increasingly coming to recognize the importance of addressing partner violence. New efforts at training providers to screen for and intervene with violence should broaden the number of people who are served. Providers are also becoming increasingly cognizant of unique safety and other issues that need to be addressed when working in the partner violence field. The importance of addressing one's personal violence histories is becoming increasingly recognized, as is the need to deal with vicarious traumatization. With this expansion of trained providers, one hopes, both prevention and intervention services will continue to develop and improve.

Recommendations

Prevention

1. Future school-based programs may benefit from being longer and more fully integrated into the curriculum.
2. Programs that focus on teaching protective factors, such as healthy relationship skills, may be more effective than programs that focus on warning about risk factors.
3. More research needs to be done on the effectiveness of communitywide prevention efforts, such as public service announcements.
4. More evaluation needs to be done on the effects of social structure changes. Such evaluations could be either longitudinal or cross-cultural (or both).
5. Future programs may encourage teenagers and others to become actively involved in community efforts to prevent violence—for example, by developing their own school awareness campaigns or by alerting them to ways they can join local community action groups.

Intervention

1. Screening for partner violence and safety planning should be fundamental components of all services, from hospital emergency rooms to individual counseling.

2. The development of programs tailored to treating victims of partner violence should receive increased attention that is on a par with the development of programs for perpetrators.

3. Victim blaming and falsely communicating a sense of safety should be strongly avoided in any service modality.

4. Respect for victims' stories, coping strategies, and self-worth should be emphasized by all service providers. Researchers should also try to increase the study of competent responses to violence (Hamby & Gray-Little, 1997).

5. Coordinated community action models (CCAMs) are the best model currently available for service provision.

6. Services should include assistance with gaining needed economic resources, social services, and legal advocacy. Services should not focus exclusively on self-esteem or other psychological issues.

7. Shortening intake assessments, explaining about the purposes of treatment, and following up on no-shows may decrease dropouts from batterers groups.

8. More attention and resources need to be devoted to comparative analyses of alternative interventions and the benefits of matching perpetrator to treatment.

9. Sanctions, especially legal sanctions, for noncompliance with treatment should be consistently applied.

10. Social impact and other forms of community assessment need to be integrated into outcome research.

11. CCAMs might develop further by encouraging the inclusion of extended family members as part of the planning and execution of the response to violence (as has been done in one province of Canada regarding community response to child abuse; Pennell & Burford, 1994).

Training

1. Although several training programs are available for providers who intervene with violent individuals and their victims, programs for those who provide preventive services could not be located. Such programs are needed.

2. Providers should receive specialized training and supervision that focus on preventing or intervening against violence. Providers in this

field should be aware of relevant social, political, and dynamic issues
that contribute to the problem of partner violence.

3. Providers should be thoroughly aware of their own victimization and
   perpetration histories, if any, and of their attitudes toward partner violence. Sufficient self-exploration, training, and personal therapy
   should take place so that transferential responses to victims and perpetrators are minimized.

4. More experienced providers should also continue to receive support
   and ongoing peer supervision to help minimize the effects of vicarious
   traumatization.

5. Safety issues, such as avoiding seeing clients at night in an otherwise
   empty office, are important considerations for all providers who work
   with partner violence.

6. Training should include an increased emphasis on cultural, religious,
   and socioeconomic issues and how such issues affect all services.

References

Abney, V. D., & Priest, R. (1995). African Americans and sexual child abuse. In L. A. Fontes (Ed.), *Sexual abuse in nine North American cultures: Treatment and prevention* (pp. 11-30). Thousand Oaks, CA: Sage.

Achenbach, T. M., & Edelbrock, C. S. (1984). *Child Behavior Checklist.* Burlington, VT: University of Vermont.

Adams, D. (1989). Stages of antisexist awareness and change for men who batter. In L. J. Dickstein & C. C. Nadelson (Eds.), *Family violence: Emerging issues of a national crisis* (pp. 63-97). Washington, DC: American Psychiatric Press.

Adams, D. (1994). *Historical timeline of institutional responses to battered women* (Available from Emerge, 2380 Massachusetts Ave., Cambridge, MA 02140).

Adams, D., Bancroft, L., German, T., & Sousa, C. (1992). *First-stage groups for men who batter.* Cambridge, MA: Emerge.

Aguilar, R. J., & Nightengale, N. N. (1994). The impact of specific battering experiences on the self-esteem of abused women. *Journal of Family Violence, 9*(1), 35-45.

Aldarondo, E. (1996). Cessation and persistence of wife assault: A longitudinal analysis. *American Journal of Orthopsychiatrics, 66*(1), 141-151.

Aldarondo, E. (in press). Perpetrators of domestic violence. In A. Bellack & M. Hersen (Eds.), *Comprehensive clinical psychology.* New York: Pergamon.

Aldarondo, E., & Straus, M. A. (1994). Screening for physical violence in couple therapy: Methodological, practical, and ethical considerations. *Family Process, 33,* 425-439.

Aldarondo, E., & Sugarman, D. B. (1996). Risk marker analysis of the cessation and persistence of wife assault. *Journal of Consulting and Clinical Psychology, 64*(5), 1010-1019.

Aldwin, C. M. (1994). *Stress, coping, and development: An integrative perspective.* New York: Guilford.

Alexander, P. C., Moore, S., & Alexander, E. R., III (1991). What is transmitted in the intergenerational transmission of violence? *Journal of Marriage and the Family, 53,* 657-668.

Allen, I. M. (1986). Violence and the American Indian woman. In M. C. Burns (Ed.), *The speaking profits us: Violence in the lives of women of color* (pp. 5-7). Seattle, WA: Center for Prevention of Sexual and Domestic Violence.

Allen, I. M. (1996). PTSD among African Americans. In A. J. Marsella, M. J. Friedman, E. T. Gerrity, & R. M. Scurfield (Eds.), *Ethnocultural aspects of post-traumatic stress disorder* (pp. 209-235). Washington, DC: American Psychological Association.

Almeida, R., Woods, R., Messino, T., Font, R. J., & Heer, C. (1994). Violence in the lives of the racially and sexually different: A public and private dilemma. *Journal of Feminist Family Therapy, 5*(3/4), 99-126.

Amaro, H., Fried, L. E., Cabral, H., & Zuckerman, B. (1990). Violence during pregnancy and substance use. *American Journal of Public Health, 80,* 575-579.

259

American Association of Retired Persons (AARP). (1992). *Abused elders or older battered women* (No. W15122 [1093]-D15218). Washington, DC: Author.

American Association of Retired Persons (AARP). (n.d.). *Spouse/Partner abuse in later life* (resource guide). Washington, DC: Author.

Ammerman, R. T., & Hersen, M. (1990). Issues in the assessment and treatment of family violence. In R. T. Ammerman & M. Hersen (Eds.), *Treatment of family violence* (pp. 3-14). New York: John Wiley.

Ammons, L. L. (1995). Mules, Madonnas, babies, bathwater, racial imagery, and stereotypes: The African American woman and the battered woman syndrome. *Wisconsin Law Review*, 1003-1080.

Anderson, M. J. (1993). A license to abuse: The impact of conditional status on female immigrants. *Yale Law Journal, 102*, 1401-1430.

Andrews, B., & Brewin, C. R. (1990). Attributions of blame for marital violence: A study of antecedents and consequences. *Journal of Marriage and the Family, 52*, 757-767.

Arey, D. (1995). Gay males and sexual child abuse. In L. A. Fontes (Ed.), *Sexual abuse in nine North American cultures: Treatment and prevention* (pp. 200-235). Thousand Oaks, CA: Sage.

Arias, I. (1984) *A social learning theory explication of the intergenerational transmission of physical aggression in intimate heterosexual relationships.* Unpublished doctoral dissertation, State University of New York.

Arias, I., Samios, M., & O'Leary, D. K. (1987). Prevalence and correlates of physical aggression during courtship. *Journal of Interpersonal Violence, 2*(1), 82-90.

Arroyo, W., & Eth, S. (1995). Assessment following violence-witnessing trauma. In E. Peled, P. G. Jaffe, & J. L. Edelson (Eds.), *Ending the cycle of violence* (pp. 27-43). Thousand Oaks, CA: Sage.

Asbury, J. (1987). African American women in violent relationships: An exploration of cultural differences. In R. L. Hampton (Ed.), *Violence in the Black family: Correlates and consequences* (pp. 86-106). Lexington, MA: Lexington.

Asbury, J. (1993). Violence in families of color in the United States. In R. L. Hampton, T. P. Gullota, G. R. Adams, E. H. Potter, & R. P. Weissberg (Eds.), *Family violence: Prevention and treatment* (pp. 159-178). Newbury Park, CA: Sage.

Ascione, F. R. (in press). Battered women's reports of their partners' and their children's cruelty to animals. *Journal of Emotional Abuse.*

Astin, M. C., Lawrence, K. J., & Foy, D. W. (1993). Post-traumatic stress disorder among battered women: Risk and resiliency factors. *Violence and Victims, 8*(1), 17-28.

Augustine, R. I. (1990–1991). Marriage: The safe haven for rapists. *Journal of Family Law, 29*(3), 559-590.

Babcock, J. C., Waltz, J., Jacobson, N. S., & Gottman, J. M. (1993). Power and violence: The relation between communication patterns, power discrepancies, and domestic violence. *Journal of Consulting and Clinical Psychology, 61*(1), 40-50.

Bachman, R. (1992). *Death and violence on the reservation: Homicide, family violence, and suicide in American Indian populations.* Westport, CT: Auburn House.

Bachman, R., & Coker, A. L. (1995). Police involvement in domestic violence: The interactive effects of victim injury, offender's history of violence, and race. *Violence and Victims, 10*(2), 91-106.

Bachman, R., & Saltzman, L. E. (1994). *Violence against women: A national crime victimization survey report* (No. NCJ 154348). Washington, DC: U.S. Department of Justice.

Bachman, R., & Saltzman, L. E. (1995). *Violence against women: Estimates from the redesigned survey* (BJS Publication No. 154-348)). Washington, DC: U.S. Department of Justice, Bureau of Justice Statistics.

Back, S. M., Post, R. D., & D'Arcy, G. (1982). A study of battered women in a psychiatric setting. *Women and Therapy, 1*(2), 13-26.

Baker, K., Cahn, N., & Sands, S. J. (1989). *Report on District of Columbia Police response to domestic violence.* Georgetown University Joint project of the DC Coalition Against Domestic Violence and the Women's Law and Public Policy Fellowship Program at Georgetown University Law Center.

Bandura, A. (1973). *Aggression: A social learning analysis.* Upper Saddle River, NJ: Prentice Hall.

Barnard, C. P. (1989). Alcoholism and sex abuse in the family: Incest and marital rape. *Journal of Chemical Dependency Treatment, 3,* 131-144.

Barnett, O. W., Miller-Perrin, C. L., & Perrin, R. D. (1997). *Family violence across the lifespan: An introduction.* Thousand Oaks, CA: Sage.

Bauserman, S. A. K., & Arias, I. (1992). Relationships among marital investment, marital satisfaction, and marital commitment in domestically victimized and nonvictimized wives. *Violence and Victims, 7,* 287-296.

Bekemeier, B. (1995). Public health nurses and the prevention of and intervention in family violence. *Public Health Nursing, 12*(4), 222-227.

Belsky, J. (1984). The determinants of parenting: A process model. *Child Development, 55,* 83-96.

Bennett, L. W., Tolman, R. M., Rogalski, C. J., & Srinivasaraghavan, J. (1994). Domestic abuse by male alcohol and drug addicts. *Violence and Victims, 9,* 359-368.

Bergen, R. K. (1996). *Wife rape: Understanding the response of survivors and service providers.* Thousand Oaks, CA: Sage.

Bergman, L. (1992). Dating violence among high school students. *Social Work, 37*(1), 21-27.

Berk, R. A. (1993). What the scientific evidence shows: On the average, we can do no better than arrest. In R. J. Gelles & D. R. Loseke (Eds.), *Current controversies on family violence* (pp. 323-336). Newbury Park, CA: Sage.

Berk, R. A., Newton, P. J., & Berk, S. F. (1986). What a difference a day makes: An empirical study of the impact of shelters for battered women. *Journal of Marriage and the Family, 48,* 481-490.

Berrios, D. C., & Grady, D. (1991). Domestic violence: Risk factors and outcomes. *Western Journal of Medicine, 155*(2), 133-135.

Bersani, C. A., & Chen, H. T. (1988). Sociological perspectives in family violence. In V. B. Van Hasselt, R. L. Morrison, A. S. Bellack, & M. Hersen (Eds.), *Handbook of family violence* (pp. 57-88). New York: Plenum.

Bodnarchuk, M., Kropp, R., Ogloff, J. R. P., Hart, S. D., & Dutton, D. G. (1995). *Predicting cessation of intimate assaultiveness after group treatment* (No. 4887-10-91-106). Ottawa: Health Canada, Family Violence Prevention Division.

Bogenschneider, K. (1996). Family-related prevention programs: An ecological risk/protective theory for building prevention programs, policies, and community capacity to support youth. *Family Relations, 45,* 127-138.

Bograd, M. (1984). Family systems approaches to wife battering. *American Journal of Orthopsychiatry, 54*(4), 558-568.

Bograd, M. (1988). Feminist perspectives on wife abuse: An introduction. In K. Yllö & M. Bograd (Eds.), *Feminist perspectives on wife abuse* (pp. 11-28). Newbury Park, CA: Sage.

Bohn, D. K. (1990). Domestic violence and pregnancy: Implications from practice. *Journal of Nurse-Midwifery, 35*(2), 86-98.

Bologna, M. J., Waterman, C. K., & Dawson, L. J. (1987). *Violence in gay male and lesbian relationships: Implications for practitioners and policy makers.* Paper presented at the Third National Conference for Family Violence Researchers, Durham, NH.

Bowker, L. H. (1983a). *Beating wife beating.* Lexington, MA: Lexington.

Bowker, L. H. (1983b, June). Marital rape: A distinct syndrome? *Social Casework,* 347-352.

Bowker, L. H. (1993). A battered woman's problems are social, not psychological. In R. J. Gelles & D. R. Loseke (Eds.), *Current controversies on family violence* (pp. 154-165). Newbury Park, CA: Sage.

Bowker, L. H., & Maurer, L. (1986). The effectiveness of counseling services utilized by battered women. *Women and Therapy, 5*(4), 65-82.

Bowker, L. H., & Maurer, L. (1987). The medical treatment of battered wives. *Women and Health, 12*(1), 25-45.

Brand, P. A., & Kidd, A. H. (1986). Frequency of physical aggression in heterosexual and female homosexual dyads. *Psychological Reports, 59,* 1307-1313.

Brice-Baker, J. R. (1994). Domestic violence in African American and African-Caribbean families. *Journal of Distress and the Homeless, 3*(1), 23-38.

Browne, A. (1987). *When battered women kill.* New York: Macmillan Free Press.

Browne, A. (1993). Violence against women by male partners: Prevalence, outcomes, and policy implications. *American Psychologist, 48*(10), 1077-1087.

Browne, A., & Williams, K. R. (1989). Exploring the effect of resource availability and the likelihood of female-perpetrated homicides. *Law and Society Review, 23*(1), 75-94.

Browning, J., & Dutton, D. (1986). Assessment of wife assault with the Conflict Tactics Scale: Using couple data to quantify the differential reporting effect. *Journal of Marriage and the Family, 48*(2), 375-379.

Bullock, L. F., & McFarlane, J. (1989). The birth-weight/battering connection. *American Journal of Nursing, 89,* 1153-1155.

Burge, S. K. (1989). Violence against women as a health care issue. *Family Medicine, 21,* 368-373.

Burns, M. C. (1986). *The speaking profits us: Violence in the lives of women of color.* Seattle, WA: Center for the Prevention of Sexual and Domestic Violence.

Burns, N., Meredith, C., & Paquette, C. (1991). *Treatment programs for men who batter: A review of the evidence of their success.* Cambridge, MA: Abt Associate of Canada.

Burt, M. R. (1980). Cultural myths and supports for rape. *Journal of Personality and Social Psychology, 38*(2), 217-230.

Bushman, B. J., & Cooper, H. M. (1990). Effects of alcohol on human aggression: An integrative research review. *Psychological Bulletin, 107*(3), 341-354.

Butke, M. (1995). Lesbians and sexual child abuse. In L. A. Fontes (Ed.), *Sexual abuse in nine North American cultures: Treatment and prevention* (pp. 236-258). Thousand Oaks, CA: Sage.

Buzawa, E. S., & Buzawa, C. G. (1993). The scientific evidence is not conclusive: Arrest is no panacea. In R. J. Gelles & D. R. Loseke (Eds.), *Current controversies on family violence* (pp. 337-356). Newbury Park, CA: Sage.

Buzawa, E. S., & Buzawa, C. G. (1996). Introduction. In E. S. Buzawa & C. G. Buzawa (Eds.), *Do arrests and restraining orders work?* (pp. 1-13). Thousand Oaks, CA: Sage.

Byrne, D. (1996). Clinical models for the treatment of gay male perpetrators of domestic violence. In C. M. Renzetti & C. H. Miley (Eds.), *Violence in gay and lesbian domestic partnerships* (pp. 107-116). Binghamton, NY: Haworth.

Cadsky, O., Hanson, R. K., Crawford, M., & Lalonde, C. (1996). Attrition from a male batterer treatment program: Client-treatment congruence and lifestyle instability. *Violence and Victims, 11*(1), 51-64.

Caesar, P. L. (1988). Exposure to violence in the families-of-origin among wife-abusers and maritally nonviolent men. *Violence and Victims, 3*(1), 49-63.

Cahoon, D. D., & Edmonds, E. M. (1992). Did rape occur? A comparison of male and female opinions concerning the definition of rape. *Contemporary Social Psychology, 16*(4), 60-63.

Cahoon, D. D., Edmonds, E. M., Spaulding, R. M., & Dickens, J. C. (1995). A comparison of the opinions of black and white males and females concerning the occurrence of rape. *Journal of Social Behavior and Personality, 10*(1), 91-100.

Campbell, D. W. (1993). Nursing care of African American battered women: Afrocentric perspectives. *AWHONNS Clinical Issues in Perinatal and Women's Health Nursing, 4,* 407-415.

Campbell, J., Poland, M., Walder, J., & Ager, J. (1992). Correlates of battering during pregnancy. *Research in Nursing and Health, 15*(3), 219-226.

Campbell, J. C. (1989a). A test of two explanatory models of women's responses to battering. *Nursing Research, 38*(1), 18-24.

Campbell, J. C. (1989b). Women's response to sexual abuse in intimate relationships. *Health Care for Women International, 10,* 335-346.

Campbell, J. C. (1991). Prevention of wife battering: Insights from cultural analysis. *Response to Victimization of Women and Children, 14*(3), 18-24.

Campbell, J. C. (1995). Prediction of homicide of and by women. In J. C. Campbell (Ed.), *Assessing dangerousness: Violence by sexual offenders, batterers, and child abusers* (pp. 96-113). Thousand Oaks, CA: Sage.

Campbell, J. C., & Alford, P. (1989). The dark consequences of marital rape. *American Journal of Nursing,* 946-949.

Campbell, J. C., Harris, M. J., & Lee, R. K. (1995). Violence research: An overview. *Scholarly Inquiry for Nursing Practice, 9*(2), 105-126.

Campbell, J. C., Oliver, C., & Bullock, L. (1993). Why battering during pregnancy? *AWHONNS Clinical Issues in Perinatal and Women's Health Nursing, 4*(3), 343-349.

Campbell, J. C., Pugh, L. C., Campbell, D., & Visscher, M. (1995). The influence of abuse on pregnancy intention. *Women's Health Issues, 5*(4), 214-223.

Caplan, P. J. (1985). *The myth of women's masochism.* New York: Dutton.

Carlson, B. (1987). Dating violence: A research review and comparison with spousal abuse. *Social Casework, 68*(1), 16-23.

Carlson, B. E. (1990). Adolescent observers of marital violence. *Journal of Family Violence, 5*(4), 285-299.

Cascardi, M., Langhinrichsen, J., & Vivian, D. (1992). Marital aggression: Impact, injury, and health correlates for husbands and wives. *Archives of Internal Medicine, 152,* 1178-1184.

Cascardi, M., & O'Leary, D. (1992). Depressive symptomatology, self-esteem, and self-blame in battered women. *Journal of Family Violence, 7*(4), 249-259.

Cazenave, N. A., & Straus, M. A. (1990). Race, class, network embeddedness, and family violence: A search for potent support systems. In M. A. Straus & R. J. Gelles (Eds.), *Physical violence in American families: Risk factors and adaptations to violence in 8,145 families* (pp. 321-340). New Brunswick, NJ: Transaction.

Center for Constitutional Rights. (1990). *Stopping sexual assault in marriage: A guide for women, counselors, and advocates* (2nd ed.). New York: Author.

Centers for Disease Control and Prevention. (1993). *HIV/AIDS surveillance report.* Washington, DC: U.S. Department of Health and Human Services.

Chan, C. S. (1987). Asian American women: Psychological responses to sexual exploitation and cultural stereotypes. *Asian American Psychological Association Journal, 12,* 11-15.

Chan, S., & Leong, C. W. (1994). Chinese families in transition: Cultural conflicts and adjustment problems. *Journal of Social Distress and the Homeless, 3*(3), 263-281.

Chapin, D. (1990). Peace on earth begins in the home. *The Circle, 14*(1).

Chen, S. A., & True, R. H. (1994). Asian/Pacific Island Americans. In L. D. Eron, J. H. Gontry, & J. P. Schleyel (Eds.), *Reason to hope: A psychological perspective on violence and youth* (pp. 145-162). Washington, DC: American Psychological Association.

Chester, B., Robin, R. W., Koss, M. P., Lopez, J., & Goldman, D. (1994). Grandmother dishonored: Violence against women by male partners in American Indian communities. *Violence and Victims, 9*(3), 249-258.

Chin, K. L. (1994). Out-of-town brides: International marriage and wife abuse among Chinese immigrants. *Journal of Comparative Family Studies, 25*(1), 53-69.

Chodorow, N. (1978). *The reproduction of mothering: Psychoanalysis and the sociology of gender.* Berkeley: University of California Press.

Christopoulos, C., Cohn, D. A., Shaw, D. S., Joyce, S., Sullivan-Hanson, J., Kraft, S. P., & Emery, R. (1987). Children of abused women: Adjustment at time of shelter residence. *Journal of Marriage and the Family, 49*, 611-619.

Coleman, D. H., & Straus, M. A. (1986). Marital power, conflict, and violence in a nationally representative sample of American couples. *Violence and Victims, 1*(2), 141-157.

Coleman, D. H., & Straus, M. A. (1990). Marital power, conflict, and violence in a nationally representative sample of American couples. In M. A. Straus & R. J. Gelles (Eds.), *Physical violence in American families: Risk factors and adaptations to violence in 8,145 families* (pp. 287-304). New Brunswick, NJ: Transaction.

Coleman, V. E. (1990). *Violence between lesbian couples: A between groups comparison.* Doctoral dissertation (University Microfilms No. 9109022).

Coleman, V. E. (1994). Lesbian battering: The relationship between personality and the perpetration of violence. *Violence and Victims, 9*(2), 139-152.

Coley, S. M., & Beckett, J. O. (1988). Black battered women: Practice issues. *Social Casework: The Journal of Contemporary Social Work,* 483-490.

Comas-Diaz, L. (1995). Puerto Ricans and sexual child abuse. In L. A. Fontes (Ed.), *Sexual abuse in nine North American cultures: Treatment and prevention* (pp. 31-66). Thousand Oaks, CA: Sage.

Common Purpose. (1996). *Common purpose training.* Boston: Author.

Conger, R. D., Elder, G. H., Lorenz, K. J., Conger, R. L., Simons, R. L., Whitbeck, L. B., Huck, S., & Melby, J. N. (1990). Linking economic hardship to marital quality and instability. *Journal of Marriage and the Family, 52*(3), 243-656.

Copelon, R. (1994). Intimate terror: Understanding domestic violence as torture. In R. J. Cook (Ed.), *Human rights for women: National and international perspectives* (pp. 116-152). Philadelphia: University of Pennsylvania Press.

Copping, V. E. (1996). Beyond over- and undercontrol: Behavioral observations of shelter children. *Journal of Family Violence, 11*(1), 41-57.

Cox, J. W., & Stoltenberg, C. D. (1991). Evaluation of a treatment program for battered wives. *Journal of Family Violence, 6*(4), 395-413.

Crenshaw, K. (1994). Mapping the margins: Intersectionality, identity politics, and violence against women of color. In M. A. Fireman & R. Mykitiuk (Eds.), *The public nature of private violence: The discovery of domestic abuse* (pp. 93-117). New York: Routledge.

Crites, L. (1990). Cross-cultural counseling in wife beating cases. *Response to Victimization of Women and Children, 13*(4), 8-12.

Cummings, E. M., Zahn-Waxler, C., & Radke-Yarrow, M. (1981). Young children's responses to expressions of anger and affection by others in the family. *Child Development, 52*, 1274-1282.

Cummings, J. S., Pelligrini, D. S., Notarius, C. I., & Cummings, E. M. (1989). Children's responses to angry adult behavior as a function of marital distress and history of interparent hostility. *Child Development, 60,* 1035-1043.

Curtis, L. A. (1976). Present and future measures of victimization in forcible rape. In M. J. Walker & S. L. Brodsky (Eds.), *Sexual assault* (pp. 61-68). Lexington, MA: D. C. Heath.

Dalton, D. A., & Kantner, J. E. (1983). Aggression in battered and nonbattered women as reflected in the Hand Test. *Psychological Reports, 53,* 703-709.

Dao, H. (1988). *The battered Southeast Asian women: Who is she?* Paper presented at the National Conference Against Domestic Violence Fourth National Conference and Membership Meeting, Seattle, WA.

D'Augelli, A. R., & Dark, L. J. (1995). Lesbian, gay, and bisexual youths. In L. D. Eron, J. H. Gentry, & P. Schleyel (Eds.), *Reason to hope: A psychological perspective on violence and youth* (pp. 177-196). Washington, DC: American Psychological Association.

Davies, D. (1991). Intervention with male toddlers who have witnessed parental violence. *Families in Society,* 515-524.

Davis, A. L. (1996). *Applying social learning theory through mass media to increase response to a domestic abuse hotline.* Unpublished master's thesis, University of Texas.

Davis, L. V., & Carlson, B. E. (1987). Observation of spousal abuse: What happens to the children? *Journal of Interpersonal Violence, 2*(3), 278-291.

Deal, J., & Wampler, K. (1986). Dating violence: The primacy of previous experience. *Journal of Social and Personal Relationships, 3,* 457-471.

DeMaris, A. (1987). The efficacy of a spousal abuse model in accounting for courtship violence. *Journal of Family Issues, 8*(3), 291-305.

DeMaris, A. (1989). Attrition in batterers' counseling: The role of social and demographic factors. *Social Service Review,* 142-154.

DeMaris, A., & Jackson, J. (1987). Batterers' reports of recidivism after counseling. *Social Casework, 68,* 458-465.

Dennis, R. E., Key, L. J., Kirk, A. L., & Smith, A. (1995). Addressing domestic violence in the African American community. *Journal of Health Care for the Poor and Underserved, 6*(2), 284-293.

DePuy, J. (1995). Power, control, and abuse against women in Swiss families. Paper presented at the Fourth International Family Violence Research Conference, Durham, NH.

Derogatis, L. R. (1977). *SCL-90 administration, scoring, and procedure, manual-1.* Baltimore: Johns Hopkins University, School of Medicine.

Deschner, J. P., & McNeil, J. S. (1986). Results of anger control training for battering couples. *Journal of Family Violence, 1*(2), 111-120.

Diamond, D. L., & Wilsnack, S. C. (1978). Alcohol abuse among lesbians: A descriptive study. *Journal of Homosexuality, 4,* 123-142.

Dibble, U., & Straus, M. A. (1980). Some social structure determinants of inconsistency between attitudes and behavior: The case of family violence. *Journal of Marriage and the Family, 42*(1), 71-80.

Dobash, R., Dobash, R. E., Cavanagh, K., & Lewis, R. (1996). *Research findings No. 46: Re-education programmes for violent men—an evaluation* (Available from the Research and Statistics Directorate, Information and Publications Group, Room 1308, Home Office, Apollo House, 36 Wellesley Road, Croydon CR9 3RR England).

Dobash, R. E., & Dobash, R. (1979). *Violence against wives.* New York: Free Press.

Dobash, R. E., & Dobash, R. P. (1992). *Women, violence, and social change.* New York: Routledge.

Dobash, R. P., Dobash, R. E., Wilson, M., & Daly, M. (1992). The myth of sexual symmetry in marital violence. *Social Problems, 39*(1), 71-91.

Dodge, K. A., Pettit, G. S., & Bates, J. E. (1994). Socialization mediators of the relation between socioeconomic status and child conduct problems. *Child Development, 65*, 649-665.

Dohrenwend, B. S., & Dohrenwend, B. P. (1982). Some issues in research on stressful life events. In T. Millon, C. Green, & R. Meager (Eds.), *Handbook of clinical health psychology* (pp. 91-102). New York: Plenum.

Donato, K. M., & Bowker, L. H. (1984). Understanding the help-seeking behavior of battered women: A comparison of traditional service agencies and women's groups. *International Journal of Women's Studies, 7*, 99-109.

Douglas, H. (1991). Assessing violent couples. *Families in Society, 525-535.*

Downs, W. R., Miller, B. A., & Panek, D. D. (1993). Differential patterns of partner-to-woman violence: A comparison of samples of community, alcohol-abusing, and battered women. *Journal of Family Violence, 8*(2), 113-135.

Drucker, D. (1979). The common law does not support a marital exception to forcible rape. *Women's Rights Law Reporter, 5*(2/3), 181-200.

Dunwoody, E. (1982). Battering in Indochinese refugee families. *Response to Victimization of Women and Children, 5*(5), 1-12.

Dutton, D. G. (1986). The outcome of court-mandated treatment for wife assault: A quasi-experimental evaluation. *Violence and Victims, 1*(3), 163-175.

Dutton, D. G. (1988). Profiling of wife assaulters: Preliminary evidence for a trimodal analysis. *Violence and Victims, 3*(1), 5-29.

Dutton, D. G. (1994). The origin and structure of the abusive personality. *Journal of Personality Disorders, 8*(3), 181-191.

Dutton, D. G., & Painter, S. (1993). The battered woman syndrome: Effects of severity and intermittency of abuse. *American Journal of Orthopsychiatry, 63*(4), 614-622.

Dutton, D. G., & Starzomski, A. J. (1993). Borderline personality in perpetrators of psychological and physical abuse. *Violence and Victims, 8*(4), 327-337.

Dutton, D. G., & Strachan, C. E. (1987). Motivational needs for power and spouse-specific assertiveness in assaultive and nonassaultive men. *Violence and Victims, 2*(3), 145-156.

Dutton, M. A. (1992). *Empowering and healing the battered woman: A model for assessment and intervention.* New York: Springer.

Dutton, M. A. (1993). Understanding women's responses to domestic violence: A redefinition of battered woman syndrome. *Hofstra Law Review, 21*, 1191-1242.

Eagly, A. H., & Steffen, V. J. (1986). Gender and aggressive behavior: A meta-analytic review of the social psychological literature. *Psychological Bulletin, 100*(3), 309-330.

Easteal, P. W., & Easteal, S. (1992). Attitudes and practices of doctors toward spousal assault victims: An Australian study. *Violence and Victims, 7*(3), 217-228.

Eby, K. K., Campbell, J. C., Sullivan, C. M., & Davidson, W. S. (1995). Health effects of experiences of sexual violence for women with abusive partners. *Health Care for Women International, 16*, 563-576.

Edleson, J. L. (1995). Do batterers programs work? In *International Study Group on the Future of Intervention with Battered Women and Their Families*, (pp. 1-10). Haifa, Israel.

Edleson, J. L., & Grusznski, R. J. (1989). Treating men who batter: Four years of outcome data from the Domestic Abuse Program. *Journal of Social Service Research, 12*(1/2), 3-22.

Edleson, J. L., & Syers, M. (1990). Relative effectiveness of group treatments for men who batter. *Social Work Research and Abstracts, 10-17.*

Edleson, J. L., & Syers, M. (1991). The effects of group treatment for men who batter: An 18-month follow-up study. *Research on Social Work Practice, 1*(3), 227-243.

Edleson, J. L., & Tolman, R. M. (1992). *Intervention for men who batter.* Newbury Park, CA: Sage.

Elinson, J., & Nurco, D. (1975). *Operation definitions in socio-behavioral drug research.* Rockville, MD: National Institute on Drug Abuse.

Elliot, D. S., Huizinga, D., & Morse, B. J. (1986). Self-reported violent offending: A descriptive analysis of juvenile violent offenders and their offending careers. *Journal of Interpersonal Violence, 4,* 472-514.

Elliot, P. (1996). Shattering illusions: Same-sex domestic violence. In C. M. Renzetti (Ed.), *Violence in gay and lesbian domestic partnerships* (pp. 1-8). Binghamton, NY: Haworth.

Elliott, D., & Guy, J. (1993). Mental health professionals versus non-mental-health professionals: Childhood trauma and adult functioning. *Professional Psychology: Research and Practice, 24*(1), 83-90.

Elliott, F. A. (1988). Neurological factors. In V. B. Van Hasselt, R. L. Morrison, A. S. Bellack, & M. Hersen (Eds.), *Handbook of family violence* (pp. 359-382). New York: Plenum.

Ellis, D. (1987). Postseparation woman abuse: The contribution of lawyers as "barracudas," "advocates," and "counsellors." *International Journal of Law and Psychiatry, 10,* 401-410.

Else, L., Wonderlitch, S. A., Beatty, W. W., Christie, D. W., & Staton, R. D. (1993). Personality characteristics of men who physically abuse women. *Hospital and Community Psychiatry, 44*(1), 54-58.

Emerge. (n.d.). *Guidelines for talking to abusive husbands.* Cambridge, MA.

Eng, P. (1995). Domestic violence in Asian/Pacific Island communities. In D. L. Adams (Ed.), *Health issues for women of color: A cultural diversity perspective* (pp. 78-88). Thousand Oaks, CA: Sage.

Estrich, S. (1987). *Real rape.* Cambridge, MA: Harvard University Press.

Eth, S., & Pynoos, R. S. (1994). Children who witness the homicide of a parent. *Psychiatry, 57*(4), 287-306.

Fagan, J. (1990). Intoxication and aggression. In M. Tonry & J. Q. Wilson (Eds.), *Drugs and crime* (pp. 241-320). Chicago: University of Chicago Press.

Fagan, J. (1993). *Set and setting revisited: Influences of alcohol and illicit drugs on the social context of violent events* (Monograph No. 24; pp. 161-191; No. 93-3496). Rockville, MD: National Institute on Alcohol Abuse and Alcoholism Research.

Fagan, J., & Browne, A. (1994). Violence between spouses and intimates: Physical aggression between women and men in intimate relationships. In A. J. Reiss & J. A. Roth (Eds.), *Understanding and preventing violence* (Vol. 3, pp. 115-292). Washington, DC: National Research Council, National Academy of Sciences.

Fagan, J. A., Stewart, D. K., & Hansen, K. V. (1983). Violent men or violent husbands? Background factors and situational correlates. In D. Finkelhor, R. J. Gelles, G. T. Hotaling, & M. A. Straus (Eds.), *The dark side of families* (pp. 49-68). Beverly Hills, CA: Sage.

Fantuzzo, J., Boruch, R., Beriama, A., Atkins, M., & Marcus, S. (1997). Domestic violence and children: Prevalence and risk in five major U.S. cities. *Journal of the American Academy of Child and Adolescent Psychiatry, 36*(1), 116-122.

Fantuzzo, J. W., DePaola, L. M., Lambert, L., Martino, T., Anderson, G., & Sutton, S. (1991). Effects of interparental violence on the psychological adjustment and competencies of young children. *Journal of Consulting and Clinical Psychology, 59*(2), 258-265.

Fantuzzo, J. W., & Lindquist, C. U. (1989). The effects of observing conjugal violence on children: A review and analysis of research methodology. *Journal of Family Violence, 4*(1), 77-94.

Farley, N. (1992). Same-sex domestic violence. In S. H. Dworkin & F. J. Gutierrez (Eds.), *Counseling gay men and lesbians: Journey to the end of the rainbow* (pp. 231-242). Alexandria, VA: American Association for Counseling and Development.

Farley, N. (1996). A survey of factors contributing to gay and lesbian domestic violence. In C. M. Renzetti & C. H. Miley (Eds.), *Violence in gay and lesbian domestic partnerships* (pp. 35-42). Binghamton, NY: Haworth.

Farrell, G., Buck, W., & Pease, K. (1993). The Merseyside Domestic Violence Prevention Project: Some costs and benefits. *Studies on Crime and Crime Prevention, 2,* 21-33.

Faulkner, K., Stoltenberg, C. D., Cogen, R., Nolder, M., & Shooter, E. (1992). Cognitive-behavioral group treatment for male spouse abusers. *Journal of Family Violence, 7*(1), 37-55.

Feld, S. L., & Straus, M. A. (1990). Escalation and desistance from wife assault in marriage. In M. A. Straus & R. J. Gelles (Eds.), *Physical violence in American families: Risk factors and adaptations to violence in 8,145 families* (pp. 489-505). New Brunswick, NJ: Transaction.

Finkelhor, D., & Dziuba-Leatherman, J. (1994). Victimization of children. *American Psychologist, 49*(3), 173-183.

Finkelhor, D., & Yllö, K. (1983). Rape in marriage: A sociological view. In D. Finkelhor, R. J. Gelles, G. T. Hotaling, & M. A. Straus (Eds.), *The dark side of families* (pp. 119-130). Beverly Hills, CA: Sage.

Finkelhor, D., & Yllö, K. (1985). *License to rape: Sexual abuse of wives.* New York: Holt, Rinehart & Winston.

Finn, J. (1987). Men's domestic violence treatment: The court referral component. *Journal of Interpersonal Violence, 2*(2), 154-165.

Fitzgerald, F. T. (1994). The tyranny of health. *New England Journal of Medicine, 331*(3), 196-198.

Fitzpatrick, J. (1994). The use of international human rights norms to combat violence against women. In R. J. Cook (Ed.), *Human rights for women: National and international perspectives* (pp. 532-571). Philadelphia: University of Pennsylvania Press.

Flournoy, P. S., & Wilson, G. L. (1991). Assessment of MMPI profiles of male batterers. *Violence and Victims, 6*(4), 309-320.

Follingstad, D. R., Brennan, A. F., Hause, E. S., Polek, D. S., & Rutledge, L. L. (1991). Factors moderating physical and psychological symptoms of battered women. *Journal of Family Violence, 6,* 81-95.

Follingstad, D. R., Wright, S., Lloyd, S., & Sebastian, J. A. (1991). Sex differences in motivations and effects in dating violence. *Family Relations, 40*(1), 51-57.

Fontes, L. A. (1995). *Sexual abuse in nine North American cultures: Treatment and prevention.* Thousand Oaks, CA: Sage.

Fontes, L. A. (1997). Conducting ethical cross-cultural research on family violence. In G. Kaufman Kantor & J. L. Jasinski (Eds.), *Out of the darkness: Contemporary perspectives on family violence* (pp. 296-312). Thousand Oaks, CA: Sage.

Foo, L., & Margolin, G. (1995). A multivariate investigation of dating aggression. *Journal of Family Violence, 10*(4), 351-377.

Ford, D. A. (1983). Wife battery and criminal justice: A study of victim decision-making. *Family Relations, 32*(4), 463-475.

Ford, D. A. (1987). *The impact of police officers' attitudes toward victims on the disinclination to arrest wife batterers.* Paper presented at the *Third National Conference for Family Violence Researchers, Durham, NH.*

Ford, D. A. (1993). *Mediating impacts on the effectiveness of policies for prosecuting wife beaters.* Paper presented at the Annual Meeting of the American Society of Criminology, Phoenix, AZ.

Ford, D. A., Reichard, R., Goldsmith, S., & Regoli, M. J. (1996). Future directions for criminal justice policy on domestic violence. In E. S. Buzawa & C. G. Buzawa (Eds.), *Do arrests and restraining orders work?* (pp. 243-265). Thousand Oaks, CA: Sage.

Forsstrom-Cohen, B., & Rosenbaum, A. (1985). The effects of parental marital violence on young adults: An exploratory investigation. *Journal of Marriage and the Family, 47*(2), 467-472.

Franco, F. E. (1996). Unconditional safety for conditional immigrant women. *Berkeley Women's Law Journal, 11,* 99-141.

Freeman, M. D. (1985). Doing his best to sustain the sanctity of marriage. *Sociological Review Monograph, 31,* 124-146.

Frieze, I. H. (1983). Investigating the causes and consequences of marital rape. *Signs, 8*(3), 532-553.

Frieze, I. H., & Browne, A. (1989). Violence in marriage. In L. Ohlin & M. Tonry (Eds.), *Family violence* (pp. 163-218). Chicago: University of Chicago Press.

Frieze, I. H., Knoble, J., Zomnir, G., & Washburn, C. (1980). *Types of battered women.* Paper presented at the Annual Research Conference of the Association for Women in Psychology, Santa Monica, CA.

Frodi, A., Macaulay, J., & Thome, P. R. (1977). Are women always less aggressive than men? A review of the experimental literature. *Psychological Bulletin, 84*(4), 634-660.

Gabbard, G. O. (1981). Masochism: Myth or human need? *American Journal of Psychiatry, 138*(4), 533.

Ganley, A. L. (1989). Integrating feminist and social learning analyses of aggression: Creating multiple models for intervention with men who batter. In P. L. Caesar & L. K. Hamberger (Eds.), *Treating men who batter: Theory, practice, and programs* (pp. 196-235). New York: Springer.

Gardner, R. (1989) *Method of conflict resolution and characteristics of abuse and victimization in heterosexual, lesbian, and gay male couples.* Unpublished doctoral dissertation, University of Georgia, Athens.

Garner, J., Fagan, J., & Maxwell, C. (1995). Published findings from the Spousal Assault Replication Program: A critical review. *Journal of Quantitative Criminology, 11*(1), 3-28.

Gayford, J. J. (1975). Wife battering: A preliminary survey of 100 cases. *British Medical Journal, 1,* 194-197.

Gayford, J. J. (1976). Ten types of battered wives. *Welfare Officer, 25,* 5-9.

Gebhard, P. H. (1997). *Memorandum on the incidence of homosexuals in the United States* Bloomington: Indiana University, Center for Sex Research.

Geffner, R., Mantooth, C., Franks, D., & Rao, L. (1989). A psychoeducational, conjoint therapy approach to reducing family violence. In P. L. Caesar & L. K. Hamberger (Eds.), *Treating men who batter: Theory, practice, and programs* (pp. 103-133). New York: Springer.

Gelles, R. (1974). *The violent home: A study of physical aggression between husbands and wives.* Beverly Hills, CA: Sage.

Gelles, R. J. (1978). Violence toward children in the United States. *American Journal of Orthopsychiatry, 48*(4), 580-592.

Gelles, R. J. (1990). Violence and pregnancy: Are pregnant women at greater risk of abuse? In M. A. Straus & R. J. Gelles (Eds.), *Physical violence in American families: Risk factors and adaptations to violence in 8,145 families* (pp. 279-286). New Brunswick, NJ: Transaction.

Gelles, R. J., & Cornell, C. P. (1990). *Intimate violence in families* (2nd ed.). Newbury Park, CA: Sage.

Gelles, R. J., & Harrop, J. W. (1989). Violence, battering, and psychological distress among women. *Journal of Interpersonal Violence, 4*(4), 400-420.

Gelles, R. J., & Straus, M. A. (1978). Violence in the American family. *Journal of Social Issues, 35*(2), 15-39.

Gelles, R. J., & Straus, M. A. (1988). *Intimate violence.* New York: Simon & Schuster.

Gentry, C. E., & Eaddy, V. B. (1982). Treatment of children in spouse abusive families. *Victimology, 5,* 240-250.

George, L. K., Winfield, I., & Blazer, D. G. (1992). Sociocultural factors in sexual assault: Comparison of two representative samples of women. *Journal of Social Issues, 48*(1), 105-125.

Giles-Sims, J. (1983). *Wife battering: A systems theory approach.* New York: Guilford.

Ginorio, A. B., Gutierrez, L., & Cause, A. M. (1995). Psychological issues for Latinas. In H. Landrine (Ed.), *Bringing cultural diversity to feminist psychology: Theory, research, and practice* (pp. 241-263). Washington, DC: American Psychological Association.

Gleason, W. J. (1993). Mental disorders in battered women: An empirical study. *Violence and Victims, 8,* 53-68.

Goldstein, M. Z. (1995). Maltreatment of elderly persons. *Psychiatric Services, 46,* 1219-1225.

Goldstein, P. J., Belluci, P. A., Spunt, B. J., & Miller, T. (1989). *Frequency of cocaine use and violence: A comparison between women and men.* New York: Narcotic and Drug Research.

Gondolf, E. W. (1987a). Changing men who batter: A developmental model for integrated intervention. *Journal of Family Violence, 2,* 335-349.

Gondolf, E. W. (1987b). Seeing through smoke and mirrors: A guide to batterer program evaluations. *Response to Victimization of Women and Children, 10*(3), 16-19.

Gondolf, E. W. (1988a). The effect of batterer counseling on shelter outcome. *Journal of Interpersonal Violence, 3*(3), 275-289.

Gondolf, E. W. (1988b). Who are those guys? Toward a behavioral typology of batterers. *Violence and Victims, 3*(3), 187-203.

Gondolf, E. W. (1990). An exploratory survey of court-mandated batterer programs. *Response to Victimization of Women and Children, 13*(3), 7-11.

Gondolf, E. W. (1992). Discussion of violence in psychiatric evaluations. *Journal of Interpersonal Violence, 7,* 334-349.

Gondolf, E. W. (1995). Discharge criteria for batterer programs. In *Fourth International Family Violence Research Conference* (pp. 1-17). Durham, NH.

Gondolf, E. W. (1997). Batterer programs: What we know and need to know. *Journal of Interpersonal Violence, 12,* 83-98.

Gondolf, E. W., & Fisher, E. R. (1988). *Battered women as survivors: An alternative to treating learned helplessness.* Lexington, MA: Lexington.

Gondolf, E. W., Fisher, E. R., & McFerron, R. (1988). Racial differences among shelter residents. *Journal of Family Violence, 3,* 39-51.

Gondolf, E. W., & Foster, R. A. (1991). Preprogram attrition in batterer programs. *Journal of Family Violence, 6,* 337-349.

Goodman, L. A., Koss, M. P., & Russo, N. F. (1993). Violence against women: Physical and mental health effects: Part I. Research findings. *Applied and Preventative Psychology, 2,* 79-89.

Goodwin, B. J. (1993). Psychotherapy supervision: Training therapists to recognize family violence. In M. Hansen & M. Harway (Eds.), *Battering and family therapy: A feminist perspective* (pp. 119-133). Newbury Park, CA: Sage.

Gordon, M. (1964). *Assimilation in American life: The role of race, religion and national origins.* New York: Oxford University Press.

Gottman, J. M., Jacobson, N. S., Rushe, R. H., Shortt, J. W., Babcock, J., La Taillade, J. J., & Waltz, J. (1995). The relationship between heart rate reactivity, emotionally aggressive behavior, and general violence in batterers. *Journal of Family Psychology, 9*(3), 227-248.

Graham-Bermann, S. A. (1996a). Family worries: Assessment of interpersonal anxiety in children from violent and nonviolent families. *Journal of Clinical Child Psychology, 25*(3), 280-287.

Graham-Bermann, S. A. (1996b). *The impact of woman abuse on children: The role of social relationships and emotional context.* Manuscript submitted for publication.

Graham-Bermann, S. A. (1996c). *The social functioning of preschool-age children whose mothers are emotionally and physically abused.* Manuscript submitted for publication.

Graham-Bermann, S. A. (1996d). *Traumatic stress symptoms in children of battered women.* Manuscript submitted for publication.

Greenblat, C. S. (1983). A hit is a hit is a hit . . . or is it? Approval and tolerance of the use of physical force by spouses. In D. Finkelhor, R. J. Gelles, G. T. Hotaling, & M. A. Straus (Eds.), *The dark side of families* (pp. 235-260). Beverly Hills, CA: Sage.

Greene, B. (1994). African American women. In L. Comas-Diaz & B. Greene (Eds.), *Women of color: Integrating ethnic and gender identities in psychotherapy* (pp. 10-29). New York: Guilford.

Groth, A. N. (1979). Patterns of rape. In A. N. Groth (Ed.), *Men who rape: The psychology of the offender* (pp. 174-180). New York: Plenum.

Grusznski, R. J., Brink, J. C., & Edleson, J. L. (1988). Support and education groups for children of battered women. *Child Welfare, 67*, 431-444.

Grusznski, R. J., & Carrillo, T. P. (1988). Who completes batterers' treatment groups? *Journal of Family Violence, 3*(2), 141-150.

Grych, J. H., & Fincham, F. D. (1990). Marital conflict and children's adjustment: A cognitive-contextual framework. *Psychological Bulletin, 108*(2), 267-290.

Gustafson, R. (1986). Threat as a determinant of alcohol-aggression. *Psychological Reports, 58*, 287-297.

Hackler, J. (1991). The reduction of violent crime through economic equality for women. *Journal of Family Violence, 6*(2), 199-216.

Hageboeck, H., & Brandt, K. (1981). *Characteristics of elderly abuse.* Unpublished manuscript, University of Iowa Gerontology Center at Iowa City.

Hamberger, L. K. (1994). Domestic partner abuse: Expanding paradigms for understanding intervention. *Violence and Victims, 9*, 91-94.

Hamberger, L. K. (1996). Intervention in gay male intimate violence requires coordinated efforts on multiple levels. In C. M. Renzetti & C. H. Miley (Eds.), *Violence in gay and lesbian domestic partnerships* (pp. 83-92). Binghamton, NY: Haworth.

Hamberger, L. K., & Hastings, J. E. (1986). Personality correlates of men who abuse their partners: A cross-validation study. *Journal of Family Violence, 1*(4), 323-341.

Hamberger, L. K., & Hastings, J. (1988a). Characteristics of male spouse abusers consistent with personality disorders. *Hospital and Community Psychiatry, 39*, 763-770.

Hamberger, L. K., & Hastings, J. E. (1988b). Skills training for treatment of spouse abusers: An outcome study. *Journal of Family Violence, 3*(2), 121-130.

Hamberger, L. K., Saunders, D. G., & Hovey, M. (1992). The prevalence of domestic violence in community practice and rate of physician inquiry. *Family Medicine, 24*(4), 283-287.

Hamby, S. L, & Gray-Little, B. (1996, July). *Labeling partner violence: When do victims differentiate among acts?* Paper presented at the Trauma and Memory: An International Research Conference, Durham, NH.

Hamby, S. L., & Gray-Little, B. (1997). Responses to partner violence. *Journal of Family Psychology, 11,* 339-350.

Hamby, S. L., Straus, M. A., & Sugarman, D. B. (1996). *Acts of psychological aggression against a partner and their relation to physical assault and gender.* Presented at the 5th International Family Violence Research Conference, Durham, NH.

Hamby, S. L., & Sugarman, D. B. (1996). Power and partner violence. Paper presented at the One Hundred Fourth Annual Meeting of the American Psychological Association, Toronto, Canada.

Hamilton, B., & Coates, J. (1993). Perceived helpfulness and use of professional services by abused women. *Journal of Family Violence, 8,* 313-324.

Hammond, W. R., & Yung, B. R. (1994). African Americans. In L. D. Eron, J. H. Gentry, & P. Schlegal (Eds.), *Reason to hope: A psychological perspective on violence and youth* (pp. 105-118). Washington, DC: American Psychological Association.

Hampton, R. L. (1987). Family violence and homicides in the Black community: Are they linked? In R. L. Hampton (Ed.), *Violence in the Black family: Correlates and consequences* (pp. 135-186). Lexington, MA: Lexington.

Hampton, R. L., & Gelles, R. J. (1994). Violence toward Black women in a nationally representative sample of Black families. *Journal of Comparative Family Studies, 25*(1), 105-119.

Hampton, R. L., Gelles, R. J., & Harrop, J. W. (1989). Is violence in Black families increasing? A comparison of 1975 and 1985 national survey rates. *Journal of Marriage and the Family, 51,* 969-980.

Hanmer, J. (1996). Women and violence: Commonalities and diversities. In B. Fawcett, B. Featherstone, J. Hearn, & C. Toft (Eds.), *Violence and gender relations: Theories and interventions* (pp. 7-21). Thousand Oaks, CA: Sage.

Hanneke, C. R., & Shields, N. A. (1985). Marital rape: Implications for the helping professions. *Social Casework,* 451-458.

Hanneke, C. R., Shields, N. M., & McCall, G. J. (1986). Assessing the prevalence of marital rape. *Journal of Interpersonal Violence, 1*(3), 350-362.

Hansen, M., & Goldenberg, I. (1993). Conjoint therapy with violent couples. In M. Hansen & M. Harway (Eds.), *Battering and family therapy: A feminist perspective* (pp. 82-92). Newbury Park, CA: Sage.

Hansen, M., Harway, M., & Cervantes, N. (1991). Therapists' perceptions of severity in cases of family violence. *Violence and Victims, 6*(3), 225-235.

Harrell, A. (1991). *Evaluation of court-ordered treatment for domestic violence offenders.* Raleigh: North Carolina Supreme Court Library.

Harrell, A., & Smith, B. E. (1996). Effects of restraining orders on domestic violence victims. In E. S. Buzawa & C. G. Buzawa (Eds.), *Do arrests and restraining orders work?* (pp. 214-242). Thousand Oaks, CA: Sage.

Harris, S. B. (1996). For better of for worse: Spousal abuse grown old. *Journal of Elder Abuse & Neglect, 8*(1), 1-33.

Hart, B. (1986). Lesbian battering: An examination. In K. Lobel (Ed.), *Naming the violence: Speaking out about lesbian battering* (pp. 173-189). Seattle, WA: Seal.

Hart, B. (1996). Battered women and the criminal justice system. In E. S. Buzawa & C. G. Buzawa (Eds.), *Do arrests and restraining orders work?* (pp. 98-114). Thousand Oaks, CA: Sage.

Hart, B. J. (1989). *Domestic violence: A model protocol for police response* (Available from B. J. Hart: justpro@aol.com).

Hart, B. J. (1990a). *Domestic violence intervention system: A model for response to woman abuse* (Available from B. J. Hart: justpro@aol.com.

Hart, B. J. (1990b). *Safety planning for children: Strategizing for unsupervised visits with batterers* (Available from B. J. Hart: justpro@aol.com).

Hart, B. J., & Stuehling, J. (1992). *Personalized safety plan* (Available from B. J. Hart: justpro@aol.com).

Hartup, W. W. (1989). Social relationships and their developmental significance. *American Psychologist, 44*(2), 120-126.

Harway, M., & Hansen, M. (1994). *Spousal abuse: Assessing and treating battered women, batterers, and their children.* Sarasota, FL: Professional Resource Press.

Hastings, J. E., & Hamberger, L. K. (1988). Personality characteristics of spouse abusers: A controlled comparison. *Violence and Victims, 3*(1), 31-47.

Hathaway, S. R., & McKinley, J. C. (1967). *MMPI inventory manual.* New York: Psychological Corporation.

Hattery Freetly, A., & Kane, E. W. (1995). Men's and women's perceptions of nonconsensual sexual intercourse. *Sex Roles, 33,* 785-802.

Hawkins, D. F. (1987). Devalued lives and racial stereotypes: Ideological barriers to the prevention of family violence among Blacks. In R. H. Hampton (Ed.), *Violence in the Black family: Correlates and consequences* (pp. 190-205). Lexington, MA: Lexington.

Helton, A. M. (1986). The pregnant battered woman. *Response to Victimization of Women and Children, 9*(1), 22-23.

Henning, K., Leitenberg, H., Coffey, P., Turner, T., & Bennett, R. T. (1996). Long-term psychological and social impact of witnessing physical conflict between parents. *Journal of Interpersonal Violence, 11*(1), 35-51.

Herek, G. M., Gillis, J. R., Cogan, J. C., & Glunt, E. K. (1997). Hate crime victimization among lesbian, gay, and bisexual adults: Prevalence, psychological correlates, and methodological issues. *Journal of Interpersonal Violence, 12*(2), 195-215.

Herman, J. L. (1992). *Trauma and recovery.* New York: Basic Books.

Herrenkohl, E. C., Herrenkohl, R. C., & Egolf, B. (1994). Resilient early school-age children from maltreating homes: Outcomes in late adolescence. *American Journal of Orthopsychiatry, 64*(2), 301-309.

Hershorn, M., & Rosenbaum, A. (1985). Children of marital violence: A closer look at the unintended victims. *American Journal of Orthopsychiatry, 55*(2), 260-266.

Heyman, R. E., O'Leary, K. D., & Jouriles, E. N. (1995). Alcohol and aggressive personality styles: Potentiators of serious physical aggression against wives? *Journal of Family Psychology, 9*(1), 44-57.

Hilberman, E., & Munson, K. (1977-1978). Sixty battered women. *Victimology, 2,* 460-470.

Hilberman, E. (1980). Overview: The "wife-beater's wife" reconsidered. *American Journal of Psychiatry, 137,* 1336-1347.

Hilton, N. Z. (1992). Battered women's concerns about their children witnessing wife abuse. *Journal of Interpersonal Violence, 7*(1), 77-86.

Ho, C. K. (1990). An analysis of domestic violence in Asian American communities: A multicultural approach to counseling. In L. S. Brown & M. Root (Eds.), *Diversity and complexity in feminist therapy* (pp. 129-150). New York: Harrington Park.

Hoff, L. A. (1990). *Battered women as survivors.* New York: Routledge.

Holden, G. W., & Ritchie, K. L. (1991). Linking extreme marital discord, child rearing, and child behavior problems: Evidence from battered women. *Child Development, 62,* 311-327.

Hollis, C. (1996). Depression, family environment, and adolescent suicidal behavior. *Journal of the American Academy of Child and Adolescent Psychiatry, 35*(5), 622-630.

Holtzworth-Munroe, A. (1992). Social skill deficits in maritally violent men: Interpreting the data using a social information processing model. *Clinical Psychology Review, 12,* 605-617.

Holtzworth-Munroe, A., Markman, H., O'Leary, K. D., & Neidig, P. (1995). The need for marital violence prevention efforts: A behavioral-cognitive secondary prevention program for engaged and newly married couples. *Applied and Preventative Psychology, 4*(2), 77-88.

Holtzworth-Munroe, A., & Stuart, G. L. (1994). Typologies of male batterers: Three subtypes and the differences among them. *Psychological Bulletin, 116*(3), 476-497.

Hornung, C. A., McCullough, B. C., & Sugimoto, T. (1981). Status relationships in marriage: Risk factors in spousal abuse. *Journal of Marriage and the Family, 43*, 675-692.

Hotaling, G. T., & Sugarman, D. B. (1986). An analysis of risk markers in husband to wife violence: The current state of knowledge. *Violence and Victims, 1*(2), 101-124.

Hotaling, G. T., & Sugarman, D. B. (1990). A risk marker analysis of assaulted wives. *Journal of Family Violence, 5*(1), 1-13.

Hotaling, G. T., Straus, M. A., & Lincoln, A. J. (1989). Intrafamily violence and crime and violence outside the family. In M. A. Straus & R. J. Gelles (Eds.), *Physical violence in American families: Risk factors and adaptations to violence in 8,145 families* (pp. 431-470). New Brunswick, NJ: Transaction.

Houskamp, B. M., & Foy, D. W. (1991). The assessment of post-traumatic stress disorder in battered women. *Journal of Interpersonal Violence, 6*, 367-375.

Hudson, W. W., & McIntosh, S. R. (1981). The assessment of spousal abuse: Two quantifiable dimensions. *Journal of Marriage and the Family, 43*, 873-885.

Hughes, H. M. (1982). Brief interventions with children in a battered women's shelter: A model preventive program. *Family Relations, 31*, 495-502.

Hughes, H. M. (1988). Psychological and behavioral correlates of family violence in child witnesses and victims. *American Journal of Orthopsychiatry, 58*(1), 77-90.

Hughes, H. M., & Barad, S. J. (1983). Psychological functioning of children in a battered women's shelter: A preliminary investigation. *American Journal of Orthopsychiatry, 53*, 525-531.

Hughes, H. M., Parkinson, D., & Vargo, M. (1989). Witnessing spousal abuse and experiencing physical abuse: A "double whammy"? *Journal of Family Violence, 4*(2), 197-209.

Huisman, K. A. (1996). Wife battering in Asian American communities. *Violence Against Women, 2*(3), 260-283.

Hyden, M. (1994). *Woman battering as marital act.* New York: Oxford University Press.

Indian Health Service. (1989). *Indian Health Service: Trends in Indian health.* Washington, DC: U.S. Department of Health and Human Services.

Isay, R. A. (1989). *Being homosexual: Gay men and their development.* New York: Avon.

Island, D., & Letellier, P. (1991). *Men who beat the men who love them: Battered gay men and domestic violence.* New York: Harrington Park.

Jackson, M., & Garvin, D. (1995). *Coordinated community action model* (Available from the Domestic Violence Institute of Michigan, P.O. Box 130107, Ann Arbor, MI 48113-0107).

Jackson, T. L. (1991). A university athletic department's rape and assault experiences. *Journal of College Student Development, 32*(1), 77-78.

Jaffe, P. G., Sudermann, M., Reitzel, D., & Killip, S. M. (1992). An evaluation of a secondary school primary intervention program on violence in intimate relationships. *Violence and Victims, 7*(2), 129-146.

Jaffe, P., Wilson, S. K., & Wolfe, D. (1988). Specific assessment and intervention strategies for children exposed to wife battering: Preliminary empirical investigations. *Canadian Journal of Community Mental Health, 7*(2), 227-233.

Jaffe, P., Wolfe, D., Wilson, S., & Zak, L. (1986). Similarities in behavioral and social maladjustment among child victims and witnesses to family violence. *American Journal of Orthopsychiatry, 56*(1), 142-146.

Jaffe, P. G., Wolfe, D. A., & Wilson, S. K. (1990). *Children of battered women.* Newbury Park, CA: Sage.

Jang, D., Lee, D., & Morello-Frosch, R. (1990). Domestic violence in the immigrant and refugee community: Responding to the needs of immigrant women. *Response to Victimization of Women and Children, 13*(4), 2-7.

Janoff-Bulman, R. (1983). A theoretical perspective for understanding reasons to victimization. *Journal of Social Issues, 39,* 2561-2617.

Janus, S. S., & Janus, C. L. (1993). *The Janus Report on sexual behavior.* New York: John Wiley.

Jasinski, J. L. (1996). *Structural inequalities, family and cultural factors, and spousal violence among Anglo and Hispanic Americans.* Unpublished doctoral Dissertation, University of New Hampshire, Durham.

Jasinski, J. L., Asdigian, N. L., & Kaufman Kantor, G. (in press). Ethnic adaptations to occupational strain: Work stress, drinking, and wife assault among Anglo and Hispanic husbands. *Journal of Interpersonal Violence.*

Jasinski, J. L., & Kaufman Kantor, G. (1997). Pregnancy-related wife assaults: Prevalence and onset in a national sample. Paper presented at the Fifth International Family Violence Conference, Durham, NH.

Jeffords, C. R., & Dull, R. T. (1982). Demographic variations in attitudes towards marital rape immunity. *Journal of Marriage and the Family, 44*(3), 755-762.

Jenkins, M., Smith, M., & Graham, P. (1989). Coping with parental quarrels. *Journal of the American Academy of Child and Adolescent Psychology, 28*(2), 182-189.

Jennings, J. L. (1990). Preventing relapses versus "stopping" domestic violence: Do we expect too much too soon from battering men? *Journal of Family Violence, 5*(1), 43-60.

Johnson, D. (1979). Abuse and neglect: Not for children only. *Journal of Gerontological Nursing, 5*(4), 11-13.

Johnson, D. (1994). Stress, depression, substance abuse, and racism. *American Indian and Alaska Native Mental Health Research, 6*(1), 29-33.

Johnson, M. P. (1995, May). Patriarchal terrorism and common couple violence: Two forms of violence against women. *Journal of Marriage and the Family, 57,* 283-294.

Johnson, S. A. (1992). *Man to man: When your partner says no.* Brandon, VT: Safer Society Press.

Jones, C. (1995, October 15). Nicole Simpson, in death, lifting domestic violence to the forefront as national issue. *New York Times,* p. A28.

Jones, L. E. (1991). The Minnesota School Curriculum Project: A statewide domestic violence prevention project in secondary schools. In B. Levy (Ed.), *Dating violence: Young women in danger* (pp. 258-266). Seattle: Seal.

Jouriles, E. N., & LeCompte, S. H. (1991). Husbands' aggression toward wives and mothers' and fathers' aggression toward children: Moderating effects of child gender. *Journal of Consulting and Clinical Psychology, 59*(1), 190-192.

Jouriles, E. N., Murphy, C. M., & O'Leary, D. (1989). Interspousal aggression, marital discord, and child problems. *Journal of Consulting and Clinical Psychology, 57*(3), 453-455.

Julian, T. W., & McKenry, P. C. (1993). Mediators of male violence toward female intimates. *Journal of Family Violence, 8*(1), 39-56.

Jurik, N. C., & Winn, R. (1990). Gender and homicide: A comparison of men and women who kill. *Violence and Victims, 5*(4), 227-242.

Kaci, J. H., & Tarrant, S. (1988). Attitudes of prosecutors and probation departments toward diversion in domestic violence cases in California. *Journal of Contemporary Criminal Justice,* 187-200.

Kalichman, S. C., Sarwer, D. B., Johnson, J. R., Ali, S. A., Early, J., & Tuten, J. T. (1993). Sexually coercive behavior and love styles: A replication and extension. *Journal of Psychology and Human Sexuality, 6*(1), 93-106.

Kalmuss, D. (1984, February). The intergenerational transmission of marital aggression. *Journal of Marriage and the Family, 46,* 11-19.

Kalmuss, D., & Seltzer, J. A. (1986, February). Continuity of marital behavior in remarriage: The case of spousal abuse. *Journal of Marriage and the Family, 48,* 113-120.

Kanuha, V. (1987). Sexual assault in Southeast Asian communities: Issues in intervention. *Response to Victimization of Women and Children, 10*(3), 4-6.

Kanuha, V. (1990). Compounding the triple jeopardy: Battering in lesbian of color relationships. In L. S. Brown & M. Root (Eds.), *Diversity and complexity in feminist therapy* (pp. 169-184). New York: Harrington Park.

Kanuha, V. (1994). Women of color in battering relationships. In L. Comas-Diaz & B. Greene (Eds.), *Women of color: Integrating ethnic and gender identities in psychotherapy* (pp. 428-454). New York: Guilford.

Kaufman Kantor, G. (1990). *Ethnicity, alcohol, and family violence: A structural and cultural interpretation.* Paper presented at the Forty-Second Annual Meeting of the American Society of Criminology, Baltimore, MD.

Kaufman Kantor, G. (1993). Refining the brushstrokes in portraits of alcohol and wife assaults. In *Alcohol and Interpersonal Violence: Fostering Multidisciplinary Perspectives* (NIH Research Monograph No. 24, pp. 281-290). Rockville, MD: U.S. Department of Health and Human Services.

Kaufman Kantor, G. (1996). Alcohol and spousal abuse: Ethnic differences. In M. Galanter (Ed.), *Recent developments in alcoholism.* New York: Plenum.

Kaufman Kantor, G., & Asdigian, N. L. (1996). When women are under the influence: Does drinking or drug use by women provoke beatings by men? In M. Galanter (Ed.), *Recent developments in alcoholism.* New York: Plenum.

Kaufman Kantor, G., & Jasinski, J. (1995). *Prevention of teen dating violence: Evaluation of a multidimensional model.* Paper presented at the *Fourth International Family Violence Research Conference, Durham, NH.*

Kaufman Kantor, G., Jasinski, J., & Aldarondo, E. (1994). Sociocultural status and incidence of marital violence in Hispanic families. *Violence and Victims, 9*(3), 207-222.

Kaufman Kantor, G., & Straus, M. A. (1987). The "drunken bum" theory of wife beating. *Social Problems, 34*(3), 213-230.

Kaufman Kantor, G., & Straus, M. A. (1989). Substance abuse as a precipitant of wife abuse victimization. *American Journal of Drug and Alcohol Abuse, 15,* 173-189.

Kellerman, A. L., & Mercy, J. A. (1992). Men, women, and murder: Gender-specific differences in rates of fatal violence and victimization. *Journal of Trauma, 33*(1), 1-5.

Kelly, C. E., & Warshafsky, L. (1987). *Partner abuse in gay male and lesbian couples.* Paper presented at the Third National Conference for Family Violence Researchers, Durham, NH.

Kemp, A., Green, B. L., Hovanitz, C., & Rawlings, E. I. (1995). Incidence and correlates of post-traumatic stress disorder in battered women. *Journal of Interpersonal Violence, 10*(1), 43-55.

Kemp, A., Rawlings, E. I., & Green, B. L. (1991). Post-traumatic stress disorder in battered women: A shelter sample. *Journal of Traumatic Stress, 4,* 137-149.

Kenning, M., Merchant, A., & Tomkins, A. (1991). Research on the effects of witnessing parental battering: Clinical and legal policy implications. In M. Steinman (Ed.), *Woman battering: Policy responses* (pp. 237-261). Cincinnati, OH: Anderson.

Kerouac, S., Taggart, M. E., Lescop, J., & Fortin, M. F. (1986). Dimensions of health in violent families. *Health Care for Women International, 7,* 413-426.

Kilpatrick, D. G., Best, C. L., Saunders, B. E., & Veronen, L. J. (1988). Rape in marriage and in dating relationships: How bad is it for mental health. In R. A. Prentky & V. L. Quinsey (Eds.), *Human sexual aggression: Current perspectives* (pp. 335-344). New York: New York Academy of Sciences.

Kilpatrick, D. G., Best, C. L., Veronen, L. J., Amick, A. E., Villeponteaux, L. A., & Ruff, G. A. (1985). Mental health correlates of criminal victimization: A random community survey. *Journal of Consulting and Clinical Psychology, 53*(4), 866-873.

Kilpatrick, D. G., Edmunds, C. N., & Seymour, A. K. (1992). *Rape in America: A report to the nation.* Charleston, SC: Medical University of South Carolina, Crime Victims Research and Treatment Center.

Kilpatrick, D. G., & Resnick, H. S. (1993). Post-traumatic stress disorder associated with exposure to criminal victimization in clinical and community populations. In J. R. T. Davidson & E. B. Foa (Eds.), *Post-traumatic stress disorder: DSM-IV and beyond* (pp. 113-143). Washington, DC: American Psychiatric Press.

Klein, A. R. (1996). Re-abuse in a population of court-restrained male batterers: Why restraining orders don't work. In E. S. Buzawa & C. G. Buzawa (Eds.), *Do arrests and restraining orders work?* (pp. 192-213). Thousand Oaks, CA: Sage.

Klinger, R. L. (1995). Gay violence. *Journal of Gay & Lesbian Psychotherapy, 2*(3), 119-134.

Knopp, F. H. (1994). *When your wife says no: Forced sex in marriage.* Brandon, VT: Safer Society Press.

Kolbo, J. R. (1996). Risk and resilience among children exposed to family violence. *Violence and Victims, 11*(2), 113-128.

Kolbo, J. R., Blakely, E. H., & Engleman, D. (1996). Children who witness domestic violence: A review of empirical literature. *Journal of Interpersonal Violence, 11*(2), 281-293.

Koss, M. P. (1990). The women's mental health research agenda: Violence against women. *American Psychologist, 45*, 374-380.

Koss, M. P., Dinero, T. E., Seibel, C. A., & Cox, S. L. (1988). Stranger and acquaintance rape: Are there differences in the victim's experience. *Psychology of Women Quarterly, 12*, 1-24.

Koss, M. P., Goodman, L. A., Browne, A., Fitzgerald, L. F., Keita, G. P., & Russo, N. F. (1994). *No safe haven: Male violence against women at home, at work, and in the community.* Washington, DC: American Psychological Association.

Kurz, D. (1987). Emergency department responses to battered women: Resistance to medicalization. *Social Problems, 34*(1), 69-81.

Kurz, D. (1989). Social science perspectives on wife abuse. *Gender and Society, 3*(4), 489-505.

Kurz, D. (1996). Separation, divorce, and woman abuse. *Violence Against Women, 2*(1), 63-81.

Lachs, M. A., Berkman, L., Fulmer, T., & Horwitz, R. I. (1994). A prospective community-based pilot study of risk factors for the investigation of elder mistreatment. *Journal of the American Geriatrics Society, 42*(2), 169-173.

Lachs, M. S., & Pillemer, K. (1995). Abuse and neglect of elderly persons. *New England Journal of Medicine, 332*(7), 437-443.

LaFromboise, T. D., Berman, J. S., & Sohi, B. K. (1994). American Indian women. In L. Comas-Diaz & B. Greene (Eds.), *Women of color: Integrating ethnic and gender identities in psychotherapy* (pp. 30-71). New York: Guilford.

LaFromboise, T. D., Choney, S. B., James, A., & Running Wolf, P. R. (1995). American Indian women and psychology. In H. Landrine (Ed.), *Bringing cultural diversity to feminist psychology: Theory, research, and practice* (pp. 197-239). Washington, DC: American Psychological Association.

Lai, T. A. (1986). Asian women: Resisting the violence. In M. C. Burns (Ed.), *The speaking profits us: Violence in the lives of women of color* (pp. 8-11). Seattle, WA: Center for the Prevention of Sexual and Domestic Violence.

Lane, G., & Russell, T. (1989). Second-order systemic work with violent couples. In P. L. Caesar & L. K. Hamberger (Eds.), *Treating men who batter: Theory, practice, and programs* (pp. 134-162). New York: Springer.

Lane, K. E., & Gwartney-Gibbs, P. A. (1985). Violence in the context of dating and sex. *Journal of Family Issues, 6*(1), 45-59.

Laner, M. R. (1983). Courtship abuse and aggression: Contextual aspects. *Sociological Spectrum, 3,* 69-83.

Laner, M. R. & Thompson, J. (1982). Abuse and aggression in courting couples. *Deviant Behavior, 3,* 229-244.

Lang, A. R., Goeckner, D. J., Adesso, V. J., & Marlatt, G. A. (1975). Effects of alcohol on aggression in male social drinkers. *Journal of Abnormal Psychology, 84,* 508-518.

Langhinrichsen-Rohling, J., Neidig, P., & Thorn, G. (1995). Violent marriages: Gender differences in levels of current violence and past abuse. *Journal of Family Violence, 10*(2), 159-176.

Langhinrichsen-Rohling, J., Smutzler, N., & Vivian, D. (1994). Positivity in marriage: The role of discord and physical aggression against wives. *Journal of Marriage and the Family, 56,* 69-79.

LaRossa, R. (1980). And we haven't had any problems since: Conjugal violence and the politics of marriage. In M. A. Straus & G. T. Hotaling (Eds.), *The social causes of husband-wife violence.* Minneapolis: University of Minnesota Press.

Lavoie, F., Vezina, L., Piche, C., & Boivin, M. (1995). Evaluation of a prevention program for violence in teen dating relationships. *Journal of Interpersonal Violence, 10*(4), 516-524.

Layzer, J. I., Goodson, B. D., & Delange, C. (1986). Children in shelters. *Response to Victimization of Women and Children, 9*(2), 2-5.

Leeder, E. (1988). Enmeshed in pain: Counseling the lesbian battering couple. *Women and Therapy, 7*(1), 81-99.

Leeder, E. (1994). *Treating abuse in families: A feminist and community approach.* New York: Springer.

Lehrman, F. L. (1996). *Domestic violence practice and procedure.* Deerfield, IL: Clark, Boardman, & Callaghan.

Leonard, K. E. (1993). Drinking patterns and intoxication in marital violence: Review, critique, and future directions for research. In *Alcohol and interpersonal violence: Fostering multidisciplinary perspectives* (NIH Research Monograph No. 24, pp. 253-280). Rockville, MD: U.S. Department of Health and Human Services.

Leonard, K. E., & Senchak, M. (1993). Alcohol and premarital aggression among newlywed couples. *Journal of Studies on Alcohol*(Suppl. 11), 96-108.

Letellier, P. (1994). Gay and bisexual male domestic violence victimization: Challenges to feminist theory and responses to violence. *Violence and Victims, 9*(2), 95-106.

Letellier, P. (1996). Twin epidemics: Domestic violence and HIV infection among gay and bisexual men. In C. M. Renzetti & C. H. Miley (Eds.), *Violence in gay and lesbian domestic partnerships* (pp. 69-82). Binghamtom, NY: Haworth.

Leventhal, F., & Chang, M. (1991). Dance/movement therapy with battered women: A paradigm of action. *American Journal of Dance Therapy, 13*(2), 131-145.

Levinger, G. (1966, October). Sources of marital dissatisfaction among applicants for divorce. *American Journal of Orthopsychiatry, 26,* 803-807.

Levinson, D. (1989). *Family violence in cross-cultural perspective.* Newbury Park, CA: Sage.

Lie, G. Y., & Gentlewarrier, S. (1991). Intimate violence in lesbian relationships: Discussion of survey findings and practice implications. *Journal of Social Service Research, 15*(1/2), 41-59.

Lie, G. Y., Schilit, R., Bush, J., Montagne, M., & Reyes, L. (1991). Lesbians in currently aggressive relationships: How frequently do they report aggressive past relationships? *Violence and Victims, 6*(2), 121-135.

Lindenbaum, J. P. (1985). The shattering of an illusion: The problem of competition in lesbian relationships. *Feminist Studies, 11*, 85-103.

Lindman, R., von der Pahlen, B., Ost, B., & Eriksson, C. J. P. (1992). Serum testosterone, cortisol, glucose, and ethanol in males arrested for spousal abuse. *Aggressive Behavior, 18*(6), 393-400.

Little, L. & Hamby, S. L. (1996). The impact of a clinician's sexual abuse history, gender, and theoretical orientation on treatment issues of childhood sexual abuse. *Professional Psychology: Research and Practice, 27*, 617-625.

Lloyd, S. A., Koval, J. E., & Cate, R. M. (1989). Conflict and violence in dating relationships. In M. A. Pirog-Good & J. E. Stets (Eds.), *Violence in dating relationships: Emerging social issues* (pp. 126-144). New York: Praeger.

Lobel, K. (1986). *Naming the violence: Speaking out about lesbian battering.* Seattle, WA: Seal.

Lockhart, L. L. (1987). A reexamination of the effects of race and social class on the incidence of marital violence: A search for reliable differences. *Journal of Marriage and the Family, 49*, 603-610.

Lockhart, L. L., White, B. W., Causby, V., & Isaac, A. (1994). Letting out the secret: Violence in lesbian relationships. *Journal of Interpersonal Violence, 9*(4), 469-492.

Loseke, D. R. (1992). *The battered woman and shelters: The social construction of wife abuse.* New York: State University of New York Press.

Loulan, J. (1987). *Lesbian passion.* San Francisco: Spinsters/Aunt Lute.

Lujan, C., DeBruyn, L. M., May, P. A., & Bird, M. E. (1989). Profile of abused and neglected American Indian children in the southwest. *Child Abuse & Neglect, 13*, 449-461.

Lystad, M., Rice, M., & Kaplan, S. J. (1996). Domestic violence. In S. J. Kaplan (Ed.), *Family violence: A clinical and legal guide* (pp. 139-180). Washington, DC: American Psychiatric Press.

Maccoby, E. E., & Jacklin, C. N. (1974). *The psychology of sex differences.* Stanford, CA: Stanford University Press.

Mahoney, M. R. (1991). Legal images of battered women: Redefining the issue of separation. *Michigan Law Review, 90*, 1-94.

Mahoney, P. (1997). *Exploring reports of wife rape from the redesigned National Crime Victimization Survey.* Master's thesis, University of New Hampshire, Durham.

Maiuro, R. D., Cahn, T. S., Vitaliano, P. P., Wagner, B. C., & Zegree, J. B. (1988). Anger, hostility, and depression in domestically violent versus generally assaultive men and nonviolent control subjects. *Journal of Consulting and Clinical Psychology, 56*(1), 17-23.

Makepeace, J. M. (1983, January). Life events stress and courtship violence. *Family Relations, 32*, 101-109.

Makepeace, J. M. (1984). The severity of courtship violence injuries and individual precautionary measures. Paper presented at the Second National Family Violence Research Conference, University of New Hampshire, Durham.

Makepeace, J. M. (1989). Dating, living together, and courtship violence. In M. A. Pirog-Good & J. E. Stets (Eds.), *Violence in dating relationships* (pp. 94-107). New York: Praeger.

Malamuth, N. M., Heavey, C. L., & Linz, D. (1993). Predicting men's antisocial behavior against women: The interaction model of sexual aggression. In G. N. Hall, R. Hirschman, J. Graham, & M. Zaragoza (Eds.), *Sexual aggression: Issues in etiology, assessment, and treatment* (pp. 63-97). Washington, DC: Hemisphere.

Malmquist, C. P. (1986). Children who witness parental murder: Post-traumatic aspects. *Journal of the American Academy of Child and Adolescent Psychology, 25*(3), 320-325.

Margolies, L., Becker, M., & Jackson-Brewer, K. (1987). Internalized homophobia: Identifying and treating the oppressor within. In B. L. P. Collective (Eds.), *Lesbian psychologies: Exploration & challenges.* Urbana: University of Illinois.

Margolies, L., & Leeder, E. (1995). Violence at the door: Treatment of lesbian batterers. *Violence Against Women, 1*(2), 139-157.

Margolin, G., John, R. S., & Gleberman, L. (1988). Affective responses to conflictual discussions in violent and nonviolent couples. *Journal of Consulting and Clinical Psychology, 56*(1), 24-33.

Markman, H. J., Renick, M. J., Floyd, F. J., Stanley, S. M., & Clements, M. (1993). Preventing marital distress through communication and conflict management training: A 4- and 5-year follow-up. *Journal of Consulting and Clinical Psychology, 61*(1), 70-77.

Marrujo, B., & Kreger, M. (1996). Definition of roles in abusive lesbian relationships. *Journal of Gay & Lesbian Social Services, 4*(1), 22-32.

Marshall, L. L., & Rose, P. (1988, May). Family of origin violence and courtship abuse. *Journal of Counseling and Development, 66*, 414-418.

Marshall, W. L. (1989). Intimacy, loneliness, and sexual offenders. *Behavior Research and Therapy, 27*, 491-503.

Martin, D. (1976). *Battered wives.* New York: Praeger.

Martinez, P., & Richters, J. E. (1993). The NIMH community violence project: II. Children's distress symptoms associated with violence exposure. In D. Reiss, J. E. Richters, M. Radke-Yarrow, & D. Scharff (Eds.), *Children and violence* (pp. 22-35). New York: Guilford.

Matlaw, J. R., & Spence, D. M. (1994). The hospital elder assessment team: A protocol for suspected cases of elder abuse and neglect. *Journal of Elder Abuse and Neglect, 6*(2), 23-37.

McCandlish, B. (1982). Therapeutic issues with lesbian couples. *Journal of Homosexuality, 7*(1), 71-78.

McCloskey, L. A., Figueredo, A. J., & Koss, M. P. (1995). The effects of systematic family violence on children's mental health. *Child Development, 66*(5), 1239-1261.

McCord, J. (1992). Deterrence of domestic violence: A critical view of research. *Journal of Research in Crime and Delinquency, 29*(2), 229-239.

McCreadie, C., & Tinker, A. (1993). Abuse of elderly people in the domestic setting: A UK perspective. *Age and Ageing, 22*(1), 65-69.

McFarlane, J., Parker, B., Soeken, K., & Bullock, L. (1992). Assessing for abuse during pregnancy. *Journal of American Medical Association, 267*(23), 3176-3178.

McKenry, P. C., Julian, T. W., & Gavazzi, S. M. (1995, May). Toward a biopsychosocial model of domestic violence. *Journal of Marriage and the Family, 57*, 307-320.

McLaughlin, I. G., Leonard, K. E., & Senchak, M. (1992). Prevalence and distribution of premarital aggression among couples applying for a marriage license. *Journal of Family Violence, 7*(4), 309-319.

McNally, R. J. (1993). Stressors that produce post-traumatic stress disorder in children. In J. R. T. Davidson & E. B. Foa (Eds.), *Post-traumatic stress disorder: DSM-IV and beyond* (pp. 57-74). Washington, DC: American Psychiatric Press.

Mendez, J. M. (1996). Serving gays and lesbians of color who are survivors of domestic violence. In C. M. Renzetti & C. H. Miley (Eds.), *Violence in gay and lesbian domestic partnerships* (pp. 53-60). Binghamton, NY: Haworth.

Mercy, J. A., & Saltzman, L. E. (1989). Fatal violence among spouses in the United States. *American Journal of Public Health, 79*(5), 595-599.

Merrill, G. S. (1996). Ruling the exceptions: Same-sex battering and domestic theory. In C. M. Renzetti & C. H. Miley (Eds.), *Violence in gay and lesbian domestic partnerships* (pp. 9-22). Binghamton, NY: Haworth Press.

Meyer, H. (1992). The billion-dollar epidemic. *American Medical News, 35*(1), 7.

Miller, J. D., Cisin, I. H., Gardner-Keaton, H., Harrell, A. V., Wirtz, W., Abelson, H. I., & Fishburne, P. M. (1982). *National survey on drug abuse: Main findings 1982* (DHHS Publication No. ADM0 84-1263). Rockville, MD: U.S. Department of Health and Human Services, Public Health Service.

Miller, P. C., Lefcourt, H. M., Holmes, J. G., Ware, E. E., & Saleh, W. E. (1986). Marital locus of control and marital problem solving. *Journal of Personality and Social Psychology, 5*(1), 161-169.

Miller, S. L. (1994). Expanding the boundaries: Toward a more inclusive and integrated study of intimate violence. *Violence and Victims, 9*(2), 183-194.

Miller, T. R., Cohen, M. A., & Wiersema, B. (1996). *Victim costs and consequences: A new look* (Research Report No. NCJ 155282). Washington, DC: National Institute of Justice.

Millon, T. (1987). *Manual for the Millon Clinical Multiaxial Inventory* (2nd ed.). Minneapolis: National Computer Systems.

Miranda, J., & Storms, M. (1989). Psychological adjustment of lesbians and gay men. *Journal of Counseling and Development, 68*, 41-45.

Mirande, A., & Perez, P. (1987). *Ethnic and cultural differences in domestic violence: A test of conflicting models of the Chicano family.* Paper presented at the Research Conference on Violence and Homicide in the Hispanic Community, Los Angeles.

Mitchell, R. E., & Hodson, C. A. (1983). Coping with domestic violence: Social support and psychological health among battered women. *American Journal of Community Psychology, 11*(6), 629-654.

Monson, C. M., Byrd, G. R., & Langhinrichsen-Rohling, J. (1996). To have and to hold: Perceptions of marital rape. *Journal of Interpersonal Violence, 11*(3), 410-424.

Morrow, S. L., & Hawxhurst, D. M. (1989). Lesbian partner abuse: Implications for therapists. *Journal of Counseling & Development, 68*, 58-62.

Morse, B. J. (1995). Beyond the Conflict Tactics Scale: Assessing gender differences in partner violence. *Violence and Victims, 10*(4), 251-272.

Moss, M., Frank, E., & Anderson, B. (1990). The effects of marital status and partner support on rape trauma. *American Journal of Orthopsychiatrics, 60*(3), 379-391.

Mrazek, P. J., & Mrazek, D. A. (1987). Resilience in child maltreatment victims: A conceptual exploration. *Child Abuse and Neglect, 11*, 357-366.

Murphy, C., Musser, P., & Maton, K. (1996, August). *Effects of coordinated community intervention on domestic violence recidivism.* Paper presented at the *Annual Convention of the American Psychological Association*, Toronto, Canada.

Murphy, C. M., Meyer, S. L., & O'Leary, K. D. (1993). Family of origin violence and MCMI-II psychopathology among partner-assaultive men. *Violence and Victims, 8*(2), 165-176.

Murphy, C. M., Meyer, S. L., & O'Leary, K. D. (1994). Dependency characteristics of partner assaultive men. *Journal of Abnormal Psychology, 103*(4), 729-735.

Murphy, C. M., & O'Leary, K. D. (1989). Psychological aggression predicts physical aggression in early marriage. *Journal of Consulting and Clinical Psychology, 57*(5), 579-582.

Myers, L. J. (1990). Understanding family violence: An Afrocentric analysis based on opitmal theory. In D. S. Ruiz & J. P. Comer (Eds.), *Handbook of mental health and mental disorder among Black Americans* (pp. 183-189). Westport, CT: Greenwood.

Narayan, U. (1995). "Male-order" brides: Immigrant women, domestic violence, and immigration law. *Hypatia, 10*(1), 104-119.

Neff, J. A., Holamon, B., & Schluter, T. D. (1995). Spousal violence among Anglos, Blacks, and Mexican Americans: The role of demographic variables, psychosocial predictors, and alcohol consumption. *Journal of Family Violence, 10*(1), 1-21.

Neidig, P. H. (1986). The development and evaluation of a spousal abuse treatment program in a military setting. *Evaluation and Program Planning, 9*, 275-280.

Neidig, P. H., & Friedman, D. H. (1984). *Spousal abuse: A treatment program for couples.* Champaign, IL: Research Press.

Neidig, P. H., Friedman, D. H., & Collins, B. S. (1988). Attitudinal characteristics of males who have engaged in spouse abuse. *Journal of Family Violence, 1*(3), 223-233.

New York Times. (1993, February 9-11). New York Times/CBS News Poll. p. A14.

NiCarthy, G. (1982). Social and political aspects of abuse. In G. NiCarthy (Ed.), *Getting free: You can end the abuse and take back your life* (pp. 3-13). Seattle, WA: Seal.

NiCarthy, G. (1987). *The ones who got away.* Seattle: Seal.

NiCarthy, G., Merriam, K., & Coffman, S. (1994). *Talking it out: A guide to groups for abused women.* Seattle, WA: Seal.

Okamura, A., Heras, P., & Wong-Kerberg, L. (1995). Asian, Pacific Island, and Filipino Americans and sexual child abuse. In L. A. Fontes (Ed.), *Sexual abuse in nine North American cultures: Treatment and prevention* (pp. 67-96). Thousand Oaks, CA: Sage.

O'Keefe, M. (1994). Racial/Ethnic differences among battered women and their children. *Journal of Child and Family Studies, 3*(3), 283-305.

Olday, D., & Wesley, B. (1983) *Premarital courtship violence: A summary report.* Unpublished manuscript, Morehead State University, Morehead, KY.

O'Leary, K. D. (1988). Physical aggression between spouses: A social learning theory perspective. In V. B. Van Hasselt, R. L. Morrison, A. S. Bellack, & M. Hersen (Eds.), *Handbook of family violence* (pp. 31-56). New York: Plenum.

O'Leary, K. D., Arias, I., Rosenbaum, A., & Barling, J. (1985). *Premarital physical aggression.* Unpublished manuscript, State University of New York.

O'Leary, K. D., Barling, J., Arias, I., Rosenbaum, A., Malone, J., & Tyree, A. (1989). Prevalence and stability of physical aggression. *Journal of Consulting and Clinical Psychology, 57*(2), 263-268.

O'Leary, K. D., & Curley, A. D. (1986). Assertion and family violence: Correlates of abuse. *Journal of Marital and Family Therapy, 12*, 281-289.

O'Leary, K. D., & Murphy, C. (1992). Clinical issues in the assessment of spousal abuse. In R. T. Ammerman & M. Hersen (Eds.), *Assessment of family violence: A clinical and legal sourcebook* (pp. 26-46). New York: John Wiley.

Oliver, W. (1989). Sexual conquest and patterns of Black-on-Black violence: A structural-cultural perspective. *Violence and Victims, 4*(4), 257-273.

Orava, T. A., McLeod, P. J., & Sharpe, D. (1996). Perceptions of control, depressive symptomatology, and self-esteem of women in transition from abusive relationships. *Journal of Family Violence, 11*, 167-186.

Orloff, L. E., Jang, D., & Klein, C. F. (1995). With no place to turn: Improving legal advocacy for battered immigrant women. *Family Law Quarterly, 29*(2), 313-329.

Owens, D., & Straus, M. A. (1975). The social structure of violence in childhood and approval of violence as an adult. *Aggressive Behavior, 1*, 193-211.

Pagelow, M. D. (1981a). Factors affecting women's decisions to leave violent relationships. *Journal of Family Issues, 2*(4), 391-414.

Pagelow, M. D. (1981b). *Woman-battering: Victims and their experiences.* Beverly Hills, CA: Sage.

Pagelow, M. D. (1984). *Family violence.* New York: Praeger.

Pagelow, M. E. (1988). Marital rape. In V. B. Van Hasselt, R. L. Morrison, A. S. Bellack, & M. Hersen (Eds.), *Handbook of family violence* (pp. 207-232). New York: Plenum.

Palmer, S. E., Brown, R. A., & Barrera, M. E. (1992). Group treatment program for abusive husbands: Long-term evaluation. *American Journal of Orthopsychiatry, 62*(2), 276-283.

Parker, R. N. (1993). The effects of context on alcohol and violence [Special issue: Alcohol, aggression, and injury]. *Alcohol Health and Research World, 17,* 117-122.

Patterson, G. R. (1982). *Coercive family process.* Eugene, OR: Castalia.

Patterson, G. R., DeBaryshe, B. D., & Ramsey, E. (1989). A developmental perspective on antisocial behavior. *American Psychologist, 44*(2), 329-335.

Patterson, G. R., & Dishion, T. J. (1988). Multilevel family process models: Traits, interactions, and relationships. In R. A. Hinde & J. Stevenson-Hinde (Eds.), *Relationships within families: Mutual influences* (pp. 283-310). Oxford, UK: Clarendon.

Paveza, G. J., Cohen, D., Eisdorfer, C., Freels, S., Semla, T., Ashford, J. W., Gorelick, P., Hirschman, R., Luchins, D., & Levy, P. (1992). Severe family violence and Alzheimer's disease: Prevalence and risk factors. *Gerontologist, 32*(4), 493-497.

Paymar, M. (1993). *Violent no more: Helping men end domestic abuse.* Alameda, CA: Hunter House.

Peacock, P. L. (1995). Marital rape. In V. R. Wiehe & A. L. Richards (Eds.), *Intimate betrayal: Understanding and responding to the trauma of acquaintance rape.* Thousand Oaks, CA: Sage.

Pearlman, L. A., & MacIan, P. S. (1995). Vicarious traumatization: An empirical study of the effects of trauma work on trauma therapists. *Professional Psychology: Research and Practice, 26,* 558-565.

Pearlman, S. F. (1989). Distancing and connectedness: Impact on couple formation in lesbian relationships. *Women and Therapy, 8,* 77-88.

Peled, E., & Davis, D. (1995). *Groupwork with children of battered women: A practitioner's guide.* Thousand Oaks, CA: Sage.

Peled, E., & Edelson, J. L. (1992). Multiple perspectives on groupwork with children of battered women. *Violence and Victims, 7*(4), 327-346.

Pence, E. (1989). Batterer programs: Shifting from community collusion to community confrontation. In P. L. Caesar & L. K. Hamberger (Eds.), *Treating men who batter: Theory, practice, and programs* (pp. 24-50). New York: Springer.

Pence, E., & Paymar, M. (1993). *Education groups for men who batter: The Duluth model.* New York: Springer.

Pennell, J., & Burford, G. (1994). Widening the circle: Family group decision making. *Journal of Child and Youth Care, 9*(1), 1-12.

Peplau, L. A. (1991). Lesbian and gay relationships. In J. C. Gonsiorek & J. D. Weinrich (Eds.), *Homosexuality: Implications for public policy* (pp. 177-196). Newbury Park, CA: Sage.

Perilla, J. A., Bakeman, R., & Norris, F. H. (1994). Culture and domestic violence: The ecology of abused Latinas. *Violence and Victims, 9*(4), 325-339.

Perry, S. M. (1995). Lesbian alcohol and marijuana use: Correlates of HIV risk behaviors and abusive relationships. *Journal of Psychoactive Drugs, 27*(4), 413-419.

Peterson, D. L., & Pfost, K. S. (1989). Influence of rock videos on attitudes of violence against women. *Psychological Reports, 64*(1), 319-321.

Pharr, S. (1986). Two workshops on homophobia. In K. Lobel (Ed.), *Naming the violence: Speaking out about lesbian battering* (pp. 202-222). Seattle, WA: Seal.

Pihl, R. O., Smith, M., & Farrell, B. (1983). Alcohol and aggression in men: A comparison of brewed and distilled beverages. *Journal of Studies on Alcohol*, 278-282.

Pihl, R. O., Zeichner, A., Niaura, R., Nagy, K., & Zacchia, C. (1981). Attribution and alcohol-mediated aggression. *Journal of Abnormal Psychology*, *90*(5), 468-475.

Pillemer, K. (1985, Fall). Social isolation and elder abuse. *Response to the Victimization of Women and Children*, 2-4.

Pillemer, K., & Finkelhor, D. (1988). The prevalence of elder abuse: A random sample survey. *Gerontologist*, *28*(1), 51-57.

Pillemer, K., & Finkelhor, D. (1989). Causes of elder abuse: Caregiver stress versus problem relatives. *American Journal of Orthopsychiatry*, *59*(2), 179-187.

Pizzey, E. (1974). *Scream quietly or the neighbors will hear.* Short Hill, NJ: Ridley Enslow.

Pleck, E., Pleck, J. H., Grossman, M., & Bart, P. B. (1978). The battered data syndrome: A comment on Steinmetz' article. *Victimology International Journal*, *2*, 680-684.

Podnieks, E. (1992). National survey on abuse of the elderly in Canada. *Journal of Elder Abuse and Neglect*, *4*(1/2), 5-58.

Pokorny, A. D., Miller, B. A., & Kaplan, H. R. (1972). The brief MAST: A shortened version of the Michigan Alcoholism Screening Test. *American Journal of Psychiatry*, *29*, 342-345.

Portes, A. (1984). The rise of ethnicity: Determinants of ethnic perceptions among Cuban exiles in Miami. *American Sociological Review*, *49*, 383-397.

Portes, A., & Truelove, C. (1987). Making sense of diversity: Recent research on Hispanic minorities in the United States. *Annual Review of Sociology*, *13*, 359-385.

Powell, C. (1991). Dealing with dating violence in schools. In B. Levy (Ed.), *Dating violence: Young women in danger* (pp. 279-284). Seattle: Seal.

Poynter, T. L. (1989). An evaluation of a group programme for male perpetrators of domestic violence. *Australian Journal of Sex, Marriage, and Family*, *10*(3), 133-142.

Prentky, R. A., & Knight, R. A. (1991). Identifying critical dimensions for discriminating among rapists. *Journal of Consulting and Clinical Psychology*, *59*(5), 643-661.

Prentky, R. A., Knight, R. A., & Rosenberg, R. (1988). Validation analyses on a taxonomic system for rapists: Disconfirmation and reconceptualization. In R. A. Prentky & V. L. Quinsey (Eds.), *Human sexual aggression: Current perspectives* (pp. 21-40). New York: New York Academy of Sciences.

Prescott, S., & Letko, C. (1977). Battered women: A social psychological perspective. In M. Roy (Ed.), *Battered women: A psychosocial study of domestic violence* (pp. 72-96). New York: Van Nostrand Reinhold.

Prince, J. E., & Arias, I. (1994). The role of perceived control and the desirability of control among abusive and nonabusive husbands. *American Journal of Family Therapy*, *22*(2), 126-134.

Ptacek, J. (1988). Why do men batter their wives? In K. Yllö & M. Bograd (Eds.), *Feminist perspectives on wife abuse* (pp. 133-157). Newbury Park, CA: Sage.

Pynoos, R., & Nader, K. (1988). Children who witness the sexual assaults of their mothers. *Journal of the American Academy of Child and Adolescent Psychology*, *27*(5), 567-572.

Pynoos, R. S., Steinberg, A. M., & Wraith, R. (1995). A developmental model of childhood traumatic stress. In D. Cicchetti & D. Cohen (Eds.), *Manual of developmental psychopathology: Risk, disorder, and adaptation* (pp. 72-95). New York: John Wiley.

Rachor, R. E. (1995). An evaluation of the First Step PASSAGES domestic violence program. *Journal of Reality Therapy*, *14*(2), 29-36.

Radloff, L. S. (1977). The CES-D Scale: A self-report depression scale for research in the general population. *Applied Psychological Measurement*, *1*, 385-401.

Randall, M., & Haskell, L. (1995). Sexual violence in women's lives. *Violence Against Women*, *1*(1), 6-31.

Rasche, C. E. (1988). Minority women and domestic violence: The unique dilemmas of battered women of color. *Journal of Contemporary Criminal Justice, 4*, 150-171.

Register, E. (1993). Feminism and recovering from battering: Working with the individual woman. In M. Hansen & M. Harway (Eds.), *Battering and family therapy: A feminist perspective* (pp. 93-104). Newbury Park, CA: Sage.

Renick, M. J., Blumberg, S. L., & Markman, H. J. (1992). The Prevention and Relationship Enhancement Program (PREP): An empirically based preventative intervention program for couples. *Family Relations, 41*, 141-147.

Renzetti, C. (1989). Building a second closet: Third-party responses to victims of lesbian partner abuse. *Family Relations, 38*, 157-163.

Renzetti, C. (1992). *Violent betrayal: Partner abuse in lesbian relationships.* Newbury Park, CA: Sage.

Renzetti, C. (1994). On dancing with a bear: Reflections on some of the current debates among domestic violence theorists. *Violence and Victims, 9*(2), 195-200.

Renzetti, C. M. (1996). The poverty of services for battered lesbians. In C. M. Renzetti & C. H. Miley (Eds.), *Violence in gay and lesbian domestic partnerships* (pp. 61-68). Binghamton, NY: Haworth Press.

Renzetti, C. M. (1997). Violence and abuse among same-sex couples. In A. P. Cardarelli (Ed.), *Violence between intimate partners: Patterns, causes, and effects* (pp. 70-89). Boston: Allyn & Bacon.

Renzetti, C. M., & Miley, C. (1996). Violence in gay and lesbian partnerships. *Journal of Gay and Lesbian Social Services, 14*(1), 1-116.

Resick, P. A. (1993). The psychological impact of rape. *Journal of Interpersonal Violence, 8*(2), 223-255.

Resnick, H. S., Kilpatrick, D. G., Walsh, C., & Veronen, L. J. (1991). Marital rape. In R. T. Ammerman & M. Hersen (Eds.), *Case studies in family violence* (pp. 329-355). New York: Plenum.

Richie, B. E., & Kanuha, V. (1993). Battered women of color in public health care systems: Racism, sexism, and violence. In B. Blair & S. E. Cayleff (Eds.), *Wings of gauze: Women of color and the experience of health and illness* (pp. 288-299). Detroit, MI: Wayne State University Press.

Riggs, D. S., Kilpatrick, D. G., & Resnick, H. S. (1992). Long-term psychological distress associated with marital rape and aggravated assault: A comparison to other crime victims. *Journal of Family Violence, 7*(4), 283-296.

Riggs, D. S., & O'Leary, K. D. (1989). A theoretical model of courtship aggression. In M. A. Pirog-Good & J. E. Stets (Eds.), *Violence in dating relationships: Emerging social issues* (pp. 53-71). New York: Praeger.

Rimonte, N. (1989). Domestic violence among Pacific Asians. In Asian Women United of California (Eds.), *Making waves: An anthology of writings by and about Asian American women* (pp. 327-473). Boston: Beacon.

Roark, M. L., & Vlahos, S. (1983). An analysis of the ego status of battered women. *Transactional Analysis Journal, 13*, 164-167.

Robertson, N. (in press). Reforming institutional responses to violence against women: A comprehensive community intervention project. In D. Thomas & A. Veno (Eds.), *Community psychology and social change: Australian and New Zealand perspectives.* Palmerston North, New Zealand: Dunmore.

Rodriguez, O., & O'Donnell, M. (1995). *Help-seeking and use of mental health services by the Hispanic elderly.* Westport, CT: Greenwood.

Rohsenow, D. J., & Bacharowski, J. A. (1984). Effects of alcohol and expectancies on verbal aggression in men and women. *Journal of Abnormal Psychology, 93*, 418-432.

Rollins, B. C., & Oheneba-Sakyi, Y. (1990). Physical violence in Utah households. *Journal of Family Violence, 5*(4), 301-309.

Root, M. P. (1996). Women of color and traumatic stress in "domestic captivity": Gender and race as disempowering statuses. In A. J. Marsella, M. J. Friedman, E. T. Gerrity, & R. M. Scurfield (Eds.), *Ethnocultural aspects of post-traumatic stress disorder: Issues, research, and clinical applications* (pp. 363-388). Washington, DC: American Psychological Association.

Roscoe, B., & Benaske, N. (1985, July). Courtship violence experienced by abused wives: Similarities in patterns of abuse. *Family Relations, 34,* 419-424.

Roseby, V., & Johnston, J. R. (1995). Clinical interventions with latency-age children of high conflict and violence. *American Journal of Orthopsychiatry, 65*(1), 48-59.

Rosenbaum, A., Hoge, S. K., Adelman, S. A., Warnken, W. J., Fletcher, K. E., & Kane, R. L. (1994). Head injury in partner-abusive men. *Journal of Consulting and Clinical Psychology, 62*(6), 1187-1193.

Rosenbaum, A., & O'Leary, K. D. (1981a). Children: The unintended victims of marital violence. *American Journal of Orthopsychiatry, 51*(4), 692-699.

Rosenbaum, A., & O'Leary, K. D. (1981b). Marital violence: Characteristics of abusive couples. *Journal of Consulting and Clinical Psychology, 49*(1), 63-71.

Rosenberg, M. (1965). *Society and the adolescent self-image.* Princeton, NJ: Princeton University Press.

Rosenberg, M. S., & Rossman, B. B. R. (1990). The child witness to marital violence. In R. T. Ammerman & M. Herson (Eds.), *Treatment of family violence.* New York: John Wiley.

Rosenfeld, B. D. (1992). Court-ordered treatment of spousal abuse. *Clinical Psychology Review, 12*(2), 205-226.

Rosewater, L. B. (1988). Battered or schizophrenic? Psychological tests can't tell. In K. Yllö & M. Bograd (Eds.), *Feminist perspectives on wife abuse* (pp. 200-217). Newbury Park, CA: Sage.

Rossman, B. B. R. (1994). Children in violent families: Current diagnostic and treatment considerations. *Family Violence and Sexual Assault Bulletin, 10*(3-4), 29-33.

Roth, K. (1994). Domestic violence as an international human rights issue. In R. J. Cook (Ed.), *Human rights for women: National and international perspectives* (pp. 326-339). Philadelphia: University of Pennsylvania Press.

Roundtree, G. A., Parker, A. D., Edwards, D. W., & Teddlie, C. B. (1982). A survey of the types of crimes committed by incarcerated females in two states who reported being battered. *Corrective and Social Psychiatry and Journal of Behavior Technology Methods and Therapy, 28,* 23-26.

Rounsaville, B. (1978). Theories in marital violence: Evidence from a study of battered women. *Victimology, 3*(1/2), 11-31.

Rounsaville, B., & Weissman, M. H. (1978). Battered women: A medical problem requiring detection. *International Journal of Psychiatry in Medicine, 8,* 191-201.

Roy, M. (Ed.). (1977). *Battered women: A psychosociological study of domestic violence.* New York: Van Nostrand Reinhold.

Roy, M. (1988). *Children in the crossfire: Violence in the home—How does it affect our children?* Deerfield Beach, FL: Health Communications.

Russell, D. E. H. (1990). *Rape in marriage.* Indianapolis: Indiana University Press.

Rutter, M. (1985). Resilience in the face of adversity: Protective factors and resistance to psychiatric disorder. *British Journal of Psychiatry, 147,* 598-611.

Ryan, K. M. (1995). Do courtship-violent men have characteristics associated with a "battering personality"? *Journal of Family Violence, 10*(1), 99-120.

Ryan, R. M. (1996). The sex right: A legal history of the marital rape exemption. *Law and Social Inquiry, 20*(4), 941-999.

Sacco, V. F., & Trotman, M. (1990). Public information programming and family violence: Lessons from the mass media crime prevention experience. *Canadian Journal of Criminology, 32*(1), 91-105.

Sakai, C. E. (1991). Group intervention strategies with domestic abusers. *Families in Society, 72*, 536-542.

Salzinger, S., Feldman, R. S., Hammer, M., & Rosario, M. (1992). Constellations of family violence and their differential effects on children's behavioral disturbance. *Child and Family Behavior Therapy, 14*(4), 23-41.

Sampselle, C. M., Petersen, B. A., Murtland, T. L., & Oakley, D. J. (1992). Prevalence of abuse among pregnant women choosing certified nurse-midwife or physician providers. *Journal of Nurse-Midwifery, 37*(4), 269-273.

Sato, R. A., & Heiby, E. M. (1992). Correlates of depressive symptoms among battered women. *Journal of Family Violence, 7*(3), 229-245.

Saunders, D. G. (1992). A typology of men who batter: Three types derived from cluster analysis. *American Journal of Orthopsychiatry, 62*(2), 264-275.

Saunders, D. G. (1994a). Child custody decisions in families experiencing woman abuse. *Social Work, 39*(1), 51-59.

Saunders, D. G. (1994b). Post-traumatic stress symptom profiles of battered women: A comparison of survivors in two settings. *Violence and Victims, 9*, 31-44.

Saunders, D. G. (1995). The tendency to arrest victims of domestic violence. *Journal of Interpersonal Violence, 10*(2), 147-158.

Saunders, D. G., & Azar, S. T. (1989). Treatment programs for family violence. In L. Ohlin & M. Tonry (Eds.), *Family violence: Crime and justice—A review of research* (pp. 481-547). Chicago: University of Chicago Press.

Saunders, D. G., & Hanusa, D. (1986). Cognitive-behavioral treatment of men who batter: The short-term effects of group therapy. *Journal of Family Violence, 1*(4), 357-372.

Saunders, D. G., & Parker, J. C. (1989, September). Legal sanctions and treatment follow-through among men who batter: A multivariate analysis. *Social Work Research and Abstracts*, 21-29.

Schecter, S. (1987). Empowering interventions with battered women. In S. Schecter (Ed.), *Guidelines for mental health professionals* (pp. 9-13). Washington, DC: National Coalition Against Domestic Violence.

Schilit, R., Lie, G. Y., Bush, J., Montagne, M., & Reyes, L. (1991). Intergenerational transmission of violence in lesbian relationships. *Affilia, 6*(1), 72-87.

Schilit, R., Lie, G. Y., & Montagne, M. (1990). Substance abuse as a correlate of violence in intimate lesbian relationships. *Journal of Homosexuality, 19*(3), 51-65.

Schmidt, J. D., & Sherman, L. W. (1993). Does arrest deter domestic violence? *American Behavioral Scientist, 36*(5), 601-609.

Seligman, M. (1975). *Helplessness*. New York: Freeman.

Selzer, M. (1971). The Michigan Alcoholism Screening Test: The quest for a new diagnostic instrument. *American Journal of Psychiatry, 127*, 1653-1658.

Serra, P. (1993). Physical violence in the couple relationship: A contribution toward the analysis of context. *Family Process, 32*, 21-33.

Shainess, N. (1977). Psychological aspects of wife battering. In M. Roy (Ed.), *Battered women: A psychosociological study of domestic violence* (pp. 111-119). New York: Van Nostrand Reinhold.

Shepard, M. (1992). Predicting batterer recidivism 5 years after community intervention. *Journal of Family Violence, 7*(3), 167-178.

Shepard, M., & Pence, E. (1988). The effect of battering on the employment status of women. *Affilia, 3*(2), 55-61.

Sheppard, M. E., & Campbell, J. A. (1992). The Abusive Behavior Inventory: A measure of psychological and physical abuse. *Journal of Interpersonal Violence, 7*, 291-305.

Sherman, L. W., & Berk, R. A. (1984, April). The specific deterrent effects of arrest for domestic assault. *American Sociological Review, 49,* 261-272.

Sherman, L. W., Smith, D. A., Schmidt, J. D., & Rogan, D. P. (1992). Crime, punishment, and stake in conformity: Legal and informal control of domestic violence. *American Sociological Review, 57,* 680-690.

Shields, N. M., McCall, G. J., & Hanneke, C. R. (1988). Patterns of family and nonfamily violence: Violent husbands and violent men. *Violence and Victims, 3*(2), 83-97.

Shiferaw, B., Mittelmark, M. B., Wofford, J. L., Anderson, R. T., Walls, P., & Rohrer, B. (1994). The investigation and outcome of reported cases elder abuse: The Forsyth County Aging Study. *Gerontologist, 34*(1), 123-125.

Shomer, A. (1997). Lesbian domestic violence: Our tragic little secret. *Lesbian News, 22*(2), 24-26.

Shupe, A., Stacey, W. A., & Hazlewood, L. R. (1987). *Violent men, violent couples: The dynamics of domestic violence.* Lexington, MA: Lexington.

Sigelman, C. K., Berry, C. J., & Wiles, K. A. (1984). Violence in college students' dating relationships. *Journal of Applied Social Psychology, 5*(6), 530-548.

Silvern, L., Karyl, J., Waelde, L., Hodges, W. F., Starek, J., Heidt, E., & Min, K. (1995). Retrospective reports of parental partner abuse: Relationships to depression, trauma symptoms, and self-esteem among college students. *Journal of Family Violence, 10*(2), 177-202.

Simons, R. L., Johnson, C., Beaman, J., & Conger, R. D. (1993, August). Explaining women's double jeopardy: Factors that mediate the association between harsh treatment as a child and violence by a husband. *Journal of Marriage and the Family, 55,* 713-723.

Sirles, E. A., Lipchik, E., & Kowalski, K. (1993). A consumer's perspective on domestic violence interventions. *Journal of Family Violence, 8*(3), 267-276.

Smith, C. (1988). Status discrepancies and husband-to-wife violence. Paper presented at the Meeting of the Eastern Sociological Society.

Smith, J. P., & Williams, J. G. (1992). From abusive household to dating violence. *Journal of Family Violence, 7*(2), 153-165.

Smith, M. D. (1990). Sociodemographic risk factors in wife abuse: Results from a survey of Toronto women. *Canadian Journal of Sociology, 15*(1), 39-58.

Snell, J. E., Rosenwald, R. J., & Robey, A. (1964, August). The wifebeater's wife. *Archives of General Psychiatry, 11,* 107-112.

Snyder, D. K., & Fruchtman, L. A. (1981). Differential patterns of wife abuse: A data-based typology. *Journal of Consulting and Clinical Psychology, 49*(6), 878-885.

Snyder, D. K., & Snow, A. (1995). Evaluating couples' aggression in marital therapy. Paper presented at a meeting of the American Psychological Association, New York.

Snyder, G. R. (1994) *Three-year trends in the use of restraining orders for protection from domestic abuse: An evaluation of the efficacy of a cooperative community program for the prevention of abuse.* Unpublished master's thesis, Massachusetts School of Professional Psychology.

Song, Y. I. (1986) *Battered Korean women in urban America: The relationship of cultural conflict to wife abuse.* Unpublished doctoral dissertation, Ohio State University, Columbus.

Sonkin, D. J., & Durphy, M. (1985). *Learning to live without violence* (2nd ed.). San Francisco: Volcano.

Sorenson, S. B., Stein, J. A., Siegel, J. M., Golding, J. M., & Burnam, M. A. (1987). The prevalence of adult sexual assault. *American Journal of Epidemiology, 126*(6), 1154-1164.

Sorenson, S. B., & Telles, C. A. (1991). Self-reports of spousal violence in a Mexican-American and non-Hispanic White population. *Violence and Victims, 6*(1), 3-15.

Sorenson, S. B., Upchurch, D. M., & Shen, H. (1996). Violence and injury in marital arguments: Risk patterns and gender differences. *American Journal of Public Health, 86,* 35-40.

Sousa, C. (1991). The dating violence intervention project. In B. Levy (Ed.), *Dating violence: Young women in danger* (pp. 223-231). Seattle, WA: Seal.

Spaccarelli, S., Sandler, I. N., & Roosa, M. (1994). History of spousal violence against mother: Correlated risks and unique effects in child mental health. *Journal of Family Violence, 9*(1), 79-98.

Spirito, A., Overholster, J., & Stark, L. J. (1989). Common problems and coping strategies: II. Findings with adolescent suicide attempters. *Journal of Abnormal Child Psychology, 17*(2), 213-221.

Star, B., Clark, C. G., Goetz, K. M., & O'Malia, L. (1979, October). Psychosocial aspects of wife battering. *Social Casework, 60,* 479-487.

Stark, E. (1993). Mandatory arrest of batterers. *American Behavioral Scientist, 36*(5), 651-680.

Stark, E., & Flitcraft, A. (1988). Violence among intimates: An epidemiological review. In V. B. Van Hasselt, R. L. Morrison, A. S. Bellack, & M. Hersen (Eds.), *Handbook of family violence* (pp. 293-317). New York: Plenum.

Stark, E., & Flitcraft, A. (1995). Killing the beast within: Woman battering and female suicidality. *International Journal of Health Services, 25*(1), 43-64.

Stark, E., Flitcraft, A., & Frazier, W. (1981). *Wife abuse in the medical setting: An introduction for health personnel* (Domestic Violence Monograph Series No. 7). Washington, DC: U.S. Department of Health and Human Services, National Clearinghouse on Domestic Abuse and Neglect.

Steinmetz, S. K. (1977). *The cycle of violence: Assertive, aggressive, and abusive family interaction.* New York: Praeger.

Steinmetz, S. K., & Straus, M. A. (Eds.). (1974). *Violence in the family.* New York: Harper & Row.

Sternberg, K. J. (in press). Fathers, the missing parents in research on family violence. In M. E. Lamb (Ed.), *The role of the father in child development.* New York: John Wiley.

Sternberg, K. J., Lamb, M. E., Greenbaum, C., Dawud, S., Cortes, R. M., & Lorey, F. (1994). The effects of domestic violence on children's perceptions of their perpetrating and nonperpetrating parents. *International Journal of Behavioral Development, 17*(4), 779-795.

Sternberg, K. J., Lamb, M. E., Greenbaum, C., Cicchetti, D., Dawud, S., Cortes, R. M., Krispin, O., & Lorey, F. (1993). Effects of domestic violence on children's behavioral problems and depression. *Developmental Psychology, 29*(1), 44-52.

Stets, J. E., & Straus, M. A. (1989). The marriage license as a hitting license: A comparison of assaults in dating, cohabiting, and married couples. *Journal of Family Violence, 4*(2), 161-180.

Stets, J. E., & Straus, M. A. (1990). Gender differences in reporting of marital violence and its medical and psychological consequences. In M. A. Straus & R. J. Gelles (Eds.), *Physical violence in American families: Risk factors and adaptations to violence in 8,145 families* (pp. 151-165). New Brunswick, NJ: Transaction.

Stevenson, H. W. (1992). Learning from Asian schools. *Scientific American, 267*(6), 70-77.

Stewart, D. E. (1994). Incidence of postpartum abuse in women with a history of abuse during pregnancy. *Canadian Medical Association Journal, 151*(11), 1601-1604.

Stith, S. M., & Farley, S. C. (1993). A predictive model of male spousal violence. *Journal of Family Violence, 8*(2), 183-201.

Strassberg, Z., & Dodge, K. A. (1992). The longitudinal relationship between parental conflict strategies and children's sociometric standing in kindergarten. *Merril-Palmer Quarterly, 38*(4), 477-493.

Straus, M. A. (1973). A general systems theory approach to a theory of violence between family members. *Social Science Information, 12,* 105.

Straus, M. A. (1976). Sexual inequality, cultural norms, and wife-beating. In E. C. Viano (Ed.), *Victims and society* (pp. 543-559). Washington, DC: Visage.

Straus, M. A. (1979). Measuring intrafamily conflict and violence: The Conflict Tactics (CT) Scale. *Journal of Marriage and the Family, 41*(1), 75-88.

Straus, M. A. (1986). The cost of intrafamily assault and homicide to society. *Academic Medicine, 62,* 556-561.

Straus, M. A. (1990). New scoring methods for violence and new norms for the Conflict Tactic Scales. In M. A. Straus & R. J. Gelles (Eds.), *Physical violence in American families: Risk factors and adaptations to violence in 8,145 families* (Appendix B, pp. 535-559). New Brunswick, NJ: Transaction.

Straus, M. A. (1992). Children as witnesses to marital violence: A risk factor for lifelong problems among a nationally representative sample of American men and women. Paper presented at the Twenty-Third Ross Roundtable on Critical Approaches to Common Pediatric Problems.

Straus, M. A. (1993). Physical assaults by wives: A major social problem. In R. J. Gelles & D. R. Loseke (Eds.), *Current controversies on family violence* (pp. 67-87). Newbury Park, CA: Sage.

Straus, M. A., & Gelles, R. J. (1986). Societal change and change in family violence from 1975 to 1985 as revealed by two national surveys. *Journal of Marriage and the Family, 48,* 465-479.

Straus, M. A., & Gelles, R. J. (1987). The costs of family violence. *Public Health Reports, 102*(6), 638-641.

Straus, M. A., & Gelles, R. J. (1990a). How violent are American families? Estimates from the National Family Violence Resurvey and other studies. In M. A. Straus & R. J. Gelles (Eds.), *Physical violence in American families: Risk factors and adaptations to violence in 8,145 families* (pp. 95-112). New Brunswick, NJ: Transaction.

Straus, M. A., & Gelles, R. J. (1990b). *Physical violence in American families: Risk factors and adaptations to violence in 8,145 families.* New Brunswick, NJ: Transaction.

Straus, M. A., Gelles, R. J., & Steinmetz, S. (1980). *Behind closed doors: Violence in the American family.* Garden City, NJ: Anchor.

Straus, M. A., Hamby, S. L., Sugarman, D. B., & Boney-McCoy, S. (1996). The Revised Conflict Tactics Scales (CTS2): Development and preliminary psychometric data. *Journal of Family Issues, 17*(3), 283-316.

Straus, M. A., & Kaufman Kantor, G. (1994). Corporal punishment of adolescents by parents: A risk factor in the epidemiology of depression, suicide, alcohol abuse, child abuse, and wife beating. *Adolescence, 29*(115), 543-562.

Straus, M. A., & Smith, C. (1990a). Family patterns and child abuse. In M. A. Straus & R. J. Gelles (Eds.), *Physical violence in American families: Risk factors adaptations to violence in 8,145 families* (pp. 245-261). New Brunswick, NJ: Transaction.

Straus, M. A., & Smith, C. (1990b). Violence in Hispanic families in the United States: Incidence rates and structural interpretations. In M. A. Straus & R. J. Gelles (Eds.), *Physical violence in American families: Risk factors and adaptations to violence in 8,145 families* (pp. 341-368). New Brunswick, NJ: Transaction.

Straus, M. A., & Yodanis, C. L. (1995). Corporal punishment by parents: Implications for primary prevention of assaults on spouses and parents. *University of Chicago Law School Roundtable, 2*(1), 35-66.

Strube, M. J. (1988). The decision to leave an abusive relationship: Empirical evidence and theoretical issues. *Psychological Bulletin, 104,* 236-250.

Struckman-Johnson, C., & Struckman-Johnson, D. (1994). Men pressured and forced into sexual experiences. *Archives of Sexual Behavior, 23*(1), 93-114.

Sugarman, D. B., Aldarondo, E., & Boney-McCoy, S. (1996). Risk marker analysis of husband-to-wife violence: A continuum of aggression. *Journal of Applied Social Psychology, 26*(4), 313-337.

Sugarman, D. B., & Hotaling, G. T. (1989). Dating violence: Prevalence, context, and risk markers. In A. A. Pirog-Good & J. E. Stets (Eds.), *Violence in dating relationships: Emerging social issues* (pp. 3-31). New York: Praeger.

Suitor, J. J., Pillemer, K., & Straus, M. A. (1990). Marital violence in a life course perspective. In M. A. Straus & R. J. Gelles (Eds.), *Physical violence in American families: Risk factors and adaptations to violence in 8,145 families* (pp. 305-319). New Brunswick, NJ: Transaction.

Sullivan, C. M., Campbell, R., Angelique, H., Eby, K. K., & Davidson, W. S. (1994). An advocacy intervention program for women with abusive partners: Six-month follow-up. *American Journal of Community Psychology, 22*(1), 101-122.

Sullivan, C. M., Tan, C., Basta, J., Rumptz, M., & Davidson, W. S. (1992). An advocacy intervention program for women with abusive partners: Initial evaluation. *American Journal of Community Psychology, 20*(3), 309-332.

Sullivan, J. P., & Mosher, D. L. (1990). Acceptance of guided imagery of marital rape as a function of macho personality. *Violence and Victims, 5*(4), 275-286.

Tan, C., Basta, J., Sullivan, C. M., & Davidson, W. S. (1995). The role of social support in the lives of women exiting domestic violence shelters. *Journal of Interpersonal Violence, 10*, 437-451.

Taylor, J., & Zhang, X. (1990). Cultural identity in maritally distressed and nondistressed Black couples. *Western Journal of Black Studies, 14*(4), 205-213.

Taylor, S. P., & Chermack, S. T. (1993). Alcohol, drugs, and human physical aggression. *Journal of Studies on Alcohol*(Suppl. 11), 78-88.

Taylor, S. P., & Leonard, K. E. (1983). Alcohol and human physical aggression. In R. G. Geen & E. I. Donnerstein (Eds.), *Aggression: Theoretical and empirical reviews.* San Diego: Academic Press.

Terr, L. (1990). *Too scared to cry.* New York: HarperCollins.

Thornberry, T. P. (1994). *Violent families and youth violence* (Fact Sheet No. 21). Washington, DC: U.S. Department of Justice, Office of Juvenile Justice and Delinquency Prevention.

Thorne-Finch, R. (1992). *Ending the silence: The origins and treatment of male violence against women.* Toronto: University of Toronto Press.

Tifft, L. L. (1993). *Battering of women: The failure of intervention and the case for prevention.* Boulder, CO: Westview.

Timmins, L. (Ed.). (1995). *Listening to the thunder: Advocates talk about the battered women's movement.* Vancouver, Canada: Women's Research Centre.

Tolman, R. M., & Bennett, L. W. (1990). A review of quantitative research on men who batter. *Journal of Interpersonal Violence, 5*(1), 87-118.

Tolman, R. M., & Edleson, J. L. (1995). Intervention for men who batter: A review of research. In S. M. Stith & M. A. Straus (Eds.), *Understanding partner violence: Prevalence, causes, consequences, and solutions* (pp. 262-273). Minneapolis, MN: National Council on Family Relations.

Tondonato, P., & Crew, B. K. (1992). Dating violence, social learning theory, and gender: A multivariate analysis. *Violence and Victims, 7*(1), 3-14.

Torres, S. (1991). A comparison of wife abuse between two cultures: Perceptions, attitudes, nature, and extent. *Issues in Mental Health Nursing, 12*, 113-131.

Trask, H. (1990). Politics in the Pacific Islands: Imperialism and native self-determination. *Amerasia Journal, 16*(1), 1-19.

Trimpey, M. L. (1989). Self-esteem and anxiety: Key issues in an abused women's support group. *Issues in Mental Health Nursing, 10,* 297-308.

Tutty, L. M., Bidgood, B. A., & Rothery, M. A. (1993). Support groups for battered women: Research on the efficacy. *Journal of Family Violence, 8*(4), 325-343.

Ucko, L. (1994). Culture and violence: The interaction of Africa and America. *Sex Roles, 31*(3/4), 185-204.

Ullman, S. E., & Siegel, J. M. (1993). Victim-offender relationship and sexual assault. *Violence and Victims, 8*(2), 121-134.

U.S. Bureau of Investigation, & U.S. Department of Justice. (1995). Crime clock (and excerpts): 1994. In *Uniform crime reports, 1994* (pp. 4, 13, 17, 19, 285, 287, 288). Washington, DC: Federal Bureau of Investigation.

U.S. Bureau of the Census (1991). *Statistical abstract of the United States: 1991.* Washington, DC: U.S. Government Printing Office.

U.S. Bureau of the Census (1992). *Statistical abstract of the United States: 1992.* Washington, DC: U.S. Government Printing Office.

U.S. Bureau of the Census. (1993). *We, the American . . . Asians.* Washington, DC: U.S. Department of Commerce.

U.S. Department of Justice. (1995). *Bureau of Justice statistics: Sourcebook of criminal justice statistics.* Washington, DC: U.S. Department of Justice.

Varvaro, F. F. (1991). Using a grief response assessment questionnaire in a support group to assist battered women in their recovery. *Response, 13*(4), 17-20.

Verlarde-Castillo, A. R. (1992) *Spousal abuse among Hopi women.* Unpublished manuscript, University of Texas at Austin.

Vitanza, S., Vogel, L. C., & Marshall, L. L. (1995). Distress and symptoms of post-traumatic stress disorder in abused women. *Violence and Victims, 10,* 23-34.

Vitanza, S. A., Rowe, K. L., Hobdy, J., & Marshall, L. L. (1990). Dimensions of dating violence, gender, and personal characteristics. Paper presented at the Ninety-Eighth Annual Convention of the American Psychological Association, Boston.

Vivian, D., & Langhinrichsen-Rohling, J. (1994). Are bi-directionally violent couples mutually victimized? A gender-sensitive comparison. *Violence and Victims, 9*(2), 107-124.

Wagar, J. M., & Rodway, M. R. (1995). An evaluation of a group treatment approach for children who have witnessed wife abuse. *Journal of Family Violence, 10*(3), 295-306.

Waldo, M. (1987, March). Also victims: Understanding and treating men arrested for spousal abuse. *Journal of Counseling and Development, 65,* 385-388.

Waldron, C. M. (1996). Lesbians of color and the domestic violence movement. In C. M. Renzetti & C. H. Miley (Eds.), *Violence in gay and lesbian domestic partnerships* (pp. 43-53). Binghamton, NY: Haworth Press.

Walker, L. E. (1979). *The battered woman.* New York: Harper & Row.

Walker, L. E. (1984). *The battered woman syndrome.* New York: Springer.

Walker, L. E. (1989). *Terrifying love: Why battered women kill and how society responds.* New York: Harper & Row.

Walker, L. E. A. (1993). The battered woman syndrome is a psychological consequence of abuse. In R. J. Gelles & D. R. Loseke (Eds.), *Current controversies on family violence* (pp. 133-153). Newbury Park, CA: Sage.

Walker, L. E. A. (1994). *Abused women and survivor therapy.* Washington, DC: American Psychological Association.

Walker, L. E. A. (1995). Current perspectives on men who batter women—Implications for and treatment to stop violence against women: Comment of Gottman et al. (1995). *Journal of Family Psychology, 9*(3), 264-271.

Wallace, A. (1986). *Homicide: The social reality.* Sydney, Australia: New South Wales Bureau of Crime Statistics and Research.

Wallace, H. (1996). *Family violence: Legal, medical, and social perspectives.* Needham Heights, MA: Allyn & Bacon.

Warnken, W. J., Rosenbaum, A., Fletcher, K. E., Hoge, S. K., & Adelman, S. A. (1994). Head injured males: A population at risk for relationship aggression. *Violence and Victims, 9*(2), 153-166.

Wasinger, L. (1993). The value system of the Native American counseling client: An exploration. *American Indian Culture and Research Journal, 17*(4), 91-98.

Waterman, C. K., Dawson, L. J., & Bologna, M. J. (1989). Sexual coercion in gay males and lesbian relationships: Predictors and implications for support services. *Journal of Sex Research, 26*(1), 118-124.

Weaver, T. L., & Clum, G. A. (1995). Psychological distress associated with interpersonal violence: A meta-analysis. *Clinical Psychology Review, 15*(2), 115-140.

Webersinn, A. L., Hollinger, C. L., & DeLamatre, J. E. (1991). Breaking the cycle of violence: An examination of factors relevant to treatment follow-through. *Psychological Reports, 68,* 231-240.

Webster, J., Chandler, J., & Battistutta, D. (1996). Pregnancy outcomes and health care use: Effects of abuse. *American Journal of Obstetrics and Gynecology, 174*(2), 760-767.

Weinberg, G. (1972). *Society and the healthy homosexual.* New York: St. Martin's.

Weingourt, R. (1985). Wife rape: Barriers to identification and treatment. *American Journal of Psychotherapy, 39*(2), 187-192.

Weis, K., & Borges, S. (1973). Victimology and rape: The case of the legitimate victim. *Issues in Criminology, 8,* 71-115.

West, C. G., Fernandez, A., Hillard, J. R., Schoof, M., & Parks, J. (1990). Psychiatric disorders of abused women at a shelter. *Psychiatric Quarterly, 61,* 295-301.

West, C. M., Jasinski, J. L., & Kaufman Kantor, G. (1997). *Predictors of help seeking by Hispanic and Anglo battered women.* Manuscript submitted for publication.

West, C. M., & Williams, L. M. (1997). *Adult sexual revictimization among Black women sexually abused in childhood: A prospective study.* Manuscript submitted for publication.

Whitbeck, L. B., Hoyt, D. R., Simons, R. L., Conger, R. D., & Elder, G. H. (1992). Intergenerational continuity of parental rejection and depressed affect. *Journal of Personality and Social Psychology, 63*(6), 1036-1045.

Whitcomb, D., Shapiro, E. R., & Stellwagen, L. D. (1985). *When the victim is a child: Issues for judges and prosecutors.* Washington, DC: National Institute of Justice.

White, E. (1994). *Chain, chain, change: For black women dealing with physical and emotional abuse.* Seattle, WA: Seal.

Widom, C. S. (1989). The intergenerational transmission of violence. In N. Weiner & M. Wolfgang (Eds.), *Pathways to criminal violence* (pp. 137-201). Newbury Park, CA: Sage.

Widom, C. S. (1993). Child abuse and alcohol use and abuse. In S. E. Martin (Ed.), *Alcohol and interpersonal violence: Fostering multidisciplinary perspectives* (NIH Research Monograph No. 24, pp. 291-314). Rockville, MD: U.S. Department of Health and Human Services.

Wilbanks, W. (1983). The female homicide offender in Dade County, Florida. *Criminal Justice Review, 8,* 9-14.

Wildin, S. R., Williamson, W. D., & Wilson, G. S. (1991). Children of battered women: Developmental and learning profiles. *Clinical Pediatrics, 30*(5), 299-304.

Williams, E. E., & Ellison, F. (1996). Culturally informed social work practice with American Indian clients: Guidelines for non-Indian social workers. *Social Work, 41*(2), 147-151.

Williams, L. S. (1984). The classic rape: When do victims report? *Social Problems, 31*(4), 459-467.

Williams, O. J. (1992). Ethnically sensitive practice to enhance treatment participation of African American men who batter. *Families in Society,* 588-595.

Williams, O. J., & Becker, R. L. (1994). Domestic partner abuse treatment programs and cultural competence: The results of a national survey. *Violence and Victims, 9*(3), 287-296.

Wilson, M., & Daly, M. (1993). Spousal homicide risk and estrangement. *Violence and Victims, 8*(1), 3-16.

Woffordt, S., Mihalic, D. E., & Menard, S. (1994). Continuities in marital violence. *Journal of Family Violence, 9*(3), 195-225.

Wolf, R., Godkin, M., & Pillemer, K. (1986). Maltreatment of the elderly: A comparative analysis. *Pride Institute of Long-Term Home Health Care, 5,* 10-17.

Wolf, R., & Pillemer, K. (1989). *Helping elderly victims.* New York: Columbia.

Wolf, R. S. (1988). Elder abuse: Ten years later. *Journal of the American Geriatrics Society, 36*(8), 758-762.

Wolf, R. S., Strugnell, C. P., & Godkin, M. A. (1982). *Preliminary findings from three model projects on elderly abuse.* No. Worcester, MA: University of Massachusetts Medical Center, Center on Aging.

Wolfe, D. A., Jaffe, P., Wilson, S. K., & Zak, L. (1985). Children of battered women: The relation of child behavior to family violence and maternal stress. *Journal of Consulting and Clinical Psychology, 53*(5), 657-665.

Wolfe, D. A., Zak, L., Wilson, S., & Jaffe, P. (1986). Child witnesses to violence between parents: Critical issues in behavioral and social adjustments. *Journal of Abnormal Child Psychology, 14*(1), 95-104.

Wolk, L. E. (1982). *Minnesota's American Indian battered women: The cycle of oppression; A cultural awareness training manual for non-Indian professionals.* St. Paul, MN: St. Paul Indian Center.

Wylie, M. S. (1996, March/April). It's a community affair. *Networker,* 58-66.

Yegidis, B. L. (1988). Wife abuse and marital rape among women who seek help. *Affilia, 3*(1), 62-68.

Yl16, K. (1984). The status of women, marital equality, and violence against wives. *Journal of Family Issues, 5*(3), 307-320.

Yl16, K. (1988). Political and methodological debates in wife abuse research. In K. Yl16 & M. Bograd (Eds.), *Feminist perspectives on wife abuse* (pp. 28-51). Newbury Park, CA: Sage.

Yl16, K., & LeClerc, D. (1988). Marital rape. In A. L. Horton & J. A. Williamson (Eds.), *Abuse and religion: When praying isn't enough* (pp. 48-57). Lexington, MA: Lexington.

Yl16, K., & Straus, M. A. (1990). Patriarchy and violence against wives: The impact of structural and normative factors. In M. A. Straus & R. J. Gelles (Eds.), *Physical violence in American families: Risk factors and adaptations to violence in 8,145 families* (pp. 383-399). New Brunswick, NJ: Transaction.

Yoshihama, M., Parekh, A. L., & Boyington, D. (1991). Dating violence in Asian/Pacific communities. In B. Levy (Ed.), *Dating violence: Young women in danger* (pp. 184-301). Seattle, WA: Seal.

Zambrano, M. M. (1985). *For the Latina in an abusive relationship.* Seattle, WA: Seal.

Zeichner, A., & Pihl, R. O. (1979). Effects of alcohol and behavior contingencies on human aggression. *Journal of Abnormal Aggression, 88*(2), 153-160.

Zimring, F. E. (1989). Toward a jurisprudence of family violence. In L. Ohlin & M. Tonry (Eds.), *Family violence* (pp. 547-569). Chicago: University of Chicago Press.

Zorza, J. (1993, Fall). Mandatory arrest for domestic violence: Why it may prove the best first step in curbing repeat abuse. *Criminal Justice, 3,* 2-9 & 51-54.

Zubretsky, T. M., & Digirolamo, F. M. (1994). Adult domestic violence: The alcohol connection. *Violence Update, 4*(7), 1-8.

Index

Abney, V. D., 202, 204, 206
Abusive Behavior inventory, 40*box*
Achenbach, T. M., 93, 103
Adams, D., 220, 222, 223, 233, 242
Adelman, S. A., 13, 24
African Americans:
  acculturation factors and, 196-197
  age factor and, 193, 194
  alcohol abuse factor and, 198, 199
  cultural factors and, 195, 202
  institutional stereotypes of, 204
  internalized stereotypes of, 204
  normative violence approval of, 199
  occupational and employment status
    factors and, 194
  population description of, 186
  social class factor and, 194
  suicide potential of, 205
  treatment recommendations for,
    206, 208
  violence prevalence of, 190-191
Aftermath of partner violence:
  clinical implications of, 67-68
    forensic investigations, 70-71
    identification and diagnosis,
      68-69, 72
    referral and services provision,
      69-70, 72
    social policy agenda, 71
  conclusions regarding, 71-72
  psychological consequences of
    battered woman syndrome, 50-51
    case examples and, 49-50
    cycle of violence concept and,
      50-51
    depression level factors and,
      61-62, 63-64
    frequency and severity factors
      and, 55-56
    gender differences in, 53-54

predictability factors and, 56-57
PTSD, 62-63
revictimization by service
  providers and, 61
self-esteem effects and, 58-59
social and demographic factors
  and, 54-55
social support factors and, 57-58
substance abuse factors and, 60-61
suicidal ideation, 63-64
survey research on, 51-53
research limitations and, 64
research measurement techniques of,
  45-47
research methods vs. perspectives on,
  47-48
social consequences of, 44-45, 46,
  64-65
  criminal justice costs, 67
  intergenerational impact, 67
  marital dissolution, 65-66
  productivity and medical costs, 66
survey research on
  on gender differences, 53-54
  national surveys on, 53-55
  on social and demographic factors,
    54-55
See also Children exposed to partner
  violence
Aggression Scale, 40*box*
Aguilar, R. J., 58, 59
Alcohol abuse. *See* Substance abuse
Aldarondo, E., 5, 13, 15, 21, 26, 28, 31,
  36, 39, 68, 120, 187, 191, 192, 193,
  195, 197, 198, 200, 201, 232, 251
Aldwin, C. M., 73, 75, 88, 89
Alford, P., 32, 128, 131, 132, 137, 142,
  145, 149, 164
Allen, I. M., 186, 192, 197, 205
Almeida, R., 164, 177

About the Editors

Jana L. Jasinski, Ph.D., is Assistant Professor in the Department of Sociology at Wichita State University. She received her doctorate at the University of New Hampshire (1996), where she was a National Institute of Mental Health Post Doctoral Research Fellow at the Family Research Laboratory at the University of New Hampshire (1997). Her research interests are in the area of interpersonal violence—in particular, partner violence among Latinos, the response of the criminal justice system to violence, and substance abuse as a negative consequence of child sexual assault. In addition, she has research interests in criminology, research methodology, and social policy development. She has presented her research at numerous conferences, published several articles, and is the coeditor of *Out of the Darkness: Contemporary Perspectives on Family Violence.*

Linda M. Williams, Ph.D., is Director of Research at the Stone Center, Wellesley Centers for Women, at Wellesley College, Wellesley, Massachusetts, and is Research Associate Professor at the Family Research Laboratory, University of New Hampshire, Durham. A sociologist who received her doctorate from the University of Pennsylvania in 1979, she has conducted research on family violence and sexual assault for 25 years. She has authored three books and many articles on sexual abuse, including *Nursery Crimes: Sexual Abuse in Day Care* (1988) and *The Aftermath of Rape* (1979). She has directed research on family violence, sex offenders, and the consequences of child abuse. She is principal investigator on grants from the National Center on Child Abuse and Neglect and the U.S. Department of the Navy. She has directed research funded by the National Institute of Mental Health, the U.S. Justice Department, and private foundations. In 1995–96, she served as president of the American Professional Society on the Abuse of Children.

About the Contributors

David Finkelhor, Ph.D., is the co-director of the Family Research Laboratory at the University of New Hampshire. He has studied the problem of family violence since 1977 and has published numerous books, including *Sourcebook on Child Sexual Abuse, Nursery Crimes, Stopping Family Violence, License to Rape,* and *Child Sexual Abuse: New Theory and Research.* He is coeditor of *The Dark Side of Families* and *New Directions in Family Violence and Abuse Research* and the recipient of grants from the National Institute of Mental Health and the National Center on Child Abuse and Neglect.

Jean Giles-Sims, Ph.D., is Professor of Sociology, Texas Christian University, Fort Worth. She received her doctorate from the University of New Hampshire, Durham, and was recently a postdoctoral research fellow at the Family Research Laboratory (FRL) there (1993-1994). She has worked extensively on family violence issues, including wife abuse and child abuse. She has also published a book on battered women, many journal articles, and participates in ongoing activities at the FRL.

Sherry L. Hamby, Ph.D., is a clinical and research psychologist for the San Carlos Apache Tribe in Arizona, where she is helping improve the coordinated community response to domestic violence and increase understanding of partner violence in Native American communities. She obtained her doctorate from the University of North Carolina in 1992. She has been working in the field of partner violence for more than 12 years and has published numerous articles in domestic and family violence. Her main areas of interest are examining the association of dominance and partner violence, examining women's responses to violence, and developing better measurement